AT THE NUCLEAR PRECIPICE

AT THE NUCLEAR PRECIPICE

Catastrophe or Transformation?

Edited by

Richard Falk and David Krieger

AT THE NUCLEAR PRECIPICE

First published in 2008 by
PALGRAVE MACMILLAN®
in the US—a division of St. Martin's Press LLC,
175 Fifth Avenue, New York, NY 10010.

Where this book is distributed in the UK, Europe and the rest of the world,
this is by Palgrave Macmillan, a division of Macmillan Publishers Limited,
registered in England, company number 785998, of Houndmills,
Basingstoke, Hampshire RG21 6XS.

Palgrave Macmillan is the global academic imprint of the above companies
and has companies and representatives throughout the world.

Palgrave® and Macmillan® are registered trademarks in the United States,
the United Kingdom, Europe and other countries.

ISBN-13: 978–0–230–60904–4 (Pbk)
ISBN-10: 0–230–60904–X (Pbk)
ISBN-13: 978–0–230–60895–5 (Hbk)
ISBN-10: 0–230–60895–7 (Hbk)

Library of Congress Cataloging-in-Publication Data

At the nuclear precipice : catastrophe or transformation? / Richard Falk and
David Krieger, editors.
    p. cm.
Includes bibliographical references and index.
ISBN 0–230–60895–7
    1. Nuclear disarmament. 2. Nuclear arms control. 3. Security, International.
4. Nuclear weapons (International law) 5. Nuclear warfare. 6. United States—
Military policy. 7. Nuclear weapons—United States. I. Falk, Richard A. II. Krieger,
David, 1942–

JZ5675.A89 2008
355.02′17—dc22   2008012358

A catalogue record of the book is available from the British Library.

Design by Newgen Imaging Systems (P) Ltd., Chennai, India.

First edition: October 2008

10 9 8 7 6 5 4 3 2 1

Printed in the United States of America.

To the courageous individuals who understand that peace is an imperative of the Nuclear Age, and who struggle, passionately and persistently, to abolish nuclear weapons and end the institution of war.

Contents

ACKNOWLEDGMENTS

This book includes the contributions of many authors. We thank them all for their commitment to the volume and to the challenge of ending the nuclear weapons threat to humanity.

Most of the chapters in the book were originally papers presented at a 2006 symposium, "At the Nuclear Precipice: Nuclear Weapons and the Abandonment of International Law," organized by the Nuclear Age Peace Foundation. We wish to express our appreciation to our fellow directors of the foundation and to its members and supporters.

The chapters added following the conference were those by Judge Christopher G. Weeramantry, the former vice president of the International Court of Justice (ICJ) and Mohamed ElBaradei, the director general of the International Atomic Energy Agency. We appreciate the support of these personalities and the International Atomic Energy Agency (IAEA).

We are indebted to Vicki Stevenson for her hard and careful work in preparing the manuscript for publication. We wish to thank Toby Wahl at Palgrave Macmillan for his support of the this book and the Palgrave Macmillan editing and production staff for their care in producing the book.

We also thank our wives, Hilal Elver, and Carolee Krieger, for their strong support on this project and many more.

Acronyms

ABM	Anti-Ballistic Missile (Treaty)
ASAT	Anti-Satellite Weapon
BMD	Ballistic Missile Defense
CBMs	Confidence Building Measures
CD	Conference on Disarmament
CISAC	Center for International Security and Arms Control
CISSM	Center for International Security Studies at the University of Maryland
CTBT	Comprehensive Test Ban Treaty
EU-3	United Kingdom, France, and Germany
FAS	Federation of American Scientists
FMCT	Fissile Material Cut-Off Treaty
GCS	Global Control System
GNEP	Global Nuclear Energy Partnership
GPALS	Global Protection Against Limited Strikes
GPS	Global Positioning System
HCoC	Hague Code of Conduct
HEU	High-Enriched Uranium
IAEA	International Atomic Energy Agency
ICAN	International Campaign to Abolish Nuclear Weapons
ICBM	Intercontinental Ballistic Missile
ICJ	International Court of Justice
IMF	International Monetary Fund
INESAP	International Network of Engineers and Scientists Against Proliferation
INF	Intermediate-Range Nuclear Forces (Treaty)
IRENA	International Renewal Energy Agency
ISG	Iraq Study Group
JDEC	Joint Data Exchange Centre
LCNP	Lawyers' Committee on Nuclear Policy
LEU	Low-Enriched Uranium
LOWC	Launch on Warning Capability
MAD	Mutually Assured Destruction
MTCR	Missile Technology Control Regime
NAM	Non-Aligned Movement
NAC	New Agenda Coalition
NAS	National Academy of Sciences
NASA	National Aeronautics and Space Administration
NATO	North Atlantic Treaty Organization
NCRI	National Council of Resistance of Iran
NGOs	Non-Governmental Organizations
NMs	Nuclear Materials
NNSA	National Nuclear Security Administration
NNWS	Non-Nuclear Weapon States

NPR	Nuclear Posture Review
NPT	Non-Proliferation Treaty
NRC	National Research Council
NRDC	National Resources Defense Council
NSAs	Negative Security Assurances
NSG	Nuclear Suppliers Group
NSS	National Security Strategy
NSWMD	National Strategy to Combat Weapons of Mass Destruction
NWC	Nuclear Weapons Convention
NWFW	Nuclear Weapon-Free World
NWFZ	Nuclear Weapon-Free Zone
NWS	Nuclear Weapon States
OPANAL	Organization for the Prohibition of Nuclear Arms in Latin America
OST	Outer Space Treaty
P5	Permanent Five (members of the UN Security Council)
P5+1	Permanent Five and Germany
PAL	Permissive Action Link
PNAC	Project for a New American Century
RNEP	Robust Nuclear Earth Penetrator
RRW	Reliable Replacement Warhead
SALT	Strategic Arms Limitation Treaty (I and II)
SIOP	Single Integrated Operational Plan
SLBM	Sea Launched Ballistic Missiles
SORT	Strategic Offensive Reductions Treaty
START	Strategic Arms Reduction Treaty (I and II)
UDHR	Universal Declaration of Human Rights
UFPJ	United for Peace and Justice
UN	United Nations
UNGA	United Nations General Assembly
UNMOVIC	United Nations Monitoring, Verification, and Inspection Commission
WHO	World Health Organization
WMD	Weapons of Mass Destruction
WMDC	Weapons of Mass Destruction Commission
ZBM	Zero Ballistic Missiles

Illegal in Any Circumstances
Whatsoever

Douglas Roche

The nuclear disarmament movement must focus on driving home a clear core message to the public and the politicians: nuclear weapons are immoral and illegal. They are a crime against humanity.

Though often treated separately, the moral and legal arguments have a common basis in humanity's long understanding that indiscriminate destruction of life violates the humanitarian value of life itself.

Two of the towering figures in the nuclear disarmament movement, the late Sir Joseph Rotblat and Judge Christopher Weeramantry, have forcefully expressed the interrelatedness of this twofold message. We ought to concentrate on what they have taught us as we ourselves explore ways to demand effectively that governments live up to their moral and legal responsibilities.

Rotblat provided an example of how to express the antihuman nature of nuclear weapons in moral language that transcends religions. Only a few months before his death, he sent a message to the 2005 Review Conference of the Non-Proliferation Treaty (NPT).

> Morality is at the core of the nuclear issue: are we going to base our world on a culture of peace or on a culture of violence? Nuclear weapons are fundamentally immoral: their action is indiscriminate, affecting civilians as well as military, innocents and aggressors alike, killing people alive now and generations as yet unborn. And the consequence of their use might be to bring the human race to an end. All this makes nuclear weapons unacceptable instruments for maintaining peace in the world.

Rotblat concluded his argument thus:

> How can we talk about a culture of peace if that peace is predicated on the existence of weapons of mass destruction? How can we persuade the young generation to cast aside the culture of violence when they know that it is on the threat of extreme violence that we rely for security?

This language crosses all boundaries and becomes inextricably interwoven with all the processes of daily life. The language can resonate with politicians, who should be able to relate to all segments of their constituencies.

NUCLEAR WEAPONS AND HUMAN SECURITY CANNOT COEXIST

Nuclear weapons and human security cannot coexist on the planet. Nuclear weapons are antihuman. That is what the moral aspect of the discussion is all about. Humanitarian law has always recognized that limitation and proportionality must be respected in warfare. But the very point of a nuclear weapon is to kill massively; the killing and the poisonous radiation cannot be contained.

The social and economic consequences of nuclear war in a world whose life-support systems are intimately interconnected would be catastrophic. The severe physical damage from blast, fire, and radiation would be followed by the collapse of food production and distribution and even water supplies. The prospect of widespread starvation would confront huge masses of people. Rampant disease would follow the breakdown in health care facilities. These immense brutalities would violate the universal norm of life—to go on living in a manner befitting a human being with the inherent right to life.

No civilization, no culture has ever denied this common foundation upon which all peoples stand. Leaving aside the massive suffering, which by itself ought to stir the consciences of the nuclear proponents, the entire question of human rights would be upended. The right to a social and international order, as set forth in the Universal Declaration of Human Rights, would be completely lost. The structures underpinning humanitarian law would be gone. Order would be inverted into disorder. What is the "self" that the proponents of nuclear use for "self-defense" supposed to mean? The only way to really uncover the hypocritical defense of nuclear weapons as instruments of self-defense is to focus on the overarching humanitarian question.

It is empowering to note that the age of weapons of mass destruction arrived just at the time when the Universal Declaration on Human Rights and its follow-up instruments were being codified. Just when we have learned that every human, without regard to the culture, religion, ideology, or geography, has the right to life, we have perfected our ability to kill massively. The United Nation's formulation of a Culture of Peace is leading us inevitably to the recognition that every human being has the right to peace, in fact, as is said in the early declarations on this subject, to the "sacred" right to peace. The gradual increase in humanity's understanding of itself will lead to a societal condemnation of nuclear weapons when it is fully understood that such instruments of evil are a violation of life itself.

The innate understanding of human rights has also been shown by Judge Weeramantry, who was vice president of the International Court of Justice (ICJ) when it issued its Advisory Opinion on the legality of nuclear weapons in 1996. His 88-page dissent deals convincingly with every last argument advanced by the nuclear weapon states in support of their position, including deterrence, reprisals, internal wars, the doctrine of necessity, and the health hazards of all, including so-called mini, nuclear weapons. He stated:

> My considered opinion is that the use or threat of use of nuclear weapons is illegal *in any circumstances whatsoever.* It violates the fundamental principles of international law, and represents the very negation of the humanitarian concerns which underline the structure of humanitarian law. It offends conventional law and, in particular, the Geneva Gas Protocol of 1925, and Article 23 (a) of The Hague Regulation of 1907. It contradicts the fundamental principles of the dignity and worth of the human person on which all law depends. It endangers the human environment in a manner which threatens the entirety of life on the planet.

While regretting that the court did not hold that the use or threat of use of nuclear weapons is unlawful "in all circumstances without exception," Judge Weeramantry said that the court's opinion does "take the law far on the road towards total prohibition."

The effect of the World Court Advisory Opinion is to provide, for the first time, a legal basis for political action to ban nuclear weapons. At first, the effect might seem minimal because the nuclear states are ignoring it, NATO is hostile to it, and the media have generally marginalized it. But the opinion is a watershed because it has made a strong statement of the law governing the threat or use of nuclear weapons. It effectively delegitimized nuclear deterrence. At the very least, nuclear proponents can no longer claim that nuclear weapons are a legitimate tool of warfare. The court forcefully identified the elimination of nuclear weapons as the true solution to the risk of planetary catastrophe posed by the existence of nuclear weapons.

It is the highest-level legal push ever given to governments to get on with nuclear disarmament. It goes beyond the NPT's Article VI, which obliges nations merely to *pursue* negotiations on nuclear disarmament: the court has deemed that such negotiations must be *concluded.* Moreover, it explicitly separated the two themes in Article VI: nuclear disarmament, and general and complete disarmament. No longer can the nuclear powers credibly state that nuclear disarmament can only come in the context of general disarmament. The "ultimate evil" must be eliminated urgently.

NUCLEAR WEAPONS ARE NOT EXEMPT

By emphasizing that nuclear weapons are not exempt from the rules of humanitarian law, the court, even though it divided on the application of certain questions of law, has brought nuclear weapons into the legal arena. It threw a spotlight on the laws of humanity and the dictates of the public conscience.

Since leaving the court, Judge Weeramantry has maintained his ardent stance on the illegality of nuclear weapons. In 2003, he said in a seminar in Colombo:

> Nuclear weapons are illegal under international law because the usages established among civilized peoples, the laws of humanity and the dictates of the public conscience of the global community of human beings would all undeniably unite in condemning this monstrosity which can obliterate entire

cities, destroy the environment and even extinguish all the culture and civilization built up by centuries of human efforts in one fell stroke. Can there be
any doubt that all civilization, all humanitarian sentiment, all dictates of this
public conscience would reject out of hand even the semblance of a contention
that such a weapon could be brought within the bound of legality?

Interpreting the law on this matter is a complex process if one takes the view
that any means of self-defense is valid. The nuclear proponents have, of course,
taken this route. The search for security through technology led to the nuclear
arms race, and the public—everywhere—was told this was necessary for self-
defense. Our common humanity was denied, as if the moral problems of the
obliteration of huge sections of humanity could be swept aside by technology. In
secular cultures, the maintenance of nuclear weapons has been rationalized away.
No law expressly forbids the threat or use of nuclear weapons; the absence of
such a law enables the nuclear proponents to drive onward. The World Court felt
that it by itself could not *invent*, so to speak, a new law. But it clearly pointed the
way to the political development of such a law, which would be built on a
common understanding that humanitarian law does not permit mass killing.
Humanitarian law must be applied to every use of every nuclear weapon. A
return to humanitarian law, not technological refinements of the act of killing,
is required for society to deal with the illegality of nuclear weapons.

A Nuclear Weapons Convention, prohibiting the production as well as use of
all nuclear weapons in all circumstances is urgently needed. Law-makers—that
is, politicians and government officials—must be awakened by public demand to
pass such legislation. An iron-clad law prohibiting all nuclear weapons must be
made. This will happen only when the evil nature of nuclear weapons is
recognized rather than being denied as it is today. By emphasizing our humanity, not our technological prowess, we can achieve a universal law criminalizing
the production and use of all nuclear weapons.

The Human Right to a Nuclear Weapon-Free World

Mairead Corrigan Maguire

I believe one of the most hopeful trends in the world today is the interconnectedness of the Human Family. Technology has made us interconnected, and trade and the movement of people have made us interdependent. Even in the past 10 years, the world has changed, and the next 20 years will bring changes that none of us can imagine. But we human beings can shape the world to a great extent. I am very hopeful for the future because I believe we are often capable of good choices, we are resilient even in the face of great disasters, and we are creative. The massive peoples' movements around the world should give us all hope. But governments must start listening and acting on what their people are saying, and particularly on such burning issues as nuclear weapons and war.

On nuclear weapons, I believe people of the world have chosen abolishment, but the governments are ignoring the wishes of their people. So we have entered the second nuclear arms race, led by the current U.S. administration and being followed by many other countries. At this point in history, if our governments don't take seriously their international obligations under the Non-Proliferation Treaty (NPT) to start decommissioning all nuclear weapons, there will be very serious proliferation within the next few years and we will truly not be able to abolish nuclear weapons. We will pass a frightful legacy onto our children and grandchildren, a legacy of nuclear weapons and nuclear debt that will endanger them and their world. It is not only the next generation we will burden, but also the cost of nuclear weapons in the past and today has robbed the materially poor of their rightful inheritance to be nurtured with basic rights of food, education and health care.

Governments are elected to take care of their citizens. But governments have not only a responsibility to nurture their own people; they have a responsibility to all of humanity. I believe this can best be done by all governments if, before taking serious policy decisions, they ask themselves, "Does this policy uphold domestic and international law, and how will it benefit our nation's people and humanity as a whole?"

This question is particularly relevant to the current U.S. administration. The whole world is now being affected by American foreign policies and American culture. All around the world, American television is beamed into billions of homes, Americanizing many peoples' way of life. This recognition places enormous responsibility upon American government, media, corporations, and people, to ask if what you are exporting is good for the world, or damaging it. What kind of ethical and moral values and example are you sending out to the world's people, particularly an impressionable and vulnerable younger generation? Is offering the example of increasing nuclearism, ongoing wars, and the ignoring of international treaties and laws really going to make the world a safer place for us all? Yes, terrorism is a threat and we all want human security, but meeting terror with terror is not an answer. I believe that such approaches to date have made the world a more dangerous place both for Americans and many people throughout the world.

After the horror of World War II, the world community recognized the need for legislation to protect citizens. Since then many international laws have entered into force. In the past, America played an important role in setting up many laws that would protect human rights. In 1945, America gave full support for the United Nations (UN). It supported the drafting of a Universal Declaration of Human Rights (UDHR), which affirmed the dignity of every human being. This declaration has affected the policies of the United States and other countries all over the earth for more than half a century. The preamble to the UDHR states: "Member States have pledged themselves to achieve, in cooperation with the United Nations, the promotion of universal respect for and observance of human rights and fundamental freedoms" and it upholds "the advent of a world in which human beings shall enjoy freedom of speech and belief, and freedom from fear and want has been proclaimed as the highest aspiration of the common people."

Under the UDHR, every citizen on the planet has a right to be free from fear of nuclear weapons, and every citizen on the planet has a right to be free from poverty, which condemns so many to lack of health care, education, shelter, and the very basic necessities that enable human beings to lead full and dignified lives.

I believe we all have a human right to a nuclear weapon-free world, and in proclaiming that right, we affirm that we have chosen to live together, as the human family and friends, and not to die together as victims in a nuclear holocaust.

Introduction

Richard Falk and David Krieger

We stand perilously at a nuclear precipice with public opinion ignorant, confused, and complacent about nuclear issues. The ignorance is associated with an absence of any widespread awareness that the U.S. government is actually intent on developing new nuclear weapons and making plans for long-term reliance on nuclear weapons as key elements of its security strategy. The confusion arises from the shift in concern away from the dangers arising from existing weaponry now possessed by nine countries to an almost exclusive preoccupation with the prevention of proliferation, which has provided a perverse pretext for the initiation of unlawful warfare, most notably in Iraq. The complacency is expressed by a public mood that both underestimates the threats associated with the existence of the weaponry, while exaggerating the threats associated with the potential acquisition of nuclear weapons, as well as a seeming indifference to any serious exploration of opportunities for total nuclear disarmament, that is, for moving back from the nuclear precipice.

We need to start our reflections by examining why the peoples of the world remain entrapped by nuclearism, which implies a willingness of governments under certain conditions to rely on weaponry of mass destruction to uphold their security. After all, the main rationale for these weapons, almost since their initial development, was their role to deter the nuclear weapons of an enemy state. This was particularly true of the United States and the Soviet Union, rival superpowers after World War II, with somewhat symmetrical visions that each was out to destroy the other, and thereby dominate the world. It was this reliance on deterrence, better described as a "balance of terror," that was the main public rationale for possessing and continuously developing these weapons, thereby producing the most costly and dangerous arms race in all of history. There were many close calls during the decades of Cold War rivalry when the world could have easily stumbled into a disastrous nuclear war. We owe our survival up to now more to good luck than to prudent governmental crisis management. Even during the Cold War there were highly persuasive political and moral reasons to have tried much harder than was the case to achieve nuclear disarmament through negotiations.

Against this background, as well as the graphic evidence provided by the charred ruins of Hiroshima and Nagasaki, we should have expected and demanded that when the Berlin Wall unexpectedly fell in 1989 and the Soviet Union collapsed two years later, and looked West for its new destiny as "Russia," there would have been a strong push toward nuclear disarmament led by Washington. At the very least, we should have expected and demanded that our leaders explore such a possibility with utmost seriousness. American prestige and influence was at its height in the early 1990s, and the world would have been excited by and responsive to nuclear disarmament proposals put forward with the serious backing of the U.S. government. But they never came, and instead, what is more revealing, and disturbing, was quiet American diplomacy encouraging Russia to sustain its arsenal of nuclear weapons. The evident intention in Washington was to avoid mounting pressure on the United States to undertake nuclear disarmament negotiations responsive to these favorable new global conditions in which there was no longer a major enemy state to deter.

It should have been obvious to any close observer that deterrence was never the whole story when explaining the retention, development, and doctrinal history of nuclear weapons in the face of their clear potential for eventually leading to catastrophic self-destruction. We should remember in this regard that atomic bombs were used against an enemy that had no retaliatory capacity, and certainly not in a deterrent role. As has been suggested, in the post–Cold War years the temptation to retain and make use of nuclear weapons may increase if an adversary state has no nuclear weapons of its own. Such a line of speculation is strengthened by recent diplomacy—Iraq was attacked allegedly because it might acquire nuclear weapons while North Korea, despite developing a small arsenal of these weapons, was only confronted diplomatically.

In light of these considerations it may seem disingenuous to be altogether shocked, or even surprised, by this failure to seize this extraordinary historic opportunity to rid the world of the menace of nuclear weapons once and for all. We need to remember that the singular use of atomic bombs in the heat of war did not occur under conditions where American survival or security was threatened. The official rationale in 1945, itself dubious in the view of most serious historians, was "to save American lives" by claiming that it induced a quick Japanese surrender that avoided the need for an invasion of the Japanese homeland. It also seemed clear that after some initial moves toward disarmament immediately after World War II, both leading nuclear powers seemed disinterested in the disarmament option throughout most of the Cold War.

There was a brief flurry of serious interest during the presidencies of Ronald Reagan and Mikhail Gorbachev, especially during their meeting in Reykjavik, Iceland, in 1986 when the two leaders seemed to agree on very substantial, phased nuclear disarmament arrangements. What was so disillusioning at the time on the American side was the surfacing of *bipartisan* hostility toward any serious consideration of such proposals, which were soon abandoned as political projects because of the futility of pushing a disarmament agenda in such resistant climate of opinion in the political leadership circles that then dominated the Washington scene. To understand this American attachment to nuclearism it is necessary to appreciate its embeddedness in American strategic thinking as well as in the linkages of the nuclear weapons establishment with the government bureaucracy and the private sector. It is this linkage that President Dwight Eisenhower famously described as "the military-industrial complex." As long as this complex remains intact and is not politically challenged by mobilized societal forces, rational argument and ethical concerns will be cast aside.

A Dangerous Inattention to Existing Nuclear Arms

There exists the illusion that with the Cold War over, the threat of an enemy state using its existing arsenal of nuclear weapons has receded so far into the background as to be of no serious concern with the notable exception of potential proliferation to countries viewed as hostile to the official American conception of world order or through terrorist acquisition of nuclear materials (NMs). Of course, the Iraq War was initiated by allegations that Iraq with an arsenal of non-nuclear weapons of mass destruction, and more remotely, with nuclear weapons of its own would pose an unacceptable threat. On similar reasoning, a war against Iran has been threatened to prevent its government from ever acquiring nuclear weapons. Public anxiety about nuclear weaponry has been cleverly manipulated to focus almost exclusive attention on *proliferation*, with corresponding inattention to *possession, continuing weapons development,* and *thinly disguised reliance on threatened use.*

This inattention is dangerous, and deeply misleading. It keeps us all unnecessarily poised at the edge of the nuclear precipice. But there exists also at this time a new awareness of national self-interest and the global setting that makes the case for the abolition of nuclear weapons more politically compelling than ever before. There exist three conditions that create this possibility: First of all, the realization that as the nuclear oligopoly slips further and further from American control, the diplomatic advantages of nuclear weapons are diminishing dramatically while the dangers are multiplying at an alarming pace. Second, there is in the global setting at the present time no major conflict between leading countries, while there is some worry that nonstate actors could somehow illicitly acquire nuclear weapons, and would have the will and capacity to inflict catastrophic harm on the United States or others. Third, the turmoil in Pakistan before and after Benazir Bhutto's assassination is a reminder that extremist elements could either gain control of the government or achieve access to the Pakistani nuclear weapons arsenal, either leading to a regional war between India and Pakistan fought with nuclear weapons or to such weapons falling into the hands of anti-Western extremists. Any one of these fundamental conditions make the stubborn refusal to pursue nuclear disarmament incredibly shortsighted and ill-conceived. This failure of political imagination can only be explained by the continuing stranglehold of the nuclear establishment on reasoned debate.

Encouraging Signs

There are some encouraging signs that there may be cracks in the consensus that has so far sustained this nuclear establishment for more than six decades of nuclearism. On January 4, 2007 the *Wall Street Journal* published a call for nuclear abolition endorsed by four of the most influential voices on national security policy in the United States: Former Secretaries of State George P. Shultz and Henry A. Kissinger, former Secretary of Defense William J. Perry, and former chairman of the Senate Armed Forces Committee Sam Nunn. What these conservative leaders say is that nuclear weapons today "present tremendous dangers" of a character that should persuade U.S. political leadership "to take the world to the

next stage—to a solid consensus for reversing reliance on nuclear weapons globally." Such a stand is justified primarily as "a vital contribution to preventing
their proliferation into potentially dangerous hands, and ultimately ending them
as a threat to the world."[1] Not unexpectedly, considerations of morality and
legality do not enter the calculations of these senior members of the inner circle
of American policymakers, devotees of hyperrealism. But this is partly what gives
their prodisarmament posture such potentially significant weight. It reflects the
calculation that given the dangers that confront the United States, this country
is better off without nuclear weapons, provided it can persuade other nuclear
weapon states to join in negotiating a reliable disarming process and, asserting
their conservative outlook, assuming that American global military superiority
can be maintained with so-called conventional weaponry.

From an objective standpoint, this statement seems as though it should have
shaken the foundations of the nuclear weapons establishment, but in fact it left
hardly a footprint on the national political consciousness. It caused far less of a
media ripple than did Jimmy Carter's warning to Israel that if its government
did not soon move toward peace with Palestinians, the likely result would be
a society inevitably based on a type of apartheid. We must ask why such a dramatic repudiation of nuclear weapons by the Kissinger group of four seemed to
be lost in the humdrum atmosphere of trivial pursuits in this country. At the
least, one might have expected and hoped for some high profile media events,
late night interviews with Charlie Rose and angry neoconservative responses,
but there did not even seem to be much inclination by advocates of reliance on
nuclear weapons to take issue with the position or to step forward and support
the changing realist calculus of costs and benefits. The best explanation is that
the nuclear weapons establishment is so deeply entrenched bureaucratically and
so supported by influential corporate actors that it is able to ignore a challenge
from these formidable public figures even when they take a step that is virtually
unprecedented, joining forces across party lines to stake out a common position
on one of the most vital issues of public policy affecting the well-being of the
peoples of the world and of future generations.

Taking account of these various developments, it seems of some urgency to
call attention to several competing realities. Most important at present is to
draw attention to the precariousness of the overall circumstances that brings us
once more to the nuclear precipice. Almost equally important is to recognize
that there may be finally an emerging ideological countercurrent to nuclearism
in influential policymaking circles that is premised on an alternate understanding of national security priorities. This revision of realism among elites should
be followed by the formation of a robust grassroots antinuclear movement in
the near future that might enjoy a broader resonance with public opinion this
time around. It is not only the significance of the Kissinger group declaring
in favor of nuclear disarmament, but it is the thrust of their argument that it
is increasingly dangerous for the security of the United States (and for other
states) to persist with its embrace of nuclear weaponry. The realist case against
further reliance on nuclear weapons by the United States arises from overlapping concerns about current thinking on proliferation, nuclear terrorism, loose
nukes, obsolescence of and the failures of counterproliferation strategy, and the
nonviability of deterrence as a means of addressing threats of future terrorist
attacks.

RATIONALIZING RELIANCE

For over six decades, the threshold leading to nuclear weapons use has not been crossed. The atomic weapons that destroyed Hiroshima and Nagasaki are small by today's standards, yet they demonstrated the enormous devastation and intense human suffering that could be caused by a single nuclear weapon on a single city. Six decades is both a short time and a long time. In the sweep of human history, six decades is incredibly brief, barely the blink of an eye. But in relation to a human lifespan it is a relatively long time, long enough for most of the people living today to be born and raised after the bombings and to know of them only by the way they are described in history books and through cultural manifestations such as movies and literature. For most of the world's inhabitants nuclear weapons are largely out of sight and out of mind. The survivors of the atomic bombings of Hiroshima and Nagasaki are a rapidly diminishing population.

There is no assurance that nuclear weapons will not be used in the future. On the contrary, continued reliance on nuclear weapons by the current nuclear weapon states almost assures that at some point in the future these weapons will be used again, by accident or design. There are unstable nuclear weapon states situated in war zones and there exists the Hiroshima temptation to use nuclear weapons for military advantage where there exists no retaliatory prospect.

During the Cold War the possession and development of nuclear weapons were justified in public by their official and nonofficial advocates primarily as instruments of deterrence to be used in restraining others from nuclear use and thus "necessary" for keeping the peace. Deterrence was never more than a label for a policy, actually a very unstable and misrepresented one, logically analyzed to death, but rarely subjected to experiential tests by reference to changing military balances, real-time accidents and misperceptions, and the recklessness of sociopathic or paranoid leaders. For deterrence to work there must be rational decision makers operating on the basis of near perfect information about the intentions and behavior of an adversary, a fanciful proposition in times of relative stability, and absurdly unrealistic in times of acute crisis. Communications must always be clear and reliable for deterrence to work, and the more countries with nuclear weapons the harder it will be to assure effective communications. The fabric of deterrence has been shredded in the most recent period of world politics where the main potential attacker is projected as a nonstate terrorist network without a homeland and led by willing martyrs who cannot be deterred.

It seems plausible that the more countries with nuclear weapons, the more likely it becomes that terrorist organizations will sooner or later obtain nuclear weapons and will use them without fear or even concern for retaliation. The use of a single nuclear weapon against any inhabited area would be a horrifying spectacle of devastating magnitude. One hardly dares imagine a nuclear 9/11 in New York City, so grotesque its occurrence and so likely the reaction would be to dwarf even the ghoulish reality of the provoking attack. Any unidentified use of a nuclear weapon would likely trigger a retaliatory nuclear attack on a state alleged to be harboring or supporting the terrorists, and would also move this country ever closer to authoritarian rule at home.

We are standing at a nuclear precipice, one which we could easily lurch across with catastrophic consequences for humankind. We missed a golden opportunity in the aftermath of the Cold War to back away from the precipice by immediately and drastically reducing reliance on nuclear weapons and making good faith efforts to achieve nuclear disarmament. We were lucky to have escaped from the Cold War without destroying civilization in a nuclear exchange, but we did not end, or necessarily even lessen, the danger of nuclear annihilation. What has happened instead has been a shift in our perception of the danger in the direction of proliferation and terrorism and, to an insufficient extent, of our own nuclearist dispositions.

At the height of the Cold War, there were some 70,000 nuclear weapons in the world, nearly all in the arsenals of the United States and Soviet Union. Today, the number has gone down, but it has made us, if anything, less secure. There are still some 26,000 nuclear weapons in the world, more than 95 percent in the U.S. and Russian arsenals. Some 12,000 of these are currently deployed, and some 3,500 of them remain on hair-trigger alert, ready to be launched within moments of an order to do so. From the narrowest perspective of avoiding nuclear accidents and strategic miscalculations in an era where there exists no war-prone rivalry among leading states, it seems to border on insanity to take such unnecessary risks. The willingness to do so makes sense only as further evidence that the one-eyed nuclear weapons establishment is primarily concerned with sustaining its role as the centerpiece of American national security strategy, an expression of bureaucratic compulsion that imperils the future and is completely hidden from public scrutiny and democratic accountability.

Russia, under President Boris Yeltsin, came close to launching a nuclear attack against the United States in 1995 when Russian officials initially mistook a joint U.S.-Norwegian weather satellite launch for a U.S. attack on Russia. Yeltsin, who often went to bed having had too much to drink, was awakened in the middle of the night and told he had only minutes to decide on whether or not to launch a devastating "retaliatory" attack against the United States.

Fortunately for humanity, Yeltsin chose to take some extra minutes to make the decision, and it became apparent that the rocket was not headed toward Russia. The result of a Russian nuclear attack on the United States, launched by mistake, could have been a full-scale nuclear war between the two countries, risking the survival of much of the world's population. This incident was caused by a failure of communication. The Russian military had been informed of the rocket launch, but this information had not been conveyed up the Russian chain of command, leading to the misconstruction of the facts at the highest levels of Kremlin authority. Such an incident is a stern reminder of how precarious life becomes on the edge of the nuclear precipice that we have all been living on, and continue to live on, despite the disappearance of the strategic and ideological pretext for doing so. This persisting nuclearism is a wildly irresponsible national posture, reinforced by the passivity of other governments and public opinion, and sustained by a sinister combination of the politics of denial and secrecy.

THE NEED FOR POLITICAL WILL

To move back from the nuclear precipice will require political will and leadership by the nuclear weapon states. At the present, there is little discernable political will, little apparent desire among political leaders to reduce significantly their reliance on nuclear weapons. This was exemplified by the overwhelming support in the U.S. Congress for the U.S.-India nuclear deal, as well as by the ongoing failure of the United States and the other nuclear weapon states to take any meaningful steps toward fulfilling their existing obligations regarding nuclear disarmament under international law, steps that would have served their interests in diminishing the various risks associated with the existing arsenals of nuclear weapons.

The Non-Proliferation Treaty (NPT) contains a long-standing and well-understood requirement for good faith negotiations to achieve nuclear disarmament. This obligation of the nuclear weapon states was a principal trade-off given to the non-nuclear weapon states in exchange for their agreement not to develop or otherwise acquire nuclear arsenals. There are no good faith negotiations at the moment, nor are there any on the horizon. It appears by now beyond doubt that the main nuclear weapon states, and not just the United States, remain opposed, or at best indifferent, to nuclear disarmament, and seem reluctant to bring the issue close to the surface of public awareness. In this self-serving way, these nuclear weapon states wish to retain the NPT while disregarding the bargain that made possible its negotiation, and enticed widespread participation, in the first place.

In 2002, the United States and Russia entered into a bilateral agreement, the Strategic Offensive Reductions Treaty (SORT), in which they pledged to reduce the number of deployed strategic nuclear weapons in their arsenals to 2,200 or less by the end of the year 2012. However, even this agreement is far *less* than it seems and claims. The parties made no commitment to dismantle the weapons removed from the arsenals, nor even to verify compliance with their removal, nor is there any transparency nor assurances against restoring the weapons to the arsenals at a later time; in fact, by the terms of the agreement the two states after December 31, 2012 are free to redeploy the weapons taken off deployed status. The treaty seems little more than diversionary window-dressing and should not be confused with a sincere effort to achieve nuclear disarmament. As long as this set of circumstances persists, the inhibitions on the acquisition of nuclear weapons embodied in the NPT are without moral and political force, and even lack legal credibility. According to international law, treaty obligations are dependent on *reciprocal* observance of key provisions.

The International Court of Justice (ICJ) considered the legality of the threat or use of nuclear weapons, and issued an Advisory Opinion on this subject in 1996. While a majority of the judges cast doubts on the illegality of nuclear weaponry under *any* circumstances, the court was unanimous when it came to the NPT obligation to negotiate disarmament, concluding "There exists an obligation to pursue in good faith and bring to a conclusion negotiations leading to nuclear disarmament in all its aspects under strict and effective international control."[2] That is the law as it stands, and it is being defied, ignored, and abandoned by the nuclear weapon states, and without any adverse publicity or mainstream criticism. Again it is notable to observe that the United States did its best to prevent the ICJ from ever addressing the question of the legality of nuclear weaponry, arguably the most important legal issue confronting humanity, and when this failed, and the court rendered its Advisory Opinion, the United States refused to pay the slightest heed, thereby demeaning the highest judicial body in the United Nations (UN) System.

The failure to fulfill their obligations for nuclear disarmament places the nuclear weapon states in peril. As much as they may want the global status conferred by possession of nuclear weapons, this symbolic attainment comes with an unacceptable substantive risk. Over time nuclear weapon states seem as likely as other states, perhaps more so, to be the victims of these weapons. Nuclear weapons cannot physically prevent a nuclear attack and they make their possessors a target of other nuclear-armed nations that seek to deter them. Deterrence does not work under present world conditions, while placing civilian society in a permanent position of catastrophic risk. General George Lee Butler, a former commander in chief of the U.S. Strategic Command, once in charge of all U.S. strategic nuclear weapons, has stated, "Nuclear deterrence was and remains a slippery intellectual construct that translates very poorly into the real world of spontaneous crises, inexplicable motivations, incomplete intelligence and fragile human relationships."[3]

Stepping Back from the Precipice

We stand at a nuclear precipice and, in our hubris, we could easily tip over the edge. It would be a dreadful calamity and a grim reminder to humanity of our frailty in the Nuclear Age. Rather than take this fall, we need to step back from the precipice as soon as possible, recognizing our current danger and seeking the safety of phased, verifiable, transparent, and irreversible nuclear disarmament under strict international control. There are many steps that can be taken on the way to signal such intent, but the first and most important step is an unconditional commitment to the total elimination of these weapons. Once this commitment is credibly made, the technical challenges of moving from where we are to a world freeing itself of nuclear weapons by stages need to be carefully considered, but it is likely that a safe and secure disarmament momentum will build confidence and support as it proceeds. This doesn't mean that such a process will be without problems, but it does mean that the goal can and should be accomplished, and that a positive experience with nuclear disarmament is likely to spill over to other demilitarizing steps that could liberate needed resources to address the growing menaces of climate change, resource depletion, disease, and poverty to a sustainable human future.

What are some of the more immediate steps that can be taken to signal the onset of a new realism with respect to nuclear weapons of the sort commended by the Kissinger group?

1. Take all currently deployed weapons off hair-trigger alert, so that decisions to use nuclear weapons cannot be made in a moment of miscalculation, intense anger, confusion, or panic.
2. Make legally binding No First-Use pledges to other nuclear weapon states and pledges of No Use to all other states.
3. Bring the Comprehensive Test Ban Treaty (CTBT) into force by ratification of all nuclear weapons–capable states, in order to put an end forever to nuclear weapons testing.
4. Negotiate a verifiable Fissile Material Cut-Off Treaty (FMCT), to place all nuclear weapons materials under strict and effective international control.
5. Finally, and indispensable, the nuclear weapon states should as a matter of highest priority negotiate a Nuclear Weapons Convention for the phased

elimination of nuclear weapons. This convention should have built-in confidence-building measures, so that as the numbers of nuclear weapons are diminished, confidence in the system of verification and control will simultaneously be increased. Great pressure should be exerted to obtain the participation of all nuclear weapon states in this historic denuclearizing process. Nuclear disarmament will only be politically feasible if it encompasses every nuclear weapon state, although the states with smaller arsenals can be allowed to defer their participation until the later stages of the process.

A TURN TOWARD NUCLEAR ABOLITION

Our assessment is consistent with what respected other initiatives have concluded, as well as takes comfort from the Kissinger group declaration of a new realism on the subject of nuclear weaponry. In 2006, the Weapons of Mass Destruction Commission, headed by Swedish diplomat Hans Blix, issues its report *Weapons of Terror, Freeing the World of Nuclear, Biological and Chemical Arms.* The report found that disarmament is in disarray. The commission stated, "Many people thought that the end of the Cold War would make global agreements on disarmament easier to conclude and implement. Many also expected that public opinion would push for this. The opposite has been the case."[4]

The report contained a total of 60 recommendations, including 30 recommendations on nuclear weapons. The final recommendation on nuclear weapons stated, "All states possessing nuclear weapons should commence planning for security without nuclear weapons. They should start preparing for the outlawing of nuclear weapons through joint practical and incremental measures that include definitions, benchmarks and transparency requirements for nuclear disarmament."[5]

In November 2006, a group of Nobel Peace Laureates convened in Rome for the Seventh World Summit of Nobel Peace Laureates. In their Rome Declaration they stated, "Nuclear weapons are more of a problem than any problem they seek to solve. In the hands of anyone, the weapons themselves remain an unacceptable, morally reprehensible, impractical and dangerous risk."[6] They concluded that the current situation regarding nuclear weapons, including the risk of these weapons falling into the hands of terrorists, "is more dangerous than during the Cold War."[7]

"We are gravely concerned," the Peace Laureates stated, "regarding several current developments such as NPT stakeholders enabling rather than constraining proliferation, modernization of nuclear weapons systems, the aspiration to weaponize space, thus making arms control and disarmament on earth all the more difficult, and the declared policy of terrorist organizations to obtain nuclear weapons."[8] The Laureates pledged their commitment to "challenge, persuade and inspire Heads of State to fulfill the moral and legal obligation they share with every citizen to free us from this threat."[9] And they called upon the citizens of the world to join them.

In one of his final speeches during his 10-year tenure as secretary general of the UN, Kofi Annan, speaking at Princeton University on November 28, 2006, focused his remarks on nuclear weapons, which he called "the greatest danger of all."[10] He supported this statement by arguing that nuclear weapons pose a unique existential threat to humanity, that the nonproliferation regime faces a major crisis of confidence, and that the rise of terrorism increases the danger that nuclear weapons will be used. Annan further argued that it is not possible to choose between preventing nuclear proliferation and nuclear disarmament. "We must tackle both tasks," he declared, "with the urgency they demand."[11]

In late 2006, James Carroll, a columnist for the *Boston Globe*, analyzed the U.S.-Iranian standoff on nuclear weapons. In a column on December 11, 2006, he wrote, "The nuclear double standard is the issue. Iran's nuclear ambition is only to have what America has. Hence, the impasse. No riddle here."[12] Of course, this presumption of Iranian ambitions is by no means accurate. The consensus of the American intelligence community, as contained in the November 2007 National Intelligence Estimate, concludes with "high confidence" that Iran abandoned its nuclear weapons program in 2003, and has not resumed.[13]

Carroll continued, "Washington must renounce the nuclear double standard, recommitting itself to nuclear abolition. The reason Iran should not have nuclear weapons is that no country should. With that one stroke, the entire dynamic would change. Negotiations with Iran would be purposeful. Iran would have reason to defuse the bomb of Iraq. The sphinx itself would be disarmed."[14] In other words, the key to preventing nuclear proliferation is the commitment to nuclear disarmament; it is ending the double standard of nuclear "haves" and "have-nots" that has stood for too long.

But even with the change in attitude exemplified by the Kissinger group, it will require strong public pressure on political leaders and a challenge to the all-powerful nuclear weapons establishment in order to succeed in achieving the necessary changes in U.S. nuclear policy. This establishment operates not only from within the Beltway, but from the deepest bowels of the governmental bureaucracy as reinforced by some titans of the private sector defense industry that use heavy lobbying to ensure their influence within the halls of Congress. To redirect the American approach to nuclear weapons will require educated and active citizens who are committed to attaining a world free of nuclear threat, and it also presupposes a strong remobilization of a grassroots campaign.

Mohamed ElBaradei, the director general of the International Atomic Energy Agency and the 2005 Nobel Peace Laureate, made a strong statement calling for a nuclear weapon-free world in early 2007. "We should always remember," ElBaradei said, "that the goal of the Non-Proliferation Treaty (NPT) is a world free from nuclear weapons."[15] He argued that it was crucial to move forward on the nonproliferation front, "but with equal force on the disarmament front" and "to build an effective system of collective security that does not rely on nuclear weapons in any way."[16]

The challenge is evident. Nuclear weapons are the problem, although far from the only problem. Certainly nuclear weapons are not the cure for twenty-first century fears and anxieties. At best, they have not yet taken us over the edge of the precipice. We have been abundantly warned of their dangers, but we still stand at the nuclear precipice. The question remains: Can the people of the planet awaken and use their imaginations to project the future we face if we do not end our reliance on nuclear weapons? It is an act of faith to believe this is possible. Although the shift in the winds of informed opinion create some basis for hope, it will be soon turned to despair if significant steps are not taken to rid the world of nuclear weapons.

We must summon our strength and persistence to achieve the political will in the nuclear weapon states, particularly in the United States, to change the course of history by eliminating nuclear weapons. Nothing less is required to bring some measure of human security to the peoples of the world. But even this will not be nearly enough. The world is deeply challenged to address also problems of climate change, disease, poverty, transnational crime, ethnic cleansing, political violence, and most of all, an addictive, dysfunctional militarism. As the world retreats from the nuclear precipice, it is important that a massive accompanying educational initiative link the repudiation of nuclear weaponry with a more generic repudiation of militarism, the war system, and political violence.

PUBLIC OPINION ON NUCLEAR WEAPONS

On the issue of nuclear disarmament, the public in the United States seems to be ahead of both the foreign policy elites and most political leaders, at least on the level of opinion. This was borne out in a poll developed by WorldPublicOpinion. org in conjunction with the Center for International Security Studies at the University of Maryland (CISSM). In November 2007, they released national polling results of Americans and Russians on nuclear disarmament issues. The poll found that 73 percent of Americans and 63 percent of Russians favored the goal of eliminating nuclear weapons. Eighty-eight percent of Americans and 65 percent of Russians support the U.S.-Russian SORT to reduce nuclear arsenals to 2,200 or less by the year 2012. Majorities in both countries would like to reach these goals even sooner and would support reductions to 400 weapons on each side. Ninety-two percent of Americans and 65 percent of Russians believe that an international body, such as the UN, should monitor and verify compliance with these reductions. In general, these numbers demonstrate that the U.S. public strongly favors steps to achieve nuclear disarmament, but even this evidence of encouraging attitudes is insufficient unless it is extended to the elimination of all nuclear weapons.

The public needs to enter the debate on the side of eliminating these weapons for the benefit of all humanity, and put pressure on leaders who are reluctant to move toward eliminating nuclear arsenals. We hope that this collection of essays will help to frame the debate and add to it the appropriate sense of urgency that the abolition of nuclear weapons demands.

EXPLORATIONS AT THE EDGE OF THE NUCLEAR PRECIPICE

This book is divided into five sections: At the Nuclear Precipice; Nuclear Weapons and International Law; Nuclear Weapons Policy; A New Direction; and Stepping Back from the Precipice. Many of the chapters were originally presented as papers at a conference organized by the Nuclear Age Peace Foundation in 2006: *At the Nuclear Precipice: Nuclear Weapons and the Abandonment of International Law.* The authors are leading analysts of nuclear dangers. Many have been leaders in the global effort to eliminate these dangers and have been strong advocates of pressing the nuclear weapon states to fulfill their obligations under international law.

The conference opened with a greeting from Tadatoshi Akiba, the mayor of Hiroshima and the president of Mayors for Peace. Mayor Akiba stated, "The human family will, in the next few years, decide what to do about nuclear weapons. Will we eliminate them? Will we allow every nation capable of making these weapons to have them? Or, will we try to make sure the good guys have them and the bad guys don't? These are our three alternatives, and two of them will lead to pain, suffering, and horror beyond our comprehension."

Mayor Akiba, whose city suffered the devastating effects of nuclear attack, saw a ray of hope in efforts to eliminate nuclear weapons. He said, "Nuclear weapons represent danger that defies description, but they also represent the best opportunity we have to shift the international community away from the deadly, competitive culture of war toward the prosperous, nonviolent, and cooperative culture of peace."

NOTES

1. Shultz, George P., William J. Perry, Henry A. Kissinger, and Sam Nunn, "A World Free of Nuclear Weapons," *Wall Street Journal*, January 4, 2007.
2. Advisory Opinion of the ICJ on the legality of the threat or use of nuclear weapons, United Nations General Assembly, A/51/218, October 15, 1996, p. 37.
3. Butler, George Lee, Speech at the University of Pittsburgh, May 13, 1999, Web site of the Nuclear Age Peace Foundation: http://www.wagingpeace.org/articles/1999/05/13_butler_upitt-speech.htm.
4. *Weapons of Terror, Freeing the World of Nuclear, Biological and Chemical Arms*, Stockholm: Weapons of Mass Destruction Commission, 2006, p. 24.
5. Ibid., p. 196.
6. The Rome Declaration of Nobel Peace Laureates, November 19, 2006, Web site of the Nuclear Age Peace Foundation: http://www.wagingpeace.org/articles/2006/11/19_romedeclaration_print.htm (Refer to Appendix C.)
7. Ibid.
8. Ibid.
9. Ibid.
10. Annan, Kofi, Lecture at Princeton University, November 28, 2006, Web site of the Nuclear Age Peace Foundation: http://www.wagingpeace.org/articles/2006/11/28_annan_abolition.htm (Refer to Appendix E.)
11. Ibid.
12. Carroll, James, "Desperate for Answers to All-Important Iraq Riddle," *The Boston Globe*, December 11, 2006, Web site of the Boston Globe: http://www.boston.com/news/globe/editorial_opinion/oped/articles/2006/12/11/desperate_for_answers_to_all_important_iraq_riddle/.
13. "National Intelligence Estimate," Web site of Wikipedia, http://en.wikipedia.org/wiki/National_Intelligence_Estimate.
14. Carroll, "Desperate for Answers to All-Important Iraq Riddle."
15. Maclean, William, "ElBaradei Renews Call for Nuclear Bomb-Free World," January 9, 2007 (Reuters), Web site of Nuclear News: http://nucnews.net/nucnews/2007nn/0701nn/070109nn.txt.
16. Ibid.

PART I

At the Nuclear Precipice

CHAPTER 1

Sleepwalking Into Our Century of Last Opportunity

Christopher G. Weeramantry

The theme of this book is that we are at the nuclear precipice. Catastrophe awaits us unless we transform ourselves. We urgently need to begin that process now.

The process of transformation is not something that will commence in the corridors of power. We, the citizenry of the world, need to transform our attitudes and carry that transformation with conviction to the corridors of power. As Mahatma Gandhi taught in so many ways, the process of transformation of society begins with transforming ourselves.

Carrying our convictions to the decision makers requires a considerable effort on the part of international lawyers in particular. The first step is to alert the citizenry of the world to the grim reality that their present attitude of resignation leads inevitably to the destruction of themselves, their civilization, their children, and all that they hold dear. No greater responsibility ever lay upon the global legal profession to explain to the global public the extent of the violations of international law embodied in every single nuclear weapon. The international legal profession cannot afford to speak upon this matter with a confused or muted voice. No greater responsibility ever rested on any previous generation in history to take steps to avoid a looming threat to civilization and to humanity itself. Indeed, no situation of greater universal danger ever existed since humans first began to live in organized society.

No less than these are the issues that we are facing. Yet, complacency is the order of the day. We have heard these notes of warning often—in fact so often that we have become accustomed to disregarding them. How do we correct this attitude of complacency in the face of the nuclear menace?

Some years ago I wrote a pocket booklet for the general public that was circulated in various languages on the imminence of the nuclear danger. In that I listed 15 reasons for the growing nuclear danger day-by-day. I would find it convenient to arrange the topics I will address in this chapter in groups of 15 as it is a convenient number to handle and, at the same time, is sufficient to convey the multiplicity of the ways in which our rights and security are being undermined.

One could start by noting that the nuclear weapon violates every precept of human compassion and morality and by recapitulating a number of them. Around 15 of them could be formulated with ease, but I shall gloss over them and get down to the more mundane level of the law and the facts.

As a prelude to the factual survey, it would be useful to recapitulate at least 15 of the basic principles of international law that are grossly violated by the retention of the bomb. Referring to principles of international law that are obviously violated by the bomb does not take us very far unless we bring home the urgency. I believe we can do so through at least 15 different grounds of urgency, which I will outline in this discussion.

The figure of 15, which has been only randomly selected, could be indefinitely expanded, for the selected items only outline the contours of the problem. These 15 categories are sufficient, however, because they are such as to send the danger signals flashing into every home around the world. It is because this message has not been adequately communicated that the citizenry of the world—loving fathers and mothers, loving grandparents and aunts and uncles—have permitted their rulers to prepare a catastrophic doom for the children they so lovingly nurture and cherish and the children of those children and all succeeding generations.

Nuclear Weapons and International Law

I begin with the principles of law that are grossly violated. The public needs to be reminded that they were all achieved through the sacrifice of millions of lives and through a succession of wars and massacres that have darkened the pages of recorded history. There were always resolutions at the end of such catastrophes that people would unite to prevent them from occurring again, but those resolutions were permitted to evaporate when the terrible events that prompted them receded into the past.

It is paradoxical also that the vast majorities of these good citizens, who by their inaction are parties to the impending destruction of civilization, also profess one or other of the great religions that have taught human beings to look to the higher values in the governance of their daily conduct—of which peace, goodwill, reconciliation, forgiveness, the peaceful settlement of disputes, the outlawing of cruelty, environmental protection, stewardship of earth's resources, human dignity, the unity of the human family, the protection of future generations, the love of children and good neighborliness are all basic teachings.

Those great reservoirs of human wisdom have also over the centuries helped to nourish and fertilize the development of the relevant principles of international law.

Here are just 15 of the basic principles of international law that the nuclear weapon grossly violates:

1. The criminality of genocide.
2. The illegality of aggression.
3. The criminality of inflicting torture and cruel and excruciating pain and distress.
4. The prohibition of weapons of excessive cruelty.
5. The prohibition of crimes against humanity.

6. The solemn duty of adherence to the Charter of the United Nations (UN) and the basic principles that it enshrines, all of them dedicated to the furtherance of human dignity and the preservation of peace. This was a charter that required the sacrifice of tens of millions of lives to achieve, and to disregard it is to betray the memory of those millions.
7. The total illegality of causing damage to states not involved in a conflict between the two combatants. This is an inevitable result of nuclear conflict.
8. The duty to discriminate between combatants and noncombatants, thereby rendering grossly illegal the indiscriminate killing of civilians.
9. The principle that proportionality needs to be established between the damage done and the cause for which the damage was inflicted.
10. The prohibition against the violation of basic principles of human rights contained in the Universal Declaration of Human Rights (UDHR) and related documents. These include the right to found a family, the right to a healthy environment, the principle of equality before the law, the principle of human dignity, the right to security, the right to a standard of living adequate to good health and well-being, the right to a social and international order in which rights and freedoms set forth in the UDHR can be fully realized and the very right to life itself. The UDHR, be it noted, was the first universally agreed document on human rights to be achieved in the long history of humanity and should as such command the respect of all right-thinking world citizens.
11. The right to a nuclear-free world ensuring to every global citizen from the unanimous decision of the International Court of Justice that meaningful steps should be taken toward the elimination of nuclear weapons from the arsenals of the nuclear powers.
12. The right to the protection of the cultural heritage—engineering and architectural marvels, works of art, historical objects, priceless manuscripts, libraries acquired over the millennia—only to be wiped out without a trace in seconds, in the event of the use of nuclear weapons.
13. The whole body of principles of international humanitarian law painfully worked out over the centuries.
14. The prohibition on causing irreversible environmental damage.
15. The prohibition on imperiling the rights of future generations.

The earlier observation about blinkered vision regarding nuclear weapons can be well illustrated in a manner that every schoolchild can understand. The civilized nations, as the major powers liked to describe themselves in the nineteenth century, have long recognized the principle that weapons that inflict cruel and unnecessary suffering on the victims are illegal and are not to be used in warfare among civilized countries. In pursuance of this principle, the dum-dum bullet that tore into the entrails of its victim was outlawed in the nineteenth century and rightly so.

It needs no legal knowledge to realize the abysmal contradiction between such pronouncements of the "civilized" nations and the argument they now advance even at the beginning of the twenty-first century. They fully accept the principle that the cruelty of the dum-dum bullet prevents it from being used by civilized nations, but at the same time assert that they may resort to the nuclear weapon even though it is a million times more devastating than the humble dum-dum bullet.

A child of 10 would see the absurdity of such a proposition but those in the highest echelons of power, in a generation that is better informed than any in human history, see no absurdity in such a proposition. On the contrary, they are prepared to stake their own reputation and that of the nation they lead upon such manifest absurdities. If humanity survives and the history of civilization is written in a later age, these attitudes will be severely condemned as one of the darkest chapters in the saga of human existence on the planet.

This becomes especially dangerous when we are in the beginning years of the last century that humanity will face before either putting its house in order or condemning civilization to extinction.

After the great Peace Conference of 1899, the twentieth century opened with high resolves of avoiding a repetition of the blood-stained record of the nineteenth century. Humanity then had the luxury of a twenty-first century to succeed it and give it another chance of putting its house in order in case it mismanaged its affairs in the ensuing century. The twenty-first century gives us no such opportunity. If we bungle our affairs in this century, as we did in the last, we shall have no twenty-second century to put our house in order. If the twentieth century was our century of *lost* opportunity, the twenty-first century is our century of *last* opportunity. Yet, we seem to be sleepwalking through its initial years, with the blinkers growing even narrower in the corridors of power.

Nearing the Nuclear Precipice

Having set out just 15 principles to show how unarguably the bomb overrides a battery of principles of established law, I now set out just 15 basic facts that show how unarguably we are getting nearer day-by-day to the nuclear precipice. These groups of 15 could be considerably lengthened if we chose.

1. Not even the most careful observer of the international weapons scene can venture to say exactly

   a. How many states actually have the weapon;
   b. How many states are close to acquiring it;
   c. How many states have launched nuclear weapons research;
   d. How many states are negotiating with smugglers or others to have access to nuclear weapons.

What is clear, however, is that all these processes are in progress, encouraged by the double standards that seem to prevail on this world-shattering issue. Those who seek to police the world to ensure that nuclear weapons are not acquired by new states are violators of the very principles of nonacquisition and nondevelopment of nuclear weapons that they seek to enforce. Domestic law enforcement conducted on such a basis would clearly attract scorn and resistance.

There are some who are thought to have nuclear weapons and are punished on this basis, but then are found not to have them—thereby proving that the enterprise of acquiring nuclear weapons is impossible to police unless all states act with one accord in pursuance of a common policy toward nuclear weapons.

At the time of Hiroshima and Nagasaki there was only one nuclear state and the weapon could be used without any fear of a nuclear retaliation. But the number soon increased to two, three, four, and five and is nine or more today. Any one or more of them could be drawn into a nuclear conflict once the first nuclear weapon is used. If there is even one irresponsible member of the nuclear group, this is a recipe for disaster.

There can be no doubt that there are states that would desire to acquire them, but would restrain that desire if the nuclear powers showed an intention to abide by their obligation to wind down their arsenals. So long as they continue in breach of their obligation to do so, other states would feel no obligation to desist from acquiring nuclear weaponry. Every passing day increases the risk that there will be an addition to the "nuclear club," thereby bringing closer the day when the nuclear weapon will be used.

2. There is a phenomenal increase in the power and spread of terrorist groups. They are often in league with arms manufacturers, drug runners, and other elements of society, which pay scant regard to humanitarian values. They are sometimes funded by interested organizations, sometimes by expatriate groups and sometimes by those with a vested interest in the conflict. Their assets run in some cases to hundreds of millions of dollars. They would dearly love to have a nuclear weapon available to them. They have the funds wherewith to purchase the necessary material and expertise and even the funds necessary to purchase a bomb itself from a derelict collection of nuclear weapons.

Indeed, it is not beyond the realm of possibility that we may wake up one morning in the near future to the news that such a weapon is in the hands of such a group that is using it as a threat. Once in their hands there will be no compunction in the use of it.

The current world situation breeds new terrorists—people who live in abject poverty when wealth is flaunted all around them, people involved in civil conflicts who see their loved ones killed before their very eyes, wedding parties destroyed, children blown to pieces, and friends and neighbors decimated. They will only be incited to fresh acts of violence and so the spiral of violence escalates.

3. The knowledge necessary to make a nuclear weapon has ceased to be the preserve of a few experts walled within the security establishments of states. With the proliferation of information technology, the know-how necessary to make a nuclear weapon has spread to the extent that a clever university student or code buster/hacker could break into the necessary information. I once made this point at a talk that I gave on the subject in London, and after the lecture, I asked a physics professor, who was present for the session, whether I had overstated the position. His answer was that in his view a physics student who was not able, if he so desired, to acquire the basic knowledge to make a crude nuclear device was unworthy of a higher degree in physics. It is an alarming thought that such perilous knowledge is so widely available.

Another danger in the area is the penetration of information codes by "hackers." Cyber warfare has been going on for several years and the knowledge necessary for destroying existing security systems has been growing by the day. Well-known incidents exist where hackers have been brought to book for breaking into the best protected data banks in the United States and Germany.

There is also the possibility of state-sponsored hackers. This is very much in the thoughts of security experts. Cyber warfare, whereby those having the information seek to keep it in closed compartments and those attempting to penetrate it are devising new means of breaking into this enclave, has been estimated as having occurred in 121 countries. If the data regarding construction of special weapons cannot be preserved from computer penetration and if even NASA and a Pentagon computer[1] have allegedly been penetrated, it is indeed a flimsy veil of security that protects the most dangerous weapons from reaching the most dangerous hands.

4. Some scientists who were once employed in nuclear programs, which have been disbanded, especially scientists of the former Soviet Union, have been on the market, offering their skills and expertise to any organization or individual who is willing to pay them adequately. To reach them is by no means an impossibility, especially because states or organizations that desire this knowledge have vast sums of money at their disposal.

The world has no inventory of these scientists, for the establishments they were involved with functioned under conditions of complete secrecy. Who they are, where they are, and what they are involved in, after their establishments were disbanded, is anybody's guess.

A case that attracted much attention in January 2004[2] was that of an eminent Pakistani scientist. There were allegations of a clandestine international network of nuclear weapons technology proliferating to countries desirous of acquiring nuclear weapons.

How many other less publicized leakages there have been is unknown. Not all cases attract international attention even if they are detected, but the majority probably are not detected at all.

AVAILABILITY OF NUCLEAR MATERIAL

5. Another head of danger is the availability of nuclear material. For example, on December 7, 2001 it was reported that Russia had foiled an illegal scheme of trading weapons-grade uranium and that the police had arrested seven men for attempting to sell two pounds of uranium.[3]

In the period immediately following the collapse of the Soviet Union, the Russian police regularly seized nuclear materials stolen by people allegedly attempting to trade them. Much of this material was low-grade nuclear material, but the danger always exists of high-grade enriched uranium being illicitly removed and sold.[4]

With the proliferation of nuclear reactors all over the world, this danger keeps intensifying dramatically. The number of nuclear reactors according to the International Atomic Energy Agency (IAEA) has now risen to 439 units,[5] of which some are Slovak Republic-5, Slovenia-1, Pakistan-2, Bulgaria-2, Czech Republic-6, India-17, and Ukraine-15.[6]

Total surveillance of their stock by the IAEA or any other authority is not a possibility. The IAEA does not have a proper record of all these materials and policing these 439 sites is a clear impossibility. Moreover, materials are frequently conveyed from one place to another in trains, ships, and motor vehicles. In the absence of specific and accurate inventories, the danger of theft, short delivery, or hijacking is ever present.

There have also been reports of Russian managers offering plutonium for sale to foreign scientists in the 1990s.[7] In an incident in 1998, Russian security forces foiled an attempt to steal weapons-grade nuclear material sufficient to create an active nuclear weapon.

Here is some data that has emerged from the Nuclear Traffic Forum held in Italy in 1997. It concerns cases of traffic in radioactive substances and nuclear materials (NMs) from 1990 to 1997: 43 in 1993, 45 in 1994, 27 in 1995, 17 in 1996, and 2 in 1997. Of 134 illegal traffic cases, 34 percent involved radioactive substances and 66 percent involved weapons-grade nuclear materials. Out of the total, only eight cases involved military NMs; that is, material that could be used to build a nuclear bomb (all of which occurred between 1992 and 1996).

- October 1992, Podolsk, Russia, HEU 1.5kg—90 percent enrichment[8]
- July 1993, Andreeve Guba, Russia, HEU 1.8 kg—36 percent enrichment[9]
- June 1994 St. Petersburg, Russia, 2.972 kg of 90 percent HEU[10]
- June 13, 1994 Landshut, Germany, 795 mg of 87.7 percent HEU[11]
- July 25, 1994 Munich, Germany, 240 mg of Pu-239[12]
- December 14, 1994 Prague, Czech Republic, 2.73 kg of 87.7 percent HEU[13]
- June 7, 1995 Moscow, Russia, 1.7 kg of 21 percent HEU[14]
- October 2, 1999 Kara-Balta, Kyrghyzstan, 1.49 g of Pu[15]
- July 22, 2001 Paris, France, 2.5 g of 72.57 percent HEU[16]

The stolen military nuclear materials come from research institutes, ships, space centers, or nuclear plants, and not from depots of nuclear weapons. There have also been cases of undetected thefts, given the lack of effective exchange of information on military depots, control systems, and nuclear stocks.

LAUNCH ON WARNING CAPABILITY

6. Some nations have put their defense systems on alert in accordance with what is known as a Launch on Warning Capability (LOWC). This means there are hair-trigger devices in those countries, which are set to detect incoming objects entering their air space of which they have no prior notice. If the object is a suspicious one and is thought to be a nuclear device, the LOWC is set to respond within minutes, if not seconds. This explodes the myth that a responsible presidential or prime-ministerial decision is required before a nuclear response is launched. It is the machine that decides, and the machine must decide within minutes. Machines can make mistakes. There can be purely mechanical mistakes and we all know that no machine is 100 percent perfect. There could also be errors of judgment, for an unannounced incoming object can be wrongly thought to be nuclear when, in fact, it could be perfectly innocent. There have been actual examples of this, as when a Russian LOWC nearly responded to an innocent observation satellite from Norway,[17] which was entering its air space and was under a wrong impression regarding its character for six of the eight minutes available before response. It was only by a happy accident that the error was detected when the time for the response had nearly run out.

Other examples include

- False Alarm of October 24–25, 1973—during the Middle East Crisis when the UN sponsored cease fire intended to end the Arab-Israeli War was in force and U.S. intelligence reports and other sources suggested that the USSR was planning to intervene to protect the Egyptians. U.S. officials ordered an alert on October 25; while it was in force, mechanics were repairing one of the Klaxons at Kinchole Air Force Base, Michigan and accidentally activated the whole base alarm system. B-52 crews rushed to their aircraft and started the engines. The duty officer recognized the alarm was false and recalled the crews before any took off.[18]

- November 1979—false alarm due to a faulty computer exercise tape mistakenly displaying a large number of Soviet missiles on a full-scale attack on the United States.[19]
- June 1980—a faulty computer chip showing warning displays of a number of missiles, resulting in preparations for retaliation including nuclear bomber crews starting their engines and U.S. Minutemen missiles being ready for launch.[20]
- January 1985—Russian army detecting an unexpected missile launch near Spitzbergn, five minutes flying time away from Moscow. It was a Norwegian missile launch for scientific measurements.[21]

In many of these, the dangers may have been small but an accumulation of these raises cause for concern. All of them could be fleshed out with considerable detail, but just one of them is expanded here by way of illustration. During the Suez crisis of November 5, 1956, messages were received of unidentified aircraft flying off Turkey, Soviet MIG-15 flying over Syria, a British Canberra bomber being shot down over Syria and a Soviet fleet moving through the Dardanelles. The four reports were all shown to have innocent explanations due to

1. A flight of swans.[22]
2. A routine airport escort for the president of Syria who was returning from Moscow.[23]

Such a response, if wrongly triggered, would mean the commencement of a real war since the missile system at the receiving end could automatically trigger off a nuclear response, thus leading to a real nuclear exchange.

Having regard to the large number of objects in air space for one reason or another, the possibility of their accidentally entering the air space of a nuclear state is ever present and the risk of unintended war is consequently ever on the rise.

NUCLEAR ACCIDENTS AND CLOSE CALLS

7. Nuclear accident is an ever-present possibility. There have been numerous such accidents in the past and considering the fact that there are tens of thousands of these weapons around, the dangers are grave. The numerous accidents that have occurred in the past are little known to the general public. Here are a few of them:

- November 10, 1950—Quebec, Canada the U.S. Defense Department, in its 1980 publication on nuclear accidents, stated the following: "A B-50, experiencing an in-flight emergency, jettisoned a bomb over water (outside the United States) from an altitude of 10,500 feet. The weapon's HE [high explosive] detonated on impact." The report failed to mention that the accident apparently took place just north of the U.S. border in Quebec. It was found the B-50 jettisoned a Mark 4 bomb over the St. Lawrence River near Riviere-du-Loup, about 300 miles northeast of Montreal. The detonation of the bomb's high explosives shook the region, scattering nearly 100 pounds (45 kg) of uranium.[24]

- January 24, 1961—a B-25 caught fire over North Carolina and accidentally dropped two H-bombs. They did not explode.[25]
- April 10, 1963—the U.S. nuclear submarine Thresher sank in Boston Harbor; 129 sailors died. This was the world's first nuclear submarine catastrophe.[26]
- January 17, 1966—a B-25 carrying H-bombs crashed while flying over Spain. Radioactive contamination.[27]
- February 1970—Explosion at Nuclear Submarine Factory at West Gorky. Several died, radioactive contamination.[28]
- October 25, 1976—underground nuclear explosion at Soviet Navy Base in Baltic. Over 40 deaths.[29]
- January 29, 1978—Soviet nuclear powered satellite crashes into a lake in North East Canada. Radioactive contamination.[30]
- July 6, 1979—Accidental explosion at French nuclear test site in Mururoa.[31]
- April 9, 1989—Soviet Nuclear Submarine burns and sinks offshore of Norway; 42 died.[32]

These are just a few from a very long list. As long as the nuclear enterprise continues, these accidents will continue to occur. Any one of them has the potential to trigger off a dangerous chain of consequences, which no one can predict.

8. The number of occasions when the world was on the verge of nuclear war in the past 60 years is considerable. In well over a dozen crises it was hovering on the brink and it was only by a series of happy accidents that the world was saved from nuclear war. Once the first bomb flew, that would be the point of no return and there would inevitably be an escalation of the conflict, with other nuclear powers being drawn in, resulting in all-out nuclear war.

Examples even from the years following World War II were numerous. For example,

The Berlin Wall Crisis 1948
The outbreak of the Korean War 1950
The Suez Crisis 1956
The Taiwan Straits Crisis 1958
The Cuban Missile Crisis 1962
The seizure of the USS Pueblo by North Korea in 1968

As everyone knows, the Cuban Missile Crisis was an eyeball-to-eyeball confrontation between the leaders of the Soviet Union and the United States. Looking back at it now, the conclusion seems inescapable that the probable outcome was certainly a confrontation and that the actual outcome was only a remote possibility. It was the world's phenomenal good fortune that it ended the way it did.

In more recent times, the Middle East, the Indian subcontinent, and North Korea have all furnished deep tensions from time to time, which have raised fears of the possible use of a nuclear weapon.

There are nuclear weapons today in the hands of unstable governments. Even in stable governments, extremists can suddenly come to power. In unstable governments, this danger is ever present. The dangers multiply as the nuclear powers increase.

9. Another reason why this danger is increasing is that the number of mini-wars throughout the world is on the increase. We live in a world that is torn with disputes, but we tend to dismiss them as being minor or as being too far removed from us. Even as this book goes to press there are several substantial conflicts in progress throughout the world, some of them capable of drawing in other participants. In such rivalries, there is always the possibility of drawing in states that have nuclear capabilities and when that will happen no one knows. Nearly every seemingly small conflict has some bigger states or interests operating behind the actual contesting parties and if they are drawn in, the proximity to nuclear weapons grows ever closer.

The list of such miniwars includes Bosnia, East Timor, Kashmir, Kosovo, Turkey (Kurdistan), Macedonia, Chechnya, Sri Lanka, Sudan, Uganda. These are just a few of many countries that can be mentioned in this context.

INCREASED DISREGARD OF INTERNATIONAL LAW

10. There have been trends in recent years for international law to be disregarded as and when it suits those who feel they are in a position to disregard it. An instance is the invasion mounted on Iraq by two of the Permanent Members of the Security Council in disregard of the several rules that have grown up in international law forbidding such action. The rule against unilateral action by individual states without Security Council authorization and the principle that architectural and historical objects and sites are to be preserved are just two, which illustrate the wide range of matters covered by these principles. These are all well-established rules of international law and some of them are enshrined in the UN Charter itself. They were built upon the sacrifice of millions of lives and need to be respected.

When international law is disregarded, especially by powerful states, it removes restraints that would otherwise operate on others who desire to use force illegally and flout the rules of international law.

BREEDING RESENTMENT

11. Another constantly increasing danger results from the growing disparity between the rich world and the poor world. As this gap widens, so grows the chance that economic iniquities could trigger acts of violence that, in turn, could trigger larger conflicts.

There are many nations in a state of desperation, unable to acquire even the basic necessities for their sustenance. A time may come when they or irresponsible groups within them seek to mount an attack on the centers of privilege, which they perceive as being the source of their privations. Hundreds of millions live below the poverty line and millions of preventable deaths continue to take place for sheer lack of resources and lack of concern on the part of the affluent world and its many multinational corporations, which operate within the poor world and, in fact, extract wealth from it. Resentment on these matters is intense among certain groups and can provoke rash actions. This is one of the most urgent global problems to which inadequate attention is presently devoted, and it affords a prolific breeding ground for terrorists and others who are prepared to take the law into their own hands.

Statistics convey a very eloquent message regarding this aspect. For example, 51 percent of the world's wealthiest bodies are corporations, thus enabling these individual corporations to command more financial power than nearly 150 states of the world. Half the world's population lives on less than two dollars a day and 20 percent of the population of the developed nations consume 86 percent of the world's goods.[33] Less than 1 percent of what the world spends every year on weapons could have put every child in the world into school by 2000, but war took priority over education.[34]

12. All this is breeding resentment on an unprecedented scale and calls for urgent attention.

Another factor to be borne in mind is that research on the improvement and refinement of nuclear weapons is proceeding across the world. The nuclear weapon is constantly being made more precise, less cumbersome, and more easy to deploy. Its portability is increasing steadily and the day is not far distant when it would be so small that it could be carried quite easily in a traveler's bag or even on his or her person. When that stage is reached, one suicide bomber—and of suicide bombers, there is no shortage—can hold the rest of the world to ransom.

Recent press reports have caused speculation that mininuclear weapons are being developed and that existing weapons are being refined through continuing research in the weapons laboratories of the nuclear powers. The nuclear weapon states tend to describe these as only feasibility studies, but this is a danger that looms large. Bunker buster weapons are some of those that have aroused these comments.

Currently available nuclear weapons, if used as bunker busters, would result in a massive amount of nuclear fallout and huge loss of civilian life. The argument is therefore used that bombs with low-explosive yields would minimize radioactive fallout and these are described as "benign earth penetrating nuclear weapons." The search seems to be on for mininuclear weapons, and in more than one way this can render the future use of the nuclear weapons both more likely and more dangerous.

A 1991 paper of the Los Alamos National Laboratory examined the possible development of low-yield nuclear weapons and three classes of nuclear weapons were mentioned as likely to meet the need of producing the necessary deterrent effect.

- "micronukes" with an explosive yield of about 10 tons of TNT
- "mininukes" with an explosive yield of about 100 tons of TNT
- "tinynukes" with an explosive yield of about 1,000 tons of TNT

13. It is fundamental to this entire discussion that any conflict of the future in which nuclear weapons are used will be totally unlike Hiroshima and Nagasaki, where there was the certainty that there would be no nuclear response. The next nuclear weapon wherever used will draw a nuclear response and this means further retaliation, multiple nuclear exchanges, a nuclear winter, and all the dreaded scenarios so often predicted of the extinction of organized life as we know it.

One of the myths of the Nuclear Age is that it was the nuclear weapon that saved the world from a major war for that past 60 years. Another myth is that even a city exposed to nuclear attack can rise from the ashes (witness Hiroshima and Nagasaki). As argued above, the avoidance of a weapons exchange has been largely fortuitous but, more important, the next nuclear engagement will assuredly be as different from Hiroshima and Nagasaki as the firearm was to the bow and arrow.

14. Nuclear stockpiles number over 26,000. Inventorying them, storing them, and policing them in a world where so many want them is becoming an increasingly difficult task. Some of the storage depots are far from the metropolis of the nuclear power as was the case with the Soviet arsenals in various distant parts of the former Soviet Union. Likewise, nuclear materials are not inventoried and are being continually produced.

As shown already, nuclear smuggling from these enormous stockpiles has also become a very real danger. The only way in which such nuclear smuggling can be thwarted and prevented is a universal agreement by all nations, nuclear and non-nuclear. This will never happen so long as the nuclear nations cling to their present policies of not keeping to their obligation to work toward the complete elimination of nuclear weapons.

15. The increasing number of suicide bombers now available for carrying out desperate tasks is a phenomenon of our times. Their ranks are being constantly increased as a result of current international events and policies.

Suicide bombers are committed persons; they are desperate and will stop at nothing. They can operate as individuals, thus diverting suspicion. They are bred by conditions in which they see all their values, all their loved ones, all their cherished hopes shattered by acts of violence. They are people fired with dedication, driven by hatred, smarting under a sense of injustice to their people and regardless of the consequences to themselves or to the thousands of innocents at the receiving end. They do not have the information that will soften their view of what has happened. Global conditions today are swelling their ranks as never before.

Nuclear Danger Is Not Remote

For all these reasons, then, the nuclear danger is not a remote problem distant from us in space and time. It is with us now and growing by the month. Complacency and indifference are the prime factors that accelerate the growth of the dangers and bring them progressively nearer to us.

The problem cannot be solved unless it is approached in good faith by all states, nuclear as well as non-nuclear. The fundamental principle of international law, namely one rule for all, needs to be observed if any credibility is to attach to the steps that need to be taken.

If nuclear and non-nuclear states join their resources, united by a resolve to banish this scourge from the face of the earth, we can control proliferation, inventory stocks, track down offenders and render planet Earth a safer place for all. If, on the other hand, the nuclear powers insist on a dual legal regime—one for themselves and one for the others—proliferation will continue, more hands will get a grip on the weapon, and irresponsible fingers will be twitching on the nuclear trigger. One incident will lead to another and a nuclear exchange could obliterate civilization and end all organized society and perhaps end all life itself.

Children in their simplicity see the enormity of this danger, without any obfuscation of the issues. As a six-year-old child once observed, "Adam was the first man. I hope I will not be the last." As a 10-year-old observed, "Everybody says they do not want nuclear weapons, yet the weapons remain. Somebody must be lying." The nuclear danger, as clearly seen through the eyes of children, needs to be more widely perceived by the adult population.

How long our luck will hold is anyone's guess. If all of humanity does not collectively act to abolish this weapon, this weapon can single-handedly destroy all of humanity. Public opinion needs to be alerted and public information needs to be stepped up. International lawyers need to play a lead role in this process, not merely by disseminating information among themselves, but also by carrying it to the public. International law is one of those areas veiled in obscurity as far as the general public is concerned. We need to make it one of the great illuminated places of the law, which it deserves to be—a place from which light and learning and hope radiate to all ranks of the public. If this is not so already, perhaps we international lawyers need to take much of the blame. If this is done, we can move forward to that sunlit plateau of justice and peace that has been the dream of the ages.

NOTES

1. *McKinnon v Government of the USA and another.* [2007] EWHC 762 (Admin), April 19, 2007, *Times* online, http://business.timesonline.co.uk/tol/business/law/reports/article1674046.ece.
2. William J. Broad, David E. Sanger, and Raymond Bonner, "A Tale of Nuclear Proliferation: How Pakistani Built His Network," *The New York Times*, February 12, 2004, http://www.nytimes.com/2004/02/12/international/asia/12NUKE.html?pagewanted=all&position.
3. BBC NEWS, Friday, December 7, 2001, http://news.bbc.co.uk/2/hi/europe/1697907.stm.
4. Steve Coll, "Stolen Plutonium Linked to Arms Labs, German Scientists Trace Origin of Nuclear Materials to Russia," *Washington Post Foreign Service*, Wednesday, August 17, 1994, A01.
5. Power reactor information system data base (PRIS database, http://www.iaea.org/programmes/a2/.
6. Ibid.
7. Rensselaer W. Lee, "The Failure of Supply-Side Nuclear Control," *Foreign Policy Research Institute (FPRI)*, FPRI Wire, 7.6 (April 1999), http://www.fpri.org/fpriwire/0706.199904.lee.supplysidenuclearcontrol.html.

8. Lyudmila Zaitseva and Friedrich Steinhausler, "Illicit Trafficking of Weapons-Usable Nuclear Material: Facts and Uncertainties First," published by the Forum on Physics & Society of the American Physical Society, January 2004, http://www.aps.org/units/fps/newsletters/2004/january/articles.cfm#3.
9. Ibid.
10. Ibid.
11. Ibid.
12. Ibid.
13. Ibid.
14. Ibid.
15. Ibid.
16. Ibid.
17. Pavel Podvig, "History and the Current Status of the Russian Early Warning System," *Science and Global Security*, 10. 1 (2002), pp. 21–60.
18. Alan F. Phillip, MD, "20 Mishaps That Might Have Started Accidental Nuclear War," http://www.wagingpeace.org/articles/1998/01/00_phillips_20-mishaps.htm.
19. Ibid.
20. Ibid.
21. Ibid.
22. Ibid.
23. Ibid.
24. CNN Interactive, http://www.cnn.com/SPECIALS/cold.war/experience/the.bomb/broken.arrows/.
25. CNN Interactive, http://www.cnn.com/SPECIALS/cold.war/experience/the.bomb/broken.arrows/.
26. SIPRI (Stockholm International Peace Research Institute) Yearbook 1977, p. 6.
27. CNN Interactive, http://www.cnn.com/SPECIALS/cold.war/experience/the.bomb/broken.arrows/.
28. Hiroshima peace site, http://www.pcf.city.hiroshima.jp/Peace/E/pNuclear3_3.html.
29. Jeffrey T. Richelson, *The U.S. Intelligence Community*, 2nd ed. (New York: Ballinger, 1989), pp. 167–197.
30. Nucleus, 14/6/1978; Burleson, C. W., "The Day the Bomb Fell," *Great Britain* (1980), pp. 227–245.
31. Channel 9 News, Perth, August 9, 1979 from A.A.P.
32. CNN Interactive http://www.cnn.com/SPECIALS/cold.war/experience/the.bomb/broken.arrows/content/1980d.html.
33. 1998 Human Development Report, *United Nations Development Programme*, http://hdr.undp.org/en/reports/global/hdr1998/. Anup Shah, "Poverty Facts and Stats," http://www.globalissues.org/TradeRelated/Facts.asp#fact8.
34. State of the World, Issue 287, February 1997, *New Internationalist*, http://www.newint.org/issue287/keynote.html. Anup Shah, "Poverty Facts and Stats," http://www.globalissues.org/TradeRelated/Facts.asp#fact8.

CHAPTER 2

Still Standing at the Nuclear Precipice after All These Years: Why?

Jacqueline Cabasso

August 2005 marked the sixtieth anniversary of the illegal and barbaric U.S. atomic attacks on innocent civilians. Let me repeat that: . . . *the illegal and barbaric United States atomic attacks on innocent civilians.* How different it sounds from the earnest, passive voice we've come to expect—even to utter ourselves—when describing those gruesome events, as we gather each year to "commemorate the anniversary of the atomic bombings of Hiroshima and Nagasaki." Whenever I hear that phrase, I am struck by the utter lack of accountability ascribed to the source of those anonymous weapons of mass destruction. We all learned about the Nazi Holocaust in high school. Yet, even today, the U.S. atomic bombings of Japan are not widely taught in our public schools. As the Mayor of Hiroshima told the International Court of Justice in 1995,

> History is written by the victors. Thus, the heinous massacre that was Hiroshima has been handed down to us as a perfectly justified act of war. As a result, for 50 years we have never directly confronted the full implications of this horrifying act for the future of the human race. Hence, we are still forced to live under the enormous threat of nuclear weapons.

We have now an important opportunity to review where we are and where we've been in terms of nuclear weapons themselves and the movements that have sought to control or eliminate them.

In this era of "messaging" and "reframing," I would like to suggest some new themes:

1. *There was more than one Holocaust in World War II.* In two blinks of an eye, over 200,000 human beings were sentenced to death by nuclear weapons dropped on Hiroshima and Nagasaki by U.S. bombers. By the end of 1945, approximately 210,000 men, women and children had perished—incinerated in an instant, or incomprehensively, slowly and painfully dying from ghastly radiation burns, unable to eat or drink, their

hair falling out in clumps, their skin hanging from their bones like shreds of fabric. Delayed effects, which continue to this day, include cancer, chromosome damage, birth defects, and immunological disorders. Harder to quantify is the legacy of destruction of traditional society, devastation of community life and social systems, and psychological trauma. Those who survived, live daily with the memory of "hell on earth." *Nothing could have justified those bombings. The United States should take responsibility for its heinous crimes and apologize to the people of Japan.*

2. *Nuclear weapons are the only true "weapons of mass destruction."* U.S. doctrine lumps nuclear, chemical, and biological weapons together, labeling them all as "weapons of mass destruction." But chemical and biological weapons, while unspeakably terrible, immoral, and illegal, are subject to the whims of weather and terrain, and difficult to deliver in sufficient quantities to kill many thousands of people. Nuclear weapons, in contrast, are orders of magnitude more destructive. According to a Princeton study, a single 150 kiloton modern nuclear warhead, 10 times larger than the Hiroshima bomb and the most numerous type in the U.S. stockpile, if detonated over Mumbai, India, could kill more than eight million people and cause untold injuries, illnesses, and genetic effects. *One* nuclear weapon is a Holocaust. There are still approximately 26,000 of them in the world, enough to destroy human civilization in a day. *Equating nuclear, chemical, and biological weapons is one way the United States is lowering the threshold for nuclear use.*

3. *Terrorists already have nuclear weapons and are making plans to use them again.* More than 15 years after the end of the Cold War, the United States, the *only* country that has used nuclear weapons in war, maintains a nuclear arsenal of some 10,000 warheads. It is the *only* state with nuclear weapons on foreign soil; 400 of them are deployed at eight bases in six NATO countries, ready for delivery by U.S. and NATO bombers. More than 1,500 U.S. strategic nuclear weapons remain on hair-trigger alert, ready to instantly target locations around the globe upon receiving a few short computer signals. Land-based nuclear missiles are ready to launch their deadly payloads within two minutes. U.S. Trident submarines continue to patrol the seas at Cold War levels, ready to fire hundreds of the most destructive weapons ever conceived, on 15 minutes notice. *The threatened first use of nuclear weapons, even against countries that don't have them, is official U.S. policy, at the highest level.*

4. *If you build it, they will come.* In a famous line from the movie, *Field of Dreams*, the protagonist declares: "If you build it, they will come." He was talking about a baseball field and the sports fans it would attract. In the same way, as we're now seeing all too clearly, *if you build a new nuclear weapons infrastructure, it will produce new nuclear weapons. On the basis of this close observation and analysis of developments at U.S. nuclear weapons labs, some of us were warning of this as early as 1993.*

5. *"National Security" is endangering our human security.* After touring the destruction left in the wake of Hurricane Katrina, Mississippi Governor Haley Barbour said, "I can only imagine that this is what Hiroshima looked like 60 years ago." Yet, as horrific as the hurricane and flooding were, the damage and suffering they caused pale in comparison to

the effects of a nuclear explosion—*a 100 percent preventable man-made event.* As the disaster of Hurricane Katrina continues to unfold, it is clear that our national priorities have run drastically off course. Katrina is a metaphor for massive government ineptitude, neglect, and racism. Katrina also illustrates that there could be no adequate response to the far larger catastrophe of a nuclear explosion in a city anywhere. *It is unconscionable that, in the name of "national security," the U.S. government is spending hundreds of billions of dollars on nuclear weapons and war while utterly failing to meet our human security needs.*

The United States is modernizing every weapon type in its still vast nuclear arsenal, in some cases giving them new or enhanced military capabilities. The 2007 National Nuclear Security Administration (NNSA) budget request confirms that "Life Extension Programs," to render the U.S. nuclear arsenal reliable for decades to come, are underway for the B61 bomb, the W76 SLBM (Sea Launched Ballistic Missile), and the W80 Cruise Missile. The budget's official policy guidance is the once-secret 2001 U.S. Nuclear Posture Review, widely dismissed by arms control analysts as a mere "wish list," when it was leaked to the *New York Times.* With the stated goal of establishing "a nuclear weapons infrastructure responsive to future needs," the proposed budget provides increased funding for the Reliable Replacement Warhead (RRW) program, explicitly intended to redesign and replace the entire U.S. nuclear arsenal. Under this program, virtually every warhead component will be redesigned, including the physics packages—the spherical plutonium cores, commonly referred to as "pits." Funding is provided to produce 30–40 new plutonium pits a year at the Los Alamos Lab. These new warheads aren't supposed to require the old-fashioned kind of explosive testing, but just in case, funding is included to maintain the Nevada Test Site in a state of readiness. Meanwhile something like 12,000 pits from dismantled weapons languish at the Pantex Plant in Texas, available for reuse, if desired by the weaponeers. And, just for good measure, the budget provides for demonstrating the ability to produce tritium—radioactive hydrogen, used to boost the explosive yield of nuclear weapons—by 2007.[1]

At the same time, the Pentagon is poised to begin development of a new generation of long-range delivery systems, capable of carrying either conventional or nuclear weapons. The Air Force has issued a "Prompt Global Strike Request for Information," beginning the process of examining alternatives for new weapons capable of hitting targets anywhere on earth. Supporting materials state that the "Prompt Global Strike Analysis of Alternatives" will examine "a range of system concepts to deliver precision weapons *with global reach, in minutes to hours.*" Such systems, intended primarily to increase the already overwhelming U.S. advantage in conventional weapons, could at the same time provide the building blocks for new nuclear capabilities, particularly in combination with the warhead modifications in progress and under consideration.

In 2007, the United States spent about $6.5 billion to maintain and modernize its nuclear warheads. Accounting for inflation, this is one and a half times the average annual spending during the Cold War years. It's difficult to calculate, but by some estimates, if you add the money going to modernize the warheads' means of delivery—ground-based missiles, submarines, and bombers—it is believed that the United States is spending about $54 billion a year on its nuclear forces, more than the entire military budget of nearly every other individual country in the world.

U.S. Nuclear Posture Review

Following the 9/11 attacks, the Bush administration openly declared the potential first use of nuclear weapons—even against countries that don't have them. The 2001 Nuclear Posture review revealed U.S. plans for first use of nuclear weapons in response to non-nuclear attacks or threats involving biological or chemical weapons or "surprising military developments," and targeted countries including Iraq, Iran, North Korea, China, Russia, Syria, and Libya. The December 2002 "National Strategy to Combat Weapons of Mass Destruction" states that the United States "reserves the right to respond with overwhelming force—including through resort to *all of our options*—to the use of WMD against the United States, our forces abroad, and friends and allies." "All of our options" include both "conventional and *nuclear* response and defense capabilities," employed "in appropriate cases through *preemptive* measures."

With war hanging in the balance, the President of the United States issued a warning: "America must not ignore the threats gathering against us. Facing clear evidence of peril, we cannot wait for the final proof—the smoking gun—that could come in the form of a mushroom cloud." President Bush *didn't* tell us that the mushroom cloud was more likely to emanate from the United States. In the run up to the U.S. attack on Iraq, a "Theater Nuclear Planning Document" was drawn up for Iraq.

Nuclear weapons provide the ultimate backup for U.S. conventional forces operating around the world, and they have, in fact, been more fully integrated into U.S. conventional war planning, as evidenced by Strategic Command's expanded portfolio. Nuclear weapons are *gaining* legitimacy, as the world's only remaining superpower blurs the distinction between nuclear and conventional weapons and expands the role of nuclear weapons in its "national security" policy. After 60 years of nonuse, it is uncertain whether these developments should be interpreted as dramatically lowering the political threshold for U.S. nuclear weapons use. What is unquestionably different now is that the United States is prepared to initiate aggressive wars with elevated risks of unintended consequences, including the creation of situations in which nuclear weapons might be used. But consider this: who would have believed 10 years ago that torture would be official U.S. policy and hundreds of people would be detained indefinitely, without trials, at Guantanamo? And, those with firsthand memories of hell on earth, the survivors of the atomic bombings of Hiroshima and Nagasaki, are dying off.

As the war in Iraq rages on, with mounting casualties, a country in ruins, and the poorest in the United States facing drastic cuts in vital services, Washington has turned its sights on Iran, seeking again to inflame public fears of a new nuclear threat. With the risk of use of nuclear weapons climbing toward levels not reached since the darkest days of the Cold War, where is the public outcry? What happened to the massive antinuclear movement of the 1980s? Why has the antiwar movement been so quiet about nuclear weapons?

When the Cold War abruptly ended with the dissolution of the Soviet Union (a spectacular, though never-mentioned failure of intelligence), activists, ordinary Americans, and people around the world breathed a huge collective sigh of relief, hoping and believing that they had walked away from a nuclear holocaust, and putting nuclear weapons out of their minds. Many activists went on to other issues—U.S. military interventions in Central America, apartheid in South Africa, saving ancient forests, and so on. Others went back to their day-to-day lives, raising families and working to make ends meet. Meanwhile, deeply embedded in the military-industrial-academic-corporate complex, the nuclear juggernaut rolled on, as militarists in the Pentagon and scientists at the nuclear weapons labs conjured up new justifications to project the nuclear weapons enterprise into the future. In 1991, Colin Powell, then chair of the Joint Chiefs of Staff, explained: "We no longer have the luxury of having a threat to plan for. What we plan for is that we're a superpower. We are the major player on the world stage with responsibilities...[and] interests around the world." In the early 1990s, "nonproliferation"—stopping the spread of nuclear weapons—was turned on its head. The new buzzword was "counterproliferation"—including the threat of a nuclear strike to dissuade other countries from even thinking about developing nuclear, chemical, or biological weapons that could threaten the United States or its allies.

Nuclear Weapons Off the Radar Screen

During the 1990s, nuclear weapons—especially U.S. nuclear weapons—fell off the public's radar screen. As the Dr. Strangeloves at the nuclear weapons labs got back in the saddle, questions of nuclear arms control, nonproliferation, and disarmament became increasingly isolated from issues of concern to most ordinary people—including issues of war and peace—and increasingly relegated to elite policy circles inside the beltway. This trend was exacerbated when a number of national organizations that had worked on nuclear weapons issues moved their headquarters to Washington, DC, some even closing their field offices. Professional "experts" redefined post–Cold War nuclear priorities almost solely in terms of securing Russian "loose nukes" and keeping them out of the hands of "rogue" states and terrorists.

Meanwhile, independent grassroots groups monitoring their local nuclear weapons facilities were documenting and trying to put the brakes on U.S. plans to replace full-scale underground nuclear tests with a new generation of high-tech experimental laboratory facilities and supercomputers, and proposals for new weapons production processes and capabilities. For the most part, this information was kept out of Washington, DC discourse by arms control lobbyists protecting their access to policy and decision makers. As viewed from the corridors of power, apparently, it was an "inconvenient truth" that nuclear weapons research and development was going forward hand in hand with evolving counterproliferation policies reliant on "credible" U.S. nuclear threats. To make matters worse, as the decade wore on, funding for NGOs working for arms control and disarmament began to dry up, and those funders still in the field increasingly withdrew support for independent grassroots groups advocating for the abolition of, rather than U.S. control of nuclear weapons.

Unchallenged by the arms control community, and oblivious to calls for disarmament, the Clinton administration squandered the historically unprecedented period of opportunity that appeared with the end of the Cold War. Clinton's 1994 Nuclear Posture Review was a blueprint for nuclear weapons business as usual. It was the Clinton administration that in the mid-1990s brokered the Faustian Bargain to replace full-scale underground nuclear testing with the "Stockpile Stewardship" program, at that critical juncture, making the decision to massively reinvest in, rather than begin to dismantle the nuclear weapons research and production infrastructure. Clinton's 1997 "Presidential Decision Directive-60" reaffirmed the threatened first use of nuclear weapons as the "cornerstone" of U.S. national security, and contemplated an expanded role for nuclear weapons to "deter" nuclear, chemical, or biological weapons. And Clinton signed legislation making deployment of a national missile defense system U.S. policy. Indeed, the Clinton administration laid the groundwork for the Bush administration's unilateral and aggressive foreign policy, in which the potential use of nuclear weapons is being openly considered. *If you build it, they will come.*

Thwarted in the national arena, U.S. disarmament groups gravitated toward international forums. They found, at the month-long 1995 Nuclear Non-Proliferation Treaty (NPT) Review and Extension Conference, that the United States, backed by a consortium of well-funded American arms control groups, was demanding indefinite, unconditional extension of the Treaty.[2]

CIVIL SOCIETY AND NUCLEAR DISARMAMENT

Tensions were high during the 1995 NPT Conference, as many non-nuclear states expressed their dissatisfaction with the lack of progress toward disarmament by the nuclear weapon states. They stressed the mutually reinforcing nature of the disarmament and nonproliferation obligations, and warned that an international system of nuclear apartheid was not sustainable. Frustrated and dismayed that the arms controllers were avoiding the "D" word—disarmament—dozens of NGOs from around the world adopted a comprehensive nuclear disarmament platform calling for the "definite and conditional" extension of the NPT and immediate commencement of negotiations on a verifiable treaty to eliminate nuclear weapons, with the treaty to be completed by the year 2000. By the end of the conference, hundreds of groups had signed the Abolition 2000 Statement, and the Abolition 2000 Global Network to Eliminate Nuclear Weapons was born. Today, more than 2,000 groups in over 90 countries are affiliated with Abolition 2000, and the founding statement is more relevant than ever.[3]

In the run up to the U.S. attack on Iraq, premised in part on the wholly unsubstantiated claim that Iraq had an active nuclear weapons program, a new antiwar movement began to coalesce, with a heightened sensitivity to the domestic impacts of the "war on terror," including attacks on immigrants, and drastic cuts to social services for the poorest members of our population. The first National Assembly of United for Peace and Justice (UFPJ), held in Chicago in June 2003, seemed like a good opportunity to reclaim nuclear disarmament as a peace and justice issue and to reintegrate it into the broader antiwar movement. A proposal from U.S. Abolition 2000 groups to make nuclear disarmament a UFPJ priority was adopted, with little discussion or controversy. It was striking, however, that several delegates voiced objections to the effect that "nuclear disarmament is the *Bush* agenda!" They were apparently referring to the Bush administration's preventive war doctrine, carried out against Iraq and threatened against North Korea and Iran. This turned out to be the tip of an iceberg, exposing a vast lack of awareness in the new antiwar movement—reflecting the general lack of public awareness—about the post–Cold War realities of U.S. nuclear weapons. And it marked the beginning of a continuing internal education process in UFPJ, the largest antiwar coalition in the country, with over 1,400 member groups.[4]

In August 2004, on the fifty-ninth anniversary of the U.S. atomic bombings, the mayors of Hiroshima and Nagasaki, urged on by the aging *hibakusha*—survivors—in their cities, launched the Mayors for Peace Emergency Campaign to Ban Nuclear Weapons, and announced a Year of Remembrance and Action for a Nuclear Weapon-Free World. Revisiting the Abolition 2000 agenda, they presented their "2020 Vision," a timetable for the elimination of nuclear weapons by 2020, which they would bring as a demand to the NPT five-year Review Conference in May 2005. By the time they got to New York, well over 500 Mayors from 32 countries—65 of them from the United States—had signed onto the Mayors' campaign. On May 1, the day before the 2005 NPT Review Conference began, Abolition 2000 and United for Peace and Justice joined forces to demand: *End the War in Iraq. Abolish All Nuclear Weapons. NO NUKES! NO WARS!* Forty thousand people marched past United Nations headquarters in New York City and rallied in Central Park. The Mayors of Hiroshima and Nagasaki and dozens of *hibakusha* carried the lead banner, flanked by city officials and NGO leaders from around the world. Behind them, spirited antinuclear and antiwar activists filled more than 13 city blocks.

On September 26, 2005, following a massive weekend protest organized by UFPJ in the nation's capital, I was arrested in front of the White House, with nearly 400 others, for nonviolently "demonstrating without a permit" against the war in Iraq. As I languished in a holding cell with several Gold Star mothers, women who had lost sons and daughters in Iraq, I was again reminded of the *hibakusha* and their haunting message: *What happened to us is so terrible, it must never happen to anyone again.*

COMPETITION BETWEEN THE NUCLEAR WEAPONS LABORATORIES

During the Cold War years, a weapons designer at the Lawrence Livermore National Laboratory reportedly said, "Remember: the Soviets are the competition. Los Alamos is the enemy." Today, the Los Alamos and Livermore National Laboratories are engaged in the latest variant of their ongoing arms race. The Livermore Lab was founded in 1952 to compete with Los Alamos—the permanent home of the Manhattan Project—to develop a hydrogen bomb, orders of magnitude more powerful than the atomic bombs that destroyed Hiroshima and Nagasaki. Now, while the United States accuses Iran of seeking nuclear weapons and President Bush declares that a nuclear-armed Iran would pose "a grave threat to the security of the world"—the same language he used prior to attacking Iraq—under the ill-defined RRW program, the Labs are working on competing designs for new warheads, involving entirely new pits, and a new facility to manufacture them.

With no apparent sense of irony or responsibility, Ambassador Linton Brooks, the then head of the National Nuclear Security Administration, began a January 2006 presentation on the future of the U.S. nuclear weapons stockpile this way:

> First, I assume that the United States will, for the foreseeable future, need to retain both nuclear forces and the capabilities to sustain and, if necessary, modernize those forces. *I do not see any chance of the political conditions for abolition arising in my lifetime, nor do I think abolition could be verified if it were negotiated.* Second, I see no conflict between our plans for our own nuclear weapons and our strong support for nonproliferation.

Sixty years later, this is the same kind of dangerous language the great humanist social critic, Lewis Mumford, warned about in 1946:

> You cannot talk like sane men around a peace table while the atomic bomb itself is ticking beneath it. Do not treat the atomic bomb as a weapon of offense; do not treat it as an instrument of the police. Treat the bomb for what it is: the visible insanity of a civilization that has ceased to worship life and obey the laws of life.

NOTES

I would like to thank my colleague Andrew Lichterman for his exhaustive research and analysis, which I have drawn upon here. For more in-depth analysis and source documents, see www.wslfweb.org. Specific references are available upon request: wslf@earthlink.net

1. Tritium production was halted in the United States in 1988, and plutonium pit production in 1989, due to environmental and public health hazards.
2. The NPT, which entered into force in 1970, becoming part of domestic law, manifests a bargain struck between the original nuclear weapon states and non-nuclear states. The nuclear weapon states agreed to negotiate in good faith the elimination of their nuclear arsenals. In exchange, the non-nuclear states promised not to acquire nuclear weapons. As an incentive, they were promised an "inalienable right" to "peaceful" nuclear technology, "without discrimination." By 1995, nearly every county in the world had ratified the NPT, and only the United States, Britain, Russia, France, and China had nuclear weapons. (Nuclear-armed India, Pakistan, and Israel remain outside the treaty.) At the 25-year mark, the treaty was subject to a review of its operation and negotiation of the terms for its extension.
3. The Abolition 2000 Statement is included as Appendix B. See also: www.abolition2000.org.
4. See www.unitedforpeace.org.

PART II

Nuclear Weapons and International Law

CHAPTER 3

Non-Proliferation Treaty Illusions and International Lawlessness

Richard Falk

The abandonment of international law by the nuclear weapon states in relation to nuclear weapons is nothing new though it is a serious issue. And it is nothing that we can situate in time as it was never so acknowledged for obvious reasons, and yet the practice of those governments that have acquired nuclear weapons has clearly been shaped by nonlegal assessments of their perceived security and national interests without any expression of concern about whether such weapons are legal or not. It is true that in the mid-1990s when an effort gathered momentum in the United Nations General Assembly to request an Advisory Opinion from the International Court of Justice ("World Court") as to the legality of the threat or use of the weapons, the United States and other nuclear weapon states used their influence and diplomatic leverage to discourage such a determination of legality. Such an effort suggested that at least a public relations concern existed in government circles about how the World Court would treat the legal status of the weaponry. It is chastening to realize that this American opposition to a judicial assessment of the legal status of nuclear weapons was not one more neoconservative slap at international law and the United Nations, but took place during the supposedly liberal presidency of Bill Clinton.

The General Assembly to its credit disregarded the pressure from the nuclear weapon states, and went ahead with its effort to obtain an authoritative ruling from the World Court. When the Advisory Opinion was finally issued in 1996 the majority of judges supported the view that any threat or use of nuclear weapons was unconditionally illegal unless possibly in exceptional circumstances where the very survival of the state in question. Even then the World Court did not conclude that such a use would be legal, but only that such a conclusion was a possibility. With an ill-disguised disdain for the pronouncements of international law that run counter to national security policy, the U.S. government, as well as the other nuclear weapon states, made no effort whatsoever to follow the guidelines set forth by the World Court, which were more sympathetic with the claims of these states than was the view of the three dissenting judges who favored an unconditional legal prohibition.

This assertion of an abandonment of international law when it comes to nuclear weapons must be understood as referring only to the governments of the nuclear weapon states and their supporters. By and large, neither the non-nuclear weapon states nor public opinion has abandoned international law on these questions, but they lack the capacity, and possibly the will, to work meaningfully for compliance. And certainly those groups in civil society concerned with world peace have not abandoned international law in the context of nuclear weapons. Far from it. The legal condemnation of the nuclear weapon states by civil society actors has been a consistent theme of transnational activism ever since the use of atomic bombs to attack two Japanese cities at the end of World War II. The intensity of this civic campaign has ebbed and flowed over time, corresponding roughly with periods when fears rose about risks of nuclear war, although not surprisingly the popular movement has been most sustained over time in Japan. Organizations such as the Nuclear Age Peace Foundation have always believed that any threat or use of nuclear weapons would be unlawful and would constitute a crime against humanity, and that the United States, along with the other nuclear weapon states, deserves censure for this failure to respect international law. Despite their inability to end reliance, the views of public opinion have established a climate of illegitimacy with respect to nuclear weaponry that may have added to governmental reluctance to open the Pandorra's Box of actual usage, although such governments have not over the years resisted altogether the temptation to gain diplomatic advantage by threatening use.

This abandonment challenge directed at international law by the most powerful states thus sets up a sharp tension between the imperatives of geopolitics and the requirements of international law on what is arguably the most severe danger to the future of humanity. This conclusion about the legal status of nuclear weapons is as legally unambiguous in my judgment as was the determination after 1945 that genocide should be treated as illegal and criminal. In the Genocide Convention, the language of Article 1 reminds the world that genocide was illegal before the treaty existed, as genocide was considered a crime in customary international law, although not so named: "The Contracting parties confirm that genocide, whether committed in time of peace or in time of war, is a crime under international law which they undertake to prevent and punish."

As mentioned, the Genocide Convention was not needed to establish the illegality and criminality of genocide, although the formalities of a treaty-making process added moral and political weight to the law, as well as drawing media and public attention to the crime. The treaty also established that the terminology of "genocide" would be used to delimit the crime of deliberate mass killing based on ethnic, racial, and religious identity, in a forceful, large-scale, and clearly documented fashion. An even greater benefit would result from converting existing norms of illegality relating to nuclear weapons into a widely ratified international treaty. Of course, the obstacles are far greater. In the case of genocide, the historic crime that gave rise to the treaty was the work of the Nazi regime that had been totally defeated and repudiated by the outcome of World War II. The victors reinforced this assessment of criminality by establishing the Nuremberg Tribunal that imposed responsibility on surviving Nazi military and political leaders. Although genocide was not part of the prosecution case at Nuremberg, it was an unspoken premise of the whole undertaking, and the Holocaust was never defended by postwar German leaders. On the contrary, a variety of reparations were paid to Jewish and other survivors and their descendants by the German government. In contrast, the crime of the atomic attacks have never been formally acknowledged by the American government, and has to this day been defended on the grounds of "saving American lives" as if that offers an ample explanation even if its factual assumptions are accepted as accurate. The only formal legal assessments of these attacks was made by a Japanese lower court in the Shimoda case decided in 1963 in a case seeking symbolic monetary damages that was initiated by six Hiroshima and Nagasaki survivors. This judicial body after consulting three Japanese international law experts did reach the conclusion that the attacks were unlawful, but also ruled that even nominal damages could be awarded to the complainants as the rights of Japanese citizens had been legally waived in the treaty of surrender ending the war. Another more general legal assessment was made by a civil society tribunal set up in London by British lawyers; the tribunal was presided over by four judges, three of whom had been recipients of the Nobel Prize. Its judgment provides the most extended analysis of the legal status of these weapons of mass destruction prior to the World Court Advisory Opinion, but of course, lacks any hope of implementation beyond its appeal to public opinion and even this received only scant media attention.

Against this background it remains important to evaluate the extent to which a legal assessment of nuclear weaponry has continuing relevance to policy discussions. In this sense, the absence of an international treaty of prohibition, such as outlaws any use of chemical or biological weapons, underscores both the weakness of the prohibition directed at nuclear weapons and the unwillingness of the nuclear weapon states to inhibit their discretion to possess, develop, and possibly threaten or use the weapons. Even with respect to objecting governments the absence of a treaty does not mean that nuclear weapons are unregulated by international law. We need to realize that until recently most of international law relating to uses of force was not embodied in international treaties. The law of war in its entirety was premised on the primacy of customary international law until the end of the nineteenth century. Customary international law is grounded in natural law, and ultimately derives its authority from the ethical teachings of the great world religions. Until the twentieth century, governments accepted the customary international law of war as providing a legal framework for their relations with one another. Starting in 1899 at the Hague Peace Conference, governments periodically gathered at lawmaking conferences, to codify, and in a few instances, modify and enhance, the content of customary international law and to render legal requirements in a treaty format.

The relevance of international customary law extends to new weapons and tactics that have not been explicitly regulated, but are nevertheless subject to general principles governing the behavior of states in wartime. The famous Martens Clause underscored this understanding, and has been inserted in various treaties, including the four Geneva Conventions of 1949 that provide the framework for international humanitarian law. The language is contained in the preamble to each of the Geneva treaties: "Until a more complete code of the laws of war has been issued, the High Contracting Parties deem it expedient to declare that, in cases not included in the regulations adopted by them, the inhabitants and belligerents remain under the protection and the rule of the principles of the law of nations, as they result from the usages established among civilized peoples, from the laws of humanity, and the dictates of public conscience." Such an assertion also incorporates the principles of just war as applied to the conduct of war, which disallow indiscriminate, disproportional, and inhumane weapons and tactics to be relied upon even if a military justification can be provided. It is notable that every major state has formally subscribed to this language, which undermines any argument that these weapons are legally permissible until such time as they are prohibited by treaty.

The particular dilemma faced by critics of nuclearism is that international law so clearly points in one direction and is reinforced by the even clearer imperatives of international morality and elementary prudence, while international politics continues to move decisively in an opposite direction. That is the troubling situation that we confront, and raises for all of us concerned with the menace posed by nuclear weaponry the question of what should be done in the face of such a divergence. This is not the only important global policy context in which this divergence is so vivid and pronounced. It similarly characterizes the Israeli-Palestine conflict, where impartial international legal assessments of the critical issues—be it the occupation of Palestinian territories, the status of Jerusalem, the settlements, refugees, or the security wall—is clearly on the side of the Palestinians but the political realities are on the side of the Israelis. As with the status of nuclear weapons, on all of the most contentious issues, the conclusion reached from any perspective reflective of an objective understanding of international law, the basic claims of the Palestinians enjoy roughly on the order of 90–95 percent support from the relevant provisions of international law. Because the Palestinians are politically weak and legally strong, the Israelis (with American backing) have been successful in preventing the peace process established to resolve the conflict from taking into account the bearing of international law on a determination of what constitutes a fair and just peace.

THE PRIMACY OF GEOPOLITICS

We are unfortunately living in a world where the primacy of geopolitics often suppresses the relevance of international law in those settings where the political actors who are in a situation to exert this kind of overbearing influence can shape the way in which conflicts are perceived, and either resolved or perpetuated. Whether in relation to nuclear weaponry or the rights of self-determination of a people, this vulnerability to geopolitics is responsible for much of the injustice and danger in the world. It is up to us as citizens to do our best to close these gaps between what law and morality prescribe and what dominant political forces favor.

One of the darkest shadows overhanging the nuclear weapons issue since 1945 is that the atomic bomb was used in a victorious war that was widely and, in my view, correctly appreciated as a just war in its goals, although not in its essential methods. The justifications for the horrendous atomic bombings of Japanese cities do not overcome the unavoidable legal conclusion that these attacks remain unacknowledged crimes against humanity of the greatest magnitude. The use of the atomic bomb in World War II was not merely a violation of the laws of war, a conclusion confirmed in a historic and persuasive judicial decision in the Shimoda case in 1963, but was also a criminal act of the greatest severity for which the perpetrators were given impunity.

Dropping atomic bombs on Hiroshima and Nagasaki were crimes against humanity by any reasonable understanding of international law, even without taking account of the absence of major military targets in the two Japanese cities that were attacked or the documented willingness of the Japanese government at the time to end the war on terms satisfactory to the victors. Not only has there been a virtual taboo placed on any official scrutiny of the use of atomic weapons from an international law standpoint (aside from the court case referred to above), but there has remained a widely disseminated justification relied upon by American leaders at the time that these atomic attacks saved lives, especially American lives, by inducing Japan to surrender rapidly, thereby eliminating the need for an invasion of the islands that would have caused heavy casualties on both sides.

Even overlooking the substantial historical evidence suggesting that Japan was willing and ready to surrender in any event, and granting that lives were saved, it still doesn't justify what was done any more than torturing a terrorist suspect in post-9/11 detention centers would justify torture to gain useful information. A major undertaking of international law as written into the Torture Convention of 1984 was to establish legally that torture constitutes an *unconditional* prohibition for which there are no legal exceptions. Whenever the language of "saving lives" is used by public officials to justify atrocious behavior, it should serve as a chilling warning that normally dastardly deeds are desperately seeking justification. It should be obvious that any actor using violence can always claim, often sincerely and plausibly, that the tactics relied upon, however gruesome, do save lives because they persuade the adversary to give in earlier than would otherwise occur. Such a rationalization is available to any strategic planner, resistance fighter, or suicide bomber, in virtually any circumstance, and its acceptance would nullify every effort over the centuries to set certain limits that cannot be set aside for pragmatic reasons even in the heat of battle.

There are many parts of international law and human rights that are conditional, subject to what international lawyers call derogation—that is, in times of emergency, these rights may be suspended or limited to address unusual circumstances. But the prohibition on torture has been explicitly made unconditional in both the Universal Declaration of Human Rights and the Torture Convention of 1984. It is always possible, as already mentioned, to put forward a justification for behavior of whatever character, but that's not at issue. What I am arguing is that we need to recognize the *intrinsic* criminality of any threat or use of nuclear weaponry, its nonderogability, whether we look backward in time to World War II or forward to possible situations where it serves political or military goals to threaten or actually use such weaponry.

At present we are challenged to realize with eyes wide open that an unacceptable gap continues to exist between the legal and moral imperatives prohibiting these weapons and the operational code that controls their possible use. If our leadership and citizenry were truly respectful of international law, this gap would create an obligation to pursue nuclear disarmament with a sense of urgency, or at the very least unilateral declarations renouncing first use. Unfortunately, the political culture does not yet move in this direction, and this retention and stockpiling of these weapons in large numbers for possible threat or use remains part of the geopolitical reality of contemporary world politics. These weapons of mass destruction remain essential components of the strategic planning of the major states in the world, and none more than the United States, which has been sending a regressive message in the past several years by embarking on programs to develop new categories of nuclear weapons with practical relevance to battlefield situations, and even openly discussing the military advantages of using nuclear weapons under certain combat conditions.

THE UNITED STATES IS NOT
THE ONLY OBSTACLE

Having so harshly criticized the U.S. government, I feel obliged to acknowledge that the United States is not the only obstacle to getting rid of nuclear weapons, although it is true that if the American government had vigorously pursued disarmament option either immediately after 1945 when it possessed a monopoly over the weaponry and technology, or later when the Soviet Union seemed receptive, the world might now be altogether free of the menace. Certainly, the United States bears a heavy responsibility for its failure to advocate and push for the elimination of nuclear weapons arsenals immediately following the dissolving of the Soviet Union in the early 1990s. A window of opportunity was definitely open for several years. But the United States failed to act, and even discouraged any nuclear disarmament push by others, and no government seized the opportunity to exert denuclearizing pressures.

By now several other governments seem almost as strategically attached to nuclear weapons as is the United States. Former President Jacques Chirac said a few years ago that if there was some kind of terrorist attack targeting France, he would feel free to order an attack with nuclear weapons in response. It is notable and disturbing that even such a provocative and irresponsible embrace of nuclearist diplomacy by a prominent world leader caused virtually no dismay in the media and elsewhere. Such threats, although rarely as crude and overt as voiced by Chirac, have become an acceptable form of coercive diplomacy in the Nuclear Age.

In addition, there has never been significant pressure, or even real encouragement, from the other nuclear weapon states to initiate and pursue disarmament negotiations, or even to declare formally that such weapons will never be used except conceivably in response to a nuclear attack. The United States would find itself in a very isolated and uncomfortable position if the other lesser nuclear weapon states were advocating disarmament and putting forward detailed proposals to eliminate by phases all weaponry of mass destruction and establish a trustworthy inspection and verification system. But this has yet to happen, and until it does we need to broaden our understanding of why this unlawful weaponry remains essentially unchallenged. *All* actual and potential members of the nuclear weapons club share responsibility, as do other political actors on the world stage that have done far too little to shake the foundations of nuclearism. The retention and acquisition of nuclear weapons is certainly reinforced by militarist elements in the political culture of most countries. This unfortunate reality reminds us of the need for a robust peace education throughout the world that would stimulate citizens here and elsewhere to rethink the foundations of security in the twenty-first century, pull out the roots of militarism deeply embedded in public consciousness, and build popular support for state policies that conform to international law, especially in relation to concerns about peace and security.

Secondary nuclear weapon states have become dependent on the possession of such weaponry. This means that even if the United States were to become devoted to nuclear disarmament, there would likely be strong resistance from several of the governments that now possess these weapons. It is partly that some countries have grown reliant on nuclear weapons, and could not easily replace them with conventional weapons at acceptable costs, but there are also psychological and emotional attachments that would probably impede a commitment to get rid of the weaponry altogether. Also, some countries, such as Pakistan, India, Israel, have come to think of nuclear weapons as contributing to their immediate security.

David Krieger has called attention to the jubilant mass celebrations in the streets of India after the nuclear weapons tests took place in India back in 1998. This reflected the widespread belief that a country gains stature and respect globally only when it joins the nuclear club. This nuclearist pride is something that the United States helped teach the world—that to possess these weapons is an indispensable precondition for achieving the highest rankings among sovereign states. This surge of national pride has the tendency of overlooking, or at least understating, the risks of "going nuclear." As should have been fully expected, India's entry to the nuclear club would immediately induce Pakistan to follow suit, thereby raising greatly the risk that these two adversaries would find themselves locked in a devastating future war, quite possibly fought with nuclear weapons. This seemed to have almost happened in 2002 during the border crisis in the Kargil region. At the same time, since India and Pakistan became nuclear weapon states their presence has been taken much more seriously on the global stage—leading diplomats and journalists visit, Western scholars and policymakers are more attentive, especially in the case of India. There are reinforcing factors, including India's impressive recent record of economic growth and post-9/11 security concerns in Southeast Asia, but clearly the possession of the nuclear weapons in the region has upgraded the status of both of these countries.

Converting this assessment of the illegality and criminality of nuclear weapons into a *political* project is a difficult undertaking at this time. Moral and legal pieties will not get the job done. In 1996 the World Court eloquently and definitively reinforced the consensus among scholars and activists that nuclear weapons are illegal in almost every conceivable context. Some nuclear apologists in this country have argued to the effect that if nuclear weapons arsenals are stabilized at agreed levels that this would fulfill the Non-Proliferation Treaty (NPT) commitment to achieve nuclear disarmament. Peace activists were very enthusiastic about the impact of the nuclear freeze movement in the 1980s, which in its historical setting did respond usefully to the distinctive risks of nuclear arms race at a time of Cold War tensions. It was a constructive initiative in this limited sense, but it was also detrimental to the extent that it implied an acceptance of the long-term possession of nuclear weapons and appeared to abandon an insistence of total denuclearization as an essential ingredient of a peaceful and just world order. The NPT legal obligation clearly intended to push the nuclear weapon states much beyond arms control or the freeze movement. It regarded even nuclear disarmament as only the first step in a comprehensive and agreed disarmament process designed to dismantle the whole military machine. States were and are legally required to seek general and complete disarmament, which is to address the war system as such, and to take seriously the promise of the UN Charter preamble "to save succeeding generations from the scourge of war."

THE DYSFUNCTIONALITY OF WAR AND MILITARISM

I believe that the dysfunctionality of war and militarism is one of the most important undiscovered realities of our time. Let us consider the recent efforts by governments, especially that of the United States, to solve security problems by relying on recourse to war. Such reliance in the struggle against international terrorism after 9/11 has turned out to be a very costly and unsuccessful course of action, especially in Iraq. It seems plain that if the U.S. government had accepted the constraints on policy imposed by international law it would have avoided the Vietnam War, and the Iraq War would never have happened. Of course, looking further backward, respect for international law would have meant that the atomic attacks would not have taken place, and possibly the Nuclear Age would not have materialized. And looking even further into the darkness of the historical past, Germany and Japan would not have endured such a devastating experience if their leaders had pursued national goals in a manner respectful of international law constraints. More recently, Iraq would never, in all likelihood, have been exposed to the two wars mounted against it by the United States if it had not itself waged an aggressive war against Iran in the 1980s, and then sought in 1990 to conquer Kuwait.

As a priority for national security, we require a crash program designed to reeducate our societies to understand that power and influence in the twenty-first century no longer correlates with the discretion to violate international law. In effect, realism counsels an acceptance of the constraints of international law as the basis for a prudent and effective foreign policy. The gains associated with recourse to war are largely illusory in the twenty-first century. We need to convince our leaders and citizens that adherence to international law in the conduct of foreign policy has practical advantages for even the most militarily dominant states. Until this new condition becomes widely understood it is almost certain that we will continue to have this gaping cleavage separating geopolitical imperatives to seek military solutions from legal and moral imperatives to find peaceful means to resolve international conflicts. Such a separation, in turn, means accommodating many forms of injustice, as well as keeping humanity vulnerable beneath a still dangling nuclear sword of Damocles. For several decades the states of Western Europe that were instrumental in the construction of the war system have seemed, at least partially, to have grasped this reality, refusing to invest very heavily in building a military capability. To some extent, their security was provided by the American nuclear umbrella, but the European turn toward a peace culture is more genuine than such a cynical observation implies. European borders are minimally monitored and guarded, and the new

Europe seems to have no fears that continental antagonisms that produced so many bloody wars in the past will recur in the future.

There is also a need to evaluate whether the NPT as interpreted is advancing the cause of world peace. In my opinion the NPT has long been a diversion from the core issue of nuclear abolition, but since 9/11 counterproliferation has become the leading pretext for aggressive war, which is itself a serious problem. We have yet to appreciate this link between aggressive war (or "wars of choice" as it was felicitously labeled by prowar hawks prior to the 2003 invasion of Iraq) and the NPT, although after the Iraq War and the ongoing Iran confrontation, the connection should have become unmistakable.

Beyond this current concern, the NPT from its inception has provided a way to discriminate between those countries that are allowed to be part of a second-tier nuclear geopolitics and those countries that will be destroyed because they aspire to acquire nuclear weapons and, thus, are seen as standing in the way of a broader American project to administer control over the entire global security system, with a special priority accorded to the Middle East. Putting my position provocatively, I have come to believe it is necessary to repudiate the NPT, although not nonproliferation as a policy, if our goal is to have a peaceful and just world. Perhaps, the NPT legal regime is already legally dead, given the failure of the nuclear weapon states to fulfill their end of the bargain and considering its selective implementation over the years. If material obligations in a treaty are not being fulfilled, then the treaty loses its binding character. It seems time to put the burden of risk stemming from nuclear weapons where it belongs, namely, on the principal nuclear weapon states and, especially, the United States, whose practice and doctrine seems more disposed than other nuclear weapon states to develop new types of nuclear weapons for actual battlefield use and whose history includes a persisting refusal to repudiate the past uses of such weapons.

CHAPTER 4

U.S. Nuclear Weapons Policy
and International Law

Thomas Graham, Jr.

Paul Nitze was the archetypical Cold Warrior and nuclear weapon strategist. As the author of NSC-68 commissioned by President Truman in 1950 he helped set the ground rules for the Cold War and the thermonuclear confrontation. In this report, he wrote in 1950: "In the absence of effective arms control it would appear that we had no alternative but to increase our atomic armaments as rapidly as other considerations make appropriate." But in addition to being an outstanding national leader, Paul Nitze was someone who could recognize change and respond to it. In the last op-ed that he wrote at the age of 92 in 1999 entitled "A Danger Mostly To Ourselves" he said:

> I know that the simplest and most direct answer to the problem of nuclear weapons has always been their complete elimination. My "walk in the woods" in 1982 with the Soviet arms negotiator Yuli Kvitsinsky at least addressed this problem on a bilateral basis. Destruction of the arms did not prove feasible then but there is no good reason why it should not be carried out now.

Senator Sam Nunn, in an article in the *Financial Times* in December 2004, pointed to the immense danger that exists as a result of the fact that 15 years after the end of the Cold War the United States and Russia still maintain, on 15-minutes alert, long-range strategic missiles equipped with immensely powerful nuclear warheads capable of devastating each other's societies in 30 minutes. In 1995, Russia mistook the launch of a test rocket in Norway as a submarine launched nuclear missile aimed at Moscow and came within two minutes of ordering a retaliatory nuclear strike on the United States. Senator Nunn said in his article that current U.S. nuclear weapon policies, which in effect rely on the deteriorating Russian early warning system continuing to make correct judgments as it did during the Cold War "risks an Armageddon of our own making."

In addition, former Defense Secretary William Perry, a scientist not given to exaggeration, has said that in his judgment there could be a greater than

50 percent chance of a nuclear detonation on U.S. soil in the next decade. And assuming effective international verification, a recent poll indicates that 73 percent of Americans and 63 percent of Russians favor the complete worldwide elimination of nuclear weapons.

In January 2007, in an op-ed article published in the *Wall Street Journal* by George Shultz, William Perry, Henry Kissinger, and Sam Nunn (and signed on to by a number of other former senior officials in the Reagan, first Bush, and Clinton administrations) the authors contend that reliance on nuclear weapons for deterrence "is becoming increasingly hazardous and decreasingly effective" and that "unless new actions are taken, the U.S. soon will be compelled to enter a new nuclear era that will be more precarious, psychologically disorienting, and economically even more costly than was Cold War deterrence." Noting that President Ronald Reagan had called for the abolishment of "all nuclear weapons," which he considered to be "totally irrational, totally inhumane, good for nothing but killing, possibly destructive of life on earth and civilization," and that President Reagan and General Secretary Mikhail Gorbachev shared this vision, the four authors call for "reassertion of the vision of a world free of nuclear weapons and practical measures toward achieving that goal." This op-ed article is most significant in that it represents the national security establishment, far beyond the four distinguished authors, coming to the realization that the world has become so dangerous that nuclear weapons are a threat even to their possessors. This group met at Stanford in October 2007 for the second time at the invitation of George Shultz. The four authors and a number of others recommitted themselves to pursue the vision of President Reagan. In January 2008, a second op-ed was published.

The individuals involved are serious and committed and more is going to happen. There is full agreement that the vision of a nuclear weapon-free world and the associated practical steps, such as the ratification of the Comprehensive Nuclear Test Ban Treaty (CTBT) must be pursued simultaneously for either to be viable.

THE CENTERPIECE OF WORLD SECURITY

The nuclear Non-Proliferation Treaty (NPT) is the centerpiece of world security. President John F. Kennedy truly feared that nuclear weapons might well sweep all over the world. In 1962, there were reports that by the late 1970s there would be 25–30 nuclear weapon states in the world with nuclear weapons integrated into their arsenals. If that had happened, there would be many more such states today. More than 40 countries now have the capability to build nuclear weapons. Under such conditions, every conflict would carry with it the risk of going nuclear and it would be impossible to keep nuclear weapons out of the hands of international terrorist organizations since they would be so widespread.

But such weapon proliferation did not happen and the principal reason that it did not was the negotiation of the NPT and its entry into force in 1970, buttressed by the policies of extended nuclear deterrence—the nuclear umbrella—followed by the United States and the Soviet Union with their Cold War Treaty Allies. Indeed, since 1970, at least until now, there has been very little nuclear weapon proliferation. In addition to the five nuclear weapon states recognized by the NPT—the United States, Britain, France, Russia, and China—four states, India, Pakistan, Israel, and North Korea, have built nuclear weapon arsenals, but

India and Israel were already well along in 1970. This is far from what President Kennedy feared.

But the success of the NPT was no accident. It was rooted in a carefully crafted central bargain. In exchange for a commitment from the non-nuclear weapon states (today more than 180 nations, most of the world) not to acquire nuclear weapons and to submit to international safeguards to verify compliance with this commitment, the NPT nuclear weapon states pledged unfettered access to peaceful nuclear technologies and undertook to engage in nuclear disarmament negotiations aimed at the ultimate elimination of their nuclear arsenals. It is this basic bargain that for the past three decades has formed the central underpinnings of the international nonproliferation regime.

However, one of the principal problems with all this has been that the nuclear weapon states have never really delivered on the disarmament part of this bargain and in recent years it appears to have been largely abandoned. The essence of the disarmament commitment was that pending the eventual elimination of nuclear weapon arsenals, the nuclear weapon states would agree to a treaty prohibiting all nuclear weapon tests, that is a Comprehensive Test Ban Treaty; undertake obligations to drastically reduce their nuclear arsenals; negotiate an agreement prohibiting the further production of nuclear bomb explosive, or fissile, material; and give legally binding commitments that they would never use nuclear weapons against NPT non-nuclear weapon states. None of this has been accomplished over 35 years later. The CTBT was negotiated and signed in 1996, but the U.S. Senate rejected it in 1999. There have been no negotiated reductions since 1994; nothing has ever happened on an agreement prohibiting the further production of fissile material for weapons and even though political commitments were made by the NPT nuclear weapon states in 1995 in effect not to use nuclear weapons against their NPT non-nuclear weapon treaty partners, the national policies of the United States, Britain, France, and Russia are the opposite—holding open this option.

As the Director General of the International Atomic Energy Agency (IAEA) Mohamed ElBaredi has said, "We must abandon the unworkable notion that it is morally reprehensible for some countries to pursue weapons of mass destruction and acceptable for others to rely on them for security . . . if the world does not change course, we risk self-destruction."

THE BARGAIN IS FALLING APART

And now the other side of the bargain has begun to fall apart. India and Pakistan eroded the NPT from the outside by each conducting a series of nuclear weapon tests in 1998 and declaring themselves to be nuclear weapon states. India, Pakistan, and Israel maintain sizable unregulated nuclear weapon arsenals outside the NPT. North Korea withdrew from the NPT in 2003 and may have built up to eight or ten nuclear weapons. The DPRK has now agreed in principle to return to the NPT and to negotiate an end to its nuclear weapon program, and significant progress has been made toward this objective, but probably the elimination of these weapons is years away and under current international arrangements can we ever be certain that North Korea has in fact declared and eliminated whatever nuclear weapons they may have? The A. Q. Khan secret illegal nuclear weapon technology transferring ring based in Pakistan has been exposed, but who can be sure that we have seen more than the tip of the iceberg? Iran is suspected of having a nuclear weapon program and admitted in late 2003 that contrary to its IAEA safeguards agreement, it failed to report its acquisition of uranium enrichment technology.

And why might Iran want the nuclear fuel cycle and the attendant option to construct nuclear weapons? The nuclear program is very popular in Iran. It appears that some countries believe that ultimately the only way that they can gain respect in this world, as President Lula of Brazil declared during his first election campaign, is to acquire nuclear weapons—or at least be seen as able quickly to do so. During the Cold War, nuclear weapons distinguished Great Powers from others countries. The permanent members of the Security Council are the five recognized nuclear weapon states. Forty years ago Great Britain and France both asserted that status was the real reason that they were building nuclear weapons. This high political value of nuclear weapons has not changed since the Cold War. India asserted in 1998 that it was now a big country; it had nuclear weapons. The world significantly lost interest in Ukraine once it gave up the nuclear weapons left on its territory after the collapse of the Soviet Union. The political value of nuclear weapons probably will remain high and may in the end cause the NPT to fail, unless of course over time it can be drastically reduced. Likely the only way that this can happen is for nuclear weapons to be delegitimized and over time eventually eliminated. This is what was supposed to happen pursuant to the central bargain of the NPT.

A POSSIBLE COURSE OF ACTION

But how could nuclear weapons actually be eliminated? A possible course of action could be for the United States to first work quietly with Russia to try to reach an understanding. Then, if successful, the French, British, and Chinese could be brought in. Eventually the Indians, Pakistanis, and Israelis could be included. If a general coincidence of view could be achieved among these eight states—over several years—then the project could be brought to the United Nations. The president of the United States and others of the leaders of the eight states could request an extraordinary session of the United Nations General Assembly and ask to address the assembly. In their speeches the leaders could call for the worldwide elimination of nuclear weapons (as well as all other weapons of mass destruction) and request that the Security Council be charged to carry out this task. The Security Council could then call for the negotiation of a treaty to eliminate nuclear weapons. The five permanent members of the council with right of veto would already be committed. Such a treaty would require worldwide intrusive on-site inspection and probably security guarantees for a number of states, such as Israel, Iran, Pakistan and North Korea on the edge of conflicts and where nuclear programs are or may be present. North Korea would return to the NPT as a verifiable non-nuclear weapon state. There would need to be an agreement by all states to apply economic and, if necessary, military pressure to any state that did not comply with this program or that subsequently violated the negotiated arrangements. In a first stage to be negotiated, the five NPT nuclear weapon states (the United States, Great Britain, France, Russia, and China) and the three other long-time holdouts from the NPT (India, Pakistan, and Israel) would over a period of a few years take all of their nuclear weapons off operational status. Then, in a second stage, these eight states would be required to eliminate almost all of their arsenals down to very low levels over a number of years. A third and later stage would require the complete elimination of weapons, but these eight states would be allowed to keep a relatively limited amount of nuclear explosive material (i.e., as fissile material, including both highly enriched uranium [HEU] and plutonium), which could be converted into a small number of weapons as a hedge against failure of the regime. This could amount to roughly enough material for five weapons each for India, Pakistan, and Israel, 15 weapons each for Britain, France, and China, and 30 weapons each for the United States and Russia. The material would be maintained under very high levels of national security protection at designated depositories and also be under international safeguards implemented by IAEA inspectors. Under various programs all other nuclear explosive material would be eliminated throughout the world. Missile defense systems could be developed by the world's leading powers on a cooperative basis as a further hedge against failure of the regime.

Nuclear power production would be reconfigured so as to make no more plutonium by the use of nonproliferative fuels and eventually advanced nonproliferative reactors. The plutonium in existing spent nuclear fuel around the world would have to be eliminated as well. Such an arrangement as described here would take a long time to negotiate and even longer to implement, but we must try for the hour is late. A final stage, years in the future, could be the verifiable elimination of the fissile material retained by the eight nuclear states, once the issue of "missing" fissile material, a feature of the nuclear weapon inventories in several of the nuclear weapon possessing states, has been effectively addressed.

Some might say that this is unrealistic; how could we ever hope that the U.S. government or any other government of a state possessing nuclear weapons would even contemplate such a thing? But we must press for and hope for the best and remember that nothing good is ever impossible. Who would have thought that the zero missile option proposed by President Reagan in 1981 would ever happen? Who would have thought the Cold War would end in the foreseeable future? Who would have thought that the Soviet Union would cease to exist? But all of these things did happen.

THE UNITED STATES MUST LEAD

To achieve President Reagan's dream, the worldwide elimination of nuclear weapons, and to establish a peaceful and secure world community in the twenty-first century, the United States must lead; there is no alternative. But for this to happen, the United States must be believed and trusted. On September 12, 2001 the United States had the trust and support of the entire world. Now, in the wake of exaggerated intelligence claims; rejection of international treaty arrangements such as the CTBT, the Ottawa Convention on land mines, the International Criminal Court, the Kyoto Protocol on global warming, and others; an invasion and occupation of Iraq opposed by the world community; what appears to many as an overreliance on force rather than diplomacy, as with the escalating rhetoric over Iran; rejection by some of the rules of international humanitarian law and the Geneva Protocols on the treatment of prisoners of war; that support and trust is gone and the United States is reviled and feared in many quarters of the world. Senator John McCain said last year that "America's position in the world is at an all-time low." A major worldwide poll released not long ago indicated that a substantial number view the United States as a negative influence in the world. How can we regain the trust of the world community? How can we return to our historic destiny of keeping the peace and fostering the development of the community of nations, democracies, free market economies, the international rule of law, international institutions and treaty arrangements?

Among other things, we should, first, end our intervention in Iraq in the best way that is possible and practical. The future of Iraq belongs to the Iraqis; we cannot ensure it for them. Only the Iraqis can build a new Iraq. At an early date we must take the decision to firmly, gradually, and carefully turn over the struggle against the insurgency and chaos to the Iraqis as urged by former Defense Secretary Melvin Laird in his article in an issue of *Foreign Affairs* in the summer of 2006. Our presence is what fed the insurgency and it did little to prevent the civil war. Our steady but inexorable withdrawal, while at the same time doing our best to train the Iraqi forces, would strengthen the confidence and ability of the Iraqi security forces to stand up to the forces of disorder.

Second, to recognize that in the wake of the Cold War the world has fundamentally changed, the nation-state system that has dominated international life for the past 350 years is rapidly deteriorating. Perhaps some 50–70 nations around the world are inexorably slipping into the category of failed states. We cannot go it alone. Since the end of the Cold War there has been roughly one major nation building intervention every two years. Poverty, disease, cultural misunderstandings, and machine-gun societies around the world are central national security threats; these are the principal causes of international terrorism, and the primary weapons in the battle against terror and declining world order are economic, political, social, cultural, and diplomatic and only rarely military. Reconstruction in failed states is one thing; it is relatively well understood but, in many cases, development, of necessity involving institution building, is essential to return failed states to a level where they can function. But to quote the well-known historian Francis Fukayama, "Any honest appraisal of where the 'state of the art' lies in development today would have to conclude that although institutions may be important, we know relatively little about how to create them." But one thing that we do know Dr. Fukuyama says is that "Coalitions, in the form of support from a wide range of other countries and international organizations... are important for a number of reasons."

And third, for over 50 years the United States pursued a world order built on rules and international treaties that permitted the expansion of democracy and the enlargement of international security. Over two years ago in a speech before the American Society of International Law, the secretary of state said that when the United States respects its "international legal obligations and supports an international system based on the rule of law, we do the work of making this world a better place, but also a safe and more secure place for America." We should take such steps as ratifying the CTBT, joining the Ottawa Land Mine Convention, becoming a part of the International Criminal Court and establishing ourselves once again as leading advocates of the international rule of law.

In this way the United States can regain its historic role and effectively lead the world community to take the urgent steps toward eventual elimination of nuclear weapons advocated by Presidents Reagan and Gorbachev and now pursued by Messrs. Shultz, Perry, Nunn, and Kissinger, and many others, and provide for the safety of us all in a stable and secure twenty-first century.

CHAPTER 5

The "Inalienable Right" to Peaceful Nuclear Power: A Recipe for Chaos

Alice Slater

The drums of war are sounding yet again as we read reports about preparations and rehearsals for a U.S. military strike against Iran to "take out" its nascent bomb-making capability, as Iran asserts its inalienable right under the Non-Proliferation Treaty (NPT) to enrich uranium for "peaceful" nuclear power. North Korea manufactured its bomb material for its underground nuclear tests from the plutonium produced in its "peaceful" reactor. As we watch the planned transformation of the imperial U.S. military into a "global strike force," seeking "full spectrum dominance," its abhorrent willingness to wage illegal preemptive wars, the recent Nuclear Posture Review (NPR) that would authorize the use of nuclear weapons even against non-nuclear weapon states, its 2030 plan for new, more useable nuclear weapons, and its designation of so-called rogue states as the "axis of evil" we are reaping the grim whirlwind of these policies. Iran is relying on Article IV of the NPT to develop what is ostensibly described as "peaceful" nuclear technology, which would give them the capacity and materials they need to build bombs of their own as a deterrent against U.S. threats.

It's ironic that just about the same time the *real politique* old Cold Warriors like Kissinger, Nunn, Perry, and Shultz finally woke up to the bankruptcy of their past policies to "control" the spread of nuclear weapons, raising the alarm and calling for their elimination, the Western network of industrialized nations is now vigorously promoting a "nuclear renaissance" of civilian power. They have the hubris to think they can manage a whole new regime of nuclear apartheid, despite their recent and most welcome acknowledgment of the breakdown of the nuclear weapons arms control regime. When will they ever learn? They're planning a top-down, hierarchical, central control of the nuclear fuel cycle, in a mad plan to reprocess the irradiated fuel rods in 17 countries, including the United States, Russia, China, United Kingdom, France, Japan, Australia, Bulgaria, Ghana, Hungary, Jordan, Kazakhstan, Lithuania, Poland, Romania, Slovenia, Ukraine, Italy, and, most recently, Canada, that are to be members of a new Global Nuclear Energy Partnership.[1] The partnership will ship toxic bomb-ready materials to the four corners of the world and back, in a nightmare scenario of plutonium in constant transit, subject to terrorist theft and negligent accidents on land and on sea, while creating a whole new class of nuclear "have-nots" who can't be trusted not to turn their "peaceful" nuclear reactors into bomb factories. *It's just so twentieth century!* Time for a paradigm shift to safe, sustainable energy.

ARTICLE IV OF THE NPT

Article IV of the NPT provides an "inalienable right to peaceful nuclear technology" and was offered as a sweetener to the countries that agreed to sign the treaty and forego the acquisition of nuclear weapons. But "peaceful" nuclear technology is an oxymoron for the twenty-first century. The international community had clearly acknowledged that peaceful nuclear technology is a gateway to nuclear weapons proliferation when it required the signatures of 44 "nuclear-capable" nations on the Comprehensive Nuclear Test Ban Treaty (CTBT) before the treaty could enter into force.

There are now 440 "peaceful" reactors in 31 countries[2]—all producing deadly bomb materials with 272 research reactors in 56 countries, some producing highly enriched uranium (HEU).[3] The signers of the CTBT were well aware that by having a nuclear reactor, a nation had been given the keys to a bomb factory and would need to be included in any effort to ban nuclear tests, regardless of whether they proclaimed any intention to develop weapons. And U.S. CIA director, George Tenet, said, "The difference between producing low-enriched uranium and weapons-capable high-enriched uranium is only a matter of time and intent, not technology."[4]

There are nearly 200 million kilograms of reactor wastes in the world—with only five kilograms needed to make one nuclear bomb. The United States is planning to build 50 more reactors by 2020; China plans 30; with 32 more now under construction—to churn out more toxic poisons; on tap for bomb-making, with no known solution to safely containing the tons of nuclear waste that will be generated over the unimaginable 250,000 years it will continue to threaten life on earth.[5] New projects are underway to mine uranium on every continent,[6] mostly on indigenous lands, where first peoples have suffered inordinately from radiation poisoning.[7]

Countless studies report higher incidences of birth defects, cancer, and genetic mutations in every situation where nuclear technology is employed—whether for war or for "peace." A National Research Council (NRC) 2005 study reported that exposure to X-rays and gamma rays, even at low-dose levels, can cause cancer. The committee defined "low-dose" as a range from near zero up to about…ten times that from a CT scan. "There appears to be no threshold below which exposure can be viewed as harmless," said NRC panelist, Herbert Abrams, professor emeritus of radiology at Stanford and Harvard universities.[8] Tens of thousands of tons of nuclear waste accumulate at civilian reactors with no solution for its storage, releasing toxic doses of radioactive waste into air, water, and soil and contaminating our planet and its inhabitants for hundreds of thousands of years.

The industry-dominated International Atomic Energy Agency (IAEA) has been instrumental in covering up the disastrous health effects of the Chernobyl tragedy, understating the number of deaths by attributing only 50 deaths directly to the accident. This was a whitewash of health studies performed by Russia and the Ukraine, which estimated thousands of deaths and tens of thousands who suffered thyroid cancer and leukemia as a result of the accident.[9] This cover-up was no doubt due to the collusive agreement between the IAEA and the World Health Organization (WHO), which under its terms provides that if either of the organizations initiates any program or activity in which the other has or may have a substantial interest, the first party shall consult with the other with a view to adjusting the matter by mutual agreement. Thus, our scientists and researchers at the WHO are required to have their work vetted by the industry's champion for "peaceful" nuclear technology, the IAEA.

For example, WHO abandoned its original 1961 agenda for research on the basic human health implications of food irradiation. It ceded to the IAEA, whose mission is preserving the nuclear industry, not the health of people, the ultimate power of researching the safety of irradiated foods. The IAEA is leading a global campaign to further the legalization, commercialization, and consumer acceptance of irradiated foods. "We must confer with experts in the various fields of advertising and psychology to put the public at ease," one IAEA report states, also recommending that the process "should not be required on the label."[10] Yet, the NRC study, stating that there is no safe dose of radiation, clearly justified the public's rational fear of radiation. It is time for the IAEA to give up its dual mission in nuclear technology. While the agency plays an indispensable role in inspecting and verifying compliance with nuclear disarmament agreements, it should not continue to act with a manifest conflict of interest as a shill for the nuclear industry.

Whatever naiveté may have existed in the world about the potential of harnessing nuclear technology for benign purposes, in 1953, when President Eisenhower made his Atoms for Peace speech to the United Nations General Assembly, we can no longer turn a blind eye to the terrifying consequences of the Nuclear Age. At that time, Eisenhower said,

> It is not enough to take this weapon out of the hands of the soldiers. It must be put into the hands of those who will know how to strip its military casing and adapt it to the arts of peace. The United States knows that if the fearful trend of atomic military build up can be reversed, this greatest of destructive forces can be developed into a great boon, for the benefit of all mankind. The United States knows that peaceful power from atomic energy is no dream of the future. That capability, already proved, is here—now—today. Who can doubt, if the entire body of the world's scientists and engineers had adequate amounts of fissionable material with which to test and develop their ideas, that this capability would rapidly be transformed into universal, efficient, and economic usage.[11]

Interestingly, in Eisenhower's famous farewell address, in which he warned the country of the military-industrial complex, in a little noted aside, he also cautioned, presciently, against the abuse of science, warning that

> [I]n holding scientific research and discovery in respect, as we should, we must also be alert to the equal and opposite danger that public policy could itself

become the captive of a scientific-technological elite. It is the task of states-manship to mold, to balance, and to integrate these and other forces, new and old, within the principles of our democratic system—ever aiming toward the supreme goals of our free society.[12]

Can there be any doubt that the "scientific-technological" elite at Los Alamos and Livermore Laboratories have been driving the nuclear arms race, squandering lost opportunities for nuclear disarmament since the end of the Cold War, and developing new untested weapons designs that create the need for more tests that are used as an excuse to block U.S. ratification of the CTBT and serve to provoke other states, threatened by the United States, to develop their own nuclear weapons?

What does it take for a country to be willing to inflict the toxic assault of nuclear waste on its own people in light of the lessons we have learned during the past 60 years of the Nuclear Age? One delegate at the disastrous 2007 NPT Review shared quite frankly, at an NGO panel, that his country was unwilling to forego its "inalienable right" under the treaty because their scientists wouldn't want to be left behind in state-of-the-art knowledge. They need to play in the major leagues of science with the big boys. It is noteworthy that one of the sanctions proposed by the Bush administration against North Korea, for having dared to join the nuclear club, was a prohibition on their scientists studying in our universities. So despite the promise of clean, safe abundant energy from the sun, the wind, the tides, many non-nuclear weapon states have underscored their equal rights to the dark fruits of nuclear technology. Will this kind of scientific machismo, which has created so many gruesome chapters in world history, be supported at the expense of the health of so many people and of the very survival of our biosphere? Will we satisfy our scientists' dangerous thirst for knowledge and status despite the obvious possibility that the peaceful nuclear reactor can readily be converted to weapons manufacture?

The nuclear crisis we face today is a direct result of the exportation of peaceful nuclear technology to countries such as Iraq, Iran, and North Korea. Indeed, every nuclear reactor enables a country to develop its own nuclear weapons, as we have seen in the case of India, Pakistan, and Israel, who never joined the NPT and North Korea, which exploited the fruits of "peaceful" technology and then quit to develop its own deterrent against U.S. bullying. Under the guise of "peace," other countries, such as South Africa, Argentina, Brazil, and Libya were also well on their way to developing nuclear bombs, which they later abandoned.

WE CANNOT CONTINUE BUSINESS AS USUAL

IAEA Director, Mohamed ElBaradei recently stated,

We just cannot continue business as usual that every country can build its own factories for separating plutonium or enriching uranium. Then we are really talking about 30, 40 countries sitting on the fence with a nuclear weapons capability that could be converted into a nuclear weapon in a matter of months.[13]

The current flurry of negotiations and the move to try to control the production of the civilian nuclear fuel cycle in one central place, as proposed by ElBaradei, simply will not fly. It would be just another discriminatory aspect of the NPT, creating yet another class of "haves" and "have-nots" under the treaty, as was done with those permitted to have nuclear weapons and those who are not. Now it is proposed that some nations be permitted to make their own nuclear fuel, while others, such as Iran, would be precluded from doing so. And in the wake of the stern warnings to Iran, and the referral of the issue to the Security Council, which has provoked Iran to begin reprocessing of nuclear fuel under its "inalienable" right, the United States has incomprehensibly announced its Global Nuclear Energy Partnership to control the spread of nuclear materials in which "supplier" nations would manufacture nuclear fuel rods, ship it to other countries, by rail, road, and sea, to use in their reactors and then take back the irradiated fuel and reprocess it, breaking a 30-year taboo in the United States on turning irradiated reactor fuel into weapons-grade material. Brazil too, recently got into the action, firing up its own major uranium enrichment plant while we were warning Iran that such action would be viewed as hostile.[14] And six new Arab nations—Egypt, Algeria, Saudi Arabia, Morocco, Tunisia, and the United Arab Emirates—have announced their intention to develop "peaceful" nuclear technology, no doubt in response to the dominant industrial nations now announcing their intention to put the nuclear fuel cycle under their exclusive control.[15]

We think we can control the atom, while in reality we have been pushing our luck since 1945 when we unleashed its awful power and created jerry-built structures to contain its terrifying consequences. As more countries acquire nuclear power, against a backdrop of unauthorized preemptive war to strike at "rogue" nuclear weapons—the nuclear phantoms are chasing us—we imagine them where they aren't and fail to see them under our very noses; or we deliberately turn a blind eye for geopolitical reasons or commercial greed. Trying to exercise control over the reprocessing and distribution of nuclear fuels would be like going down the same path we've been on for the past 50 some odd years for nuclear arms control. Do you think France, Japan, or the United States, for example, will surrender control of nuclear materials production, any more than the nuclear powers have surrendered control of atom bombs? It would be a long drawn-out effort with discriminatory rules in the end—when, instead, we could be expending our energy and intellectual treasure on shifting the energy paradigm to make nuclear and fossil fuel obsolete.

But there are commercial interests that don't want to lose their ability to continue to profit from the human misery caused by nuclear and fossil fuels. The sun, the wind, the tides, and geothermal energy are here in abundance for all the world's people and they are *free*. We already have the technology to harness the bounty of the earth. And we know how to store it when the sun doesn't shine and the wind doesn't blow, by using hydrogen fuel cells. It is clearly not beyond our financial means, as argued by the corporate supporters of toxic fuel industries—particularly when you compare the costs of clean, safe energy to the more than 200 billion dollars spent annually to subsidize fossil and nuclear fuels, while renewable energies receive less than a tenth of that amount worldwide.[16] Not to mention the cost of war to protect those poisonous energy sources, or even the military infrastructure and naval operations operating during peacetime, on guard duty for the oil tankers plying the seas with their noxious cargo.[17]

So why don't we have a 10-year crash program to achieve a nuclear, fossil-free, and biomass-free energy transition? It is because of the corporate interests that insist on peddling their polluting and proliferating sources of energy—their "cash cows." Once the infrastructure to harness the energy of the sun, wind, tides, and geothermal is constructed, there will be no fuel stock to sell. It would probably be the best way to end poverty on the planet as well—since poor countries can get free, clean earth energy, abundantly available, and will not have to spend their meager budgets for their critical power needs. We need new thinking and it has to start with us—ordinary people who have no corporate axe to grind in perpetuating disastrous forms of energy on the planet. We mustn't buy into the propaganda that clean safe energy is decades away or too costly. We need to be vigilant in providing the ample evidence in its favor to counter the corporate forces arguing that it's not ready, it's years away, it's too expensive—arguments made by companies in the business of producing dirty fuel. Here's what Franklin Delano Roosevelt had to say about similar forces in 1936:

> We had to struggle with the old enemies of peace—business and financial monopoly, speculation, reckless banking, class antagonism, sectionalism, war profiteering. They had begun to consider the Government of the United States as a mere appendage to their own affairs. We know now that Government by organized money is just as dangerous as Government by organized mob.[18]

There are mountains of evidence that the corporate spin machine deliberately disseminates falsehoods about sustainable energy to keep their profits coming and to oil the war machine. And don't be fooled by industry deceptions about "clean" nuclear power being carbon free. Fossil fuel is used in every step of the process of creating these standing bomb factories—from the mining, milling, and reprocessing of uranium to the decommissioning of aging plants and the transporting and storing of nuclear waste.[19]

If, as we work to phase in safe, clean energy, eliminating the evil twin of nuclear weapons—so-called peaceful nuclear technology—as we continue to press ahead for weapons abolition, we'll have a real road map to a nuclear-free world. Otherwise, I fear we would not be dealing with a full deck and are doomed to failure in two ways—halting nuclear weapons proliferation and saving our planet from the ravages of climate change caused by massive carbon releases into our atmosphere. The proposals to try to *control* civilian nuclear fuel production suggested by ElBaradei and the Blix Commission cannot succeed.

It is unjust for certain favored nations to make their own nuclear fuel, without world condemnation, such as Brazil and Japan, while others, such as Iran and North Korea, are threatened for doing so. We must supersede the "inalienable right" to peaceful nuclear technology by supporting Germany's new initiative to establish an International Renewable Energy Agency (IRENA), funded by the more than $250 billion in annual subsidies to nuclear and fossil fuel.[20] Just as the CTBT rendered the NPT's Article V guaranteed right to "peaceful nuclear explosions" inoperative, the establishment of IRENA would make the inalienable right to peaceful nuclear technology inoperative as well.

IRENA

Let us support a protocol to the NPT establishing the IRENA and begin to rely on the safe abundant energy of our earth from the sun, wind, tides, and geothermal sources, averting the catastrophe of climate change and avoiding nuclear proliferation and resource wars. Whoever heard of a terrorist attacking a windmill? Clean safe energy is available to us now. It is an idea whose time has come. If we fail to accomplish this, it will not be because we lack the technology, but because of a scarcity of democracy.

NOTES

1. http://www.gnep.energy.gov/gnepReliableFuelServices.html.
2. http://www.euronuclear.org/info/encyclopedia/n/nuclear-power-plant-world-wide.htmm.
3. http://www.rertr.anl.gov/RERTR25/PDF/Ritchie.pdf.
4. http://www.cia.gov/cia/public_affairs/speeches/2004/tenet_testimony_03092004.html.
5. http://www.euronuclear.org/info/encyclopedia/n/nuclear-power-plant-world-wide.htm.
6. http://www.wise-uranium.org/indexu.html.
7. http://www.sric.org/uraniumsummit/.
8. http://cisac.stanford.edu/news/611/.
9. "Rethinking Nuclear Energy and Democracy After September 11, 2001," *IPPNW Global Health Watch Report*, Number 4, 2004.
10. http://www.citizen.org/documents/nukes-FI%20fact%20sheet%20-%20PDF.pdf.
11. http://www.atomicarchive.com/Docs/Deterrence/Atomsforpeace.shtml.
12. http://coursesa.matrix.msu.edu/hst306/documents/indust.html.
13. *Agence France Press*, February 23, 2005.
14. www.realcities.com/mi/krwashington/13842944.htm.
15. http://www.timesonline.co.uk/tol/news/world/middle_east/article624855.ece.
16. www.sonoma.edu/users/f/freidel/global/372gelbspan1.htm.
17. See generally, "A Sustainable Energy Future is Possible Now," www.abolition2000.org.
18. http://millercenter.virginia.edu/scripps/digitalarchive/speeches/spe_1936_1031_roosevelt.
19. www.greatchange.org/bb-thermochemical-nuclear_sustainability_rev.pdf.
20. www.irena.org.

PART III

Nuclear Weapons Policy

CHAPTER 6

Rethinking U.S. Nuclear Weapons Policy

Michael D. Intriligator

INTRODUCTION

There have been remarkable changes in recent years in U.S. nuclear weapons policy under the administration of President George W. Bush that have not been adequately analyzed and that call for serious reconsideration. These changes were announced in 2002 in three official documents and they constitute a new doctrine, the *Bush doctrine*, ending the security system and nuclear weapons policies of the Cold War period and creating the basis for the U.S. invasion and occupation of Iraq starting in March 2003. They represent a discontinuous sea change in the international security system that calls for discussion, debate, and analysis, none of which has taken place so far. The earlier bipolar world has been replaced by a proposed unipolar world with the United States under President Bush seeing itself as the dominant power or sole superpower. The mutual deterrence system that was part of the Cold War has been replaced by U.S. unilateral actions against possible rivals, including "regime change" as seen in Afghanistan and Iraq. Cooperative approaches to national and international security and alliance systems that had existed in the earlier epoch have been replaced by unilateral U.S. policies and actions. Arms control has been replaced by unilateral U.S. arms initiatives.

The purposes of this chapter are to present these current concepts related to U.S. nuclear weapons doctrine; to evaluate them; and to consider an alternative approach, that of global security. The current concepts as well as alternatives, such as global security, call for a wide-ranging debate both nationally and internationally. Unfortunately, this has not happened, possibly due to the concern over the U.S. wars in Afghanistan and Iraq that were, ironically, examples of these new policies put into action. Both the new policies and their underlying goals should be subjects of intense scrutiny and they call for rethinking in Washington and elsewhere.

BACKGROUND TO THE NEW BUSH POLICY

The background to these new nuclear weapons doctrines include the end of the Cold War in 1989; the dissolution of the Soviet Union on Christmas day 1991; the Project for a New American Century (PNAC) that was established in 1997 "to promote American global leadership" (www.newamericancentury.org); the advent of the new Bush administration in January 2001, which included many of the PNAC individuals in major leadership positions (Cheney, Rumsfeld, Wolfowitz, Perle, Armitage, Bolton, Khalilzad, Libby, Zakheim, Zoellick, and others); the September 11, 2001 terrorist attacks on the World Trade Center and the Pentagon; and the ensuing declaration by the Bush administration of a "War on Terrorism" later broadened to a "Global War on Terrorism [GWOT]." Following on the adoption of these new policies were the invasion and occupation of Afghanistan and Iraq.

CHANGES IN POLICY ANNOUNCED IN THREE MAJOR POLICY DOCUMENTS IN 2002

The changes in U.S. nuclear weapons policy were announced in three official documents that were released by the Bush administration in 2002. The first of these documents is the U.S. *Nuclear Posture Review* (NPR) that was delivered to the U.S. Congress by the U.S. Department of Defense in January 2002. It is a classified document that is mandated by Congress and produced periodically, the last one having been that of the Clinton administration in 1994. The *Los Angeles Times* leaked the latest version in March 2002. According to the NPR, "A combination of offensive and defensive, and nuclear and non-nuclear capabilities is essential to meet the deterrence requirements of the twenty-first century." It is a wide-ranging analysis of the requirements for deterrence in the twenty-first century. It states that it does not provide operational guidance on nuclear targeting or planning. Rather, it states that the Department of Defense continues to plan for a broad range of contingencies and unforeseen threats to the United States and its allies in order to deter such attacks in the first place. It does, however, refer to the "possible use of nuclear weapons in an Arab-Israeli conflict, in a war between China and Taiwan, or in an attack from North Korea on the South." It also refers to the possible use of nuclear weapons against targets able to withstand non-nuclear attack, in retaliation for attacks by nuclear, biological, or chemical weapons, or "in the event of surprising military developments." Thus, it calls for possible plans for the use of nuclear weapons in various contingencies, including against non-nuclear weapon states and in response to conventional weapons. It also states that the administration is fashioning a more diverse set of options for deterring the threat of Weapons of Mass Destruction (WMD), which emerged as the last of these three policy documents in December 2002.

Overall, according to the NPR, nuclear weapons play a critical role in the defense capabilities of the United States, its allies, and friends. They provide credible military options to deter a wide range of threats, including WMD and large-scale conventional military force. The NPR states that these "nuclear capabilities possess unique properties that give the United States options to hold at risk classes of targets [that are] important strategic and political objectives." This document calls for the integration of nuclear weapons into conventional strike options, thus diminishing the firewall separating nuclear and conventional weapons and the development of new nuclear weapons to provide a wider range of options to defeat hardened and deeply buried targets. It also calls for a reduced reliance on nuclear weapons via missile defense and non-nuclear strike forces, including precision conventional forces, but, at the same time an indefinite retention of nuclear weapons under the 2002 Strategic Offensive Reductions Treaty (SORT)—the Moscow Treaty.

The second of these documents is the *National Security Strategy of the United States of America* (NSS) that was issued by the office of the then national security advisor to the president, Condoleeza Rice, in September 2002. It is an unclassified and open public document that is available on the White House Web site. According to the NSS, there are plans to ensure that no nation could rival U.S. military strength. Its emphasis is on defeating rogue states and global terrorists, noting that deterrence will not work against such enemies. It proclaims the doctrine of U.S. preemption, where it states that the United States "cannot let our enemies strike first" and gives arguments for such preemption. (Some scholars and analysts have noted, correctly, that this is not a doctrine of *preemption* but rather one of *preventive war.*) For example, it notes that, "For centuries, international law recognized that nations need not suffer an attack before they can lawfully take action to defend themselves against forces that present an imminent danger of attack." It further states that "The U.S. has long maintained the option of preemptive actions to counter a sufficient threat to our national security." It should be noted, however, that the United States did not preempt in most of the recent wars it has fought, including World War I and II, Korea, Vietnam, and the Gulf War, while its attempt at preemption in the Bay of Pigs invasion of Cuba was a total failure. Far from there being historical precedents, this new policy represents a fundamental shift from a U.S. policy of reaction to a new policy of initiation—from wars of necessity to wars of choice. It is too early to say that this policy of preemption in the Iraq War was a success or failure, but the costs in terms of both casualties and dollar spending have been immense and much larger than expected. Indeed, this war is being seen more and more as a quagmire and likened to the Vietnam War. As to its dollar cost, a careful accounting of its costs in January 2006 by Nobel Laureate economist Joseph E. Stiglitz and Linda Bilmes, former assistant secretary of commerce who now teaches public finance and government budgeting at the Kennedy School of Government at Harvard, estimated its cost as much higher than previously reckoned, amounting between $1 trillion and $2 trillion, depending primarily on how much longer it lasts. This study provides an important analysis of the cost of Bush's preemption strategy in Iraq (see www.informationclearinghouse. info/).

The NSS notes that "To forestall or prevent such hostile acts by our adversaries, the United States will, if necessary, act preemptively." Such a policy of preemption is, however, a violation of the United Nations (UN) system that was set up in large part to prevent precisely such preemption, as in Hitler's invasion of Poland or Japan's invasion of China. The UN Charter forbids a member state from taking military action against another member state unless it has itself been attacked or has the authorization of the Security Council. The United States acted preemptively in the current Iraq War, which represented the first application of the NSS policy, but, at the same time, also represented a violation of the

UN Charter. In terms of international law, the United States was as much an outlaw in its attack on Iraq as Saddam Hussein was in his attack on Kuwait.

President Bush's West Point Commencement Speech of June 2002 articulates many of the points in the NPR and the NSS. In fact, this speech set the stage for the NSS, which quotes at length from it.

The third of these documents is the *National Strategy to Combat Weapons of Mass Destruction* (NSWMD) that was issued by the White House in December 2002. As in the case of NSS, NSWMD is an unclassified and open public document that is available on the White House Web site. It notes that WMD, including nuclear, biological, and chemical weapons in the possession of states hostile to the United States or terrorists represents one of the greatest security challenges facing the United States. It states that an effective strategy for countering WMD, including their use and further proliferation, is an integral component of the National Security Strategy of the United States. It states that, as in the war on terrorism, the strategy for homeland security, and the new concept of deterrence, this new approach to WMD represents a fundamental change from the past. It affirms that the highest priority is accorded to protection of the United States and its allies from the threat of WMD. The three pillars it announces are *counterproliferation* to combat WMD use, *strengthened nonproliferation* to combat WMD proliferation, and *consequence management* to respond to WMD use. It discusses such policies as interdiction of WMD; new methods of deterrence with threats of overwhelming force; and defense mitigation, including the destruction of an adversary's WMD before their use, on a first-strike attack as in the preemptive policy enunciated in NSS, as well as traditional nonproliferation approaches. It does not exclude the use of nuclear weapons to destroy facilities that could produce nuclear weapons.

The policies set out in NSWMD were further elaborated by President George W. Bush in his February 11, 2004 speech at the National Defense University, in which he developed a seven-point agenda, including international cooperation against proliferation, requiring all states to criminalize proliferation, an expansion of the Nunn-Lugar Cooperative Threat Reduction program, the required renunciation of reprocessing and enrichment for non-nuclear weapon state parties to the nuclear Non-Proliferation Treaty (NPT), a required additional protocol for states to import equipment for civilian nuclear reactors, the formation of a special committee of the International Atomic Energy Agency (IAEA) Board to focus on safeguards and verification, and a requirement that states under investigation for violations of the NPT not be allowed to serve on the IAEA Board of Governors.

TARGETS FOR NUCLEAR WEAPONS

According to the NPR, the United States reserves the right to use nuclear weapons, thereby possibly breaking the long-standing taboo against their use that has existed since their first and only use—by the United States against Japan in August 1945. According to this statement of U.S. policy, they are to be treated like any other weapon, with no sharp distinction from non-nuclear weapons, unlike traditional doctrine that sees them as weapons of last resort.

Nuclear targeting discussions have been a part of U.S. military strategy for some time, but the leak of the NPR reveals for the first time an official "hit list" of targets for nuclear weapons. The NPR lists seven nations as possible targets for U.S. nuclear weapons. First are the two "old" enemies: Russia and China. Second are the three countries listed as members of the "Axis of Evil" in President Bush's 2002 State of the Union speech, namely Iran, Iraq, and North Korea. Third are two countries that are listed by the United States as terrorist states: Syria and Libya.

Of these seven nations that could be targets of U.S. nuclear weapons, three are non-nuclear weapon states that are parties to the treaty on the Non-Proliferation of Nuclear Weapons, the NPT; namely, Iran, Syria, and Libya. ("Regime change" has occurred in Iraq as a result of the U.S. invasion, while North Korea has withdrawn from the NPT.) The United States, along with other nuclear weapon states that are parties to the NPT, however, gave so-called negative security assurances to non-nuclear weapon state parties to the NPT in 1978, pledging that it would not use nuclear weapons against such non-nuclear states unless they were allied with nuclear powers. The most recent such pledge was given on April 5, 1995 during the Clinton administration by Secretary of State Warren Christopher, who stated,

> The United States reaffirms that it will not use nuclear weapons against non-nuclear weapon states parties to the treaty on the Non-Proliferation of Nuclear Weapons except in the case of an invasion or any other attack on the United States, its territories, its armed forces or other troops, its allies, or on a State toward which it has a security commitment, carried out or sustained by such a non-nuclear weapon state in association or alliance with a nuclear-weapon State.

This pledge was reiterated by the U.S. State Department spokesman Richard Boucher on February 11, 2002 but undermined by his saying that if WMD were used against the United States, the administration would not rule out any specific type of military response.

Thus, targeting any of these three nations with nuclear weapons would be a violation of these U.S. negative assurances that provided an inducement for these states to join the NPT and that were reiterated at the time of the NPT Review and Extension Conference in 1995.

The NPR also calls for lesser reliance on the massive stockpiles of nuclear weapons as a deterrent to attack, with greater reliance on precision-guided weapons to deter attacks. It states that because of improvements in precision-guided weaponry, as demonstrated in the war in Afghanistan, the U.S. military can now rely more on powerful, highly accurate conventional bombs and missiles.

A New Triad

According to the NPR there is a new triad. The old triad consisted of three different basing modes for nuclear weapons: long-range bombers, land-based missiles, and submarine-launched ballistic missiles.

By contrast, the NPR refers to a new triad with three component parts of the U.S. strategic system. First are *offensive strike weapons*, both nuclear and non-nuclear, including all three components of the old triad. Second are *defenses*, both active and passive, including the new national missile defense system that is currently under construction despite repeated failures in tests of the system. Third is a *revitalized defense infrastructure* that could "design, develop, manufacture, and certify new warheads in response to new national requirements and maintain readiness to resume underground testing [at the Nevada Test Site] if required."

The Bush administration had obtained agreement from Congress to lift its ban on the design of new nuclear warheads, and there were plans to develop two such weapons. One is a low-yield weapon, a "mininuke," that could potentially be used as a weapon in regional conflicts, thus possibly changing the role of nuclear weapons from that of deterring war to that of an instrument of war. The other is the Robust Nuclear Earth Penetrator (RNEP), a "bunker buster," that can destroy underground facilities, including missile silos in Russia, China, and elsewhere. At this point, however, in 2006, the mininuke and RNEP are probably defunct, and the new concern is with the Reliable Replacement Warhead (RRW).

The Bush administration has already started to construct a missile defense system at Fort Greeley, Alaska, and the secretary of defense has asked his Science Board to look into the possibility that the new system might use nuclear-tipped interceptors. Such interceptors would be much more effective in destroying incoming missiles than the more conventional hit-to-kill interceptors that are being tested now, and they could even neutralize a Russian second-strike deterrent.

Thus, the NPR is a strategy for indefinite reliance on nuclear weapons with plans to improve the capabilities of the existing arsenal and to revitalize the infrastructure for improving U.S. nuclear forces in the future. It promotes a nuclear strategy of maximum flexibility as opposed to measures for irreversible nuclear disarmament as agreed to at the 2000 NPT Review Conference in the form of "13 Practical Steps" related to Article VI of the treaty that calls for the elimination of nuclear weapons. The United States and the other nuclear weapon states that are parties to the treaty agreed to these steps. They included "an unequivocal undertaking to accomplish the total elimination of their nuclear arsenals"; an early ratification of the Comprehensive Test Ban Treaty (CTBT); and a diminishing role for nuclear weapons in security policies, including irreversible and verifiable reductions of both strategic and tactical nuclear weapons. According to NSWMD and the other 2002 documents, however, the United States has no intention of giving up its nuclear weapons but rather sees them as playing an even more important role in its security strategy and as part of a continuum of weapons, with no clear breaks or taboos against their use. Indeed, it is clear that the Bush administration is totally opposed to Article VI of the NPT, with the United States planning to use nuclear weapons for many decades. Ambassador Linton Brooks, the then administrator of the Department of Energy National Nuclear Security Administration (NNSA), told attendees at a panel discussion on "The Future of the U.S. Nuclear Weapons Stockpile" on January 25, 2006 in Washington, DC, sponsored by the Arms Control Association:

> I don't believe I will live to see the political conditions for abolition [of nuclear weapons], and I don't believe that if I live to see the political conditions that

abolition will be technically verifiable in my lifetime … I am assuming that the real issue that faces the U.S. is not whether we have nuclear weapons, but what kind and for what purpose and under what conditions.

On the other hand in the op-ed "A World Free of Nuclear Weapons," published in the January 4, 2007 issue of the *Wall Street Journal*, George Shultz, William Perry, Henry Kissinger, and Sam Nunn called for the abolition of nuclear weapons, a call echoed shortly thereafter by Mikhail Gorbachev in his own op-ed on this topic.

PREEMPTION AND ITS DANGERS

The NSS places major emphasis on preemption (more properly, as already noted, a preventive war) and calls for preemption rather than deterrence as the fundamental basis of national security. The Iraq War is the initial case of such preemption, with the United States retaining its right to preempt in defending its vital interests. (The Afghanistan War can be more properly interpreted as a retaliatory strike for the September 11, 2001 attacks on the United States.)

Such a policy of preemption requires massive defense spending, and the United States now spends more than $400 billion annually on defense, more than most of the rest of the world combined. In his budget for the fiscal year that begins in October 2006, President Bush called for defense spending amounting to $439 billion and that does not include most of the cost of the ongoing military operations in Iraq and Afghanistan. This Bush military budget request for FY-2007 is, in fact, even higher than anticipated.

In addition to its costs, there are significant dangers associated with preemption. First, it creates antagonism toward the United States and possible further terrorist attacks. Second, it sends a message to the rest of the world, that they should not attempt to fight the United States with conventional weapons, leading to the proliferation of nuclear weapons and other weapons of mass destruction. Third, this policy sets a precedent for other nations to also engage in similar preemption, including China in Taiwan and India in Pakistan. Fourth, there are dangers stemming from U.S. hubris after its quick defeat of Saddam Hussein's forces in Iraq, with the next step possibly being an invasion of the other nations on President Bush's "axis of evil" list: Iran and North Korea, or possibly others on the NPR nuclear hit list, such as Syria or Libya, or yet others, such as Sudan or Cuba. These nations will see such a possibility as looming and try to protect themselves, possibly by building their own nuclear weapons, as has already happened in North Korea. According to *The New York Times* editorial of March 12, 2002,

> If another country were planning to develop a new nuclear weapon and contemplating preemptive strikes against a list of non-nuclear powers, Washington would rightly label that nation a dangerous rogue state. Yet, such is the course recommended to President Bush by a new Pentagon planning paper … Nuclear weapons are not just another part of the military arsenal. They are different, and lowering the threshold for their use is reckless folly.

A New Nonproliferation Agenda

The new nonproliferation agenda included "old approaches" such as controls on materials and technology and "new approaches" such as reserving the right to destroy facilities used to make WMD. A precedent for the latter was the Israeli destruction of the Osirak reactor near Baghdad in 1981 before it could be used to make nuclear weapons. Many nations criticized Israel for this action that was in violation of international law, including the UN Charter, given that the Security Council did not authorize it. Similar criticisms could be directed at the United States if it were to engage in such acts. Furthermore, if the United States claims a right to such acts then other nations could also make such a claim, creating very dangerous situations. For example, India might claim the right to destroy Pakistani nuclear facilities using the same logic or China could claim a right to destroy the nuclear infrastructure of Taiwan or Japan. Such policies and actions would make the world a much more dangerous place.

One could also argue that the "old" problem of proliferation was that of nations acquiring nuclear weapons, while the "new" problem is one of terrorist groups acquiring such weapons. More should be done on a cooperative international basis to deny such weapons to terrorist organizations or subnational groups in general. This should be done under the auspices of the UN as a truly international cooperative effort. As to the old problem, involving such nations as Iran and North Korea, a case could be made that their acquiring such weapons could, in fact, be stabilizing rather than destabilizing if the effect is to deter the United States from using its weapons against these nations, seeking further "regime change" in these nations. The world has noted that the United States invaded and occupied two non-nuclear nations, Afghanistan and Iraq, but that it did not invade North Korea or Iran, nations that were on President Bush's axis of evil list in his January 2002 State of the Union address, possibly since the former already has nuclear weapons while the latter could possibly acquire them in the near future. Indeed, the U.S. 2002 documents on nuclear policy create powerful incentives for states to proliferate to deter a U.S. preemptive strike.

An Alternative Approach:
Global Security

There is an alternative to the policies that are enunciated in the NPR, the NSS, and the NSWMD, namely *global security*. The concept refers to security for the planet as a whole to replace the concept of national security, which is outmoded. National security, which is defined up to certain well-defined borders, makes little sense given the globalization that has occurred. The goal of global security would be that of protecting the planet as a whole from threats to its vital interests. This approach recognizes the value of global cooperation, in particular, the value of cooperative efforts among the current great powers of the United States, the European Union, Japan, Russia, China, India, Indonesia, Brazil, Argentina, South Africa, and others.

The concept of global security recognizes the need to create a new global system comparable to the creation of a new world system after World War II, one that would encompass not only security but also economics, politics, and other issue areas. This new global system would treat problems of security, both military and nonmilitary, through strengthening existing international institutions or creating new global institutions. These new institutions could be built, in part, on the UN system and its components. They would involve supranational decision making and authority, with enforcement capabilities, transparency, and accountability and with global perspectives and responses. Participation in the global decision-making process would be through close international cooperation. There would be a prohibition against preemption by any one nation, no matter how powerful, in favor of collective action. Such a system of global security should be preferred to the current system of the United States as a hegemonic global power.

Among the specific steps that might be taken in an agenda to foster such a system of global security are reducing world stockpiles of nuclear weapons and other WMD, especially the enormous stockpile of chemical weapons in Russia; a ratification of the CTBT; taking nuclear weapons off hair-trigger alert and generally de-alerting WMD; a reaffirmation of the moratorium against nuclear testing; international cooperation to prevent nuclear proliferation; implementation of the 13-steps program under the NPT with specific timetables for each of these steps, including an abandonment of all plans to develop new nuclear weapons; a sharing of Permissive Action Link (PAL) technology with all nuclear weapon states to reduce the chance of accidental nuclear war; a U.S. renunciation of its policy of preemption and its reaffirmation of the UN Charter; and cooperative efforts against terrorism, especially the acquisition of WMD by terrorist groups.

Domestic Strategies for Changing U.S. Nuclear Policy

Domestic strategies could result in a change in U.S. nuclear policy and a move to its replacement by the concept of global security and the above action items. First must be an educational program letting the public know about the nuclear strategies now being followed by the Bush administration and their consequences. This can be done, for example, through articles, op-eds, speeches, and courses by those aware of the current policy, such as those mentioned above of George Shultz, William Perry, Henry Kissinger, and Sam Nunn as well as Mikhail Gorbachev. Second, political leaders of both parties must be informed about these matters and prodded to work to change the current policy. Foreign leaders can also play an important role in urging a change in this policy that could have disastrous consequences.

The September 2002 document, which marked the most profound shift in U.S. foreign and security policy since President Harry S. Truman in 1947 laid out the strategy of containing the Soviet Union, provoking controversy by claiming the right to strike unilaterally and preemptively against hostile states and terrorist groups seeking to develop weapons of mass destruction. The United States invaded Iraq six months later.

One can only hope that a rethinking of our nuclear policy will take place despite the opposition of the neoconservatives and will be approved by the president. Otherwise we will have to wait until a new administration takes office in Washington and reconsiders this policy with the hope that the current policy will not lead to further disaster before that takes place.

REFERENCES

Allison, Graham, *Nuclear Terrorism: The Ultimate Preventable Catastrophe* (New York: Times Books, 2004).

Arkin, William M., "Secret Plan Outlines the Unthinkable," *Los Angeles Times* (March 10, 2002).

Cushman, John H., Jr., "Rattling New Sabers," *The New York Times* (March 10, 2002).

Gaddis, John Lewis, "A Grand Strategy of Transformation," *Foreign Policy* 133 (2003), pp. 50–57.

Gordon, Michael R., "U.S. Nuclear Plan Sees New Weapons and New Targets," *The New York Times* (March 10, 2002).

———— "Nuclear Arms for Deterrence or Fighting?" *The New York Times* (March 11, 2002).

Gould, Robert M. and Patrice Sutton, "Global Security: Beyond Gated Communities and Bunker Vision," *Social Justice* 29.3 (2002), p. 1.

Guoliang, Gu, "Redefine Cooperative Security, Not Preemption," *The Washington Quarterly* 26.2 (2003), p. 135.

Heisbourg, Francois, "A Work in Progress: The Bush Doctrine and Its Consequences," *The Washington Quarterly* 26.2 (2003), p. 75.

Hoffman, Stanley, "The High and the Mighty: Bush's National Security Strategy and the New American Hubris," *The American Prospect* 13.24 (2003), p. 28.

Intriligator, Michael D., "Global Security After the End of the Cold War," Presidential Address, Peace Science Society (International), Conflict Management and Peace Science, 13.2 (1994), pp. 1–11.

Intriligator, Michael D. and Abdullah Toukan, "Terrorism and Weapons of Mass Destruction," forthcoming in Peter Katona, John Sullivan, and Michael D. Intriligator, eds., *Creating a Global Counter-Terrorism Network* (London: Taylor & Francis, 2006).

Levi, Michael A., "The Case against New Nuclear Weapons: New Tactical Bombs Would Have Little Military Value and Would Undercut U.S. Nonproliferation Efforts," *Issues in Science and Technology* (March 2003).

McGwire, Michael, "Shifting the Paradigm (Western Ideology of the Cold War)," *International Affairs* 78.1 (2002), p. 1.

O'Hanlon, Michael E., Susan E. Rice, and James B. Steinberg, "The New National Security Strategy and Preemption" Policy Brief #113, *Brookings Institution* (December 2002).

U.S. Department of Defense, Nuclear Posture Review, *The Pentagon* (January, 2002). Excerpts available at http://www.globalsecurity.org/wmd/library/policy/dod/npr.htm.

U.S. Office of the National Security Advisor, The National Security Policy of the United States of America, The White House (September 2002). http://www.whitehouse.gov/nsc/nss.html.

U.S. Office of the President, National Strategy to Combat Weapons of Mass Destruction, The White House, December 2002. http://www.whitehouse.gov/news/releases/2002/12/WMDStrategy.pdf.

NATO Nuclear Weapons: The International Face of U.S. Nuclear Policy

Matthew Martin

A credible Alliance nuclear posture and the demonstration of Alliance solidarity and common commitment to war prevention continue to require widespread participation by European Allies involved in collective defense planning in nuclear roles, in peacetime basing of nuclear forces on their territory and in command, control and consultation arrangements.

—NATO's Strategic Concept (1999)

INTRODUCTION

Americans and Europeans alike could be forgiven for attributing this policy statement to perhaps the Cold War of the 1960s. Sixteen years after the end of the Soviet Union and the breakup of the Warsaw Pact, most of the populations on both sides of the Atlantic would be surprised to learn that this is current doctrine.

International leverage points for changing U.S. nuclear policy are difficult to quantify. Not only do international actors hold no official standing—they do not hold elected office in the United States, they are not constituents to any U.S. elected official—but we live in an age that seems particularly hostile to international armchair quarterbacking. In searching for strategies to affect U.S. nuclear policy then, it may be helpful to turn attention to fora in which international actors wield decision-making power cooperatively with the United States—and one of the most recognizable of these institutions is North Atlantic Treaty Organization (NATO). As it happens, NATO is also an integral component of U.S. nuclear policy.

BACKGROUND

Nuclear weapons have played a key role in NATO's military strategy since its inception in 1949. NATO's current Strategic Concept (1999) states that the "fundamental purpose of the nuclear forces of the Allies is political: to preserve peace and prevent coercion and any kind of war." And NATO substrategic weapons not only provide a nuclear umbrella for Europe, they are also seen as symbolic of the transatlantic link between the United States and its European allies.

In 2007, the United States is the only country that bases any portion of its nuclear arsenal on foreign soil. According to a February 2005 report by the Natural Resources Defense Council, the United States continues to deploy approximately 480 nuclear weapons at eight bases in six NATO countries. Five of these six countries—Belgium, Germany, Italy, the Netherlands, and Turkey—are Non-Nuclear Weapon States under the terms of the Non-Proliferation Treaty (NPT). These countries host U.S. B61 "gravity" bombs that, in the event of nuclear war, could be delivered by aircraft and pilots belonging to the host nation. Previously Greece also participated in nuclear sharing, but in 2003 U.S. nuclear weapons were reportedly withdrawn from the country. The United Kingdom also hosts U.S. nuclear weapons, U.S. Air Force aircraft, and pilots. Along with its ballistic missile submarines, NATO nuclear weapons are the forward tip of the U.S. nuclear arsenal.

Legal Issues

The question of the legality of NATO nuclear weapons hinges on the interpretation of several of the articles of the nuclear NPT. There is a long history of debate surrounding the question of transferring nuclear weapons to non-nuclear states. NATO's nuclear sharing arrangements were at the center of negotiations between the United States and Russia on Articles I and II of the NPT in the mid-1960s. Article I of the NPT states: "Each nuclear-weapon State Party to the Treaty undertakes not to transfer to any recipient whatsoever nuclear weapons or other nuclear explosive devices or control over such weapons or explosive devices directly, or indirectly."

Article II completes the circle by imposing similar restrictions from non-nuclear states on the receiving end: "Each non-nuclear-weapon State Party to the Treaty undertakes not to receive the transfer from any transferor whatsoever of nuclear weapons or other nuclear explosive devices or of control over such weapons or explosive devices directly, or indirectly."

NATO nuclear sharing expressly bases U.S. nuclear weapons within five non-nuclear countries and explicitly sets out a chain of command instructions whereby those nuclear weapons would be transferred to the basing countries in time of need. As such, NATO nuclear sharing appears to breach both Article I and II of the NPT. For its part, NATO asserts that nuclear sharing is compatible with the NPT, based on a U.S. interpretation that it does "not involve any transfer of nuclear weapons or control over them unless and until a decision were made to go to war, at which time the treaty would no longer be controlling."

In the past 10 years, this interpretation has become increasingly controversial. At the 1995 NPT Review Conference, Mexico asked in Main Committee 1 for clarification on whether nuclear sharing breached Articles I and II. Mexico's concerns were taken up by the Non-Aligned Movement (NAM). As a result, several proposals for language questioning the U.S. interpretation were put forward for inclusion in the committee's final report, including

> The Conference notes that among States parties there are various interpretations of the implementation of certain aspects of articles I and II which need clarification, especially regarding the obligations of nuclear weapon States parties…when acting in cooperation with groups of nuclear-weapon States parties under regional arrangements…

Similarly, at the 1998 Preparatory Committee meeting, Egypt proposed a way to close the loophole on nuclear sharing by suggesting that

> The PrepCom recommend that the 2000 Review Conference state in clear and unambiguous terms that Articles I and II of the Treaty on the Non-Proliferation of Nuclear Weapons allow for no exceptions and that the NPT is binding on States Parties at all times.

At the 1999 PrepCom, a statement on behalf of the New Agenda Coalition (NAC) stated that "all the articles of the NPT are binding on all States Parties and at all times and in all circumstances."

NATO also asserts that nuclear sharing is in compliance with the NPT because it predates the NPT. However, not all parties to the NPT were made aware of the NATO arrangements at that time. Although nuclear sharing was not challenged in the 1960s, it has been subsequently challenged and is being questioned today.

DEVELOPMENTS SINCE THE 2000 REVIEW CONFERENCE

The 1995 NPT Principles and Objectives for Nuclear Non-Proliferation and Disarmament contain a number of commitments relevant to NATO, such as the establishment of additional Nuclear Weapon-Free Zones (NWFZ) and the need for strengthened security assurances for non-nuclear weapon states. Similarly, the 2000 NPT Final Document includes

- the need for further unilateral reductions in nuclear arsenals;
- increased transparency;
- further reduction of nonstrategic nuclear weapons;
- measures to reduce the operational status of nuclear weapons systems; and
- a diminishing role for nuclear weapons in security policies.

This call for a "diminishing role for nuclear weapons in security policies" followed concerns about NATO's Strategic Concept, which describes nuclear weapons as the "supreme guarantee" of Allied security.

In June 2004, NATO published two fact sheets, which it claims demonstrate the "radical" and "far reaching" steps the alliance has taken to adapt its nuclear policy, by reducing the number of nuclear weapons in Europe since the end of the Cold War. However, recent figures published by the National Resources

Defense Council (NRDC) indicate that the number of U.S. nuclear warheads based in Europe has remained static at about 480 since the 1994 U.S. Nuclear Posture Review. After three subsequent NPT Review Conferences, 16 years past the end of the Cold War, and 6 years after 9/11, official NATO nuclear policy has remained static for the past 13 years.

However, U.S., UK, and French nuclear policies have not remained equally static. Far from reducing the role of nuclear weapons, the United States is now pursuing the development of new nuclear weapons under the aegis of the Reliable Replacement Warhead program and enlarging the roles of nuclear weapons in counterproliferation and preventive war strategies. The United Kingdom has announced its intention to replace its sole nuclear platform—four Vanguard-class submarines—with new Trident-capable submarines and preparations would seem to indicate a path closely hewing to the U.S. position. Indeed, the United States and United Kingdom have conducted subcritical nuclear tests at the Nevada Test Site as part of ongoing cooperative efforts. France has matched these actions with rhetoric, with President Chirac stating in January 2006 that France reserves the right to use nuclear weapons against any who would threaten the use of WMD against it. France has also announced that it has modified its nuclear arsenal to improve its strike capability and increase missile range. NATO may come under pressure to adopt similar policies.

Taken as a whole, these activities bring into serious question the commitment of the United States, the United Kingdom, and France toward fulfilling their obligations under Article VI of the NPT, which mandates pursuing in good faith negotiations toward disarmament.

INTERNATIONAL STRATEGIES FOR INFLUENCING U.S. NUCLEAR POLICY

Perhaps surprisingly, there has recently been considerable grumbling among high-level European officials on the subject of the continuing presence of U.S. nuclear weapons in Europe. In March 2005, the Belgian Senate unanimously adopted a resolution calling for "the gradual withdrawal of the American tactical nuclear weapons from Europe as fulfillment of Article VI of the NPT." In April 2005, the German Liberal party, the FDP, introduced a resolution to the Bundestag similarly calling for the removal of U.S. nuclear weapons from Germany. Subsequently, a number of prominent German politicians have repeated the call and a new resolution was introduced in 2006. The same month, a Norwegian Parliament Foreign Affairs Committee member from the ruling party reiterated the desire to see U.S. nuclear weapons removed from European soil.

PROSPECTS FOR PROGRESS

NATO does not publish details on the number of nuclear weapons remaining in Europe, despite the member states' commitment to transparency in the 2000 NPT Final Document. The continued presence of U.S. nuclear weapons has, in part, also resulted in Russia declining to discuss their "tactical" nuclear weapon holdings and dismantlement. NATO claims that it is in "full compliance" with the Negative Security Assurances (NSAs) issued by the United States, the United Kingdom, and France on the eve of the 1995 NPT Review Conference.

However, NATO's refusal to rule out first use of nuclear weapons is a major obstacle to further steps to strengthen NSAs. It also effectively gives a green light to NATO military planners to prepare for the option of using nuclear weapons first. NATO's policies have also proved a serious obstacle to any possibility of a NWFZ in Central Europe.

NATO could play an important role in strengthening the NPT by supporting

- ratification of the Comprehensive Test Ban Treaty (CTBT);
- efforts to negotiate a Fissile Material Cut-Off Treaty (FMCT);
- the establishment of an ad hoc committee on nuclear disarmament at the Conference on Disarmament;
- the adoption of a no-first use policy;
- negotiations with Russia on the verifiable elimination of substrategic nuclear weapons and on warhead accounting; and
- the withdrawal of the remaining U.S. nuclear weapons from Europe.

Unfortunately, the latest communique from the ministerial meeting of the Defense Planning Committee and the Nuclear Planning Group from June 2005 upheld NATO's nuclear role and failed to mention any of these issues. It is clear from continuing European actions, however, that these concerns remain very much alive.

A 2005 poll shows that three quarters of the German public wants nuclear weapons out of Germany. In January 2006, the Norwegian Ministry of Finance excluded seven companies from the country's Government Pension Fund-Global—selling approximately $500 million in shares—due to their involvement in the production of nuclear weapons. A majority in the United Kingdom oppose the development of a follow-on to Trident, when presented with the estimated cost. Also, the current SNP Scottish government opposes the proposed replacement of the Trident system, as well as the basing of nuclear submarines on its soil (the UK nuclear submarine fleet is stationed at Faslane Naval Base in Scotland).

In the challenging realm of international influences on U.S. nuclear policy, changing U.S. policy through NATO may be one of the more attainable goals. Prominent European government officials are already sympathetic and activated; significant portions of European populations are uncomfortable with the current posture; the current policy is hampering nonstrategic reductions in Russia and harming our overall relationship with Russia; nuclear sharing makes broader negotiations on nonproliferation (i.e., Iran) more difficult; forward-based nuclear weapons have little or no strategic value in the current political environment; and even U.S. military officials have questioned the continued utility of NATO nuclear sharing.

Scaling back and eliminating NATO nuclear policies would be a significant change in U.S. nuclear policies. It would realign U.S. nuclear forces on a footing much more in keeping with the other nuclear powers and also necessarily change the role of nonstrategic nuclear weapons in U.S. nuclear planning. Further, continued efforts on the part of European leaders and those who support and influence them may actually provide a bright spot in otherwise disturbing and worrisome trends in nuclear weapons policies.

NOTE

This chapter borrows heavily from British American Security Information Council papers and presentations that I coauthored with Nigel Chamberlain and Carol Naughton for the 2005 NPT Review Conference.

CHAPTER 8

Ending Nuclear Terrorism:
By America and Others

Daniel Ellsberg

Long after the ending of the Cold War, the chance that some nuclear weapons will kill masses of innocent humans somewhere, not far in the future, may well be higher than it was before the fall of the Berlin Wall.

One phase of the Nuclear Age, the period of superpower arms race and confrontation, has indeed come to a close (though the possibility of all-out, omnicidal exchange of alert forces triggered by a false alarm remains, inexcusably, well above zero). But another dangerous phase now looms, the era of nuclear proliferation and with it, an increased likelihood of regional nuclear wars, accidents, and nuclear terrorism. And the latter prospect is posed not just by "rogue" states or substate terrorists but by the United States, which has both led by example for 60 years of making nuclear first-use threats that amount to terrorism and may well be the first or among the first to carry out such threats.

Averting catastrophe—not only the spread of weapons but also their lethal use—will require major shifts in attitude and policy in every one of the nuclear weapon states, declared and undeclared. But such change is undoubtedly most needed, and must come first, in the United States and Russia. Despite important and creditable moves, both unilateral and negotiated, since 1991 to reverse their bilateral arms race, and piecemeal measures to restrain proliferation, none of their initiatives and proposals has shown a decisive shift away from Cold War notions of the broad functions of and requirements for nuclear weapons in "superpower" arsenals.

Neither country has adopted—even as a goal—a nuclear posture that is remotely appropriate, let alone adequate, to discourage proliferation effectively. On the contrary, as in the past, their joint declaratory position against proliferation is at odds with their operational doctrines and nuclear weapons programs that continue, on balance, to stimulate the spread and possible use of nuclear weapons. And that is true of all the declared nuclear powers, which not coincidentally make up the permanent membership of the United Nations (UN) Security Council.

With each month and year that these states maintain large nuclear arsenals, postpone ratification of the Comprehensive Test Ban Treaty (CTBT) and sustain nuclear policies that suggest that such weapons convey major power status and are useful for political and military purposes, other nations can only conclude that acquiring and in some circumstances using nuclear weapons may well be in their national interest.

U.S. NUCLEAR POLICIES ENCOURAGING PROLIFERATION

Looking specifically at the United States, a whole set of policies persist that have long tended to *encourage* proliferation. These have included long-term selective blindness and tolerance for some covert nuclear weapons programs, Israel's in particular, but also that of India, South Africa, Pakistan, and in earlier periods, Iran and Iraq.

Moreover, the United States maintains a massive nuclear arsenal after the end of the Cold War, resists radical cuts, and insists on its right, and that of its North Atlantic Treaty Organization (NATO) allies, to threaten or implement initiation of nuclear attack ("first use") against non-nuclear challenges. Beyond this, U.S. policies continue to endorse the notion that the relative size of nuclear arsenals is an essential badge of status. Just like their predecessors—and with the support of most elite opinion makers and mainstream arms control analysts—the Clinton and the two Bush administrations have declared themselves resolved to maintain nuclear superpower standing, insisting on a U.S. arsenal that will remain for the foreseeable future an order of magnitude larger than all others apart from Russia, and that is projected to remain "Number One" in the world indefinitely.

The need for U.S. nuclear "superiority" goes unquestioned, while these same administrations along with members of Congress and editorial writers lecture potential "rogues" among the non-nuclear weapon states on the anachronism of their fantasy that having some nuclear weapons rather than none will confer on them any prestige, status, or influence.

All these expressions of nuclear policy—what we do, and what we say to ourselves, as opposed to what we say others should do—especially in the absence now of any serious military threats to U.S. national security, can only encourage potential nuclear states to regard nuclear weapons in the same way that the United States and its major allies, along with Russia, evidently do: as having vital, multiple, legitimate uses, as well as being unparalleled symbols of sovereignty, status, and power.

Perhaps most dangerously, such potential proliferators are led by past and present American doctrine and behavior to consider—among the possible, acceptable, and valuable uses of nuclear weapons—the issuance and possible execution of nuclear first-use threats: that is, the "option" of threatening to initiate nuclear attacks and, if necessary, of carrying out such threats.

The threat of first use (against a country without nuclear weapons) is intentionally implicit in the repeated statements of President Bush and Secretary of State Rice over the past year, echoed by leading members of Congress, that "all options are on the table" with respect to preventing Iran from acquiring nuclear weapons. Such threats have the perverse effect of challenging other states, including Iran itself, to acquire nuclear capabilities of their own, perhaps stimulating a regional nuclear arms race—mimicking past superpower folly—to be able likewise to threaten, to deter, or to preempt nuclear attack.

Years after the former members of the Warsaw Pact, including Russia, began asking to be admitted to NATO, and after China has acquired most-favored-nation status, the United States still refuses to adopt a policy of "no-first use." This means that the United States refuses to make a commitment never under any circumstance to initiate a nuclear attack. This is also true of Britain, France and now Russia, which abandoned its no-first-use doctrine in late 1993, citing the U.S.-NATO example and reasoning in doing so.

This is not only a matter of words, as some suppose. Despite sensible moves on both sides beginning in late 1991 to remove tactical nuclear weapons from the surface navy and from ground units—responding to realistic fears in both leaderships of "loose nukes" in the Soviet Union—both states continue to deploy sizeable numbers of tactical weapons on air bases and still larger numbers in reserve storage. Virtually all of these weapons are vulnerable to nuclear attack. Thus, they are weapons *only* for first use or for use against non-nuclear opponents.

So long as these continue to be components of the nuclear arsenals of both the United States and Russia, even after their own overarching confrontation has ended, there is simply no logical argument for denying either the legitimacy or reasonableness of nuclear arsenals sized and shaped to the same ends in other countries. This is especially true for countries such as Pakistan and Israel, who face regional opponents with much larger conventional forces. This, after all, was the historic rationale for NATO's reliance on first-use nuclear threats.

In May 1990, a nuclear conflict between India and Pakistan over Kashmir was plausibly feared by U.S. officials, and little has happened since to reduce the prospect of a recurrence. But neither then nor later was the United States in a position to invoke an internationally accepted norm against Pakistan's tacit first-use threats, since Pakistan was so clearly imitating U.S. and NATO behavior.

U.S. Nuclear Weapons Use

Later in 1990, after Saddam Hussein attacked Kuwait, not one of the four nuclear states militarily arrayed against Iraq in the Gulf War—the United States, Britain, France, and Israel—refrained from tacit threats to initiate nuclear attacks under some circumstances. Under public questioning, high U.S. and other Allied officials—including Vice President Quayle, Secretary of Defense Cheney, and General Schwarzkopf—pointedly refused to rule out the possible first use of nuclear weapons against Iraq: in particular, if the Iraqis used chemical weapons extensively, which was regarded as highly possible. Thus, nuclear weapons *were used* as a threat against a non-nuclear opponent during the Gulf War.

By the same token, contrary to the belief of most Americans that U.S. nuclear weapons have never been used in the 50 years since Hiroshima and Nagasaki, American presidents have employed nuclear threats over a dozen times, generally in secret from the U.S. public, in crises and limited wars in Indochina, East Asia, Berlin, Cuba, and the Middle East.[1] The Soviet Union, Israel, and Pakistan have used nuclear weapons in the same way.

In each of these cases, nuclear weapons were *used* in the exact sense in which a gun is used when it is pointed at someone's head in a confrontation, whether or not the trigger is pulled. To get one's way without having to pull the trigger is a major reason for acquiring the gun and, often, for brandishing it.

Some of these nuclear threats were probably bluffs, some probably not. Most were ambiguous, some were rejected, some were believed to be successful, including those in the Gulf War. But all of them involved real dangers, short run or long, to some degree for both sides; intimidation on this scale is never without mutual risk.

One of the successes, the Pentagon concluded, was the Gulf War. Saddam Hussein did not, after all, use the chemical weapons he then possessed—some on alert missiles—either against Allied troops or against Israel. Fear of Israeli nuclear reprisal may have been an especially effective deterrent. But this success, if true, came at a high price. The message that the United States and its allies regarded such threats both as legitimate and as successful was not lost on potential proliferators, who could imagine themselves either as receiving or as imitating such threats themselves in the future.

Yet another spur to proliferation was the accompanying thought, among third world observers, that Iraq might have been spared both these nuclear threats and the heavy conventional bombing it received if Saddam Hussein's efforts to acquire a nuclear weapon had already been successful. That inference became inescapable after 2003, with the dramatic difference in the U.S. responses to a supposed nuclear weapons program in Iraq and an actual successful one in North Korea. (A conventional or nuclear U.S. attack in the near future on a yet-non-nuclear Iran would underline that point once again for the rest of the world.) And once proliferation has occurred, new nuclear states are likely to use the same ambiguous first-use threats, in the same ways and with the same risks of provocation, commitment, and of possible failure and escalation.

This observation rejects the common, condescending implication that significant risk of nuclear war will emerge for the first time only with the acquisition of nuclear weapons by "irresponsible, immature" leaders in the third world. But it also presumes that the risk of nuclear war has been higher over the past 60 years than the world public was allowed to learn.

With nuclear weapons in the hands of a greater number of leaders, individually no more but *no less* reckless than most American presidents of the past 60 years, the long-term risk of nuclear explosions launched by nuclear weapon states is higher still. There is no basis here for limiting the danger of such attacks exclusively to nonstate, "terrorist" groups. The latter real and growing danger must be seen not as replacing but as adding to (and being enhanced by) the dangers of existing and broadened possession of nuclear weapons by states, led by our own.

FAILURE TO MAKE NUCLEAR DISARMAMENT IRREVERSIBLE

Equally foolish and dangerous is the failure of the Clinton and George W. Bush administrations to require Russian commitment—at the price of reciprocal American commitment—to immediate deactivation of strategic weapons to be dismantled under arms control agreements; and to the dismantling, under reciprocal, bilateral controls, of warheads as well as vehicles; and to international control of all the fissile material from these warheads. Only such a combination of measures could lock in the reductions verifiably and irreversibly. Yet these administrations have hung back from proposing, let alone demanding, such bilateral commitments at the cost of U.S. freedom of action to maintain huge stockpiles of warheads and material "in reserve."

There isn't any national security rationale, or any excuse, for U.S. failure to press Russian leaders now, and on every occasion, to commit Russia to reduce *and dismantle* its nuclear forces, both strategic and tactical, as far and as fast as they can be induced to go on a mutual and reciprocal basis. Yet because of reluctance to cut our own forces as deeply as Yeltsin, for one, actually proposed— down to 2,000 in 1992, and reportedly to 1,000 in 1994—high-level officials under Clinton, as under George H. W. Bush, bargained Yeltsin *up* in terms of joint levels of strategic forces to be negotiated.

The present administration of George W. Bush has actually announced that the most recent agreed reduction schedule—down to 1,700–2,200 "operation-ally deployable" warheads by December 2012 with no provision for destruction of warheads or missiles or for detailed verification, and with many thousands each in reserve[2]—is to be the last they envision negotiating.

The risks of such fecklessness are incalculable. The unprecedented opportuni-ties that emerged in late 1991 (or even earlier, under Gorbachev) for reducing and eliminating nuclear weapons and for changing long-standing Cold War policies were and are obviously subject to continuous erosion and challenge. Warnings by Secretary of Defense Cheney at that time—reiterated by Secretary Perry and then by Secretaries Rumsfeld and Gates—that the Russian future is highly uncertain are self-evidently realistic. (Likewise, arms policies in China.) But the conclusions they have all drawn from this, serving to preserve swollen defense budgets and nuclear arsenals on both sides, seem perversely implausible.

It is true that there is a continuing danger of a shift to a more authoritarian, militarist regime within Russia, which would close down such opportunity as still might be nurtured for greatly increased trust and cooperation, openness to international inspection, and reductions in arms. (This may, or may not, already have happened under Putin, but the contrary possibility has scarcely been explored by the United States.)

But that is precisely why reciprocal commitments to inspection and disarma-ment should have been sought urgently throughout this period, and at present. No matter how fascistic its future or even present leadership might become, Russian need for credits and trade would make its leaders extremely reluctant to disavow formal undertakings that had been ratified. The logic of these ominous uncertainties points in exactly the opposite direction from maintaining insanely high levels of nuclear weaponry in Russian, along with American, hands.

Nuclear Insanity

"Insane" is not too strong a word for arguments that occupy planners in the Pentagon and otherwise serious arms control analysts in favor of maintaining thousands of thermonuclear warheads in the U.S. arsenal—hence thousands in Russia—in a world where neither any longer has a superpower adversary. After two generations of a strategic nuclear arms race that was the clearest example in human history of a social process psychotically divorced from reality or an urge to survive, such advisors have clearly lost any conception of what a nuclear bomb is or does.

They have forgotten, if they ever knew, that pictures of Nagasaki in the late summer of 1945 show what happens to a medium-sized city when just the detonator to a modern, thermonuclear weapon is exploded in its midst. Almost no Americans are aware of the elementary fact that every thermonuclear fusion weapon, or H-bomb—which comprise all of our strategic arsenal, still over 6,000 warheads—requires a Nagasaki-type fission warhead, or A-bomb, to set it off.

The earliest thermonuclear blasts released 1,000 times the explosive power of the A-bomb detonator that triggered it, which was in turn 2,000 times more powerful than the largest "blockbuster" of World War II. The latter destroyed a city block with 10 tons of TNT. The second fusion explosion, in February 1954, had a yield equivalent to 15 million tons of TNT, over seven times greater than the tonnage of all the bombs dropped by the United States in World War II, including the A-bombs on Hiroshima and Nagasaki. That single bomb—the first test of a droppable H-bomb—had greater explosive power than that of all the shells and bombs together in all the wars of human history.

It is in that unearthly light that bomb designer Herbert York, the first director of Livermore Nuclear Weapons Laboratory and later President Carter's test ban negotiator, gave an unfamiliar but plausible answer to the Cold War question: How many survivable, deliverable nuclear warheads would it take to deter an adversary rational enough to be deterred at all? York's answer was: "Somewhere in the range of 1, 10, or 100"; and, he conjectured, "I think it is closer to 1 than it is to 100."

York also suggested another way of arriving at an upper limit for an appropriate nuclear arsenal. He proposed that we ask ourselves what the upper limit of destructive power is within a short period of time that we would want a single state, or a single individual heading that state, to control. Suppose that upper limit was the ability to inflict, in a day or two, the full scale of destruction of World War II. Surely it would be challenging to justify a capability to inflict immediate damage that was greater than that. The criterion would imply, York calculated, an upper limit to a survivable nuclear force of about 100 thermonuclear warheads. It might be as many as 200. It would certainly not allow 1,000 warheads, or 500.

Thus, even by Cold War standards of requirements for deterring nuclear attack, applied to present and foreseeable conditions: what nuclear weapon state can really make a plausible case for possessing as many nuclear weapons as the 200 deployed by Britain or China, or the 348 deployed by France? Not France, or Britain, or China; nor the United States, nor Russia.

Even the smaller of these states continue to maintain and to expand arsenals so large as to mock intolerably the presumption of the Non-Proliferation Treaty (NPT) that none of the other states of the world, the non-nuclear weapon states, has any compelling or legitimate reason to possess even one nuclear weapon. That can be said even of India (40–50 assembled warheads), or Israel (commonly estimated at 200 warheads, but with other estimates ranging from 300 to 600).

Meanwhile, the U.S. arsenal—10,000 warheads, nearly 6,000 operational—is *one hundred times* the maximum suggested by York. The Russian stockpile—16,000 warheads, over 7,000 operational—is even larger. Even after reductions currently agreed under the current Strategic Offensive Reductions Treaty by 2012, the operational warheads alone—1,700–2,200 "operationally deployable" warheads, for each (apart from the much larger number of inactive/reserve weapons "on the shelf")—will be 10–20 times the York levels.[3] And they will still be larger in 2013 and beyond than the arsenals that either deployed in 1968, when they signed the NPT. By their behavior, the two nuclear superpowers have been saying to every non-nuclear weapon state over the 40 years since then: "You don't need a single nuclear weapon ever. We need thousands indefinitely."

By the time of the 1995 NPT Review and Extension Conference, it seemed obvious (to this writer, among many others) that this contradiction could not be sustained much longer (even though, under intense diplomatic pressure from the United States, the non-nuclear members of the NPT did renew the treaty indefinitely). The situation looked, and remains, unstable. At a time when fissile materials and nuclear weapons were becoming widely available, the nuclear weapon states, led by the United States and Russia, could not continue to maintain and flaunt the privileges of the nuclear "club" without membership in that club eventually expanding.

It did not take long. In retrospect, the Indian decision to test, inevitably triggering Pakistani tests, followed quickly on that NPT conference performance by the nuclear weapon states. Before long, North Korea was the first to join them (and Israel) outside the treaty, and proceeded to test (followed by a sudden renunciation of military threats and a willingness to negotiate by the United States: a sequence from which Iran, for one, may have drawn dangerous conclusions).

The Need for an Effective International Norm and Practical Disincentives

Without an effective international norm against both acquisition and threat/use of nuclear weapons, there cannot be an adequate basis for consensual, coordinated international action to prevent such acquisition or use, including intrusive inspection "any time any place," with comprehensive sanctions against violators of the norm. But there cannot be such a norm, a true international consensus on values and obligations, so long as the current nuclear weapon states project an indefinite extension of a two-tier system in which they are subject to a different set of rules, or in effect, no rules at all.

At the same time, trying to close off all technological access to nuclear weapons will never be enough to discourage others from following America's and NATO's nuclear example. The "supply side" approach, by itself, cannot succeed in stopping proliferation. Nor can the current threats of military preemption. In the immediate case of Iran, in the absence of a ground invasion—of incalculable cost, length, and consequences—a full-scale air assault could actually speed up, over a period of years, Iran's acquisition of nuclear weapons. It would replace any prospects of negotiating intense inspection and restraint of the Iranian nuclear energy program by an uninhibited, totally *uninspected* crash pursuit of nuclear weapons outside the NPT, in underground, dispersed sites.

Meanwhile, this very prospect of an eventual Iranian bomb would encourage nuclear weapons programs throughout the Middle East. This already seems to be occurring, with sudden interest in "nuclear energy" programs in Egypt, Saudi Arabia, Turkey, and the Gulf States. Which of these would be subject to threats of an American preemptive attack? For that matter, which of the more than 40 states that could pursue a near-term nuclear capability with the breakdown of the NPT that would almost surely follow an American attack on Iran would be plausibly deterred by the prospect of American military preemption? Japan? Brazil (followed by Argentina)? Taiwan? South Korea?

Discouraging Iran now and in the future—by a variety of diplomatic means—from leaving the NPT, rejecting international inspection or acquiring nuclear weapons is thus extremely important. But by the same token, foregoing military assault on Iran is essential. For all the severe limitations of the existing "nonproliferation regime," which have brought us to this point, its breakdown would surely be even more dangerous. An American attack on Iran would be a fatal attack on the NPT.

More generally, there must be a successful effort to reduce the *incentives*, the demand for acquiring nuclear weapons. This must include resolving existing regional conflicts as in the Middle East and South Asia, providing effective alternatives to military means, and reducing decisively global causes of war.

Simultaneously, without further delay, there must be drastic changes in official nuclear policies of the United States and other nuclear weapon states that now *enhance* the demand for nuclear weapons by creating incentives for proliferation or by making it seem legitimate. The nuclear weapon states, led by the United States and Russia, can only adequately reduce incentives to join the club by moving convincingly toward its eventual dissolution, and meanwhile giving up decisively the discriminatory privileges of membership: freedom to test, to expand and modernize arsenals, to threaten first use, to flaunt status differentials, to be free of international inspection and accountability.

Only in the context of normative and practical disincentives to acquire or threaten to use nuclear weapons can there be effective international collaboration in verifying and enforcing global bans on such activities. Such norms have to be universal: one set of rules for everyone.

It is urgent for the nuclear weapon states to acknowledge the reality that they have been denying and the non-nuclear weapon states have been proclaiming for almost 40 years: that in the long run—and that time has arrived—effective nonproliferation is inescapably linked to nuclear disarmament.

It is all or none. Eventually—indeed, very shortly—either all nations forego the right to possess and threaten others with nuclear weapons or every nation will claim that right, and actual possession and use will be very widespread.

It was observed earlier that no nuclear weapon state has ever had an appropriate posture from which to discourage proliferation. (Indeed, nearly every one has actively stimulated efforts toward proliferation in at least one neighbor or rival.) A shift toward such a posture awaits fundamental changes in the present policies of all nuclear weapon states, which must rest on a new way of thinking about nuclear weapons and weapons-usable fissile materials.

No longer can we afford to think of such permanently toxic, provocative, and dangerous objects and materials as "national treasure"—as Russian officials have described Russian plutonium. We must come to see the existence of nuclear stockpiles in any country, starting with the United States and Russia, as a threatening and urgent international problem, akin to global warming and ozone depletion, or to radioactive waste (literally) that needs to be dealt with cooperatively by humanity as a whole, led by the countries that are themselves the greatest contributors to the problem.

Thus, there should be a global, verified cutoff in the production of fissile materials for weapons purposes and a program for monitoring all existing military stocks and safeguarding all civil stocks; likewise, an immediate moratorium on programs for the civilian production and use of weapons-usable fissile materials—separated plutonium and highly enriched uranium (HEU)—with the longer-term goal of a complete ban on the production, stockpiling, and use of such material for any purposes including civilian energy or research, along with verified declarations and reductions of existing stocks under international safeguards or possible custody.

We must shift the focus of the creative energies of the military and the laboratories in all the nuclear weapon states to ways of quickly and irreversibly disabling the weapons under multilateral safeguards, and guarding them safely until they can be dismantled. Planning should begin now to safeguard the radioactive residues indefinitely under international supervision.

Only if those of us in the United States act decisively and consistently on such a reconceptualization can we ask other countries to forego nuclear weapons altogether, or ask other nuclear weapon states to restrain their buildup or use of threats, or expect effective international collaboration on enforcement. We cannot hope for any of these so long as we continue to develop new nuclear warheads while we insist on our freedom to threaten and initiate nuclear warfare—"all options are on the table"—and to maintain massive nuclear arsenals or in the longer run, any nuclear arsenal at all.

A COMMITMENT TO NUCLEAR WEAPONS ABOLITION

It is true that even the most radical disarmament effort cannot uninvent nuclear weapons. It cannot permanently assure that later generations of humans will never resume development and testing of nuclear weapons, once ended. Even physical elimination of all existing weapons, adequately inspected and verified, cannot guarantee that they will never return. The work of the Manhattan Project will not be entirely undone. The danger it bequeathed can never be reduced permanently to zero. Nor can abolition be achieved in one leap; or, ever, simply by demanding or promising it, with no specification of a constructive path toward it.

But these truisms do not mean that anything like the present levels of danger must or should be tolerated any longer: even for another year, let alone indefinitely. In a meaningful sense, near-abolition of nuclear weapons—95–99 percent dismantlement of current stockpiles—is an appropriate goal to be achieved *within a decade*. Concretely, that would mean that United States and Russia would aim in that time to reduce their arsenals to the neighborhood of the other declared nuclear states—around 500 warheads or less—calling on these others not to increase or modernize their arsenals while awaiting multilateral reductions to lower levels. And they would call on all to make early commitments to seek multilateral ceilings—on the way eventually to a nuclear weapon-free world—on the order of tens to hundreds of nuclear weapons.

To be credible enough to avert further proliferation in the short run, the goal of abolition needs not only to be proclaimed at the outset but also to be demonstrated immediately by practical steps in that direction, including both progressive reductions and steps to make these reductions irreversible. These must include commitments to *de-alert* and, progressively, deactivate and dismantle warheads and missiles, with bilateral or international monitoring of this process. Both superpowers should move quickly toward "zero alert" for operational missiles and aircraft, taking land-based missiles off alert and adopting zonal and other restrictions on missile submarine patrols and antisubmarine-warfare operations. Steps like these, either unilaterally or bilaterally, could reduce the danger of nuclear war radically in the very short run, weeks to months.

The presumption here is that abolition must come in stages. But if proliferation in the near future is to be averted, a true commitment to total abolition of nuclear weapons—banning and eliminating their use and possession—as the goal is no longer to be delayed or equivocated. We must begin now the effort to explore and to immediately help bring about conditions that will make a world of zero nuclear weapons feasible.

We cannot accept the conclusion that abolition must be ruled out "for the foreseeable future" or put off for generations. There will not be a truly long-run human future without it. In particular, it seems more naïve than realistic to believe that large cities can coexist indefinitely with nuclear weapons. If human civilization in the form that emerged 4,000 years ago (in Iraq!) is to persist globally even another century or two, a way must be found to make the required transformations ultimately practical.

The program spelled out below can be seen as the early and middle stages of the phased elimination of nuclear weapons. It does not assume that any nuclear state is now ready to commit itself to achieving total abolition by a definite deadline. Yet it does represent a belief that quite drastic steps in this direction— going far beyond the current proposals of any nuclear state, to a state that could reasonably be called "near-abolition"—are both urgently desirable and physically possible in the relatively short run.

Whether they are *politically* possible in the world as it is in 2007 is another question. For the immediate future, through 2008, that question can be answered definitely: No. For most of these measures, negotiations toward them are now actively opposed, or stalemated, by the Bush administration.[4] The CTBT remains unratified, and the Anti-Ballistic Missile Ban Treaty rescinded in 2002. Unilateral steps that could reduce nuclear dangers within days or weeks, like dealerting, are not even considered. All this places an extremely high premium on averting, during that interval, an attack by the Bush administration on Iran, or the occurrence of a new 9/11 in the United States. Either of these, in my opinion, would launch a dynamic—including a resumption of nuclear testing by the United States and thence by many other countries—that would put nuclear disarmament permanently beyond reach.

But the replacement of this administration in 2009 by another, Democrat or Republican, will not, in the light of past experience, make the fundamental changes in U.S. posture that are necessary to prevent widespread nuclear proliferation or use easy to achieve or even likely. Only, possible.

The obstacles to achieving these changes even after the departure of President Bush and Vice President Cheney are not posed by the majority of the American public (or the publics of any of the major nuclear weapon states), but by officials and elites in both parties, and by major institutions supporting militarism and empire.

No First Use

It is not only Bush and other Republicans who are *using* nuclear weapons against Iran at this time—to reinforce threats of military force if Iran does not give up uranium enrichment—by declaring that *"all* options are on the table." (All options, for Bush, except direct negotiations, assurances against American attack, expanded trade, or diplomatic recognition.) Although they would favor broader negotiation, the president has been joined in these expressions of first-use nuclear threats, if diplomacy fails, by each of the leading candidates for the Democratic nomination in 2008: Hillary Clinton, John Edwards, and Barack Obama.

No major candidate in either party has been willing to undercut the president's "bargaining hand" by insisting that initiating *or threatening* a nuclear attack is not a legitimate "option" for the president of the United States or for any other national leader: above all, against a non-nuclear adversary that has not launched an overwhelming attack.

It should be self-evident that a nation that is currently using nuclear weapons for national purposes, and has traditionally defended the legitimacy of doing so, is devoid so long as that persists of any moral authority, or really, much hope of any effective influence of any kind, toward averting either proliferation or similar use by others. Indeed, it cannot fail to promote both spread and use.

Yet it will take more than a change in administration or party for the U.S. government to join China and most of the non-nuclear states of the world in rejecting the legitimacy of first-use threats or attacks under any circumstances. The opposite of that proposition has been fundamental to U.S. nuclear policy, and to its military policy as a whole, every year since 1945.

Few Americans in or out of government are aware of the extent to which the United States and NATO first-use doctrine has always isolated the United States and its Western allies morally and politically from world opinion. Nor are they familiar with the sharpness of the language used by majorities in the UN General Assembly in resolutions condemning the policies on which NATO has long based its planning.

UN Resolution 36/100, the Declaration on the Prevention of Nuclear Catastrophe, was adopted on December 9, 1981. It declares in its preamble:

> Any doctrine allowing the first use of nuclear weapons and any actions pushing the world toward a catastrophe are incompatible with human moral standards and the lofty ideals of the UN.

The body of the UN Resolution 36/100 declares:

> States and statesmen that resort first to nuclear weapons will be commit-ting the gravest crime against humanity. There will never be any justification

or pardon for statesmen who take the decision to be the first to use nuclear weapons.

Eighty-two nations voted in favor of this declaration. Forty-one (under heavy pressure from the United States) abstained; 19 opposed it, including the United States and most NATO member nations.

That the dissenters were allies of the United States is no coincidence. The first-use doctrine denounced here in such stark terms underlies the basic strategic concept of NATO, devised and promoted by the United States from the early 1950s to the present. (Most Americans, polls show, have been unaware of this.) NATO plans and preparations not only "allow" first use of nuclear weapons, if necessary to defeat an overwhelming attack; they promise it. They always have, and they still do.

This remains true despite the fact that the possibility of an overwhelming conventional attack against NATO no longer exists. Nineteen years after the fall of the Berlin Wall, hundreds of U.S. tactical nuclear weapons remain in Europe to carry out first-use nuclear attacks as a "last resort," although the Warsaw Pact is no more and all its former members, including Russia, have indicated desire for membership in NATO. In 1997, a serious effort to promote consideration of a no-first-use doctrine by Germany—West Germany was the strongest European supporter of the first-use policy during the Cold War—was shelved after intense opposition by the United States.

Only China, of the five declared nuclear weapon states, has made the simple, unqualified commitment that it would never, under any circumstances, be the first to use a nuclear weapon, and that it would not use nuclear weapons against a non-nuclear weapon state. The United States should join China, and call on Russia and other nuclear states to do likewise.

As concrete implementation of this shift (apart from rejecting immediately declarations that "all options" including nuclear first use "are on the [bargaining] table") the United States and Russia should agree to withdraw from deployment all tactical nuclear weapons, seeking a global ban, dismantling both weapons systems and nuclear warheads under bilateral safeguards.

With an era of widespread proliferation threatening, it should be unmistakably clear that accepting UN resolution 36/100 as a universal principle would be in the best interests of the United States and the rest of the world. The United States and its allies would join, at last, in a moral judgment that is already asserted by the majority of governments of the world.

What is at issue here is more than the practical benefits of joining in a consensus. It has been argued above that the United States—along with the other nuclear weapon states—has failed to do remotely as much as it could and must do to motivate and to organize an effective nonproliferation regime. In particular, *none* of these nuclear weapon states (with the exception of China, on first use) have been unwilling—in order to motivate a true international taboo against nuclear acquisition and acceptance of a strong inspection regime—to negotiate the necessary constraints on their own freedom of action, to develop, test, deploy, and threaten nuclear weapons, in order to motivate a true international taboo against nuclear acquisition and acceptance of a strong inspection regime. The costs of this folly will be measured in otherwise avoidable regional nuclear wars and nuclear terrorism, the latter potentially threatening all states.

The Moral Cost of Continued Reliance on Nuclear Arms

But there is a moral cost, as well, in reliance by the United States and others on threats and readiness to initiate such slaughter by state action. It was suggested earlier that many strategic planners and even many arms control analysts have lost track of the reality of what a nuclear bomb is, and what it does. In the light of that reality, plans and doctrines for the use of nuclear weapons, and resistance to the goal of eliminating them, raise questions about who we are—as a nation, as citizens, as a species—and what we have been doing and risking, what we have a right to do, or an obligation, and what we should not do.

Speaking personally, I have always shared President George W. Bush's blanket condemnation, under all circumstances, of terrorism, defined as the deliberate slaughter of noncombatants—unarmed civilians, children and infants, the old and the sick—for a political purpose. The destruction of the World Trade Center buildings with their inhabitants on September 11, 2001 was rightly recognized as a terrorist action, and condemned as mass murder, by most of the world.

But in contrast, most Americans have never recognized as terrorist in precisely the same sense the firestorms caused deliberately by U.S. firebombing of Tokyo, Dresden, or the atomic bombings of Hiroshima and Nagasaki. These deliberate massacres of civilians, though not prosecuted after World War II like the Japanese slaughter at Nanking, were by any prior or reasonable criteria war crimes, wartime terrorism, crimes against humanity.

Just like the bombs that destroyed Hiroshima and Nagasaki—which would be considered, in terms of scale, tactical nuclear weapons today—any attack by a single tactical nuclear weapon near a densely populated area would kill tens to hundreds of thousands of noncombatants.

Virtually any threat of first use of a nuclear weapon is a terrorist threat. (Exceptions might be tactical antisubmarine weapons underwater, or weapons in space, or air-bursts against military targets in a desert: but even these would be highly likely to lead to less discriminating exchanges.) Any nation making such threats—that means the United States and its allies, including Israel, along with Russia, Pakistan, and India—is a terrorist nation.

But the same is true of threats of nuclear retaliation to nuclear attack. To threaten second use—above all with thermonuclear weapons, like the five permanent members of the Security Council—is to threaten counterterrorism on the largest of scales: retaliatory genocide. To possess a nuclear weapon is to be a terrorist nation.

To reject terrorism—as we should, as moral beings—is to reject the possession of nuclear weapons. The elimination of nuclear weapons, of nuclear terrorism, will have to be accomplished by multilateral collaboration. But it must be accomplished. To recover fundamental moral bearings, as well as to preserve life and civilization, the United States, Russia, Britain, France, China, Israel, India, Pakistan, and North Korea must cease to be terrorist states.

The challenge especially to citizens of these states, in company with others around the world, is to bring their national policies into line—overcoming the resistance of their present national leaderships—with fundamental morality, and thus with the global goal, the species-task, defined by the then UN Secretary

General Boutros Boutros-Ghali in his inaugural address to the NPT Review and Extension Conference in May 1995:

> The most safe, sure and swift way to deal with the threat of nuclear arms is to do away with them in every regard. This should be our vision of the future. No more testing. No more production. No more sales or transfer. Reduction and destruction of all nuclear weapons and the means to make them should be humanity's great cause.

Notes

1. See Daniel Ellsberg, "Call to Mutiny," Introduction to Protest and Survive, ed. E. P. Thompson and Dan Smith (Monthly Review Press, 1981): http://www. ellsberg.net/content/view/16/32/. For a more recent list of threats, see "U.S. Nuclear Threats: Then and Now," Robert S. Norris and Hans M Kristensen, *Bulletin of Atomic Scientists*, September/October 2006, pp. 69–71: http://www. thebulletin.org/print_nn.php?art_ofn=so06norris.
2. Joseph Cirincione, *Bomb Scare* (New York, 2007), p. 42.
3. All estimates, except for Israel, from Cirincione, *Bomb Scare,* Table 5.5, p. 98.
4. See the detailed critique of the current status of negotiations in *Nuclear Disorder or Cooperative Security: A Civil Society Assessment of the Final Report of the Weapons of Mass Destruction Commission,* by John Burroughs, Michael Spies, Jacqueline Cabasso, Andrew Lichterman, and Jennifer Nordstrom. Copies available from Lawyers' Committee on Nuclear Policy, Michael@lcnp.org.

CHAPTER 9

At the Nuclear Precipice: Iran

Aslı Ü. Bâli

IRAN AND THE DUAL-USE DILEMMA

The Nuclear Non-Proliferation Treaty (NPT) underwent its most recent five-year review session in May 2005. There were numerous proposals on the table to consider how to strengthen nonproliferation mechanisms, reinforce disarmament commitments, close loopholes in the verification and monitoring procedures associated with the regime, and create more effective multilateral arrangements for the management of fissile materials. Despite the urgency of the issues addressed by these proposals, none was adopted and the review session was widely regarded as a failure.[1]

The source of the dispute at the conference was the bargain at the heart of the NPT framework: nonproliferation in exchange for disarmament and civilian nuclear energy cooperation. The debate during the month-long conference centered ultimately on non-nuclear weapon states demanding the strengthening of the disarmament provisions of the treaty, while the United States, backed to some extent by its European allies demanded a focus on reinforcing verification of treaty compliance and nonproliferation requirements. With North Korea still withdrawn from the NPT, as of May 2005, American nonproliferation concerns centered on the Iranian case. Indeed, the failure of the conference was interpreted by at least one analyst as a consequence of disagreements between the United States and Iran.[2] More broadly, the breakdown of the conference reflects an international climate in which non-nuclear weapon states are unwilling to accede to additional demands for the limitation of their access to the nuclear fuel cycle, while the nuclear weapon states fail to implement their disarmament commitments under Article VI of the NPT and, more specifically, those commitments undertaken at the 2000 NPT Review Conference.

The role of the United States in undermining progress at the 2005 NPT review session despite the priority placed by the American administration on nonproliferation raises an interesting question: why would the chief architect of the multilateral nonproliferation regime resist the strengthening of a framework that preserves the current status quo of nuclear weapons "haves" and "have-nots"? Furthermore, how can we reconcile the priority given to nonproliferation enforcement in U.S. policy statements with the international record of inconsistent enforcement of the nonproliferation norm, with some known proliferators escaping any consequence and other suspected proliferators facing severe, punitive sanctions?

The Iranian case is conventionally understood as an enforcement problem. Iran, like all non-nuclear weapon state parties to the NPT, has two obligations under the treaty: not to manufacture or acquire nuclear weapons (Article II) and to accept safeguards, implemented by the International Atomic Energy Agency (IAEA), to prevent the diversion of nuclear energy from peaceful uses to weapons (Article III). Because enforcement of the Article II obligations of non-nuclear weapon states would require unacceptably intrusive inspections, there is no specific enforcement mechanism for this obligation. Rather, the reporting obligations of countries and the IAEA's monitoring and verification authority associated with Article III is designed to ensure that declared nuclear energy facilities are being operated according to relevant safety requirements and that there is no diversion of fissile materials from permitted civilian facilities. The IAEA has found since 2002 that Iran has failed, over a period of nearly two decades, to comply with some of its reporting obligations. On the other hand, there has been no concrete evidence of the diversion of nuclear materials to weapons programs or other military use. Thus, Iranian noncompliance has not been with its principal obligations under the NPT but, rather, of its Safeguards Agreement. Further, the clandestine nuclear enrichment program that the Iranians developed has not been more advanced than the declared enrichment programs of other non-nuclear weapon state parties to the NPT such as Japan and Brazil. These other enrichment programs have been treated as permissible under Article IV of the NPT, subject to strict monitoring and inspection by the agency.

Following the revelations that other countries developed clandestine nuclear weapons programs—notably Iraq and North Korea—the IAEA adopted an Additional Protocol for broader inspections that would enable the Agency to monitor not only declared facilities but also to uncover the presence of undeclared facilities. Beginning in 2003, Iran voluntarily complied with the Additional Protocol inspections regime, though the breakdown of negotiations over its nuclear program led to the suspension of its compliance in 2006. It is now argued that the NPT should develop stronger safeguards requirements, more aggressive inspection protocols, and more stringent limitations on the development of civilian nuclear energy programs specifically to prevent such reporting violations in the future. If these steps were taken, it is argued, they would lead to stricter controls that would reduce proliferation concerns with respect to problem states. While a stricter inspections regime would certainly be desirable, a more consistent and nondiscriminatory approach to enforcement would also greatly improve the current nonproliferation regime's capacity to command compliance. In particular, measures to address the deterioration of the bargain underlying the regime as a result of the focus of enforcement efforts on the non-nuclear weapon states to the exclusion of the obligations of the nuclear weapon states would be helpful. Further, attention should be paid to the potential damage done to nonweapons' states incentives to remain within the regime as access to nuclear energy technologies is increasingly curtailed, before the nonproliferation regime is further weakened.

This chapter will outline the context for nonproliferation enforcement with respect to Iran and alternatives to the course currently being adopted by the IAEA, with a view to considering measures to strengthen the nonproliferation regime while resolving the Iranian nuclear dispute. A significant portion of this chapter will trace recent developments in the Iranian nuclear dossier since the revelation in 2002 that Iran had a clandestine nuclear energy program, with a particular emphasis in the most recent period. This review will include an evaluation of the record of Iranian violations of NPT obligations in light of Iranian explanations as well as the politics of negotiations within the IAEA board. After an assessment of the current approach adopted by the international community, the remainder of the chapter will turn to a discussion of alternative approaches to promoting nonproliferation objectives in the Iranian case.

CHRONOLOGY OF THE DISPUTE OVER
IRAN'S NUCLEAR PROGRAM: 2002–2006

Claiming that it wishes to produce Low-Enriched Uranium (LEU) containing about 4 percent U-235 fuel for nuclear power reactors, Iran is pursuing the development of a domestic centrifuge enrichment plant. The international community is concerned that such a centrifuge enrichment plant would have an inherent dual-use capability that would render it capable of also producing weapon-grade uranium containing more than 90 percent U-235. Iran's 18-year clandestine enrichment efforts, which were revealed in August 2002 by the National Council of Resistance of Iran (NCRI), and subsequently subjected to IAEA monitoring and verification, have brought back into international focus the difficulty raised by Article IV of the NPT.[3] Article IV of the NPT gives nonweapons state parties to the treaty the "inalienable right" to enjoy the benefits of the peaceful uses of nuclear energy. Iran has interpreted this provision (as have several other nonweapons states, including Japan, South Korea, and Brazil) as entitling it to build enrichment and other sensitive fuel cycle facilities provided that those facilities are placed under IAEA verification. The IAEA maintains that the reference to inalienable rights does not encompass the right to develop enrichment facilities, but simply to operate nuclear reactors for energy purposes and to have access to enriched uranium on open markets.

The reason that Iran's development of an enrichment capability raises serious nonproliferation concerns is that an ostensibly peaceful civilian enrichment program can provide the basis for a latent nuclear weapons capability. First, once a country masters the technology for its overt civilian enrichment program, it might build a parallel covert program that would be used to enrich uranium for military purposes. Second, after developing an overt civilian enrichment capability, a country might exercise its rights under the NPT withdrawal clause to terminate IAEA safeguards and enrich either natural uranium or further enrich the LEU produced in its civilian program to weapons grade.[4] Among non-nuclear weapon states, Brazil, Japan, the Netherlands, Germany, and South Africa all have enrichment facilities.[5]

While several non-nuclear weapon states have enrichment facilities, Iran has been singled out for developing facilities that raise specific nonproliferation concerns. In this section, I will review the sources of these concerns and the recent trajectory of the confrontation between the IAEA board of governors and Iran concerning its nuclear energy activities.

REVELATIONS

The NCRI revelations and the subsequent IAEA inspections disclosed the existence of two undeclared nuclear facilities in Iran: a centrifuge-based uranium enrichment plant at Natanz and a heavy water production plant at Arak.[6] Following the revelations, the Iranian representative to the regular session of the IAEA General Conference in September 2002 declared Iran's intention to embark on a "long-term plan to construct nuclear power plants with a total capacity of 6000 MW within two decades...[including] all out planning, well in advance, in various fields of nuclear technology such as fuel cycle, safety and waste management."[7] While the goals of the current Iranian energy program are significantly more modest than the nuclear energy program that had been undertaken, with American approval, in the 1970s by the Shah, they are considerably more advanced than anything the Islamic Republic had publicly stated previously.

In the aftermath of its declaration of its civilian uranium enrichment program, Iran's approach toward intensified IAEA inspections and its own obligation to take corrective actions and provide comprehensive declarations of its current nuclear activities has been somewhat ambivalent. In the fall of 2003, Iran entered into negotiations with the governments of the United Kingdom, France, and Germany (the so-called EU-3) to engage in confidence-building measures, including the temporary, voluntary suspension of its uranium conversion and enrichment programs while negotiating arrangements to establish "objective guarantees" that its nuclear activities cannot be diverted to military uses. The most recent round of negotiations with the EU-3 failed in August 2005, resulting in Iranian resumption of uranium conversion activities at its Isfahan facility followed by a strongly worded resolution issued by the IAEA board of governors in September. Since the September IAEA Resolution, there have been no further negotiations between Iran and the EU-3 and relations between the Iranian government and the IAEA board have further deteriorated. By January 2006, it was evident that further progress in negotiations with the EU-3 was unlikely and Iran took the next step toward reversing the confidence-building measures that it had undertaken for the duration of the negotiations by requesting that the IAEA remove its seals from the Natanz uranium enrichment facility. This move prompted intensive diplomatic efforts among the EU-3, the United States, Russia and China, culminating in an emergency session of the IAEA board from February 2 to 4, 2006, which issued a resolution reporting the Iranian nuclear file to the United Nations (UN) Security Council.

To better understand the trajectory of events that led from the 2002 revelations concerning the clandestine Iranian enrichment program to the 2006 IAEA board resolution reporting the matter to the Security Council, it will be helpful first to examine the Iranian explanation for its clandestine program and then the course of negotiations with the EU-3 from 2003 to 2005. A useful starting point would be a brief analysis of the relationship between Iran's clandestine facilities and its NPT obligations.

IAEA inspections in Iran beginning in 2002 have confirmed the existence of a uranium enrichment program and a heavy water production program in Iran.[8] The heavy water reactor program consists of a heavy water production plant under construction at Arak and a planned 40 MW heavy water reactor on which construction has not yet begun. The uranium enrichment program consists of a pilot-scale gas centrifuge enrichment plant that went into operation in June 2003 but was suspended following an agreement with the EU-3 in December 2003 and became operational again in mid-February 2006. A commercial-scale enrichment facility is also under construction at Natanz, the site of the pilot-scale plant. Iran's failure to report the construction of these facilities was not in itself a violation of its safeguards obligations provided no fissile materials were present. In the case of the Arak facilities, which are still under construction or in the planning phase, fissile materials cannot yet be introduced. In the case of the uranium enrichment facilities, the status of Iranian compliance depends crucially on whether nuclear material was introduced into the pilot-scale Natanz facility prior to the plant going into operation (e.g., for testing purposes). If so, the introduction of nuclear material into the plant without informing the IAEA would constitute a serious violation of Iran's reporting obligations under the Safeguards Agreement. Iran has denied that any nuclear material was introduced into the facility prior to the first IAEA inspection at the facility in February 2003. In its June 2003 report following initial inspections of both sites, the IAEA did not report violations of Iranian reporting obligations related to the construction of facilities at either Natanz or Arak.[9]

The intense three-year inspection process that ensued following the 2002 revelations have, however, revealed numerous reporting violations. The record of covert Iranian nuclear activities uncovered by the IAEA inspectors includes the conduct of undeclared enrichment activities, the conduct of undeclared reprocessing experiments, and the import of undeclared fissile materials from foreign suppliers.[10] In addition, evidence revealed by IAEA inspections led to the discovery of Iranian ties to the A.Q. Khan black market nuclear supply network. The principal areas in which Iran was discovered to have undeclared nuclear activities during the course of three years of inspections by the IAEA, from 2002 to 2005, are the following: the import, manufacture, and use of P-1 and P-2 centrifuge designs; the one-time import of fissile materials in 1991; the testing of a pilot centrifuge enrichment facility; work on a laser enrichment program; the conduct of plutonium reprocessing experiments and limited polonium production. There have also been reports that additional nuclear activities might be taking place at military sites at Parchin and Lavizan. The IAEA has made what it has described as "good progress" in investigating each of these categories of violations and its secretariat has taken the position that nonproliferation objectives are better served by ongoing inspections, and negotiations with the Iranian government for a suspension of its enrichment program than by a referral to the Security Council.[11]

Iran's explanation for the clandestine development of these programs is that it has been systematically barred from transparently developing a civilian nuclear energy program, principally by U.S. efforts to prevent it from making necessary purchases. To substantiate this claim, Iran has pointed to U.S. pressure that blocked its efforts in the late 1980s and throughout the 1990s to enter into talks with German, Argentine, Brazilian, Chinese, and Russian companies for completion of work on the Bushehr nuclear reactor, begun under the Shah, and to acquire additional research reactors.[12] Further, Iran claims that it requires an independent and indigenous nuclear fuel cycle because it has also faced systematic discrimination in its efforts to purchase nuclear fuel to power its nuclear reactors.[13] This discrimination is both as a result of direct American intervention to cancel contracts and sanction firms that do business with Iran and of the indirect effects on foreign companies' calculations of the impact on their access to American markets should they enter into transactions with Iran.[14] The restriction of Iranian access to open market sources for its civilian nuclear energy program, and particularly efforts to block its development of a light water reactor at Bushehr, have clearly contributed to Iranian arguments in favor of developing a domestic fuel cycle that would provide it with nuclear energy independence. Although motivated by nonproliferation concerns, the blocking of Iranian access to civilian technologies and nuclear fuel to which it is entitled under the NPT has been counterproductive.

EU-3 NEGOTIATIONS

Iran's arguments for developing a domestic nuclear fuel cycle suggest the basic prerequisites of any negotiation for the suspension of its enrichment program. Logically, such prerequisites would include fuel supply guarantees, guarantees of the right to acquire light water reactors for energy production purposes,[15] and security guarantees that will dissuade Iran from the view that it requires a latent nuclear capacity as a virtual deterrent. Unfortunately, in both the areas of guaranteed open market access to dual-use technologies and in terms of a security guarantee, the nonparticipation of the United States in the negotiations to suspend Iran's enrichment program limited the offer that the EU-3 was able to provide Iran. The course of the negotiations between the EU-3 and Iran underscores the significance of the U.S. position in undermining progress, first by virtue of the U.S. decision to withhold its support from the discussions and then as a result of direct American intervention with the Europeans to alter their position.

The EU-3 negotiations with Iran were premised on the framework set forth in the Paris Agreement of November 2004.[16] The purpose of the negotiations were to find a formula, satisfactory to the Europeans, for "objective guarantees that Iran's nuclear program was exclusively for peaceful purposes." Both sides entered negotiations with a recognition of Iran's rights to pursue the acquisition of civilian nuclear technology, provided such rights were exercised in conformity with its obligations under the treaty "without discrimination." What this signaled was that a formula could be reached that would acknowledge Iran's right to enrich uranium while also satisfying the demands of the international community that such enrichment be conducted under tight controls that would prevent the diversion of materials or technology to military purposes. However, in March 2005, the negotiating position of the Europeans changed. Under pressure from the United States, the EU-3 revised their strategy, adopting the new position that the only acceptable "objective guarantee" would be the total cessation of enrichment in Iran.

The signing of the Paris Agreement had coincided with a positive development in the Iranian IAEA dossier: the November 2004 IAEA report found that all nuclear materials in Iran had been accounted for and that no evidence had been uncovered of any military nuclear program. While the report cautioned that the existence of a weapons program could not be discounted as a result of incomplete information and a series of unresolved questions, it seemed that serious progress was being made with Iran. A series of unilateral U.S. actions between January and March 2005 altered the negotiating climate.

As negotiations between Iran and the EU-3 were getting underway, the U.S. State Department announced that it was penalizing eight foreign companies under the Iran Nonproliferation Act of 2000 for transferring to Iran technologies deemed restricted by the U.S. legislation.[17] Secondary sanctions imposed by the United States on foreign companies engaging in trade with Iran were an important source of frustration for Iranian diplomats relying on the Paris Agreement for improved access to open market sources for technology and nuclear cooperation.[18] Similarly, Secretary of State Condoleezza Rice's statement in February that the Untied States would withhold its support from the incentives package offered to Iran by the EU-3 was also a blow to the credibility of European commitments.[19] Following President George W. Bush's late February trip to Europe, senior Iranian officials concluded that the Paris Agreement was dead for lack of U.S. support and because the EU-3 was perceived to have accepted the U.S. condition of a permanent cessation of all uranium enrichment activities in any long-term agreement with Iran.[20]

The Iranian conclusion that the Paris Agreement was a dead letter by March 2005 did not, however, prompt an immediate withdrawal from negotiations or a resumption of enrichment activities. Rather, Iranian officials continued to press to see whether "objective guarantees" short of complete permanent cessation of enrichment activities were attainable. For instance, President Khatami publicly stated that although ending Iran's uranium enrichment program would be "completely unacceptable," Iran would be willing to provide any "objective guarantees" of the peaceful uses of enrichment requested by the EU-3 or the IAEA.[21] Iran proposed a package to the EU-3 in late March, agreeing to a permanent halt of its broader uranium enrichment program and of its planned reprocessing program in exchange for economic and technical assistance and the continued operation of its pilot enrichment facility with a ceiling of enrichment at the LEU level under a system of "objective guarantees" implemented by the IAEA to ensure that no materials or activities would be diverted to nonpeaceful uses. The key technical elements of the Iranian proposal that would address proliferation concerns were acceptance of an open fuel cycle, permanently committing to forgoing reprocessing, setting a ceiling of enrichment at LEU levels that could not be weaponized, placing of all uranium hexafluoride produced at the Isfahan facility under IAEA seal and immediate conversion of all enriched uranium into fuel rods. Another key element of the proposals put forth by the Iranian side was a strengthened verification mechanism with a "phased approach including enhanced monitoring and technical guarantees."[22] Iran also offered to permit on-site IAEA inspectors to be permanently stationed at the enrichment facility and to continue to implement the Additional Protocol.[23] Finally, the Iranians offered to accept a permanent ban on nuclear weapons together with the enforcement of Iranian export controls on sensitive nuclear technologies.

The March 2005 offer was far reaching and addressed several key proliferation concerns while also permitting the establishment of an important precedent with a significantly strengthened inspection regime. The Europeans, however, were reportedly not prepared to accept any measure short of complete cessation of enrichment activities as an adequate "objective guarantee," following an understanding reached with the United States.[24] The Iranians followed up with a second proposal presented in London on April 29, 2005, in which they offered a six-month extension of their ongoing suspension of enrichment activities and requested that the EU-3 work toward the implementation of steps to undertake an EU-Iran energy partnership and move forward on technical and economic cooperation.[25] The Iranian proposals of March/April did not advance discussions with the Europeans. Following the clarification of the new EU-3 position requiring permanent cessation of enrichment—interpreted by the Iranians as the adoption of an American position—both sides engaged in a series of unilateral actions that undermined the likelihood of any further progress in negotiations.

Iranian negotiators imposed a July 31 deadline on the EU-3 to prepare a counterproposal to the March/April Iranian proposals. In May 2005, reports emerged suggesting that the EU-3 had reached an agreement with the United States to call for UN Security Council action if their negotiations with Iran failed to secure an agreement to full cessation of enrichment activities.[26] Despite these reports, Iran again offered a proposal to the European delegation in July to try to break the impasse in negotiations. Iran's then chief nuclear negotiator, Hassan Rowhani, offered a proposal on July 18 reiterating the spring Iranian proposals, and proposing the phasing of permitted experimental enrichment activity to prevent sufficient quantities of nuclear material from accumulating to levels that might be deemed to pose a proliferation risk. The proposal also offered multinational participation in the enrichment pilot project to add an additional layer of international supervision and control.[27] Dr. Rowhani also made reference to earlier statements by the EU-3 suggesting that they would present a bridging proposal and requested that they come forward with their draft. He noted Iranian concerns based on information they had received from "public and diplomatic channels" that following Iranian presidential elections, the EU-3 might withhold their proposal.

Rumors at the time suggested that the EU-3 had held off submitting a proposal in the hope that their favored candidate in the 2005 Iranian presidential election, Akbar Hashemi Rafsanjani, would be elected and be more amenable to a nuclear deal. When, instead, the conservative candidate, Mahmoud Ahmadinejad, was elected, there was concern that the EU-3 might no longer be willing to offer a far-reaching counterproposal. Rowhani did not succeed in securing a response from the EU-3 negotiators, who later reported that they were aware that Rowhani was desperate to achieve a breakthrough within the existing negotiating framework in the summer of 2005.[28] When the EU-3 finally offered their counterproposal on August 5, 2005, five days after the Iranian deadline had expired, the context for an agreement had seriously deteriorated. Iran viewed the failure of the EU-3 to respond to the spring proposals within the agreed timeframe as undermining the Paris Agreement. In the interim, Iran announced on August 1 that it would resume uranium conversion activities under IAEA supervision.[29] The resumption of uranium conversion by Iran was treated by the EU-3 as a violation of the Paris Agreement. Both sides viewed the other as having abrogated the agreement and negotiations came to an end.

The EU-3 counterproposal of August 2005 had several significant weaknesses.[30] The first serious drawback was its failure to engage with Iranian proposals to limit nuclear fuel cycle activities and place their nuclear program under an enhanced inspection regime. The second weakness was the imbalance between incentives and demands—the demands reflected the American position that Iran would be required to completely shut down all of its nuclear fuel cycle activities including uranium conversion, enrichment, and reprocessing, as well as the closure of the heavy water facility at Arak. The Iranians would only be permitted to continue plans for light water power reactors for which fuel would have to be procured from abroad under an agreement that would require return of spent fuel to the supplier. In addition, the Iranians were asked to resolve all outstanding issues with the IAEA, ratify the Additional Protocol, adopt strict national export controls in compliance with Security Council Resolution 1540 and accept a legally binding commitment not to withdraw from the NPT.

In exchange for these detailed and concrete demands, the incentives offered by the EU-3 were a combination of mutually beneficial cooperative measures in the areas of trade and investment, combating terrorism and drug trafficking, on the one hand, and vague offers for future negotiation on frameworks to provide Iranian access to international nuclear technologies markets on the basis of competitive tenders and Russian fuel supply for Iranian use. Without offering detailed proposals on arrangements for such incentives, the proposal did not address key Iranian concerns about lack of access to technology markets and reliable fuel supply. Similarly, to the extent there were security guarantees offered in the August counterproposal, they were reaffirmations of existing international obligations rather than security guarantees involving the United States. As such, the security component of the package was far too weak to address Iranian strategic threat perception and the associated incentive to develop a virtual nuclear deterrent.

The Iranian response to the counterproposal came in less than a week and was categorical in its denunciation of the package as a violation of the spirit of the Paris Agreement and an insult to negotiators who had worked in good faith to find an acceptable compromise with the Europeans.[31] The European demand for Iranian cessation of all fuel cycle activities was, from the Iranian perspective, a capitulation to an American position external to the understanding on the basis of which the Iranians had originally entered into discussions with the Europeans, namely that the modality for a limited Iranian enrichment program was negotiable, provided that "objective guarantees" of the civilian nature of the program were put in place through the IAEA.

STALLED DIPLOMACY

The course of events between August 2005 and January 2006 suggest that the Iranians came to the conclusion that confidence-building measures and negotiations with the Europeans had weakened their position. With conservative Mahmoud Ahmadinejad having replaced reformist Mohammad Khatami as president of Iran following the June 2005 presidential elections, changes were made in the Iranian nuclear negotiating team and Iranian diplomacy took a tougher turn. While talks with the EU-3 were suspended, Russia emerged with a new offer for Iranian consideration. Although the details of the Russian proposal were to be determined upon future negotiations, the basic contours of the proposal involve a joint venture between Iran and Russia, whereby Iranian uranium would be enriched in a jointly operated facility in Russia. The degree of permitted Iranian participation in the enrichment process, whether some enrichment research would be permitted on Iranian soil and various other aspects of the proposal, remained open, negotiating points to be discussed should Iran act on the Russian offer. By January 2006, the Russian proposal was the only serious diplomatic option available to Iran to negotiate a solution to objections to its enrichment activities. This option led some commentators to note that despite the adoption of a more confrontational approach by the United States and the Europeans, a nonconfrontational solution was still achievable.[32]

Unfortunately, January 2006 witnessed a new round of unilateral actions on both sides that led to a serious escalation of the situation. Beginning with Iran's announcement of its decision to resume activity at the Natanz enrichment facility in early January, the United States initiated negotiations first with the EU-3, then with China and Russia, to prompt an emergency session of the IAEA board of governors in order to refer the Iranian file to the UN Security Council. As discussed above, the IAEA board adopted a resolution to report the Iranian file to the Security Council on February 4, 2006.[33] The resolution itself was the product of extremely aggressive diplomatic efforts, principally on the part of the U.S., to bring Russia, China, India, and other Non-Aligned Movement (NAM) countries into line with its strategy on Iran. While the director general of the IAEA continued to hope for a negotiated solution, the United States secured Russian and Chinese support by offering a compromise on the speed with which the council would address the matter,[34] and Indian support by linking the country's IAEA vote to the promise of a civilian nuclear technology cooperation agreement between the United States and India.[35] Finally, the United States initially resisted the Egyptian demand that language indirectly referring to the Israeli nuclear program be included in the resolution. However, the United States ultimately relented and agreed to language on a "Middle East free of weapons of mass destruction" to maintain the support of the NAM countries.[36] In the end, the resolution passed with the support of 27 countries, five abstentions and only Venezuela, Cuba, and Syria voting against.[37]

Following the issuance of the IAEA Resolution, Iran made good on its promise to decrease the degree of its cooperation with IAEA inspectors, specifically by suspending its voluntary compliance with inspections pursuant to the Additional Protocol to the NPT.[38] Despite the deterioration of relations between Iran and the IAEA, Iran appeared willing to continue negotiations on the Russian proposal and offered to resume compliance with inspections under the Additional Protocol were it permitted to enrich limited quantities of uranium for research purposes under stricter IAEA controls.[39] However, the negotiations with the Russians later stalled over the question of whether Iran would be permitted under the deal to engage in limited uranium enrichment research experiments under IAEA monitoring on its own soil.[40]

THE ROAD TO CONFRONTATION: 2006–2007

The overview provided to this point sets forth the background against which the developments over the rest of 2006 through the spring of 2007, including repeated Security Council action on the Iranian nuclear file, increased chatter about a possible military option and the apparent decline of prospects for a negotiated solution, must be understood. This section will set forth a somewhat more detailed account of the recent trajectory of negotiation and confrontation over the Iranian nuclear file.

Moving the Iranian File to the Security Council

In late February 2006 reports emerged that Iran had reached a basic agreement with Russia on a joint venture to enrich uranium, with some Iranian technical participation.[41] Initial reports left unclear whether some portion of the activities of the joint venture would take place on Iranian soil, but it was suggested that the deal would permit Iran some limited face-saving enrichment activity. The acceleration of diplomacy between Iran and Russia in February was designed to take advantage of the unusual provision of the February IAEA Resolution that provided that the "reporting" of Iran to the Security Council would not take place until the completion of the March IAEA board meetings. The window of opportunity provided by this month would close with the IAEA board meetings on March 6–8, and the presentation of the comprehensive report prepared by the IAEA secretariat summarizing the results of three years of intensive inspections in Iran.

The weekend preceding the March IAEA board meetings was characterized by furious diplomacy between the Russians and Iranians to iron out the terms of their basic agreement. As the meetings began on Monday, March 6, 2006, IAEA Director General Mohamed ElBaradei publicly expressed optimism that "'an agreement could be reached' within a week to bring Iran into compliance with international demands."[42] His comments were widely interpreted as an endorsement of the leaked account of an Iranian-Russian deal, reached over the weekend, which would have permitted Iran to retain a small research enrichment facility. The United States immediately balked at any agreement that would leave Iran with an enrichment capacity, however small, and it was even rumored in some circles that Condoleezza Rice personally contacted ElBaradei to rebuke him for his comments. Within two days of the reported deal, both Secretary of State Rice and President Bush held meetings with Russian Foreign Minister Sergei Lavrov, signaling the importance the United States attached to blocking any such compromise. At a joint press conference on March 7, Lavrov flatly denied that any new Russian proposal had been tabled. The possibility of a Russian-Iranian deal to avoid Security Council action came to an end with the Lavrov-Rice press conference. With the close of the IAEA board meetings the next day, IAEA chief ElBaradei publicly confirmed that the agency would forward its report concerning outstanding Iranian verification issues to the Security Council.

The submission of the Iranian file to the council was marked by an escalation of the rhetoric of confrontation by both the United States and Iran. In response to heated rhetoric from U.S. Vice President Dick Cheney and the then U.S. ambassador to the UN, John Bolton, calling for the world to confront Iran, the head of Iran's delegation to the IAEA responded by warning that "the United

States may have the power to cause harm and pain but it is also susceptible to harm and pain."[43] Veiled threats of sanctions and coercive action on the part of U.S. officials were met by equally veiled references on the Iranian side to the potential pain that might be inflicted through an Iranian oil embargo. In this tense context, the discussions on the Security Council of next steps on the Iranian file were even more sensitive and complex than the negotiations that yielded the February IAEA Resolution. As early as March 9, 2006, a day after the close of the IAEA board meetings, the text of a draft Security Council Resolution on Iran was circulating among the 15 members of the council.[44] What followed were three weeks of intense bargaining, with substantial resistance from the Russians and Chinese to elements of the Franco-British draft resolution. As the prospect of consensus on the language of a resolution gave way, an intermediate measure short of a resolution but articulating the position of the council through the issuance of a presidential statement was adopted.[45] As a nonbinding declaration, the March 29 presidential statement did not have the coercive force the United States desired. All reference to a threat to international peace and security, which would have foreshadowed an invocation of the council's coercive authority under Chapter VII of the UN Charter, was dropped. The language adopted for the presidential statement urged Iran to suspend its uranium enrichment activities and asked the IAEA to report back on Iran's compliance with the IAEA's board resolution within 30 days.[46] A new 30-day window was thus opened by the council's action.

The aftermath of the presidential statement further aggravated tensions over the Iranian nuclear program. On the one hand, April heralded credible revelations by an American journalist that the Bush administration was contemplating military action to deter Iran's nuclear program. On the other hand, the Iranian government announced on April 11, 2006 that it had succeeded in using its pilot 164-centirfuge cascade to enrich a small quantity of uranium to the 3.5 percent level for use in fuel production. Each of these developments merits brief consideration. First, the revelation by veteran journalist Seymour Hersh tended to support the long-standing Iranian complaint that the United States is using the nuclear issue as a cover for its broader regime change ambitions in Iran. For instance, Hersh reported that

> The Bush Administration, while publicly advocating diplomacy in order to stop Iran from pursuing a nuclear weapon, has increased clandestine activities inside Iran and intensified planning for a possible major air attack. Current and former American military and intelligence officials said that Air Force planning groups are drawing up lists of targets and teams of American combat troops have been ordered into Iran, under cover, to collect targeting data and to establish contact with antigovernment ethnic-minority groups.[47]

The allegations of advanced military planning for air strikes, the covert infiltration of Iran by "teams of American combat troops," and the attempts to establish contact with Iranian ethnic minorities to foment antigovernment tensions within Iran all echo Iranian fears of an American regime change agenda. As if to underscore the validity of Iranian concerns, Hersh's piece specifically noted that there is a "growing conviction among members of the United States military, and in the international community, that President Bush's ultimate goal in the nuclear confrontation with Iran is regime change." Perhaps even more worryingly, Hersh also reported that one of the military options considered by the White House and the Pentagon in considering possible air strikes against Iran called for "the use of a bunker-buster tactical nuclear weapon, such as the B61-11, against [suspected Iranian] underground nuclear sites."[48]

To dampen anxieties about a military option, IAEA Director General ElBaradei repeatedly publicly stated that coercion would be unlikely to produce a solution on Iran, that the only solution would have to be negotiated and that all parties needed to "lower the pitch" on this issue.[49] But ElBaradei's emphasis on a negotiated solution did not gain much traction in the United States. Hersh's revelations were not the only indication that the United States remained attached to a strategy of regime change rather than diplomacy with Iran. Spring 2006 also witnessed the announcement of new offices in the State Department and the Department of Defense on Iran, and the creation of an Office of Iranian Affairs out of the U.S. embassy in Dubai, designed to monitor Iran and promote democratization.[50]

The other significant development in April 2006 was the Iranian announcement that they had successfully used their pilot centrifuge cascade to enrich small quantities of uranium to reactor-levels suitable for use as nuclear fuel. President Ahmadinejad's announcement that Iran had mastered the nuclear fuel cycle "at the laboratory level" and had attained an enrichment level of 3.5 percent for a tiny quantity of uranium was not especially surprising.[51] The Iranians were known to have assembled a 164-centrifuge pilot cascade and had been working on enriching a small quantity of uranium for some time. While President Ahmadinejad used the announcement to gain political credit domestically—with a nationalist-themed televised ceremony to celebrate the success—from the perspective of concerns related to the imminence of a potential nuclear weapons program, this announcement was not particularly significant. Indeed, nuclear analysts were quick to note that despite the Iranian announcement "nothing had changed to alter current estimates of when Iran might be able to make a single nuclear weapon assuming that is its ultimate goal. The United States government has put that at five to ten years, and some analysts have said it could come as late as 2020."[52]

While arguably technically modest, the Iranian announcement had great diplomatic significance. The timing of the announcement fell within the 30-day period for Iranian compliance with the Security Council's presidential statement. The Iranian rejection of this demand was clearly signaled by President Ahmadinejad's announcement and confirmed soon after by an IAEA report to the council confirming that Iran had enriched a miniscule quantity of uranium to the 3.5 percent level and that there had been no suspension of enrichment activities.[53] The tone of the IAEA report was unusually bleak, noting the reduction in Iranian cooperation with nuclear inspectors, a consequence of Iran's suspension of its voluntary compliance with the requirements of the Additional Protocol in response to the February IAEA Resolution. The report also catalogued the continuing refusal of Iran to provide information to the agency regarding certain long-standing questions concerning different aspects of its nuclear program. The ominous tone of the report reflected the agency's concern that confrontation at the council would yield even less Iranian cooperation on the ground.[54]

Forging International Consensus

By the beginning of May, then, the scene was set for a serious diplomatic confrontation. Iran had met the council's presidential statement with defiance, the United States had stepped up its own efforts to isolate Iran diplomatically and possibly undermine the regime politically. With the IAEA report confirming Iran's noncompliance with suspension demands, the question of next steps arose. From the perspective of the Bush administration, sanctions were clearly the preferred means of increasing pressure on the regime to comply with enrichment suspension demands. However, divisions on the Security Council regarding sanctions persisted, with China and Russia both reluctant to approve such a measure without definitive evidence of a military component to Iran's nuclear program or a showing of an imminent threat.

The first half of May witnessed American efforts, supported by Britain, France, and Germany, to gain support for a resolution imposing sanctions on Iran for its failure to comply with the calls for the suspension of its enrichment program.[55] By the middle of the month, however, reports emerged of a new approach. For instance, IAEA Chief ElBaradei heralded renewed negotiations, commenting that the Security Council was "holding off from sanctions against Iran as Europeans work on a package of benefits to induce Tehran to cooperate."[56] Even more surprisingly, at the end of a month that began with American efforts to impose sanctions on Iran, Condoleezza Rice announced a significant policy shift, stating American willingness to join direct negotiations with Iran over a European package of incentives.[57] Secretary Rice's offer of direct talks, however, came attached to a precondition requiring the full and verifiable suspension of all enrichment and reprocessing activities on the part of Iran. The Iranians viewed such a precondition as requiring Iran to comply with the very demands that were subject to negotiation *prior to* any negotiation. Nonetheless, the Iranians were interested in learning the terms of the package of economic and commercial incentives for enrichment suspension that would follow the American announcement.

The Iranians did not wait long for the package to be presented to them. The day after Secretary Rice's announcement, Britain, France, Germany, Russia, China, and the United States (or the council's five permanent members and Germany, frequently referred to as the P5+1) came to an agreement on the terms of the package of incentives to be proposed to the Iranians.[58] The package was designed to offer Iranians a choice parallel to the one described by Rice in her press conference: accept inducements to return to negotiations with the precondition of suspension or face Security Council action. But the package itself reportedly included only the terms of the incentives, with no mention of possible penalties. A subsequent description of the consequences of declining the package was to be provided orally. Thus, the package represented an offer to suspend consideration of Security Council action if Iran would suspend enrichment and resume negotiations. The American offer of talks was reportedly designed more to forge international consensus on this incentives-or-coercion approach, keeping the Chinese and Russians on board, than as a conciliatory gesture toward Iran.[59]

Elements of the incentives package, presumably the only portion of the package that was delivered in writing, were subsequently published by the

French Foreign Ministry, but the description of the released document does not make clear whether it represents the entire written proposal submitted to the Iranians or a redacted version or summary.[60] The advantages of the proposal as compared to the August 2005 EU-3 proposal were significant. First, this proposal includes the participation of three additional key players: Russia, China, and, most importantly, the United States. Russian involvement makes proposals concerning Iranian participation in a fuel center in Russia more compelling than the allusions to such a possibility in the August 2005 package, which did not include Russia. Similarly, American participation offers some reassurance to the Iranians that the terms of the proposal will not be subject to subsequent revision or revocation based on the objections of a third party outside of the negotiations. Because the Iranians believe that the unraveling of the Paris Agreement negotiations with the EU-3 was a result of American indirect intervention and the alteration of the terms of negotiation, direct American participation in this proposal would render it more reliable from their perspective. Finally, the proposal offered more concrete incentives than the August 2005 version, while modifying some of the demands. In particular, the increased specificity of fuel supply provisions, the recognition of Iran's conversion facility at Isfahan and the possibility that limitations on the Iranian fuel cycle might be reviewed and modified following IAEA confirmation of full Iranian compliance were all significant improvements on the August 2005 proposal.

Unfortunately, however, the final proposal presented to the Iranians was considerably weaker than a leaked earlier draft.[61] The reversal on some of the key points in that leaked draft proposal was apparently made following discussions between the Europeans and Americans in which the United States insisted on diluting provisions, particularly as regards security guarantees. The key features of the final version of the proposal entailed reaffirmation of Iran's inalienable right to nuclear energy for peaceful purposes; support for Iranian plans to develop new light water power reactors; acceptance of the Isfahan uranium conversion plant; the establishment of an international fuel center in Russia with Iranian participation; a buffer stock to hold a reserve of up to a five-year supply of nuclear fuel dedicated to Iran; review of the terms of the agreement following IAEA verification of all unresolved issues; and a long-term energy partnership between Iran and the EU. Missing from the proposal was the all-important reference to security guarantees. In the place of the security guarantees referred to in the original draft of the proposal, the final draft incorporated a vague reference to a "new conference to promote dialogue and cooperation on regional security issues." The elimination of the security guarantee provision of the proposal coupled with the imposition of a precondition that Iran must suspend all uranium enrichment activities generated a fundamental weakness in an otherwise significantly improved proposal.

By June 9, European and American officials declared that Iran had three weeks to respond to the package or face the reinitiation of Security Council consideration of a sanctions resolution.[62] The timing of the deadline was related to the schedule for a Group of 8 meeting in early July at which the P5+1 group of nations (with the exception of China, which is not in the G8) might resume discussions of their options on the Iranian nuclear file. Iran's initial response to the incentives package was relatively warm—perhaps in part because the package was presented through public diplomacy that emphasized incentives and soft-pedaled disincentives, an approach more attentive to Iranian sensitivities. However, the absence of an American security guarantee left Iran searching for a mechanism to signal its enthusiasm for some of the elements of the proposal while finding a face-saving formula to finesse the suspension issue.[63] Iran responded negatively to the imposition of a three-week deadline for it to provide a response to a package that took more than three weeks to be negotiated among the P5+1. Iran's counteroffer was to provide a response by August 22, the beginning of a new month in the Iranian calendar, which was dismissed by the P5+1 as too long a period.[64] By July 12, it was clear that a consensus position among the Iranian leadership was not going to emerge in time to meet the deadline.[65] As the deadline passed and positions hardened, the focus of the Security Council shifted to the outbreak of a war in Lebanon.

Despite the Lebanon War, however, Iran's failure to meet the July 12 deadline did eventually result in the return of the Iranian file to the Security Council and the resumption of negotiations over the language of a resolution. While Russia continued to balk at any suggestion of sanctions or the invocation of the Security Council's coercive authority under Chapter VII, language of a new resolution, weaker than the one tabled in May, but still including a demand of enrichment suspension, was circulated to the council in the last week of July.[66] The council ultimately adopted Resolution 1696, demanding that Iran suspend enrichment by August 31 or face unspecified appropriate measures.[67] The resolution passed with only one vote cast in opposition by Qatar, the sole Arab state on the council.

The particular framing of this resolution raises several important issues. First, the resolution provided a new deadline of August 31 for Iranian suspension of enrichment—this deadline was over a week beyond the date by which Iran had pledged to respond to the package. To preempt the Iranian response with a Security Council Resolution only to provide a deadline that gave Iran a longer window for a suspension decision than the time Iran had requested, suggests that an objection to the Iranian timeframe was not the driver of the resolution. Given that Iran had not rejected the incentives package and had even characterized it in positive terms, the decision to resume a confrontational path before receiving the Iranian response suggests that the commitment to a negotiated solution was relatively weak.

If the U.S. motivation for lending its support to the incentives package was to forge greater international consensus on the Security Council, the imposition of a unilateral precondition of suspension of the enrichment program, particularly in the absence of security guarantees, increased the likelihood of that eventuality. The resolution ultimately adopted, once the issue came before the council, did little to address the obstacles to renewed negotiations. While on its face it would appear that the resolution altered Iran's international legal obligations, weakening Iran's claim that any suspension would be voluntary on its part, on closer examination the Iranian claim may have partially survived the resolution.

The resolution avoids several of the key features that would have altered Iran's underlying legal obligations. First, it relies on an IAEA board resolution that itself did not purport to make mandatory under international law, a suspension obligation for the Iranians, but rather requested that they suspend their program. Second, nowhere in the resolution does the council make a finding that the Iranian nuclear program represents a threat to international peace and security (a finding no doubt resisted by the Russians and Chinese). Without such a finding, it is unclear how the council can claim to act under its Chapter VII authority. Finally, the reliance on Article 40 of the UN Charter, which governs the use of interim measures to prevent the aggravation of a situation rather than authorizing sanctions or other forms of coercion, suggests that the council wished to limit its coercive authority in this instance. Although the preambular language concludes with the statement that the resolution was issued "to make mandatory the suspension required by the IAEA," the absence of the predicates necessary to give the resolution the force of mandate draws into question the legal status of the obligation created by the resolution for Iran. This is further reinforced by the fact that the resolution does not adopt the conventional language of "deciding" that Iran must suspend its enrichment and reprocessing activities, but rather demands that Iran do so, introducing the possibility that the resolution amounts to a forceful request rather than a determination of a legal obligation.[68] Nonetheless, like the IAEA board resolution and the presidential statement, the resolution reflects a diplomatic victory for the United States and a blow to Iran's efforts to keep its nuclear program out of the purview of the Security Council.

Building Momentum for Sanctions

The remainder of the summer and fall brought few developments that genuinely impacted the standoff reached with Resolution 1696. August saw further revelations by the American journalist, Seymour Hersh, that the United States encouraged broad air strikes by the Israelis in Lebanon as a sort of "dry run" of a war using a similar tactic against Iran.[69] This claim reignited debates in the United States as to whether a military option against the Iranian nuclear program is either desirable or feasible. On August 22, Iran did provide a 21-page counteroffer to the incentives package it received from the P5+1 in June: the Iranians offered to engage in serious talks over nuclear activities and to consider new formulas to satisfy international concerns about fuel cycle-related proliferation.[70] One such formula offered by the Iranians was a joint venture with the European nuclear energy consortium Eurodif operating on Iranian soil. After a day of consideration of the counterproposal, American officials announced that it was inadequate because it failed to specify that Iran would suspend enrichment,[71] while Javier Solana declined to give an immediate public reaction on behalf of the EU, suggesting there was enough in the Iranian position to merit consideration.[72] A leaked copy of the document showed that the Iranians had indicated a willingness to discuss suspension of enrichment in the course of negotiations (though not as a precondition).[73] The American conception of next steps following the Iranian counteroffer focused on sanctions, but emphasized a "low-key" strategy to dealing with the Iranian counteroffer precisely to give the appearance of a "patient and measured" approach in order to keep the Russians and Chinese on board as the council contemplated penalties against Iran.[74]

In the meantime, elements in the U.S. government appeared to step up domestic efforts to portray the Iranian nuclear program as an imminent threat. A congressional staff report from the House of Representatives' Intelligence Committee issued in mid-August alleged that Iran was enriching uranium to weapons' grade, a charge that was rejected internationally as unsubstantiated. The report was widely seen as an attempt to prompt U.S. intelligence agencies to produce more aggressive intelligence on Iran. Because the staff report was unclassified, however, it was also available to the IAEA to review. The IAEA formally responded to the report in a letter dated September 12 to the Chair of the House Intelligence Committee. The letter stated that the report was "outrageous and dishonest" and cited five specifically incorrect or unsubstantiated claims made in the report.[75] Analysts examining the report also concluded that it was written with the clear purpose of exaggerating the intelligence on the Iranian nuclear program. For instance, David Albright, president of the Institute for Science and International Security and a well-regarded nuclear proliferation expert, said in an interview that "this is like prewar Iraq all over again...You have an Iranian nuclear threat that is spun up, using bad information that is cherry-picked and a report that trashes the inspectors."[76] Following the debacle of the public rejection of the report's findings by the IAEA, the report was shelved, but public perception in the United States of an Iran determined to acquire nuclear weapons remained otherwise well-entrenched.

September witnessed a series of diplomatic initiatives by Iran, in conjunction with the annual meeting of the NAM, and the meeting of heads of state at the UN General Assembly. In Cuba, Iran enjoyed the reaffirmation of the NAM countries' support for the right to a peaceful nuclear energy program and the final declaration of the summit included specific criticism of American unilateralism, critiquing the American Nuclear Posture Review as undermining the security guarantees provided by Nuclear Weapon States (NWS) to non-NWS under the NPT.[77] In New York, President Ahmadinejad took the opportunity to try to address the American people directly by participating in as many interviews and public presentations as possible, including a tense meeting at the Council on Foreign Relations.[78] This wave of Iranian public diplomacy was coupled with two Iranian offers to engage in temporary suspensions of enrichment to facilitate negotiations. As Ahmadinejad began meetings in Havana, Ali Larijani, the chief Iranian nuclear negotiator, offered a two-month suspension for the first time during meetings with European negotiators.[79] This initial offer, which was met with some interest on the part of the United States, was followed by a second offer made directly by President Ahmadinejad. While still at the UN General Assembly meetings, Ahmadinejad told reporters on September 21 that the Iranian position on suspension is that it is negotiable under "fair and just conditions."[80] In light of the flexibility on this same point included in the Iranian counteroffer in August, genuine space appeared to exist by the early fall for serious negotiations.

Reports also emerged in this period that there had been a slowing down of Iranian efforts on enrichment after the initial success with the first 164-centrifuge cascade due to technical difficulties with the centrifuges.[81] The combination of potential political will to find a compromise solution in Tehran, the technical slowing of enrichment progress and the concrete proposal and counterproposal on the table, gave rise to a new window of opportunity for progress despite ongoing discussions among the Security Council P5 regarding sanctions. But as with the unexpected Lebanon War of the summer, so negotiations may have stalled after the first week of October over the external shock of a North Korean nuclear test on October 9. Much of the aftermath of the North

Korean test focused on interpreting sanctions against the DPRK as a message to Iran. Political tensions flared, the muted deliberate diplomacy of the late summer and early fall fell away, and immoderate claims about the threat posed by Tehran were resumed, first in Tel Aviv,[82] then in Washington.[83]

By late fall, it appeared that early progress in talks between Iran and the Europeans may have been undermined by American demands. Reports suggested that talks between the EU's high representative, Javier Solana, and Iran's chief nuclear negotiator, Ali Larijani, had resulted in a "Gentleman's Agreement" that would involve a temporary partial suspension of enrichment-related activities in order to enter negotiations. This agreement was apparently scuttled by the American insistence on the sequencing of suspension as a *precondition* to negotiations.[84] In the meantime, the United States also suggested that some accord had been reached among the permanent members of the Security Council regarding possible sanctions against Iran.[85]

With the apparent collapse of talks with the Europeans, Iran resumed its domestic enrichment activities by bringing a second cascade on line on October 27.[86] Though the addition of a second cascade did not significantly increase Iran's enrichment capacity or the quantities of enriched uranium produced, it was nonetheless attributed diplomatic significance as another example of Iranian defiance. The next IAEA report on Iran, issued on November 14, did nothing to change the calculus on Iranian compliance either. In keeping with the Iranian announcement of a second cascade, the report found that Iran was making progress on work at its pilot enrichment facility at Natanz and noted that Iran had provided no new cooperation with inspectors in the period covered by the report on outstanding verification questions.[87]

Further undermining prospects for negotiations were reciprocal public displays of willingness to resort to force, with U.S.-led naval war games in the Persian Gulf at the end of October followed by Iran revolutionary guard war games in Qom.[88] A war of words also ensued, with President Bush calling for the global isolation of Iran in a joint press conference with Israeli Prime Minister Ehud Olmert in mid-November and President Ahmadinejad retorting in an address to the General Assembly of the Association of Asian Parliaments for Peace that the Security Council was being improperly used by powerful nuclear-armed states to threaten developing countries in pursuit of alternative fuels.[89] Despite the standoff, however, some progress was made in Iranian cooperation with the IAEA, including an agreement by Iran to allow the agency to take more environmental samples from the Lavizan-Shian site for its inspections.[90] Iran also agreed to allow the agency to inspect its operating records related to the pilot enrichment facility at Natanz.[91] Surprisingly enough, the gestures took place at the same time that the IAEA board took the unusual step of declining a request for technical assistance lodged by the Iranians regarding safety precautions at their heavy water reactor facility at Arak. The decision was taken despite the fact that the IAEA deputy director for technical cooperation, Ana Maria Cetto, reportedly told the IAEA technical cooperation committee that the project was not at odds with Resolution 1696 and that there was no legal basis for refusing Iran's request.[92]

The back and forth on the Iranian nuclear program, the possibility of a sanctions resolution in the Security Council and the question of cooperation between the IAEA and Iran remained open issues throughout November. At the same time, the mid-term elections in the United States brought significant changes to the American legislative branch, with both the Congress and Senate coming under the control of the Democrats, who have been frequently critical of the Bush administration's foreign policy. On November 20, Seymour Hersh published his third article of the year related to the American administration's planning on Iran. In the article, Hersh reported the existence of a classified draft report on Iran prepared by the Central Intelligence Agency (CIA) that challenged the administration's assessment of Iran's nuclear ambitions. More specifically, the report, according to Hersh, "found no conclusive evidence, as yet, of a secret Iranian nuclear-weapons program running parallel to the civilian operations Iran has declared to the [IAEA]."[93] The challenge to intelligence concerning the potential weapons capabilities of Iran conjured haunting echoes of the prewar American planning for Iraq.

Three initially promising signs in December that there might be an opening for engagement were comments by the newly designated U.S. secretary of defense, Robert Gates, the publication of the recommendations of the Iraq Study Group (ISG), and the results of the Iranian municipal elections. At his confirmation hearing, then designate Secretary of State Gates stated his view that the purpose of an Iranian nuclear weapons capability would be as a deterrent in the first instance, suggesting greater American appreciation for Iranian threat perception.[94] Gates' comments were closely followed by the publication of the recommendations of the ISG, a bipartisan panel that had been convened at the request of the U.S. Congress, to assess the situation in Iraq and make policy recommendations.[95]

Among the 79 recommendations offered in the report was a proposal that the United States engage Iran, Syria, and other regional powers in efforts to stabilize Iraq. At a news conference responding to the publication of the ISG's recommendations, President Bush warned that he would not consider talks with Iran unless they met the precondition of enrichment suspension.[96] Nonetheless, the bipartisan support for the recommendation of talks with Iran reflected in the ISG report was significant. On the Iranian side, the outcome of municipal council elections and an election for the Assembly of Experts on December 15, 2006, represented an electoral upset for the hard-line President Ahmadinejad's bloc, with major electoral gains for reformists and pragmatic conservatives aligned with former Presidents Khatami and Rafsanjani and was interpreted as a repudiation of Ahmadinejad's domestic populism and aggressive foreign policy stance.[97] Together with the November mid-term elections in the United States, the December Iranian elections suggested that the people of both countries had no appetite for the confrontational foreign policies of their governments.

Against the backdrop of these developments, talks over a new Security Council Resolution finally bore fruit in December 2006. Following two months of intensive negotiations, a compromise was reached involving a much more limited package of initial sanctions than had originally been tabled. The watering down of the provisions as related to the scope of an arms embargo, the inclusion of a travel ban, and the possibility of sanctions on the Iranian oil and gas sectors were all seen as necessary to win Chinese and Russian support. Nonetheless, insofar as the resolution established a framework for a series of incrementally enhanced sanctions against Iran's nuclear program should Iran refuse to suspend its fuel cycle activities, each of the elements removed from the initial sanctions package remained on the table for discussion of future measures. The compromise sanctions package was unanimously adopted by the Security Council in a vote on December 23, 2006.[98]

Resolution 1737 requires that Iran suspend its enrichment activities, any plutonium reprocessing activities, and its heavy water–related activities, the last of which had been omitted from the terms of the previous resolution.[99] The principal terms of the sanctions component of Resolution 1737 were the following: a prohibition on the sale to Iran of technologies or materials that may be used in Iran's nuclear program, including anything that might "contribute to enrichment-related, reprocessing or heavy water-related activities,"[100] the freezing of the assets belonging to 10 Iranian government officials and 12 institutions or entities associated with the nuclear program;[101] a ban on the transfer of technologies that may have applications in Iran's missile delivery systems;[102] a restriction on permitted IAEA technical cooperation with Iran;[103] and the demand that states "exercise vigilance regarding the entry into or transit through their territories" of designated Iranian officials and the provision of specialized training to Iranian nationals that might have an application for Iran's nuclear activities.[104] The resolution explicitly excludes the construction of the Bushehr light water reactor that Iran is building with Russian assistance from the terms of the sanctions, but demands the suspension of virtually all other aspects of Iran's nuclear program. The Iranian response to the resolution maintained the country's systematic position that progress toward an agreement on their nuclear file would not be attained through coercion. The country's chief nuclear negotiator, Ali Larijani, stated that the resolution would only bolster the Iranian nuclear position and the Iranian Parliament immediately adopted a bill demanding that the government "revise its cooperation" with the IAEA and "accelerate" its nuclear activities.[105] While the bill stopped short of calling on the Iranian government to withdraw from the NPT, the domestic pressure on the government to resist council demands was pronounced. As numerous experts on all sides had warned, the adoption of sanctions by the council closed yet another window of opportunity for a negotiated settlement of the Iranian nuclear file.

Escalation in the Aftermath of Sanctions

The beginning of 2007 witnessed the emergence of an increasingly aggressive American posture toward Iran. In a series of policy statements, U.S. President George W. Bush effectively announced a military and diplomatic escalation against Iran. In a speech on January 10, 2007, President Bush vowed to "seek out and destroy" networks providing "material support for attacks on American troops," singling out Iran and Syria as the source of such support.[106] Less than two weeks later, the president once again focused on Iran in his State of the Union Address, characterizing Iran as the backer of Shia extremists in Iraq and equating such support to that for "Sunni extremists backed by Al Qaeda."[107] Following the president's suggestion that Iran represents a threat on a par with al Qaeda, came reports of a new "kill or capture" policy toward Iranian "agents" found by American forces in Iraq.[108] At least one intelligence officer reportedly commented that the new lethal force policy toward Iranians operating in Iraq "has little to do with Iraq. It's all about pushing Iran's buttons. It's purely political."[109] In a third January statement on Iran, the president gave an interview on National Public Radio threatening a firm American response to any evidence of Iranian activities detrimental to U.S. forces in Iraq.[110] Bush's comments were mirrored by those of other members of his administration, including an interview granted by Vice President Dick Cheney to *Newsweek* magazine in which he characterized a decision to send a second American aircraft carrier force to the Gulf as a "very strong signal" that the United States is committed to working with regional allies to "deal with the Iranian threat,"[111] and testimony by Condoleezza Rice to the U.S. Senate Foreign Relations Committee in which she described American policy as fostering a new alignment of forces in the Middle East to counter Iran and other regional "extremists."[112]

Beyond official statements, there were numerous developments demonstrating that the new aggressive policies were being rapidly put into practice. These included the deployment of a new battery of Patriot missile units to the Middle East;[113] the deployment of the second aircraft carrier battle group to the Persian Gulf (referred to by Vice President Cheney); the appointment of a naval aviator, Admiral William Fallon, as the new commander of the American military's Central Command (or CentCom);[114] American allegations of Iranian arms being smuggled to insurgents in Iran,[115] and the ongoing detentions of Iranian officials and personnel in Iraq.[116] There were also reports that the United States was quietly seeking approval for "significant new military sales" to Gulf Arab states, in a bid to arm Iran's neighbors as part of its containment strategy.[117]

Alongside these concrete developments on the ground came the proliferation of reports in the international media of impending American strikes against Iran.[118] Some commentators noted the resemblance between the build-up to the war with Iraq and the escalation of American rhetoric and activities against Iran in January and February 2007, noting in particular that "allegations against Iran are similar in tone and credibility to those made four years ago by the U.S. government about Iraq possessing weapons of mass destruction in order to justify the invasion of 2003."[119] The positioning of significant American military assets in the Persian Gulf in possible preparation for air strikes was also seen as eerily reminiscent of American prepositioning of forces in the region in 2003, while the Bush administration continued to deny that a decision to attack Iraq had been taken.[120]

Despite repeated denials of attack plans against Iran by administration officials, and particularly by Secretary of Defense Gates, multiple reports emerged over the course of January and February of contingency planning by the Pentagon for a bombing campaign against Iran, the most detailed of which suggested that "a special planning group has been established in the offices of the Joint Chiefs of Staff charged with creating a contingency bombing plan for Iran that can be implemented, upon orders from the President, within twenty-four hours."[121] Additional reports suggested that the plans would target not only Iran's nuclear program but also its military infrastructure,[122] and possibly even its oil infrastructure.[123] Some reports suggested that the United States has also been positioning a defensive ring of bases around the Black Sea in preparation for an attack on Iran,[124] or that the Israelis might engage in an initial strike followed by a more extensive American aerial campaign that would be easier to justify domestically as assistance to a vulnerable ally.[125] Other reports suggested that the United States was already engaged in covert operations in Iran,[126] with

Iran alleging that there may have been American assistance to separatist groups in Iran behind a recent bombing campaign.[127] At least one report predicted that the United States would be in a position to commence air strikes against Iran as early as the spring of 2007.[128]

Detailed reports also emerged of independent Israeli strike plans against Iran, involving the potential use of nuclear-tipped bunker-busters to destroy Iranian underground enrichment facilities.[129] There was also some speculation that the United States or Israel might be pursuing tactics to sabotage the Iranian nuclear program and/or assassinate Iranian nuclear scientists along the lines of earlier Israeli efforts to disrupt the Iraqi nuclear program prior to the Israeli strike on the Osiraq facility.[130] A prominent Iranian nuclear scientist died under mysterious circumstances in January, while a former Iranian deputy defense minister disappeared during a private trip to Turkey in February.[131] By the end of January, the accumulation of leaked reports of military planning, combined with developments on the ground, had reached a pitch that led numerous analysts and commentators to warn of the risk of accidental conflagration and concern that the American government was having difficulty "calibrating its message" to distinguish between "a stern message and a warning of attack."[132]

The Iranian response to American escalation was to step up its own military exercises in a bid to demonstrate that it retained a deterrent capacity. Following the November missile tests and war games that Iran had undertaken, it also conducted short-range missile tests in January, followed by the testing of a Russian-supplied air defense missile system in early February. These moves were followed by war games in mid-February involving three days of ground maneuvers and tests of various Iranian missile systems. In comments obviously intended as a response to concerns about the possibility of American air strikes, The Guards' ground forces commander, Mohammed Reza Zahedi, was quoted by the official Iranian news agency, IRNA, as stating that "[t]he message of this maneuver shows the whole Iranian nation's readiness for defending their sacred country."[133] While the military exercises were clearly intended as a show of force in response to the new American offensive against Iran in 2007, the emphasis placed by Iran on the defensive nature of their exercises was likely a measure of their concern not to provoke further American escalation.

Two readings of the increasingly aggressive posture toward Iran adopted by the United States in 2007 are possible. The first is the straightforward reading that the United States is planning an attack on Iran and is, therefore, positioning its forces to enable it to implement military plans for such an offensive. The second is that the United States is engaging in actions to generate a credible threat of military action against Iran in order to increase its leverage in the dispute with Tehran. The measures taken by American officials lend themselves to both interpretations, with some commentators pointing to the actual planning underway at the Pentagon as evidence of preparation for an attack and others pointing to the multiple leaked stories of American and Israeli military planning as evidence of a psychological campaign to intimidate Iran.

The view that American moves in January were intended to improve its leverage was rendered more plausible by a surprise policy reversal, when Secretary Rice announced in February that the United States had agreed to attend a conference on Iraqi security together with representatives of Iran and Syria. The decision was described by Secretary Rice as "supporting the Iraqis in a new diplomatic offensive: to build greater support, both within the region and beyond for peace and prosperity in Iraq."[134] That position echoed the ISG recommendations, suggesting that the delay in adopting the ISG position may have been related to efforts to strengthen the American negotiating position. The announcement of U.S. participation at the Baghdad summit also served to allay growing public and congressional concern about the administration's intentions toward Iran.[135] In the end, U.S. representative Zalmay Khalilzad exchanged greetings and shook hands with the Iranian representative, Abbas Araghchi, but little substantive interaction took place during the Baghdad summit. Nonetheless, and despite reports of a tense exchange between another American official in attendance, David Satterfield, and Araghchi concerning allegations of Iranian arms smuggling to Iraqi militias, both the American[136] and the Iranian[137] envoys reported positive assessments of the first meeting. The promise of a subsequent, ministerial-level meeting in Istanbul in April, with Secretary Rice and Iranian Foreign Minister Mottaki in attendance, left the door open to further dialogue.[138] The Baghdad summit will only prove to have been a meaningful first step toward engagement if it is followed by direct bilateral talks between the United States and Iran, something that did not materialize at the first meeting.

Irrespective of the interpretation of American ratcheting of military pressure on Iran, other measures were also unilaterally undertaken by the United States to increase the costs of continuing Iran's enrichment program. The United States adopted aggressive measures to bolster the limited 1737 sanctions with a campaign to dry up financing for the Iranian energy sector. A restrictive domestic American sanctions regime that prohibits investments of more than $20 million in Iran's oil industry had been in place since the late 1990s, but was limited in its application to American oil companies.

Following the passage of Security Council sanctions, the United States began to frame its objections to international investments in the Iranian energy sector in terms of international law and placed significant pressure on international banks and companies to curtail investments or risk possible American financial sanctions applied extraterritorially.[139] According to at least one report, the American strategy is to "use the language of the resolution to help persuade foreign governments and financial institutions to cut ties with Iranian businesses.... The new strategy builds on the Treasury Department's efforts over the past few months to get Western banks to scale back business with Iran or risk running afoul of American laws."[140]

The United States also took steps to individually impose sanctions on major Iranian banks, with penalties imposed on Bank Saderat in September 2006 and similar sanctions imposed on Bank Sepah in January 2007. While Iran appealed these measures to the International Monetary Fund (IMF), complaining that they contravened the Fund's foreign exchange rules, the IMF issued a determination in March that found no violation, leaving two of Iran's principal banks excluded from dollar markets.[141] American legislators also debated the adoption of even tougher unilateral sanctions against Iran during the spring,[142] yielding additional warnings to foreign companies that they might face secondary sanctions for investments in the Iranian energy sector.[143]

The American strategy also focused on maintaining low oil prices, with Saudi cooperation, to cut the levels of revenue available in Iran for domestic investment.[144] Indeed, it was suggested that the meeting of the World Economic Forum at Davos in January served as a venue for the United States to reveal a new strategy to advance an "anti-Iranian policy nexus" using financial diplomacy, energy policy, and assistance from Saudi Arabia to thwart Iranian regional influence and damage its economy.[145] One result of American efforts to discourage investment in Iran was the reduction of a Japanese stake in the development of an Iranian oil field from 75 percent to 10 percent. Another indication that pressure was being felt was the warning issued by Chinese officials to the United States to "stop interfering in its trade affairs with Iran, after Washington raised concerns over a planned energy deal with Tehran."[146]

Reports of serious damage to the Iranian economy as a result of the American campaign emerged in 2007, with the greatest strains in the Iranian energy sector as a result of declines in foreign investment.[147] Indeed, reports published between December 2006 and February 2007 suggested that Iran faced a serious energy crisis that was feeding in a significant way into the nuclear issue by generating a genuine demand for new sources of energy. In late December 2006, the National Academy of Sciences released a report indicating that Iran's declining oil and gas infrastructure may leave it with a real need for nuclear energy to meet its domestic energy consumption needs. The study's author, Roger Stern, a researcher at Johns Hopkins University, was quoted in an interview as stating that according to the study's projections, oil exports, which currently account for 70 percent of Iranian government revenue, "may be less than half their present level, and could drop to zero by 2015. 'It therefore seems possible that Iran's claim to need nuclear power might be genuine, an indicator of distress from anticipated export revenue shortfalls,' [Stern] wrote. 'If so, the Iranian regime may be more vulnerable than is presently understood.'"[148] By February 2007, with the decline of foreign investment in its energy sector, projections about the long-term decline in Iran's oil production confirmed the National Academy of Sciences' grim conclusions.[149] By March, Iran was even forced to implement serious measures for petrol rationing to offset the strain on its energy sector.[150]

No Imminent Threat of an Iranian Nuclear Capacity

With mounting evidence that the sanctions regime was having a significant impact on the Iranian economy, there was also news that Iran's enrichment program had encountered new obstacles. Following the Iranian Parliament's December bill demanding that the government accelerate its nuclear program, Iran announced that it intended to commence the installation of centrifuge cascades at its industrial-scale commercial enrichment facility at Natanz, which stood empty as of the end of 2006.[151] But Iran had earlier announced its intention to run six cascades at its experimental pilot enrichment facility and to install 3,000 centrifuges at the commercial facility by the end of 2006. Instead, in January 2007, Iran appeared to have abandoned its plan of installing more than the two cascades it had been able to run intermittently at the pilot facility and had shifted emphasis to beginning the assembly and installation of centrifuges at the commercial facility. By early February it had installed two cascades at the underground Natanz facility, though it had not moved beyond the phase of dry-spinning the centrifuges to test them and no uranium hexafluoride gas had been fed into the centrifuges by March.[152]

The Iranian announcement was met with analysis that the activity at the Natanz facility was more for public relations purposes than a real indication of an advance in Iran's enrichment capabilities. Sources familiar with the Iranian program reported a growing recognition that Iran was further from mastering centrifuge technologies than had been realized.

The consensus view among analysts was that even if Iran were able to install 3,000 centrifuges at the Natanz facility, given its struggle to run even a single pilot cascade smoothly, the country would likely run into numerous technical delays before it would be able to link the newly installed cascades or run them smoothly. It was also argued that Iran had had difficulty procuring materials after the nuclear smuggling network run by A. Q. Khan was shut down.[153] In light of these technical difficulties, at least one report argued that the acceleration of activity at Natanz "may be aimed as much as enriching Iran's political leverage as enriching uranium."[154] In part as a result of the realization of significant delays in the progress of the Iranian enrichment program, IAEA Director General ElBaradei argued at the end of January that the Iranian nuclear file did not represent an imminent threat and that the lack of urgency left plenty of time to find a negotiated solution.[155]

In addition to the evidence of technical difficulties at Natanz, another development mitigated urgency with respect to the Iranian nuclear file. February witnessed the emergence of reports casting doubt on claims of an active Iranian nuclear weapons intent. The evidence of the existence of a parallel Iranian nuclear program with military applications or a decision on the part of the Iranian government to acquire a nuclear weapon had always been weak.

In general, concerns have focused on the possibility that an Iranian enrichment program might subsequently enable Iran to develop a virtual deterrent insofar as the country would have mastered the necessary technology to be nuclear weapons "capable," in the language of the Bush administration. It is such a nuclear weapons capability, rather than concrete evidence of a nuclear weapons program or the diversion of nuclear material to military purposes, that has driven much of the international efforts to limit the Iranian nuclear program. Building a case against the Iranian nuclear program principally on concerns about the intentions of the government and, in the case of the United States, concerns about the nature of its regime, has proven difficult under international law, leaving Iran with numerous counterarguments.

Accordingly, the intelligence agencies of numerous countries have aggressively pursued any tangible evidence of the existence of a parallel nuclear weapons program in Iran or a decision to adapt the safeguarded nuclear program to military purposes. Such a "smoking gun" would resolve all ambiguity concerning the status of the Iranian nuclear program and furnish a clear basis to demand the cessation of Iranian nuclear activities. One such potential "smoking gun" was a laptop allegedly stolen from the Iranian nuclear program, which came into American possession through an informant in Iran and contained records of plans for a nuclear weapon.

After American intelligence officials shared printed versions of the material with the IAEA, agency officials approached the Iranians about the information. Iran rejected the material as a forgery. More recently, it emerged that IAEA officials also have reservations about the authenticity of the material. The doubts are based principally on two factors; first, IAEA officials regard it as unlikely that plans related to a nuclear warhead would be kept on a laptop for security reasons. Second, they find it suspicious that all the documents on the computer were in English with neither Farsi language files nor even notes contained anywhere among the materials on the laptop.[156] It was also reported that "most of the tip-offs about supposed secret weapons sites provided by the CIA and other U.S. intelligence agencies have led to dead ends when investigated by IAEA inspectors, according to informed sources in Vienna."[157] In a separate report, diplomats at the IAEA were quoted as saying that "most U.S. intelligence shared with the UN nuclear watchdog agency has proved inaccurate and none has led to significant discoveries inside Iran."[158] These doubts combined with the November report from a leaked CIA assessment concluding that there is no evidence of a secret Iranian nuclear weapons program separate from the IAEA safeguarded activities[159] lend further credence to IAEA Director General ElBaradei's oft-stated view that the Iranian nuclear program does not represent an imminent threat.

A final development that may have diminished the apparent urgency of concerns about Iran's nuclear program was evidence of moderation in the Iranian position. Whereas President Ahmadinejad had promised a significant announcement regarding the nuclear program at the celebrations of the twenty-eighth anniversary of the Iranian Revolution, no such announcement occurred. In contrast to the lavish April 2006 ceremony at which the president had announced that Iran had enriched to low levels a small quantity of uranium, the February event was marked with a speech in which Ahmadinejad reiterated Iran's right to enrich uranium but also expressed an openness to talks and Iran's determination to remain within the NPT rules. The fact that the expected announcement was not made was widely interpreted as a concession and step backward by Iran in its aggressive nuclear posture.[160]

In another move designed to calm international fears, the country's chief nuclear negotiator, Ali Larijani, speaking at an international security conference in Munich, stated that Iran would be open to accepting some limits on its enrichment program, explicitly disavowed any Iranian threat to Israel and affirmed that Iran would not engage in any act of aggression against any country.[161] While reiterating that Iran would not accept the suspension of enrichment activities as a precondition, Larijani also took the opportunity of his attendance at the Munich conference to call for renewed talks and to hold meetings with German Foreign Minister Frank-Walter Steinmeier and the EU's High Representative for Foreign Affairs, Javier Solana, both of whom reported that they had had a "good and constructive" meeting and believed the Iranians had a "new ambition for talks."[162]

Larijani's offer at Munich of limiting the enrichment program was later clarified by comments made by Iranian foreign minister, Manouchehr Mottaki, indicating that Iran would accept a permanent cap on enrichment levels at its facilities to between 3.5 and 5 percent, coupled with strict IAEA monitoring to guarantee that the fuel produced for the civilian program would not be diverted to other uses.[163] While none of these offers for limiting the enrichment program would be sufficient to meet Western demands, the conciliatory tone struck by Iranian officials nonetheless signaled a shift away from President Ahmadinejad's earlier, more aggressive posture. This shift was further confirmed when Ahmadinejad granted an interview to the television program, "Good Morning America," Ahmadinejad emphasized to Diane Sawyer the Iranian view that the world's problems are best solved through dialogue and that the Iranian tradition is one of conflict avoidance.[164]

Analysts viewed much of this moderation as a response to increasing domestic challenges to Ahmadinejad's handling of the nuclear file. This pressure ranged from criticism of the president's provocative rhetoric in the diplomatic arena by conservative newspapers in Iran usually identified with the country's supreme leader, Ayatollah Ali Khamenei, to direct criticism by high-level Iranian officials.[165] There were even reports that Khamenei had refused to meet with Ahmadinejad for a period to convey a rebuke to his aggressive policies.[166] The results of the domestic pressure were evident both in the government's more moderate stance on the nuclear issue and its muted response to new American policies permitting the detention or use of lethal force against Iranians present in Iraq. Despite the persistence of occasional rhetorical flourishes by the Iranian president—including a February speech that occasioned widespread criticism in Iran in which he likened the Iranian nuclear program to a train without brakes[167]—the overall direction taken by Iranian nuclear negotiators was far more tempered in 2007 than Ahmadinejad's earlier tone.

February and March saw Iranian nuclear negotiator Larijani proposing that Iran limit its enrichment activities to the dry-spinning of centrifuges in order to begin talks, a compromise rejected by the United States, but indicative of further efforts by the Iranians to return to negotiations. These efforts were bolstered by Foreign Minister Mottaki's call for a peaceful resolution to the dispute with the United States over preconditions to negotiating[168] and by the reported remarks of a senior Iranian official that the United States and Iran should restore relations through direct talks, which would illustrate that despite their mutual recriminations, Iran and the United States are "natural allies."[169]

In sum, then, a combination of technical obstacles to advances in the Iranian enrichment program, reports of newfound skepticism concerning allegations of Iranian efforts to divert nuclear materials to military purposes, and a moderation in the Iranian stance on its nuclear program all suggested that the Iranian nuclear program was less urgent of a concern than had previously been feared and created a more propitious environment for direct engagement. In addition to these developments on the Iranian side, heightened international concerns about increasingly aggressive American policies gave rise to numerous high-profile statements calling for deescalation and warning of the disastrous consequences of any attempt to resolve the conflict over the Iranian nuclear program by force.

While several prominent Iranians made conciliatory statements at, or coincident with, Davos,[170] other groups and nations represented at Davos were at pains to denounce any military option against Iran. The Arab League's Secretary General Amr Moussa warned that he believed there was a 50 percent probability of an attack on Iran, which he categorized as highly "counterproductive."[171] Striking a similar note, IAEA Director General ElBaradei spoke at Davos warning that a military strike on Iran would "absolutely counterproductive and it would be catastrophic" and calling for negotiations to end the impasse over the Iranian nuclear file.[172]

From "Timeout" to a New Resolution

ElBaradei also used the Davos meeting to introduce a new proposal calling for a "time out" whereby negotiations would begin with a simultaneous suspension of the 1737 sanctions and the Iranian enrichment program.[173] The proposal was an attempt to create a face-saving solution to the timing hurdle associated with the American demand that a suspension in uranium enrichment be a *precondition* to talks and the Iranian unwillingness to engage in a unilateral concession as the price to enter negotiations. Given earlier expressions of Iranian willingness to suspend enrichment within the context of negotiations, ElBaradei's proposal held out the possibility of satisfying the requirement of suspension while also enabling the Iranians to claim that the concession was not unilateral but exchanged for a suspension of the sanctions.

While the Iranians showed interest in the proposal and stated that it was under consideration, the Americans appeared to rule out any consideration of modifying the sequencing contemplated in 1737 of the suspension of enrichment *prior to* the suspension of sanctions.[174] Several American experts lamented the U.S. position as once again undermining prospects for negotiation in the face of mounting international and Iranian calls for talks, but a subsequent European endorsement of the timeout proposal was not sufficient to overcome the American objection.[175]

The deadline for Iranian compliance with 1737 approached in February against a backdrop of American escalation and apparent Iranian moderation. In advance of the deadline, the IAEA circulated a separate report concerning reductions in the agency's technical assistance to Iran in compliance with the Security Council sanctions. The report identified 22 out of 55 technical assistance programs that would have to be suspended under the terms of 1737.[176] The United States had earlier proposed more extensive aid cuts, a proposal that had drawn an adverse reaction from NAM countries, but the American ambassador to the agency, Greg Schulte, indicated that the United States was satisfied that the reductions identified by the IAEA met the requirements of 1737.[177]

In a separate indication of the deterioration of relations between the IAEA and Iran, the Iranian government requested that the agency withdraw the designations of 38 inspectors for work on the Iranian nuclear file.[178] IAEA Director General ElBaradei discussed the Iranian request in an interview with CNN in which he stated that while the barring of these inspectors reduced some of the agency's flexibility, that there remained over 100 inspectors able to travel to Iran, which was enough to continue inspections without difficulty.[179] Reports suggested that the Iranian objection to the 38 inspectors, all from Western countries, was based on espionage concerns in a climate of escalating military threats.[180] An additional request by Iran led the IAEA to reassign the inspector in charge of the agency's work with Iran, also on the basis that the inspector was suspected by the Iranians of having leaked information.[181]

The moves were likely a combination of measured retaliation by the Iranian government for the imposition of the Security Council Resolution and real Iranian concerns that agency inspections might be facilitating targeting plans in light of frequent reports that the United States was drawing up military contingency plans for aerial strikes against Iranian nuclear and other infrastructure. Despite these adverse developments in the Iranian relationship with the agency, however, IAEA Director General ElBaradei remained a consistent voice cautioning against relying on sanctions or coercion to resolve the Iranian nuclear issue and strongly advocating direct talks between Iran and the United States. For example, on the eve of the agency's release of its report on Iranian compliance with 1737, ElBaradei gave an extended interview to the British *Financial Times* in which he warned against the "hype" concerning Iran's nuclear program, cautioned that the international community should address Iran's legitimate security concerns and called specifically on the United States to assist efforts to resume negotiations by dropping preconditions and engaging directly with Iran.[182] ElBaradei's comments were timed to give the agency's view in anticipation of a push for a second set of sanctions against Iran that would predictably result from the impending IAEA report on Iranian compliance with the Security Council mandate to suspend its nuclear activities.

The IAEA circulated its fifteenth report on Iran's nuclear program on February 22. The report described Iran's failure to implement Security Council Resolution 1737 and detailed the status of Iran's safeguarded activities. Specifically, the report found that Iran had continued its uranium enrichment and heavy water–related activities and had not extended the additional cooperation to the IAEA necessary to resolve all of the outstanding issues related to its past activities for the agency to certify that there are no undeclared nuclear activities in Iran.[183] The report noted that Iran had continued to feed uranium hexafluoride into the centrifuges at its pilot facility and had proceeded to install centrifuges in its industrial-scale enrichment plant, with two cascades installed and operating under vacuum at the underground Natanz facility and an additional two cascades nearing completion.[184] The agency also reported that there were no reprocessing activities at any of Iran's facilities, but that Iran had continued with construction of a heavy water research reactor at Arak and the operation of a nearby heavy water production plant, in contravention of the requirements of Resolution 1737.[185] While the report noted that Iran had been complying with its Safeguards Agreements in providing sufficient access to inspectors to complete verification, Iran had not agreed to remote monitoring arrangements through the installation of cameras in the cascade halls of the commercial enrichment plant, which will become required should Iran install more than 500 centrifuges at the facility.

The report reiterated earlier agency certifications that it had been "able to verify the nondiversion of declared nuclear material in Iran" and noted that Iran "has provided the Agency with access to declared nuclear materials and facilities and has provided the required accountancy reports" under its Safeguards Agreement.[186] However, the agency was unable to confirm the absence of undeclared nuclear activities in Iran, something that can only be accomplished through the implementation of the Additional Protocol.[187] Iran suspended its voluntary implementation of the Additional Protocol following the referral of its nuclear file to the Security Council in 2006, and has repeatedly stated that it would only be willing to resume implementation of the Protocol measures if its file was returned from the council to the sole authority of the agency, a position reaffirmed in its correspondence with the IAEA as mentioned by the report.[188]

The overall conclusion, then, of the report was that while Iran was meeting its obligations under its Safeguards Agreement, it had not complied with the requirements of Resolution 1737 nor had it resumed implementation of measures under the Additional Protocol. As the board of governors began meeting to discuss the report in early March, IAEA Director General ElBaradei reported that Iran appeared to have temporarily halted its enrichment work, with no increase in the number of centrifuges at the Natanz facility.[189] Thus, despite the report's conclusions with respect to 1737 compliance, both the report and ElBaradei's comments reflected important areas of Iranian compliance with NPT obligations and moderation in its nuclear drive.

While the report laid the groundwork for the resumption of Security Council deliberations on the Iranian nuclear file, ElBaradei's admonishment against the sole reliance on sanctions to resolve the Iranian nuclear dispute was telling. From the agency's perspective, negotiations to cap Iranian enrichment activities coupled with a return to Iranian implementation of the Additional Protocol would be the most constructive means of resolving the dispute with Iran while strengthening the nonproliferation regime. By reducing the agency's technical cooperation with Iran and imposing reporting demands on the inspectors that are not derived from the NPT or other agreements governing the agency's relationship with the country, Security Council action was not only penalizing Iran but also risked undermining the agency's stature and independence.

The discussion of the IAEA report at the board of governors meeting occasioned NAM countries to raise concerns that a negative precedent was being set by the Security Council's demand that the agency limit technical cooperation with Iran, which amounted to subjecting the agency's technical activities to "political conditions."[190] Concerns were also raised that "double standards" were being applied whereby Iran was penalized for having a safeguarded enrichment program while Israel did not face technical aid cuts despite its apparent admission of operating a clandestine nuclear weapon program.[191] The appearance of politicization of the agency's work is one adverse consequence of transferring the Iranian nuclear file to the Security Council. Another adverse consequence is that the incremental escalation of measures against Iran at the council has set the Iranian nuclear dispute on a path of coercion not negotiation.

With the IAEA report confirming Iranian noncompliance with Security Council Resolution 1737, the permanent members of the council together with Germany (the so-called P5+1) resumed meetings to discuss a new resolution to incrementally strengthen sanctions against Iran. The first such meeting was held in London on February 26 with Under Secretary of State Nicholas Burns representing the United States.[192] Subsequent meetings and conference calls, at the ministerial level and later between the P5+1 ambassadors to the UN in New York, took place over the next three weeks with reports suggesting significant progress toward identifying an additional set of limited measures to implement against Iran. The sticking points in discussions were Chinese and Russian opposition to the expansion of an arms ban on exports to Iran, Chinese concerns about the extent of additions proposed to the asset-freeze list and European hesitation over further restrictions on export credits to companies trading with Iran.[193]

By March 15, 2007, there was news that the P5+1 had agreed to the terms of additional sanctions and would be circulating their draft text for a resolution to the full Security Council within a week.[194] According to leaked drafts, the terms of the new sanctions package would include the following five elements: (1) a ban on Iranian export of any arms or related materials; (2) expansion of the list of Iranian individuals and firms that will be subject to an assets freeze, to 15 additional individuals and 13 additional companies; (3) a call on all nations to exercise "vigilance and restraint" in selling tanks, combat aircraft, and other heavy weapons to Iran; (4) vigilance and restraint in allowing members of the expanded asset-freeze list to travel; and (5) the urging of all governments and financial institutions to desist from any new commitments "of grants, financial assistance, or concessional loans" to the Iranian government.[195] As with Resolution 1737, the new resolution would provide for a 60-day compliance window for Iran to suspend its nuclear activities, following which additional measures would be considered. There was some resistance to the terms of the sanctions package voiced by the nonpermanent members of the council, including South African objections to penalties beyond the nuclear sphere and the insistence of Qatar and Indonesia that the resolution include language encouraging a nuclear-free zone in the Middle East. Despite this back and forth, it was reported that the draft text would be debated by the Security Council on March 21 and that a vote would likely take place before the end of the month at the latest.[196]

The terms of the new sanctions package reflect concessions to allay Russian, Chinese, and European concerns. The continued exclusion of the light water reactor at Bushehr being constructed by Iran with Russian assistance is an example of such a concession. However, despite the carve-out, the effects of Resolution 1737 have reportedly endangered the continuation of Russian work on the project, both as a result of Iranian payment difficulties as the country's banking system absorbed restrictions in its access to dollars due to American unilateral financial sanctions on Iranian banks, and as a result of Russian procurement difficulties with third party subcontractors refusing to supply parts for the project, possibly as a result of unilateral American and European measures.[197]

In one counterproductive consequence of the sanctions, the Russian delay of nuclear fuel delivery for the Bushehr plant was cited by Iran as vindication of its position that it requires an indigenous nuclear fuel cycle because it is systematically blocked from nuclear fuel supply on international markets.[198] As additional reports emerged that the Russians were withholding the fuel supply to generate political pressure on Iran to suspend its enrichment activities, the Iranian argument was reinforced.[199] More generally, both the impact of the 1737 sanctions and the prospect of ratcheting up of restrictions on Iranian markets through a second resolution have clearly adversely impacted the Iranian economy and the progress of its nuclear program. What sanctions have not accomplished is bringing the parties any closer to negotiations, widely agreed to be the only viable avenue for a resolution to the nuclear standoff. With the council poised to adopt a second resolution in late March and the Iranian President Ahmadinejad suggesting that there might be a new announcement concerning advances in the Iranian nuclear program in April,[200] there seems little basis for optimism about renewing stalled negotiations.[201]

ALTERNATIVES TO THE CURRENT APPROACH IN THE IRANIAN CASE

The back-and-forth trajectory of the Iranian nuclear dispute described in the foregoing sections suggests the wisdom of the initial international response to revelations concerning an Iranian nuclear program in 2002. That initial response comprised a combination of heightened IAEA inspections and multilateral negotiations as the only means to resolve international nonproliferation concerns while respecting Iranian sovereign rights and preserving the integrity of the nonproliferation regime.

IAEA Director General Mohamed ElBaradei, in an interview with the *Financial Times*, made clear that he continues to believe that the only means to break the deadlock over the Iranian nuclear dispute is through multilateral engagement. Specifically he called for the Iranian nuclear file to be returned to the parallel tracks of agency inspections and negotiations, rather than further council action. By creating an environment in which Iran is isolated and potentially subject to further sanctions, ElBaradei argued that continuing down the path of sanctions might encourage some of the "worst case scenarios" from materializing. Rather, he argued, the international community should prioritize preventing Iran from developing an industrial-scale enrichment program, deterring additional limitations on the work of agency inspectors and avoiding an Iranian withdrawal from the NPT.[202]

Each of these priorities would involve stepping away from council action, returning to negotiations and allowing the IAEA to resume principal control of monitoring the Iranian nuclear file. In identifying these priorities, ElBaradei was focusing on the nonproliferation goals of the international community with respect to Iran. While the path of coercion might serve other ends—ranging from containment of Iranian regional influence to laying the groundwork for regime change—it is serving to undermine nonproliferation objectives by delaying a negotiated solution to the dispute. Because the contours of such a negotiated solution have been evident since 2005, if not earlier, such postponements are particularly frustrating from a nonproliferation perspective.

There have been several avenues of multilateral engagements proposed since the first revelations concerning the Iranian nuclear program in 2002. Iran, for its part, has made numerous overtures, including notably in 2003, to engage in comprehensive talks with the United States, including on the nuclear issue. The history of the circumstances in which these efforts were rebuffed has recently emerged and caused some discomfort for Bush administration officials.[203] In a clear earlier effort to engage with the Americans, the Iranians cooperated with the 2001 invasion of Afghanistan. Instead of being rewarded for their assistance, they believed their gesture was met with the insult of being designated as a member of the "Axis of Evil."[204] The Iranians then entered into multilateral negotiations with the Europeans and demonstrated willingness to be flexible on the question of suspension of enrichment. But their key concerns—fuel supply guarantees, the lifting of American sanctions, and, most crucially, security guarantees—have gone unaddressed, largely as a result of the American refusal to even join talks.

As detailed in the chronology provided above, when the United States decided to endorse the EU-3 negotiating track, it did so by imposing a new condition that altered the terms of the talks. The Iranian negotiations with the EU-3 foundered in large measure as a result of that condition—the complete cessation of Iranian enrichment activities—and later, when the United States agreed to join talks with Iran directly, insistence on a precondition of Iranian enrichment suspension achieved much the same effect of stalling negotiations.

IAEA Director General ElBaradei conveyed the core of the argument for engagement without preconditions in an October 2006 *Newsweek* interview while visiting the United States.

> We need to move away from the idea that dialogue is a "reward" for good behavior. You need dialogue when you have bad behavior, because the purpose of the dialogue is to change the behavior. As former [U.S.] Secretary of State James Baker said recently, talking to your enemy is not appeasement.

The insight that talking to or engaging with an adversary is not the equivalent of appeasement should be internalized by American policymakers and their Western counterparts if there is to be any hope of a negotiated solution. The dropping of preconditions and pursuit of reciprocal concessions, as with the "timeout" proposed by the director general, is the only way to signal a meaningful commitment to a negotiated track and hence pave the way for a resolution to the Iranian nuclear dispute.

Options for the UNSC

With the European negotiating track suspended, the United States insisting that no solution permitting even limited enrichment research on the part of the Iranians would be acceptable, and Russia and China opposing significantly strengthened sanctions to coerce Iranian suspension of enrichment, the stage has been set for ongoing confrontation over Iran's nuclear file in 2007. It is worth noting, however, that the Security Council's options are quite narrow. Given that sanctions have now been imposed on Iran and negotiations are advanced for the strengthening of the 1737 sanctions regime, scenarios for Security Council action are limited to a continued reinforcement of sanctions to coerce Iran into abandoning its nuclear program, or further escalation. Beyond sanctions, the only remaining option for ratcheting up coercive pressure on Iran would be the authorization of multilateral coercive intervention to forestall Iran's nuclear ambitions. Let us consider both of these options.

The likeliest scenario at this point is the incremental strengthening of the sanctions first imposed by the council in December 2006. This approach has a few potential benefits and many potential risks. On the plus side, by virtue of their presence on the council, the United States, Russia, and China are brought directly into discussions over the Iranian nuclear file, as the P5+1 initiative of this summer suggested. This creates a more multilateral context for the dispute so that if an understanding is ultimately reached through negotiations, it will have the support of all relevant actors.

The sanctions might also have the benefit of strengthening the IAEA's hand in demanding greater transparency from Iran. But this potential benefit has a double-edged quality. First, the resolution's requirements exceed those mandated by the NPT framework, extending to complete cessation of fuel cycle activities that are otherwise permitted under the treaty. The additional requirements imposed by the council are ones that might actually undermine the agency's activities in the long run by downgrading the significance of agency certification of Iranian compliance with its obligations under the NPT. Further, by taking the Iranian file out of the agency's hands and leaving final determinations of Iranian compliance in the hands of the Security Council, the sanctions undermine Iranian incentives to comply with the agency's current inspection efforts and technical work. Finally, by subjecting agency technical cooperation with Iran to new standards imposed by Security Council Resolution, an appearance of politicizing the agency's work may arise in ways that are criticized not only by Iran but also by other nonweapons states party to the NPT.

Sanctions also bear the risk of having detrimental effects on the prospects for a negotiated settlement. The concern that sanctions are an impediment to engagement between the parties has repeatedly been expressed by the IAEA director general, as well as numerous other international officials. Because they are drawn from the arsenal of coercive measures, sanctions inherently represent a move away from the negotiating track of reciprocal concessions and mutually agreed compromise. Instead, they have escalated the confrontational dimension of the standoff. On the Iranian side, sanctions have caused a measure of alarm among moderate and pragmatic elites, but they have also occasioned increased nationalist support for a hard-line insistence on accelerating the nuclear program, as evidenced by the Iranian Parliament's swift action to endorse the nuclear program and call for reduced cooperation with the IAEA following the adoption of Security Council Resolution 1737. While Iran has responded with relatively measured retaliation to the resolution and subsequent IAEA reduction of technical assistance to Iran, the banning of 38 IAEA inspectors is clear indication that the sanctions are neither strengthening the inspection regime nor encouraging greater compliance on the part of the Iranians. Further, Iran's threat perception—a factor that is perhaps the strongest rationale for Iran's current pursuit of nuclear energy—is also exacerbated as it braces for potentially coercive Security Council action against it.

More generally, the international record suggests that sanctions are a blunt and time-intensive instrument for altering state behavior. In the Iranian case, sanctions are likely to be even less effectual for a number of specific reasons. First, the council is unlikely to augment sanctions to the point that they would have the necessary coercive impact on Iran. It is extremely unlikely that the council would impose full economic or trade sanctions, and indeed current efforts at imposing more limited sanctions face significant opposition not only from Russia and China, but also from European nations, each time that export credit bans or trade embargos are contemplated. The areas that can conceivably be impacted by sanctions in the near-term remain limited to discussion of travel bans on certain regime officials, possible measure to limit cultural and educational exchanges, the slow expansion of freezes on Iranian government assets, and other forms of targeted, symbolic sanctions designed to isolate the Iranian government and tarnish its image without causing disruption to the world economy by impacting Iranian oil exports.

Second, with American unilateral sanctions already in effect, Iran is also extremely adept at evading the harshest impact of sanctions through recourse to black market channels. Iranian officials have often noted that they have been forced to create back channel access for their import needs, particularly where goods are perceived by the United States as dual use. American secondary sanctions have seriously impeded open market transactions for Iran in light of the costs such transactions impose on their trading partners. As a result of its experience with U.S. sanctions, the Iranian economy is unusually resilient in the face of sanctions; the effects of broad economic sanctions, were they to be imposed, would likely be offset to some degree by Iranian preparedness. In the end, continuing and incrementally strengthening sanctions through actions taken by the council is as likely to escalate tensions and undermine diplomatic options as it is to provide any benefit.

The option of multilateral coercive intervention is an even more potentially damaging option and one with considerably grimmer prospects. While the council has the authority to find the Iranian nuclear program to represent a threat to international peace and security triggering coercive intervention under its Chapter VII powers, this is an unlikely scenario. Russia and China are not likely to support any council-led military action against Iran. Indeed, in the aftermath of the debacle of the American and British efforts to secure council support for their intervention in Iraq, it is extremely unlikely that either country would once again seek authorization to use military force from the council so soon after their failed 2003 effort.

Finally, there is no good military option to deter the Iranians from pursuing nuclear energy or a latent nuclear weapons capacity. Despite the persistence of periodic American calls to bomb Iran,[205] or analysts' arguments that the Bush administration is on the verge of approving an air campaign against Iran,[206] this option remains an extremely poor one even from the perspective of a unilateralist American military planner.[207] Numerous reports have outlined the drawbacks of a military option for reasons ranging from the dispersion of Iranian facilities to the unreliable intelligence for targeting purposes to the destabilization of the region following such an attack to concerns about civilian casualties and environmental harm to the damage an attack would do to the NPT regime.[208] In part because of the limitations of each of the options available to the council, several prominent international figures including both Hans Blix, the former head of UNMOVIC that led weapons inspections in Iraq, and former UN Secretary General Kofi Annan had publicly warned at the beginning of 2006 that they consider referral to the council both premature and potentially counterproductive.[209]

As this review of the course of the Iranian nuclear file has sought to demonstrate, the degeneration of negotiations to limit Iran's nuclear enrichment program and place it under international controls was avoidable and may still be repairable. The relegation of the Iranian nuclear file to the Security Council followed by the imposition of sanctions has, however, further undermined prospects for a negotiated settlement. The best alternative remains a negotiated settlement through direct engagement between the parties involved, and most importantly between the United States and Iran. There remains the question, however, of what formulas are available that represent an acceptable compromise for the parties, satisfying international proliferation concerns while enabling the Iranian government to claim that it has not foregone its rights to nuclear energy under the NPT. In the following section, I will consider the available compromise *alternatives* that might be pursued through direct engagement and comprehensive negotiations in lieu of Security Council action.

Negotiations Based on Common Interests

Negotiations, to succeed, require the identification of areas of common interest and mutual benefit in addition to specifying the areas where positions diverge. Fortunately, the area of overlapping interests and the potential for mutually beneficial arrangements abound in the Iranian case. The starting point for any negotiation at this stage is to pick up from where talks broke off in the fall of 2006, namely the P5+1 proposal and the Iranian counterproposal of August 2005. Much useful ground is covered in these proposals, leaving only small issues that should be relatively easy to tackle. Chief among these issues is the modality and timing of an Iranian suspension of current enrichment and reprocessing activities and a medium- and long-term agreement regarding the conditions under which Iranians would be permitted to resume enrichment activities and the extent of the permissible activities. Numerous proposals on each of these issues already exist and require greater elaboration.

The principal elements of the P5+1 proposal that are promising are affirmation of Iran's right to nuclear energy; the recognition of the Isfahan conversion facility as a permissible Iranian program; the proposal for the location of an international fuel cycle in Russia with Iranian participation; the provision of a five-year nuclear fuel buffer stock dedicated to Iran; and an energy partnership with Iran permitting investment in Iran's oil and gas infrastructures, which has currently been hampered by American direct and secondary sanctions. The Iranian counterproposal, coupled with reports on the discussions between Javier Solana and Ali Larijani in the fall of 2006, suggest, on the Iranian side, a willingness to suspend enrichment activities during a negotiating period.

The first obstacle to be tackled is the question of whether Iranian suspension must be a *precondition* to negotiations, as the United States insists, or can be undertaken simultaneously with the commencement of negotiations, something the Iranians suggested in their August 2006 counterproposal and that is built into the proposal by IAEA Director General Mohamed ElBaradei's suggestion of a "timeout" that would enable negotiations through a simultaneous (rather than sequential) suspension of the Security Council sanctions and Iranian enrichment activities. Numerous American analysts and the IAEA have all suggested that a modality to deal with the timing of the suspension should not be difficult to achieve and that this is an inappropriate basis for delaying the resumption of engagement.[210] Further, it may be possible to entertain definitions of "suspension" that would satisfy the formal American demand while enabling Iran to justify the action domestically as not compromising future research activities.[211]

Assuming that the question of timing for suspension is resolved, the key remaining issues are whether the Iranians would be permitted a pilot enrichment program while implementing the Additional Protocol and permitting the IAEA to undertake the enhanced inspections, verification and monitoring activities necessary to resolve all outstanding issues and certify that there are no undeclared nuclear activities in Iran. Many nuclear analysts and diplomats have reportedly privately endorsed a face-saving compromise that would cap the Iranian enrichment program to a research capacity well short of industrial-scale production, in exchange for tight inspections that address proliferation concerns and trade benefits that end Iran's isolation.[212] Such a modality for resolving the crisis cannot be broached, however, until the United States decides whether it is committed to a negotiated solution or prefers to pursue a more aggressive policy of Iranian containment.

Indications to date have been that while the United States is willing to modify its positions to the extent necessary to maintain a relatively unified position within the P5+1, it has not been committed to finding a negotiated solution with Iran that would require a genuine compromise. On balance, this is a counterproductive approach on the part of the United States. The only purpose served by such an approach would be to generate an appearance of exhausting diplomatic options to legitimate recourse to coercion. However, this approach serves little function if there is no viable military or coercive solution.

For reasons already canvassed, a negotiated solution is the most promising alternative to strengthen the nonproliferation regime generally and control an

Iranian proliferation risk specifically. Moreover, there are a number of features of the Iranian context that make negotiations especially promising. First, despite some modest progress in the Iranian nuclear program in the past four years, there is still no urgency involved in the negotiations as the most pessimistic estimates still suggest that Iran is years away from having a nuclear weapon capacity, if indeed it is seeking one.[213] Second, the Iranian case presents an excellent opportunity for a win-win compromise outcome where permitting a highly restricted pilot enrichment facility for Iran under an enhanced inspections and verification mechanism would not only provide more reliable intelligence on the Iranian program than is currently available through the safeguards inspections, but would also set a constructive precedent for future cases in which a country might seek to acquire an indigenous fuel cycle.

Achieving such a positive negotiated outcome requires several steps that depend not only on Iran but also on the willingness of the United States to undertake meaningful negotiations. These include a willingness on the part of the United States to enter into direct negotiations, in the P5+1 framework or bilaterally, with Iran without preconditions that prejudice the likelihood of constructive engagement. The United States would also have to accept a willingness to join in discussions of a regional security framework involving, at a minimum, negative security assurances. To understand why these elements are important, it is worth considering the legitimate strategic interests of both Iran and the United States as they enter these discussions.

On the Iranian side, there are two principal interests: first, a reliable assurance of access to nuclear fuel; and second, a guarantee that it will not face coercive American intervention for the purposes of regime change. Both of these constitute legitimate concerns in light of Iranian historical experience. With respect to fuel supply assurances, no arrangement that does not permit Iran to have some minimal access to enrichment technology for the purpose of indigenous nuclear fuel production can fully address the supply concerns that have been generated by systematic actions to block Iran from open market transactions as a result of hostility to the Iranian regime. Specifically, Iran has argued that being restricted to an equity stake in a Russian enrichment facility without the right to limited enrichment research on its own soil or direct participation in the enrichment processes at the Russian facility does not offer greater security than Iran's earlier equity investment in the French Eurodif enrichment facility. In the Eurodif case, Iran had an equity stake in the facility but as a result of changes in political circumstances it was denied access to the nuclear fuel supply for which it had made payment. The recent Russian refusal to respect an agreed schedule for fuel delivery to the Bushehr light water reactor does little to assuage these Iranian concerns, particularly in light of the suggestion that fuel delivery is being withheld for political purposes.

With respect to its concerns regarding coercive American intervention, Iran points historically to Anglo-American intervention resulting in the overthrow of a democratically elected Iranian government in 1953, the more recent experience of the American intervention against Iraq—widely seen in the region as an example of using arms control concerns pretextually to engage in regime change—and the open calls by American officials for regime change in Iran.[214] By including Iran in the so-called Axis of Evil, the Bush administration gave rise to the suggestion that Iran might be a legitimate target of military intervention and the recent acceleration in speculation about American military strikes against Iran aggravate Tehran's threat perception. By repeatedly stating that all options are on the table in American policy toward Iran, and earlier raising the possibility that there might be circumstances under which nuclear strikes would be permissible against a non-nuclear weapon state, the Bush administration has generated new incentives for Iran to seek aggressive deterrents against a potential American attack.

On the American side, there are also two significant interests related to policy on Iran: the first is preventing Iran from attaining a nuclear weapon and the second is containing any threat that Iran might pose to the regional status quo, in which the United States wishes to remain, together with its principal Gulf ally, Saudi Arabia, the principal regional hegemon. Fortunately, both of these interests can readily be accommodated by seeking a negotiated solution that imposes a tight inspection and verification regime on Iran, dramatically limits the permitted extent of Iran's fuel cycle activities and involves Iran in a regional security framework that allays Iranian concerns about an American attack while drawing Iran into a web of negative security assurances that limits any Iranian capacity to threaten the regional status quo.

Elements of a Negotiated Solution

In light of the American and Iranian interests that would be served by a negotiated solution, as well as the advancement of the nonproliferation norm, identifying the minimum elements of such a solution must be the priority. As suggested above, IAEA Director General ElBaradei emphasized that any solution must prevent the development of an industrial-scale Iranian enrichment program, strengthen inspections and avoid an Iranian withdrawal from the NPT.

A cursory examination of the history of attempted multilateral negotiations have left the Iranians with the lesson that past concessions have not been rewarded by the United States. Under these circumstances, imposing a unilateral precondition that would require Iran to give up its principal bargaining chip—its current fuel cycle activities—in advance of negotiations will remain a nonstarter. It is also clear from the history of the fits and starts in negotiations since 2003 that any package without serious negative security guarantees will not address Iran's threat perception, which most analysts believe to be a major driver of their nuclear program. Finally, for the reasons surveyed in detail elsewhere, there is no military option that can do more than delay the Iranian nuclear program and do so at an enormous, catastrophic price to the region, to world markets and to the nonproliferation regime.[215] For this reason, most analysts have concluded that even should negotiations fail and the international community be faced with an Iranian nuclear weapon capacity, deterrence will be the option involving the least risk and should be preferred to any military "rollback" policy.[216] Fortunately, a Iranian nuclear weapons capacity is not inevitable and by most projections is not imminent.

At the core of a negotiated agreement that would address the legitimate interests of Iran and the United States is a package that would tightly limit Iranian fuel cycle activities to a pilot enrichment facility restricted to a low threshold of enrichment and subjected to a strengthened inspections regime to guard against proliferation risks. Uranium enrichment is already widely understood to represent a lesser proliferation risk than reprocessing activities and heavy water reactors.

An agreement under which Iran permanently forgoes any reprocessing activities (by committing to an open fuel cycle, as it had already agreed to do in the spring of 2005) and abandons construction of a heavy water facility at Arak, while agreeing to drop plans to develop an industrial-scale uranium enrichment facility would go a very long way to addressing proliferation concerns. Adding a strict inspections system to monitor enrichment activities at a pilot facility, combined with Iranian implementation of the Additional Protocol and cooperation in resolving outstanding issues related to past nuclear activities would transform the Iranian nuclear program from a challenge to the nonproliferation regime to an opportunity to strengthen it. Further, the establishment of a reliable fuel supply market mechanism for Iran—either through the envisioned joint venture in which Iran would have an equity stake in a Russian international fuel center, or through Iran participation in another multinational consortium—would also provide another constructive precedent that would allay other developing countries' concerns about their future access to supply.

The March 2007 IAEA board of governors meeting saw concerns expressed by NAM nations that restrictions on fuel supply, proposals for multilateral approaches to the fuel cycle, and new export control regimes were all lending to the entrenchment of a system of "haves" and "have-nots" that would give existing nuclear powers monopolist advantages and degenerate into get-rich-quick schemes for multinationals.[217] Establishing a clear supply precedent in the Iranian case might generate a useful counterexample.

Based on the foregoing analysis, the minimum elements of an acceptable negotiated solution to the Iranian nuclear dispute are readily attainable. These elements build on the three priorities identified by IAEA Director General ElBaradei. First among these is preventing Iran from developing an industrial-scale enrichment program. But to persuade the Iranians to accept this element, measures must be adopted that credibly address Iranian fuel supply concerns as well as their insistence of the indigenous right to technology. This would mean, first, that Iran should be given fuel supply assurances that provide a guaranteed supply insulated from political pressures, including any unilateral actions on the part of the United States. Several proposals have been floated to address the fuel supply issue, including the idea of Russian uranium enrichment joint venture with Iranian participation and a multilateral "blackboxed" enrichment facility operated by a European consortium with Iranian participation.[218]

The second measure to persuade Iranians to forgo industrial-scale enrichment is to permit them to retain a pilot-level enrichment facility. This is necessary in order to enable Iranians to sell the package domestically as having preserved their rights to a fuel cycle under the NPT. Nor is this element necessarily undesirable as it poses a minimal proliferation risk while creating an important opportunity for the international community to set a valuable precedent by establishing a strengthened inspection and verification mechanism, including the presence of on-site inspectors, remote monitoring devices, and an Iranian commitment to implement and ratify the Additional Protocol. Finally, on the Iranian side, a minimum package should entail an Iranian commitment not to withdraw from the NPT. In exchange for Iran meeting these three conditions, the package would require direct American participation in good faith negotiations,[219] abandoning any American military policy to promote regime change in Iran.

Exploration of avenues for a negotiated solution, however, currently flounder on the American "red line" of not permitting even a limited pilot or research enrichment facility to the Iranians, despite the view of the IAEA and a majority of nonproliferation analysts that such a facility, particularly under a strengthened inspections regime, would pose little proliferation risk.[220] The American opposition to limited Iranian enrichment is based on the desire to close the "loophole" in the NPT that permits countries to develop enrichment technologies within the treaty regime that might contribute to a latent weapons capacity. While this loophole is an appropriate source of concern, singling out Iran as the one case in which this loophole is to be closed is a risky strategy. Failure to secure a negotiated solution in the Iranian case will do far greater damage to the already wounded nonproliferation regime than a compromise at this stage.

To find a compromise that will take most enrichment activities out of Iran while permitting a face-saving symbolic domestic capacity is likely to be the best available course. Iran has repeatedly offered to place any limited enrichment capability it would be permitted to operate under strict IAEA in-person, on-site, 24-hour monitoring. Iran's oft-stated willingness to accept extremely intrusive inspections to meet the standards of "objective guarantees" that it is operating a proliferation-resistant nuclear energy pilot program enable the international community to set an excellent precedent for strengthening monitoring and verification standards that go further toward closing the NPT "loophole" than efforts to deprive nations of nuclear technology that will likely prompt an eventual exodus of energy-starved nonweapons states from the NPT. Strengthening the safeguards against the diversion of fissile materials under cover of a civilian energy program is the most viable means of reinforcing the NPT. The compromise of an Iranian pilot facility under enhanced IAEA monitoring should then be followed by a multilateral initiative to strengthen the regime across the board in a fashion that is equitable and nondiscriminatory.

The achievement of an acceptable medium-term solution for the Iranian nuclear file would be an important advance toward eliminating a significant risk to the current nonproliferation regime. But a more long-term option would be to seek to develop a regional or global arrangement to produce or guarantee reliable access to nuclear fuel on a proliferation-resistant basis. If such an arrangement were limited to guaranteeing supply, it would closely parallel the recent proposal by IAEA Director General Mohamed ElBaradei who has argued for the creation of a fuel bank as a last-resort supplier and the adoption of "objective, apolitical nonproliferation criteria" to guarantee fuel supplies such that a country that meets its NPT obligations should be assured of access to nuclear fuel.[221] The better alternative may ultimately be a multinational approach to limiting the spread of nuclear fuel cycle technologies by providing a multinational alternative to the indigenous fuel cycle. This would entail the creation of regional or international fuel cycle centers, either through the conversion of existing national facilities in the case of regions where such facilities exist, or through the construction of new facilities. Such centers could be developed on the Eurodif model, whereby recipient states would have an equity share in the facility but would not have access to sensitive technologies. Alternatively, they could be developed on the Urenco model that would permit members to share resources, access to technologies, and expertise on the fuel cycle. Clearly, on the basis of the course of the Iranian nuclear dispute, the United States and Europe would strongly prefer the Eurodif model while most developing countries would prefer the Urenco model. These issues would need to be tackled in the event that such multinational fuel cycle centers are adopted as a solution for meeting the increasing energy needs of developing countries while addressing concerns about the dual-use potential of sensitive enrichment technologies.

CONCLUSION: IRAN AND THE DAMAGE TO THE NONPROLIFERATION REGIME

The Iranian case has drawn attention to an issue that has been of concern to nonproliferation advocates for years—the potential to develop a civilian nuclear energy program in compliance with the NPT and then exploit the dual-use nature of nuclear fuel cycle technology to acquire a latent weapons capacity or to develop a physical arsenal. Most commentators have focused on this aspect of the Iranian case, however, to the exclusion of other, less apparent damage that has been done to the nonproliferation regime as a result of the handling of the Iranian case since 2002.

The basic bargain underlying the nonproliferation regime—already under assault as a result of nuclear weapon states' failure to disarm and the limitations on meaningful civilian nuclear energy cooperation between the weapons states and the nonweapons states—was dealt another blow as the right to civilian nuclear energy programs for nonweapons states was called into question. The energy needs of the developing world in the next century are clearly going to require the rapid development of alternatives to fossil fuel consumption. The energy needs of the developing world are therefore setting the stage for a century in which the expansion of the use nuclear energy is a near certainty.

Under these circumstances, the developing world is watching the course of the Iranian case very closely to determine the extent to which the Iranian precedent will limit their rights under Article IV of the NPT. To the extent that the developing world perceives a new form of discrimination being introduced to the NPT regime—one that distinguishes between states permitted to have a nuclear fuel cycle and others—the costs of membership in the NPT may come to be perceived as outweighing the benefits. Particularly when set beside the nuclear weapon states record of compliance with their disarmament commitments, and more recent developments in which some states are even considering expanding and modernizing their existing nuclear arsenals, further restrictions on the rights of nonweapons states under the NPT regime may undermine its legitimacy and credibility in much of the developing world. Should the current crisis with Iran result in an Iranian withdrawal from the NPT, the regime may not be able to withstand the damage associated with such a precedent. The worst fears of nonproliferation experts that the Iranian case might trigger a cascade proliferation effect, particularly in the Middle East, would then become far more plausible. As a result, the stakes of promoting a nuclear-free Middle East are higher today, perhaps, than they have ever been. Yet the prospects for a WMD-free zone in the region are grim.

For this reason, it is imperative to find a way to resolve the conflict over the Iranian nuclear file within the NPT framework. The recent moves to shift the Iranian file permanently to the Security Council are unhelpful in this regard. The council has already been weakened by the course of the military intervention in Iraq and the *ex post* UN imprimatur that was provided for the ensuing occupation. The council may be further weakened if it is perceived as an enforcement agent for American policy preferences in the Iranian case. Further, as discussed above, the council is not an attractive forum for resolving the Iranian crisis precisely because there are no good options available to the council for action to unblock the current impasse. Moving the Iranian file to the council absent an IAEA report that Iran is in violation of its Article II obligations under the NPT (to forgo acquisition or production of nuclear weapons) is premature and counterproductive.

Instead of continuing to take a relatively ad hoc approach to the Iranian case, it would be far more beneficial to view the Iranian case in the context of a broader effort to strengthen the NPT monitoring and inspections system as well as nonweapons states' incentives to remain within the treaty regime. In the words of former UN Secretary General Kofi Annan, "we cannot continue to lurch from crisis to crisis, until the regime is buried beneath a cascade of proliferation."[222]

The Iranian case represents both a serious risk to the nonproliferation regime and an important opportunity. Should the Iranian nuclear dispute ultimately escalate to the point that unilateral or multilateral military intervention is undertaken, it will likely be viewed, together with the invasion of Iraq, by much of the developing world as another instance of regime change under the pretext of arms control concerns. A military intervention to resolve the Iranian nuclear dispute will at best delay an Iranian nuclear capability while risking the unraveling of the international nonproliferation system. Similarly, by prolonging the delay in negotiations and insisting on preconditions while the Iranian nuclear program continues to progress, many NAM states may conclude that the real concerns of the United States and other parties to the negotiations are not related to proliferation but rather to regime type.

The conflation of regime change objectives with nonproliferation policy gives rise to an appearance of politicization in the nonproliferation regime, which may ultimately undermine its authority. Further, in the context of continuing international speculation about a military option against Iran, Iranian allegations that international inspections are being used for the purpose of covert intelligence gathering are also damaging the reputation of the IAEA.[223] Finally, the insistence that IAEA inspections must prove a negative—that there are not and have never been undeclared nuclear activities in a given country—that may require inspections beyond the scope of the Additional Protocol, demands a level of certainty that may undermine the sustainability of monitoring mechanisms as a reliable method of arms control. To base international nonproliferation concerns on intentions or regime type rather than actual activities is to invite the kind of bottomless inspections that left inspectors unable to certify the absence of a serious WMD program in Iraq long after they had reached a reasonable level of certainty that the country posed neither a conventional nor unconventional weapons threat. The risk of the Iranian case is not only that Iran might actually engage in proliferation but also that the measures taken to prevent Iranian proliferation will ultimately damage and undermine the nonproliferation regime itself.

Particularly in light of these risks, treating the Iranian case as an opportunity to move toward a proliferation-resistant global nuclear fuel cycle is the best alternative to the present course. By putting the emphasis on long-term solutions applicable beyond the Iranian case, a more sustainable approach to strengthening the regime as a whole may be possible. A good interim solution for the current Iranian crisis would be to limit the Iranian nuclear program to a highly restricted open fuel cycle, operating a pilot number of cascades under a tight monitoring mechanism, while providing assurances of fuel supply access, strong support from the United States and Europe, and security guarantees. But the long-term emphasis should be on a broader approach. Working toward a proliferation-resistant fuel cycle regime at the international level will require a balanced and nondiscriminatory approach. Within Iran's own region, such an approach would also have to bear in mind the present threat perceptions of the states of the region. Developing a multilateral fuel cycle solution in the Middle East will only be feasible if it is accompanied by a commitment to achieving a WMD-free zone in the region and bringing all states in the region within the NPT framework. Otherwise, incentives to defect will remain difficult to deter.

By most estimates, Iran remains at least a decade away from being able to enrich sufficient quantities of uranium for militarized use—the international community should pursue a nonconfrontational solution to the problem while time still permits. One key will be shifting Iran's threat perception both by providing it with security guarantees and by abandoning an approach that sets the Iranian case apart from all others. The IAEA's director general has publicly argued that the international community must "abandon unworkable notions that it is morally reprehensible for some countries to pursue nuclear weapons but morally acceptable for others to rely on them for security—and indeed continue to refine their capacities and postulate plans for their use."[224] Policymakers reviewing options for dealing with the Iranian case when it is next raised before the IAEA board of governors or the Security Council would do well to heed this cautionary advice. The doctrine of preemption, even where designed to curtail proliferation, will in all likelihood exacerbate proliferation as other states seek to acquire weapons to deter preemption. Rather than adopting a confrontational approach that may stimulate proliferation, the Iranian case presents an important opportunity for the international community to find a diplomatic solution within the NPT framework and to develop multilateral approaches to the management of the global fuel cycle.

NOTES

1. See, for example, David E. Sanger, "Month of Talks Fails to Bolster Treaty," *The New York Times*, May 28, 2005 at A1 (noting that the "month-long conference at the United Nations to strengthen the Nuclear Nonproliferation Treaty ended Friday in failure, with its chairman declaring that the disagreements between nuclear-armed and non-nuclear states ran so deep that 'very little has been accomplished'").

2. See Suzanne DiMaggio, "US-Iran Disagreements Play a Part in NPT Deadlock," *InterDependent* (Fall 2005) (United Nations Association of the United States of America [UNA-USA]), available at http://www.unausa.org/site/apps/s/content. asp?c=fvKRI8MPJpF&b=369041&ct=1460711.

3. The NCRI is an Iranian opposition group operating in exile and affiliated with the *Mujahideen el-Khalq* organization, based in Iraq. For the series of IAEA reports on inspection and monitoring of Iran's enrichment facilities, see www.iaea.org/ NewsCenter/Focus/IaeaIran/index.shtml.

4. It is worth noting that reprocessing plants, used to separate plutonium out of spent fuel, raise similar problems. Plutonium separated from spent field can be mixed with uranium and recycled as fuel for nuclear power reactors. However, separated plutonium can also be used for nuclear weapons purposes. Because plutonium recycling is not economical it is a less popular avenue, though some states have reprocessing facilities in order to avoid the environmental concerns raised by long-term spent fuel storage. Among non-nuclear weapon states, only Japan has both enrichment and reprocessing facilities.

5. Brazil's program was originally developed to provide fuel for its naval nuclear reactor and its now-defunct nuclear weapons program. South Africa's facility was also originally designed to provide weapon-grade uranium for its now-abandoned nuclear weapons program, as well as for its energy needs.

6. On the NCRI revelations of 2002, see, for example, Sharon Squassoni, "Iran's Nuclear Program: Recent Developments," CRS Report for Congress, *Congressional Research Service*, August 2, 2005.

7. Statement of the vice president of the Islamic Republic of Iran and president of the Atomic Energy Organization of Iran (AEOI), H.E. Mr. Reza Aghazadeh, cited in, *Implementation of the NPT safeguards agreement in the Islamic Republic of Iran*, Report by the Director General, GOV/2003/40, June 6, 2003, at para. 2.

8. See, for example, *Implementation of the NPT Safeguards Agreement in the Islamic Republic of Iran*, Report by the Director General, GOV/2003/40, June 6, 2003, at paras. 25–31.

9. The IAEA did cite five instances of reporting violations unrelated to the two sites. These violations were (1) failure to report the import of natural uranium in 1991; (2) failure to declare activities involving the use of that natural uranium; (3) failure to declare the facilities where these materials had been stored and processed (in Tehran and Isfahan); (4) failure to provide updated design information for two facilities in Tehran; and (5) failure to provide timely information concerning waste storage. *Implementation of the NPT Safeguards Agreement in the Islamic Republic of Iran*, Report by the Director General, GOV/2003/40, June 6, 2003 (hereafter "IAEA June 2003 Report") at para. 32.

10. It is important to bear in mind when assessing this record, as described in the following subsection, that none of these activities are in and of themselves prohibited under the NPT and the related Safeguards Agreements. Nor do any of these activities necessarily go beyond the requirements of a civilian energy production program. The violations of Iran's obligations are, to date, limited to *reporting* violations. Had these activities been conducted with notification to the IAEA they would not have been considered problematic from an NPT perspective. However, as Iran has consistently argued, the activities would have been deemed problematic for political reasons because the United States has opposed the provision of nuclear technologies to Iran since the early 1990s and has repeatedly pressured foreign suppliers to cancel contracts or penalized them with sanctions. As a result, while none of Iran's activities would have been proscribed legally had they been reported to the IAEA, Iran alleges that it was forced to conduct these activities clandestinely because they would not have been feasible otherwise for geopolitical reasons. Bearing in mind the distinction between the legality of the underlying activity and the obligation to report the activity is important in assessing the seriousness of Iranian violations.

11. For example, the director general of the IAEA, Mohamed ElBaradei, voiced his hope that all parties "will go back to the negotiating table" following the first suggestion that the UN Security Council might become involved following the September IAEA board resolution. Mark Landler "Nuclear Agency Votes to Report Iran to UN Security Council for Treaty Violations," *New York Times*, September 25, 2005, at Sec. 1, p. 6.

12. For a discussion of the efforts in the late 1980s to find a partner to restart work at Bushehr, see Andrew Koch and Jeanette Wolf, "Iran's Nuclear Facilities: A Profile," Center for Nonproliferation Studies (1998), *available at* http://www. iran-e-sabz.org/news/nuc1a.htm. In one example, there were numerous reports that Iran had approached Kazakhstan following an Iranian visit to the Ulba Metallurgival Plant, for the purchase of highly enriched uranium (HEU) or for the purchase of parts toward the completion of the Bushehr facility. Discovery of the Iranian interest in Ulba by U.S. officials prompted immediate American requests to the Kazakh government to block any transactions with Iran and ultimately resulted in an agreement through which the United States bought all of the Ulba HEU inventory by 1994. David Alrbight, "An Iranian bomb?" *Bulletin of the Atomic Scientist,* 51.4 (July/August 1995), pp. 20–26, at 20. See, also, Christina Lamb, "Brazilian Nuclear Deal Row," *Financial Times,* December 5, 1991, at p. 6 (noting that in the face of U.S. protests, a Brazilian report of a potential reactor sale to Iran had been retracted).

13. Comments by a senior Iranian official, October 2005 (on file with author). This observation is reinforced with the difficulty Iran has had recouping on its $1 billion investment in the Eurodif enrichment plant, which was made under an agreement that Iran would be given access to a uranium enrichment supply from the facility. Iran has sought the return of its investment in the uranium enrichment plant constructed by the French nuclear energy commission for the Eurodif consortium, and France has sought payment for the cancellation of its Shah-era contracts with Iran for the provision of two reactors. The proceedings did not result in a settlement and Iran now invokes the example of its blocked Eurodif investment as a reason that it cannot trust that it will be given open market access to nuclear fuel and must therefore develop an indigenous nuclear fuel cycle. On the Eurodif dispute, see, for example, George Graham, "Tehran Wins Ruling in French Nuclear Dispute," *Financial Times,* February 4, 1991, at p. 4; and William Dawkins, "France, Iran near Contracts Accord," *Financial Times,* October 26, 1991, at p. 3.

14. Comments by a senior Iranian official, October 2005 (on file with author).

15. The acquisition of a light water reactor is widely acknowledged to have little potential to contribute to efforts to develop a nuclear weapons program. For instance, proliferation specialist with the Center for Strategic and International Studies, Anthony Cordesman, has written that "the reactor design Russia is selling Iran produces only very limited amounts of plutonium, and no country has as yet used a similar reactor design to acquire fissile material." Anthony Cordesman, "Iran and Nuclear Weapons: A Working Draft," Center for Strategic and International Studies, February 21, 2000, *available at* http://www.csis.org/media/csis/pubs/ irannuclear.pdf, at p. 15.

16. For the text of the Paris Agreement, see IAEA INFCIRC/637 (Communication Dated 26 November 2004. Received from the Permanent Representatives of France, Germany, the Islamic Republic of Iran, and the United Kingdom concerning the agreement signed in Paris on November 16, 2004), *available at* http://www.iaea.org/Publications/Documents/Infcircs/2004/infcirc637.pdf. The Paris Agreement succeeded the earlier Tehran Agreement of October 21, 2003, setting forth a more detailed mutual understanding of the specific obligations of the Iranian government in its suspension of uranium enrichment activities as a confidence-building measure during the course of its negotiations with the EU-3.

17. David E. Sanger, "U.S. Is Punishing Eight Chinese Firms for Aiding Iran," *New York Times,* January 17, 2005, at p. A6.

18. It is worth noting that these efforts also strengthened Iranian arguments that an independent nuclear fuel cycle is necessary to its national interests because Iran

cannot rely on international markets and cooperation to meet its energy needs. Analysts have noted that U.S. efforts to block Iranian acquisition of nuclear technologies from third parties may have contributed to the Iranian decision to pursue an indigenous fuel cycle. See, for example, George Perkovich, Testimony before the United States Foreign Relations Committee, May 19, 2005, at p. 10.

19. Steven R. Weisman, Elaine Sciolino, and David E. Sanger, "Rice Says U.S. Won't Aid Europe on Plans for Incentives to Iran," *New York Times*, February 4, 2005, at p. A1.

20. Comments by a senior Iranian official, October 2005 (on file with author).

21. "Iran Offers 'Objective Guarantees' on Nuclear Program, But No End to Uranium Enrichment," *Global Security Newswire*, March 17, 2005, *available at* http://www.nti.org/d_newswire/issues/2005_3_17.html#8C76AC79.

22. Elaine Sciolino, "Nuclear Accord Eludes Iran and Europeans," *New York Times*, March 24, 2005, at p. A12.

23. Comments by a senior Iranian official, October 2005 (on file with author).

24. Sciolino, "Nuclear Accord Eludes Iran and Europeans," *supra* note 22.

25. The Iranian government has made all of the Iranian proposals that were provided to the EU-3 prior to August 2005 available through the UN in a single consolidated document that also includes numerous Iranian official statements and publications on their nuclear program. These documents are available at http://www.un.int/iran/facts_about_peaceful_nuclear_program.pdf.

26. Dafna Linzer, "Europeans Agree to Meeting with Iran on Nuclear Program," *Washington Post*, May 17, 2005, at p. A14 ("If Iran is not dissuaded from resuming the nuclear work, U.S. and European officials said its program will become the subject of discussion inside the U.N. Security Council, which can impose sanctions.").

27. "Message from Dr. Rohani to E3/EU Ministers," July 18, 2005, *available at* http://www.un.int/iran/facts_about_peaceful_nuclear_program.pdf. The emphasis in the discussions surrounding the delivery of the proposal was described by a senior Iranian official in an interview with the author, October 2005 (on file with author).

28. In one article, European diplomats report that upon telling Rowhani that "they hadn't nailed down exactly what they could offer in return for a freeze, and the Americans still weren't fully onboard," that Rowhani "'was in front of us sweating,' says the European diplomat. 'He was trapped: he couldn't go further...Psychologically he was broken. Physically he was almost broken.'" Michael Hirsh and Maziar Bahari, "Blowup? America's Hidden War with Iran," *Newsweek*, February 19, 2007.

29. Nazila Fathi and Alan Cowell, "Iran Says It Will Resume Uranium Enrichment, Jeopardizing Nuclear Talks with Europe," *New York Times*, August 1, 2005, at p. A8; Nazila Fathi and Thomas Fuller, "Iran Reopens Uranium Processing Plant as UN Agency Meets," *New York Times*, August 11, 2005, at p. A3.

30. The EU-3 counterproposal was then communicated to the IAEA on August 8, 2005. IAEA INFCIRC/651 (Communication Dated August 8, 2005 received from the Resident Representatives of France, Germany, and the United Kingdom to the IAEA), *available at* http://www.iaea.org/Publications/Documents/Infcircs/2005/infcirc651.pdf.

31. Response of the Islamic Republic of Iran to the Framework Agreement Proposed by the EU3/EU, *available at* http://www.acronym.org.uk/docs/0508/doc03.htm#iran The Iranian response opens with the statement that the "proposal presented by the E3/EU on August 5, 2005 is a clear violation of international law and the Charter of the UN, the NPT, the Tehran Statement and the Paris Agreement of November 15, 2004." It closes with the statement that the proposal "amounts to an insult on the Iranian nation, for which the E3 must apologize."

32. John Burroughs, Michael Spies, Peter Weiss, and Jacqueline Cabasso, "Letter to IAEA Board Opposing Referral to the Security Council," January 23, 2006, *available at* http://www.lcnp.org/disarmament/iaea_letter-jan06.htm.

33. The language of "reporting" rather than referral was adopted because Russia and other countries insisted that the IAEA retain its control over the Iranian nuclear file, providing information to the Security Council but not relinquishing its authority over the case. American diplomats have cast doubt on the difference between referral and reporting and suggest that regardless of the language, authority over the Iranian compliance with the NPT has now transferred to the Security Council. It is likely that there have been significant closed-door negotiations between the United States and Russian and Chinese officials over the scope of action that may be taken by the council when it receives the IAEA's report on Iranian compliance in March. It is not clear at this point whether the distinction between reporting and referral will make any material difference in the options available to the council.

34. One reason that the Russians and Chinese may have sought to delay any council consideration of the matter until March may have been to avoid having the issue arise during the American presidency of the council with Ambassador John Bolton presiding. Argentina will hold the presidency of the council in March and will be seen as a less ideologically and politically invested actor in this issue. In addition, of course, the delay was designed to create additional time and pressure for Iran to accept a version of the open Russian proposal to engage in a joint venture with Iran to enrich uranium in Russia and transfer the nuclear fuel to Iran.

35. See, for example, "US Warns India over Iran Stance," *BBC*, January 25, 2006, *available at* http://news.bbc.co.uk/2/hi/south_asia/4647956.stm.

36. Elaine Sciolino, "Dispute over Israel Delays Vote on Iran Nuclear Resolution," *New York Times*, February 4, 2006.

37. IAEA GOV/2006/14 (February 4, 2006), *available at* http://www.iaea.org/Publications/Documents/Board/2006/gov2006-14.pdf. The five abstentions were Algeria, Belarus, Indonesia, Libya, and South Africa.

38. As one of its early confidence-building measures, Iran signed the Additional Protocol—which provides for a greater scope of inspections and verification of compliance than required under the Safeguards Agreement. While the Iranian Parliament has refused to ratify the Additional Protocol, Iran had voluntarily complied with its requirements as if it were in effect from 2003 until February 2006.

39. On the NPT withdrawal threat, see "Iran 'could quit nuclear treaty," *BBC*, February 11, 2006, *available at* http://news.bbc.co.uk/2/hi/middle_east/4703434.stm; on Iranian willingness to resume spot inspections, see Steven R. Weisman, "Iran Hints at Compromise on Nuclear Inspections," *New York Times*, February 18, 2006.

40. Steven Lee Myers, "Russian Talks with Iran on Nuclear Program Stall," *New York Times*, February 20, 2006. The article also notes that while negotiations might resume before the end of February during a visit to Iran by Sergei Kiriyenko, the head of Russia's nuclear agency. However, Iranian negotiators noted that progress over the Russian proposal would, in any event, be insufficient to head off a confrontation with the IAEA and the Security Council over Iran's nuclear program in March.

41. Ian Traynor, "Iran and Russia Reach Tenuous Deal on Nuclear Programmes," *The Guardian*, February 27, 2006, *available at* http://www.guardian.co.uk/iran/story/0,,1718633,00.html.

42. Glenn Kessler, "U.S., Russia Cooperate on Iran amid Rifts," *Washington Post*, March 8, 2006, at p. A14.

43. Elaine Sciolino, "Threats Rattle at Nuclear Meeting on Iran," *New York Times*, March 9, 2006.

44. Warren Hoge, "UN Council to Chastise Iran But May Sidestep Sanctions," *New York Times*, March 10, 2006.

45. Mark John, "US Still Expects UN Statement on Iran—Envoy," *Reuters*, March 22, 2006, noting that Greg Schulte, the U.S. representative to the IAEA, had reduced expectations from a resolution to a statement.

46. S/PRST/2006/15 (2006) (March 29, 2006), *available at* http://daccessdds.un.org/doc/UNDOC/GEN/N06/290/88/PDF/N0629088.pdf?OpenElement.

47. Seymour Hersh, "The Iran Plans," *The New Yorker*, April 17, 2006.

48. Hersh, "The Iran Plans," *supra* note 47.

49. "Sanctions against Iran 'Bad Idea,'" *BBC*, March 30, 3006, *available at* http://news.bbc.co.uk/1/hi/world/middle_east/4862912.stm.

50. Various reports on the creation of these programs and their purpose to monitor Iran and open communication channels with domestic opponents of the regime were reported beginning in the early spring of 2006. See, for example, Elise Labott, "U.S. to Sharpen Focus on Iran: Office of Iranian Affairs to 'Facilitate Change in Iranian Policies,'" *CNN*, March 2, 2006, *available at* http://www.cnn.com/2006/POLITICS/03/02/us.iran/index.html; Laura Rozen, "U.S. Moves to Weaken Iran," *L.A. Times*, May 19, 2006; and Hassan M. Fattah, "US Keeps Finger on Pulse of Iran From Dubai," *International Herald Tribune*, November 20, 2006, *available at* http://www.iht.com/articles/2006/11/20/news/dubai.php.

51. Nazila Fathi, David E. Sanger, and William J. Broad, "Iran Reports Big Advance in Enrichment of Uranium," *New York Times*, April 12, 2006, at p. A1.

52. William J. Broad, Nazila Fathi, and Joel Brinkley, "Analysts Say a Nuclear Iran Is Years Away," *New York Times*, April 13, 2006, at p. A1.

53. IAEA GOV/2006/27 (April 28, 2006), *available at* http://www.iaea.org/Publications/Documents/Board/2006/gov2006-27.pdf.

54. For an account of an Iranian letter to the IAEA confirming that cooperation would be curtailed so long as the Iranian file remained before the Security Council, see Elaine Sciolino, "UN Agency Says Iran Falls Short on Nuclear Data," *New York Times*, April 29, 2006, at p. A1.

55. Colum Lynch, "Security Council Is Given Iran Resolution; Pressure Builds to End Tehran's Nuclear Efforts," *Washington Post*, May 4, 2006, at p. A18.

56. Philippe Naughton, "Iran Ready for Dialogue 'with Anybody,'" *Times (UK)*, May 11, 2006, *available at* http://www.timesonline.co.uk/article/0,,251-2175827,00.html.

57. Secretary of State Condoleezza Rice, "Press Conference on Iran," May 31, 2006, *available at* http://www.state.gov/secretary/rm/2006/67103.htm.

58. Thom Shanker and Elaine Sciolino, "Package of Terms (No Sanctions Included) for Iran," *New York Times*, June 2, 2006, at p. A12.

59. Glenn Kessler, "Rice Key to Reversal on Iran: Expected Failure of International Effort Led to US Turnaround," *Washington Post*, June 4, 2006, at p. A17.

60. "Elements of a Revised Proposal to Iran Made by the E3+3," Ministere des Affaires Etrangeres, Republique Francaise, *available at* http://www.diplomatie.gouv.fr/en/article-imprim.php3?id_article=5314.

61. The terms of the leaked draft, which was originally made available to ABC News, and subsequently published by the British American Security Information Council (BASIC), can be found as an Appendix to BASIC's analysis of the leaked document. Ian Davis and Paul Ingram, "New Proposal to Iran: Will It Be Enough to Defuse the Nuclear Crisis?" *BASIC Notes*, June 9, 2006, *available at* http://www.basicint.org/pubs/Notes,BN060609.pdf.

62. Helene Cooper and Nazila Fathi, "Iran Gets Deadline to Respond to Deal on Ending Enrichment," *New York Times*, June 10, 2006, at p. A3.
63. The spring revelations of renewed American regime change initiatives and possible military planning for airstrikes would only have reinforced the urgency of Iran's need for security guarantees.
64. Helene Cooper, "Diplomats Push Iran to Reply Soon to Incentives Offer," *New York Times*, June 30, 2006, at p. A3.
65. On the absence of consensus within Iran as an obstacle to providing a response by the deadline, see Elaine Sciolino, "At Europeans' Talks with Tehran about Its Nuclear Future, a Familiar Impasse Endures," *New York Times*, July 12, 2006, at p. A12.
66. Warren Hoge, "UN Moves toward Vote on Iran's Atom Program," *New York Times*, July 29, 2006, at p. A3.
67. NSC S/RES/1696 (2006) (July 31, 2006), *available at* http://daccessdds.un.org/doc/UNDOC/GEN/N06/450/22/PDF/N0645022.pdf?OpenElement.
68. For a detailed analysis of the shortcoming of the resolution, see Michael Spies and John Burroughs, "Commentary on Security Council Resolution 1696 on Iran," Lawyer's Committee on Nuclear Policy, July 31, 2006, *available at* http://www.lcnp.org/disarmament/iran/UNSCres-jul06.htm.
69. Seymour Hersh, "Watching Lebanon: Washington's Interest in Israel's War," *The New Yorker*, August 14, 2006, *available at* http://www.lcnp.org/disarmament/iran/UNSCres-jul06.htm.
70. Michael Slackman, "Iran Won't Give Promise to End Uranium Effort," *New York Times*, August 23, 2006, at p. A1.
71. Helene Cooper, "US Says Iranian Nuclear Proposal Is Inadequate," *New York Times*, August 24, 2006, at p. A12.
72. Solana reportedly commented that the Iranian counterproposal document was "'extensive' and required 'a detailed and careful analysis.'" "Iran Offers West 'Serious' Talks," *BBC*, August 22, 2006.
73. The full text of the Iranian counteroffer was made available on the Institute for Science and International Security website at http://www.isis-online.org/publications/iran/responsetext.pdf.
74. In the words of one author: "While the United States and its European allies appear to be united in the notion that the next step should be to impose penalties on Iran through the Security Council, Russia and China remain question marks.... 'The game is about appearing to be reasonable,' [a] Bush official said." Helene Cooper, "In Muted Response to Iran, US and Allies Seek Edge," *New York Times*, August 25, 2006, at p. A8.
75. David E. Sanger, "Nuclear Agency for UN Faults Report on Iran by US House," *New York Times*, September 15, 2006, at p. A3.
76. Dafna Linzer, "UN Inspectors Dispute Iran Report by House Panel," *Washington Post*, September 14, 2006, at p. A17.
77. NAM 2006/Doc.1/Rev.3. Final Document of the Fourteenth NAM Summit in Havana Cuba, paras. 74–76, September 16, 2006, *available at* http://www.cubanoal.cu/ingles/index.html.
78. Bernard Gwertzman, "Ahmadinejad Spars with CFR members," Council on Foreign Relations, September 20, 2006, *available at* http://www.cfr.org/publication/11498/ahmadinejad_spars_with_cfr_members.html. Later, Ahmadinejad again seized an opportunity to bypass American officials and try to reach the American public with an open letter in late November 2006. Michael Slackman, "Iran's President Criticizes Bush in Letter to American People," *New York Times*, November 30, 2006, at p. A1.

79. Glenn Kessler and Dafna Linzer, "Brief Nuclear Halt May Lead to Talks with Iran; Rice Suggests Temporary Move Could Be Enough," *Washington Post*, September 12, 2006, at p. A20.

80. Colum Lynch, "Iran Open to a Break in Nuclear Program; But Ahmadinejad Demands 'Fair, Just' Conditions for Talks," *Washington Post*, September 22, 2006, at p. A13.

81. David Ignatius, "Iran's Uranium Glitch; Technical Troubles Offer Time for Diplomacy," *Washington Post*, September 29, 2006, at p. A21.

82. Ronny Sofer, "Olmert Urges Action against Iran," *Yediot Aharonoth (Israel)*, October 12, 2006, *available at* http://www.ynetnews.com/articles/0,7340, L-3314124,00.html.

83. Barry Schweid, "Bush Calls for Global Isolation of Iran," *San Francisco Chronicle*, November 13, 2006, *available at* http://www.sfgate.com/cgi-bin/article.cgi?f=/ n/a/2006/11/13/national/w100832S24.DTL&type=politics.

84. David Ignatius reported in the *Washington Post* that Iran had been circulating a copy of the so-called "Gentleman's Agreement" in late February in an attempt to restart talks, but that the issue of suspension as a precondition continued to be an obstacle to negotiations. The language of a "partial suspension" may refer to Iranian proposals to run centrifuges in a vacuum without feeding any gas stock and thus not actually engaging in enrichment. It is also doubtful that such a "partial" suspension would satisfy American demands. David Ignatius, "Signals from Tehran," *Washington Post*, February 23, 2007, at p. A19.

85. Philip Shenon, "US Says It Has Deal with Other UN Members to Penalize Iran for Nuclear Drive," *New York Times*, October 7, 2006, at p. A6.

86. Nazila Fathi, "Using a Second Network, Iran Raises Enrichment Ability," *New York Times*, October 28, 2006, at p. A5.

87. IAEA GOV/2006/64 (2006) (November 14, 2006), *available at* http://www. iaea.org/Publications/Documents/Board/2006/gov2006-64.pdf.

88. Nazila Fathi, "Iran Revolutionary Guards Hold War Games after US Exercise," *New York Times*, November 3, 2006, at p. A12.

89. Nazila Fathi, "Iran Criticizes Security Council over Threat of Sanctions," *New York Times*, November 13, 2006, at p. A15.

90. "Iran to Let Atomic Watchdog Take More Samples," *Reuters*, November 28, 2006, *available at* http://news.yahoo.com/s/nm/20061128/wl_nm/iran_ nuclear_iaea_dc_4.

91. George Jahn, "Iran Offers Look at Uranium Program," *Associated Press*, November 23, 2006, *available at* http://news.yahoo.com/s/ap/20061123/ ap_on_re_mi_ea/nuclear_agency_iran_4.

92. "IAEA Likely to Block Aid for Iran Nuclear Reactor," *Agence France Presse*, November 20, 2006 (citing Cetto's comments that "the aid projects Iran seeks, including Arak, waste disposal, cancer therapy and human resource development, conformed to the relevant Security Council Resolution. 'Specifically, these projects do not contribute to enrichment-related or reprocessing activities in Iran,' Cetto said"). While the board did not technically reject the request but postponed consideration of it, permitting Iran to subsequently resubmit the request in 2008 or thereafter, the clear outcome was that the board would not permit the agency to provide safety expertise in regard to the development of the facility as a result of the proliferation concerns of America and its European allies. Michael Adler, "UN Agency Shelves Iranian Reactor Request," *Agence France Presse*, November 23, 2006.

93. Seymour Hersh, "The Next Act: Is a Damaged Administration Less Likely to Attack Iran, or More?" *The New Yorker*, November 20, 2006, *available at* http:// www.newyorker.com/printables/fact/061127fa_fact.

94. For a full transcript of Robert Gates' testimony at his confirmation hearing, see "Transcript: Confirmation Hearing of Robert Gates to Be Secretary of Defense," *Congressional Quarterly Transcripts Wire*, December 5, 2006, *available at* http://media.washingtonpost.com/wp-srv/politics/documents/rgates_hearing_120506.html. Gates had earlier chaired the Council on Foreign Relations task force that published a report in 2004 calling for selective engagement with Iran in areas where such engagement would better serve American national interests than a policy of nonengagement. Zbigniew Brzezinski and Robert Gates, cochairs, *Iran: Time for a New Approach* (New York: Council on Foreign Relations Press, July 2004). While his assessment of the prospects for selective engagement may have been altered by subsequent domestic changes in Iran with the election of President Ahmadinejad in 2005, his openness to the prospect in 2004, at a time when the Bush administration was equally reluctant to engage with Iran, is nonetheless indicative of a more balanced perspective.

95. The ISG, also known as the Baker-Hamilton Commission, made the report available in a print edition and also in a PDF version through the United States Institute of Peace website. James A. Baker III and Lee H. Hamilton, cochairs, *The Iraq Study Group Report: The Way Forward—A New Approach* (New York: Vintage Books, 2006), *available at* http://www.usip.org/isg/iraq_study_group_report/report/1206/. The other members of the bipartisan ISG were Lawrence Eagleburger, Vernon Jordan, Edwin Meese, Sandra Day O'Connor, Leon Panetta, William Perry, Charles Robb, and Alan Simpson. Robert Gates resigned as a member of the ISG on November 8, 2006, when he was nominated to be Secretary of Defense. It is, however, widely believed that he endorsed most of the views forwarded in the ISG recommendations.

96. Peter Barker and Robin Wright, "Bush Appears Cool to Key Points of Report on Iraq," *Washington Post*, December 8, 2006, at p. A1 (noting that the president "repeated his refusal to talk with Iran...unless Tehran suspends its uranium-enrichment program" during a press conference with British Prime Minister Tony Blair).

97. Edmund Blair, "Results in Iranian Vote Seen as Setback for Ahmadinejad," *Washington Post*, December 18, 2006, at p. A19. The Assembly of Experts is a congressional, directly elected body that oversees the selection of the Iranian Supreme Leader. In the elections for the assembly, it was particularly notable that former Iranian President Hashemi Rafsanjani, who was defeated in the 2005 presidential election by Ahmadinejad won twice as many votes as Ayatollah Mohamed Taqi Mesbah Yazdi, a hard-line cleric who is widely seen as Ahmadinejad's spiritual adviser. In total, of the 86-member assembly, 65 of the elected candidates were known to be close to the Rafsanjani bloc, giving pragmatic conservatives over 75 percent of the assembly. With a high voter turnout of over 60 percent, these results were widely interpreted as a serious rebuke of President Ahmadinejad's policies.

98. The adoption of the sanctions was confirmed in a UN press release. "Security Council Imposes Sanctions on Iran for Failure to Halt Uranium Enrichment, Unanimously Adopting Resolution 1737," United Nations Department of Public Information, December 23, 2006 (Security Council 5612th Meeting [AM]), SC/8928, *available at* http://www.un.org/News/Press/docs/2006/sc8928.doc.htm (includes full text of the resolution and statements issued by permanent representatives to the UN of the nations on the Security Council as well as the statement of Iranian UN ambassador Javad Zarif).

99. UNSC S/RES/1737 (2006) (hereafter UNSC 1737). paras. 2(a) and 2(b) (December 23, 2006), *available at* http://daccessdds.un.org/doc/UNDOC/GEN/N06/681/42/PDF/N0668142.pdf?OpenElement.

100. UNSC 1737, paras. 3, 4, 5, 6, and 7.

101. Ibid., para. 12.

102. Ibid., para. 3.

103. Ibid., para. 8.

104. Ibid., paras 10 and 17.

105. The bill passed in record time and with 161 votes in favor to only 15 votes against and 15 abstentions. The overwhelming Iranian domestic consensus in favor of resisting coercive measures designed to force a suspension of the nuclear program once again confirm analysts' views that a resolution to international concerns over the Iranian nuclear program is only possible through direct engagement and negotiations. See Nazila Fathi, "Iran Parliament Limits Nuclear Cooperation with UN," *New York Times*, December 28, 2006.

106. George W. Bush, President's Address to the Nation, White House Office of the Press Secretary, January 10, 2007, *available at* http://www.whitehouse.gov/news/releases/2007/01/20070110-7.html.

107. George W. Bush, State of the Union 2007, White House Office of the Press Secretary, January 23, 2007, *available at* http://www.whitehouse.gov/news/releases/2007/01/20070123-2.html.

108. Dafna Linzer, "Troops Authorized to Kill Iranian Operatives in Iraq," *Washington Post*, January 26, 2007, at p. A1. The policy apparently replaced an earlier "capture and release" policy whereby U.S. forces had earlier been permitted to detain Iranian "operatives" found in Iraq and subject them to DNA sampling retina scans, fingerprinting, and photographing before releasing them as part of a policy to intimidate Iranian emissaries in Iraq. The *Washington Post* reported, however, that a decision was taken in the summer of 2006 to take a more confrontational approach to counter growing Iranian regional influence. That decision apparently laid the groundwork for adoption of the new "kill or capture" policy.

109. Dafna Linzer, "Troops Authorized to Kill Iranian Operatives in Iraq," *supra* note 108.

110. For a description of the president's interview on NPR, see "Bush Warns Iran Against Action in Iraq," *Associated Press*, January 29, 2007.

111. Richard Wolffe, "Exclusive Q&A: Dick Cheney, Man without Doubt," *Newsweek*, February 5, 2007 Issue (the interview was published by the magazine's website on January 28, 2007). The full transcript of the interview was made available on the *Newsweek* website at http://www.msnbc.msn.com/16843459/site/newsweek/. In the interview, Cheney goes on to comment that the presence of two American aircraft carrier groups in the Gulf demonstrates that the United States is in the region "to stay, that we clearly have significant capabilities and that we are working with friends and allies as well as the international organizations to deal with the Iranian threat."

112. Senate Foreign Relations Committee Hearing on Iraq, Opening remarks by Secretary of State Condoleezza Rice, Congressional Quarterly Transcript, January 11, 2007, at p. 8. The transcript of the full hearing, including Secretary Rice's testimony, is available at http://www.washingtonpost.com/wp-dyn/content/article/2007/01/11/AR2007011100735.html?nav=rss_nation/nationalsecurity.

113. President Bush acknowledged that he had ordered such a new deployment of Patriot missile defense to the Middle East in his January 10 national address, *supra* note 106.

114. In describing the appointment of Fallon as the new commander of CentCom, a *New York Times* article stated that it was "classic gunboat diplomacy." John Kifner, "Gunboat Diplomacy: The Watch on the Gulf," January 14, 2007, says

that "CentCom, as it is known, has always been run by a four-star general from the Army or Marines," and that CentCom is currently involved in ground operations in two active combat theaters in Iraq and Afghanistan. Analysts have interpreted the appointment of a naval aviator as a signal to Iran that the United States is ready to employ the naval aircraft carriers now deployed in the Gulf to engage in airstrikes against Iran, should that become necessary.

115. The United States twice postponed a press briefing with evidence on alleged Iranian weapons supply to Iraqi insurgents before finally showing some materiel that were claimed to have Iranian serial markings during a press briefing in Baghdad on February 11, 2007. The postponements were occasioned by concerns that the briefing might overstate the evidence. For instance, National Security Adviser Stephen Hadley stated that: "The truth is quite frankly, we thought the briefing overstated. And we sent it back to get it narrowed and focused on the facts." Stephen Hadley, "Press Briefing by Stephen Hadley," White House Office of the Press Secretary, February 2, 2007, *available at* http://www.whitehouse. gov/news/releases/2007/02/20070202-6.html. British troops had earlier cast doubt on allegations by the American and British governments that Iran was aiding insurgents with weapons supply. Ellen Knickmeyer, "British Find No Evidence of Arms Traffic From Iran; Troops in Southeast Iraq Test US Claim of Aid for Militias," *Washington Post*, October 4, 2006, at A21. When the briefing on Iranian weapons supply was ultimately delivered, it was widely criticized both for overstating the evidence of a connection between the materiel displayed and the Iranian government and because the nature of the briefing by unnamed defense officials suggested an unwillingness on the part of the administration to take responsibility for the allegations. The day after the briefing, the chairman of the Joint Chiefs of Staff, General Peter Pace, drew into question claims of evidence of direct involvement by senior Iranian officials. "Iran government link to Iraq not clear, says US general," *Reuters*, February 13, 2007. Several commentators note that these allegations were timed in advance of the deadline set by Resolution 1737 for a suspension of the Iranian enrichment program and may be designed to place additional pressure on Iran. See, for example, Paul Reynolds, "New Tensions over Iran's Nuclear Plans," *BBC*, February 20, 2007. Skeptics also pointed to the recent American National Intelligence Estimate on Iraq, which judged that the involvement of Iran and other neighbors "is not likely to be a major driver of violence" in Iraq, for further evidence that the heightened American allegations against Iran were motivated not security-related concerns but for political reasons. For the National Intelligence Estimate, see "Prospects for Iraq's Stability: A Challenging Road Ahead," Office of the Director of National Intelligence, January 2007, *available at* http://hosted. ap.org/specials/interactives/wdc/documents/nie020207.pdf (the position that Iraq's neighbors are not a major driver of the violence there is at page 8).

116. The December detention of Iranian officials during a Baghdad raid on the Hakim compound was followed up immediately after Bush's January 10 address, by a Special Forces raid on an Iranian liaison office in Iraqi Kurdistan. The Irbil office was described by Iraqi Foreign Minister Hoshyar Zebari as "an Iraqi-government-approved liaison office," which was "set up to become a diplomatic consulate." Dafna Linzer and Ann Scott Tyson, "Lethal-Force Order Justified, Bush Says," *Washington Post*, January 27, 2006, at p. A12. Iran objected to the detentions as a "kidnapping," but their response was generally seen as muted as a result of growing concerns in Tehran that the United States might be searching for a pretext to engage in air strikes against the country. On this point, see Azadeh Moaveni, "The Jitters in Tehran," *Time*, February 1, 2007, *available at* http://www.time.com/time/world/article/0,8599,1584842,00.html.

Following the U.S. detention of Iranian security officials in Baghdad and the raid on the liaison office in Irbil came the abduction of Jalal Sharafi, second secretary at the Iranian embassy in Baghdad, by 20 gunmen in Iraqi National Guard uniforms. The Iranian embassy charged that the group who abducted Sharafi were under direct American supervision. *Newsweek* later quoted a "senior Coalition adviser" who said that the idea the group was under U.S. supervision was "plausible" because such a unit does exist that specializes in "snatch operations." In the same article, Hillary Mann, the Bush administration's former National Security Council director for Iran and the Persian Gulf stated that the abduction fit into an escalating pattern driven by some Bush advisers who wish to generate a pretext for an attack on Iran: "They intend to be as provocative as possible and make the Iranians do something [America] would be forced to retaliate for." Michael Hirsh and Maziar Bahari, "Blowup? America's Hidden War With Iran," *Newsweek*, February 19, 2007.

117. The arms sales contemplated reportedly include "sophisticated air and missile defense systems, advanced early warning radar aircraft that could detect low-flying missiles and light coastal combat ships that could sweep the Gulf for mines and help gather underwater intelligence." The sales were described by acting assistant secretary of state for political-military affairs, Stephen D. Mull as part of the "broader context of what Secretary Rice calls the looming confrontation between extremists and moderates," alluding to American coordination of a new alignment against Iran, involving the Gulf Cooperation Council states, Egypt and Jordan (the so-called 6+2). More specifically, the arms sales were described as part of a "Gulf Security Dialogue" launched in May 2006 to "bolster the defenses of Saudi Arabia, Qtara, Kuwait, the United Arab Emirates, Bahrain and Oman." Farah Stockman, "US Looks to Sell Arms in Gulf to Try to Contain Iran," *Boston Globe*, March 21, 2007.

118. See, for example, Philip Giraldi, "Next Stop: Tehran," *The American Conservative*, February 12, 2007.

119. See, for example, Patrick Cockburn, "Target Tehran: Washington Sets Stage for New Confrontation," *The Independent (UK)*, February 12, 2007.

120. One prominent skeptic of the administration's moves against Iran was the Senate Intelligence Committee Chairman, Senator John D. Rockefeller, who was widely quoted as stating: "To be quite honest, I'm a little concerned that it's Iraq again. This whole concept of moving against Iran is bizarre." Mark Mazzetti, "Leading Senator Assails Bush Over Iran Stance," *New York Times*, January 20, 2007. On the argument that the Bush administration's escalation may be deliberately designed to provoke a confrontation with Iran, see Joseph Cirincione, "Taunting Iran," *American Progress*, January 16, 2007.

121. Seymour Hersh, "The Redirection," *The New Yorker*, March 5, 2007 (online version available February 25, 2007), at 3 (online version), *available at* http://www.newyorker.com/reporting/2007/03/05/070305fa_fact_hersh.

122. "US 'Attack Plans' Revealed," *BBC*, February 20, 2007, *available at* http://news.bbc.co.uk/2/hi/middle_east/6376639.stm.

123. Ahmed Al-Jarallah, "US Military Strike on Iran Seen by April '07; Sea-Launched Attack to Hit Oil, N-Sites," *Arab Times* (Kuwait), January 14, 2007.

124. Gabriel Ronay, "America 'Poised to Strike at Iran's Nuclear Sites' from Bases in Bulgaria and Romania," *Sunday Herald UK*, January 28, 2007.

125. Robert Parry, "Iran Clock Is Ticking," *Consortium News*, January 31, 2007.

126. Hersh, "The Redirection," *supra* note 121; see also Dan Plesch, "American Preparations for Invading Iran Are Complete," *New Statesmen*, February 19, 2007, *available at* http://www.newstatesman.com/200702190014.

127. Nazila Fathi, "Iran Says Insurgent Bombers Are Trained in Pakistan." *International Herald Tribune*, February 19, 2007; see also, Kim Murphy, "Iran Alleges US Link to Militant Attack," *LA Times*, February 19, 2007.
128. Ewan MacAskill, "Target Iran: US Able to Strike in the Spring," *Guardian*, February 10, 2007.
129. Uzi Mahnaimi, "Revealed: Israel Plans Nuclear Strike on Iran," *Sunday Times* (UK), January 7, 2007. This report also noted that military analysts believed the disclosure of the plans to the newspaper was "intended to put pressure on Tehran to halt enrichment," suggesting that the proliferation of leaks to the media about military planning might be deliberate as part of a psychological campaign to pressure Iran.
130. See, for example, Terrence Henry, "Can Sabotage and Assassination Stop Iran from Going Nuclear?" *Atlantic Monthly* (December 2005).
131. On the mysterious death of Iranian senior nuclear physicist, Ardashir Hosseinpour, see Yossi Melman, "US Website: Mossad Killed Iranian Nuclear Physicist," *Haaretz (Israel)*, February 4, 2007. On the disappearance of former Iranian deputy defense minister, Ali Reza Asghari, see Vincent Boland and Gareth Smyth, "Former Iranian Defence Minister 'Missing,'" *Financial Times*, March 6, 2007. It is worth noting that a campaign of sabotage, abduction or other measures, while it may have some effect on the margins, also carries some of the risks associated with a military option, including the possibility of retaliatory actions on the part of Iran.
132. The concern about the calibration of the American message was voiced by Lee Feinstein, Senior Fellow for U.S. Foreign Policy and International Law at the Council on Foreign Relations and former Defense and State Department official in the Clinton Administration. The article citing Feinstein's concerns also canvassed Iran expert Ray Takeyh and Columbia University professor Gary Sick, both of whom reported similar concerns. "US—Iran Tensions Could Trigger War," *Associated Press*, February 1, 2007.
133. "Iran Fires Missiles in New Round of War Games," *Reuters*, February 19, 2007.
134. Helene Cooper and Kirk Semple, "US Set to Join Iran and Syria in Talks on Iraq," *New York Times*, February 28, 2007.
135. Jim Lobe, "Washington Get 'Neighborly' over Iraq," *IPS/Asia Times*, March 1, 2007.
136. Anne Gearan, "US Calls Iran, Syria Talks Cordial," *Associated Press*, March 10, 2007.
137. Nasser Karimi, "Iran Calls Baghdad Talks Constructive," *Associated Press*, March 11, 2007.
138. "US, Iran Have History of Contact Since Cutting Ties," *Reuters*, March 9, 2007.
139. On U.S. unilateral efforts to impede investments in the Iranian energy sector, see Kim Murphy, "US Puts Squeeze on Iran's Oil Fields," *LA Times*, January 7, 2007.
140. Helene Cooper and Steven R. Weisman, "The West Revises Its Strategy for Halting Iran's Nuclear Program," *International Herald Tribune*, January 2, 2007.
141. Lesley Wroughton, "US Embargo against Iran Bank Not a Violation: IMF," *Reuters*, March 12, 2007.
142. "US Senators Mulling Tougher Iran Sanctions Bills," *Dow Jones Newswire*, March 21, 2007.
143. Steven Weisman, "US Cautions Foreign Companies on Iran Deals," *New York Times*, March 21, 2007.

144. Louis Charbonneau, "EU, Russia Resist US on Iran Sanctions: Diplomats," *Reuters*, January 30, 2007.

145. According to one report, Davos revealed a new U.S. strategy to curtail Iranian influence: "the idea is to thwart Iran's threatened hegemony with an economic pincer movement consisting of financial diplomacy on one side and energy policy on the other." According to reports, the main responsibility for this strategy rests with Saudi Arabia. The key element of the policy, reportedly, is the maintenance of low oil prices. The article notes that "since July a barrel of oil has fallen from $78 to just over $50, reducing the Government [of Iran]'s revenues by one third. If the oil price fell into the $35–$45 range, Iran would shift into deficit, and with access to foreign borrowing cut off by UN sanctions." Anatole Kaletsky, "New US Strategy on Iran Emerges from Davos," *Times (UK)*, January 25, 2007.

146. "China Defends Iran Gas Deal Talks," *BBC*, January 11, 2007. The dispute involved plans by a Chinese oil firm to invest in Iran's Pars gas field in a deal reportedly worth as much as $16 billion.

147. Simon Tisdall, "US Financial Squeeze on Iran Yields Results," *Guardian (UK)*, February 13, 2007.

148. Jim Wolf, "Iran May Need Nuclear Power, Study Says," *Reuters*, December 26, 2006. For the full report, see Roger Stern, "The Iranian Petroleum Crisis and U.S. National Security," *Proceedings of the National Academy of Sciences 2007*, 104, pp. 377–382 (originally published online December 26, 2006), *available at* http://www.cfr.org/publication/12539/.

149. See, for example, Jad Mouawad, "West Adds to Strains on Iran's Lifeline," *NYT*, February 13, 2007 (citing an analyst who stated that "Iran might have no more oil to export around 2015 if it did not rein in runaway consumption and reverse the long-term decline in its oil production," something that would be virtually impossible absent foreign investment in Iranian energy infrastructure).

150. Stuart Williams, "Iran's Motorists Face Petrol Rationing," *Agence France Presse*, March 7, 2007.

151. "Iran Has Begun Assembling Centrifuges at Natanz Site," *Agence France Presse*, February 1, 2007.

152. "Iran Installs More Centrifuges," *Global Security Newswire*, February 5, 2007.

153. For reports on Iran's technical difficulties in running centrifuges, see Peter Beaumont, "Nuclear Plans in Chaos as Iran Leader Flounders," *The Observer (UK)*, January 28, 2007; "Status of Iranian Uranium Enrichment Activity Remains Unclear," *Global Security Newswire*, January 29, 2007; and "Iran Sets Up 328 Centrifuges at Big Atom Site: Sources," *Reuters*, February 1, 2007.

154. William J. Broad and David E. Sanger, "Iranian Boast Is Put to Test," *New York Times*, February 4, 2007.

155. "Iran Sets Up 328 Centrifuges at Big Atom Site: Sources," *Reuters*, February 1, 2007.

156. Julian Borger, "US Iran Intelligence 'Is Incorrect,'" *Guardian (UK)*, February 22, 2007.

157. Julian Borger, "US Iran Intelligence 'Is Incorrect,'" *supra* note 156. The article also cites a diplomat at the IAEA "with detailed knowledge of the agency's investigations," as stating that the Americans "gave us a paper with a list of sites. [The inspectors] did some follow-up, they went to some military sites, but there was no sign of [banned nuclear] activities. Now [the inspectors] don't go in blindly. Only if it passes a credibility test."

158. A senior diplomat at the IAEA was further quoted as stating that "[s]ince 2002, pretty much all the intelligence that's come to us has proved to be wrong." The article also reports that "American officials privately acknowledge that much

of their evidence on Iran's nuclear plans and programs remains ambiguous, fragmented and difficult to prove." Bob Drogin and Kim Murphy, "UN Calls US Data on Iran's Nuclear Aims Unreliable," *LA Times*, February 25, 2007.

159. Seymour Hersh, "The Next Act," *supra* note 93.

160. Nazila Fathi, "No News from Iran's Leader on Nuclear Program," *NYT*, February 12, 2007.

161. Slobodan Lekic, "Envoy: Iran Poses No Threat to Israel," *Associated Press*, February 11, 2007; and "Iran Offers Hope to Ease Nuclear Impasse," *Global Security Newswire*, February 12, 2007.

162. Solana and Steinmeier's comments on the meeting were widely reported. See, for example, Molly Moore, "EU Nations to Impose Limited Sanctions on Iran," *Washington Post*, February 13, 2007, at A18.

163. "Iran Keeping Enrichment to Low Levels: FM," *Agence France Presse*, February 13, 2007.

164. "We shy away from any kind of conflict...we think the world problem can be solved through dialogue, the use of logic and a sense of friendship." For the full transcript of the Ahmadinejad interview, see "Exclusive: Iranian President Ducks Charges That Iran Is Arming Iraqi Insurgents," *ABC*, February 12, 2007, *available at* http://abcnews.go.com/GMA/story?id=2868077. For commentary on the Ahmadinejad interview, see Ali Akbar Dareini, "Iran Leader Softens His Tone on Iraq," *Associated Press*, February 12, 2007.

165. The criticisms were published in editorials in January and February in the conservative Iranian newspapers, *Jomhouri Eslami*, *Etemad-e Melli* and *Hamshahri*. For an example of one such editorial, see *Etemad-e Melli*, "Nuclear Issue," February 26, 2007. Translation of Reformist Etemad-e Melli editorial in Mideast Mirror 26.02.07 Section C (Turkey and Iran), (Part 2—From today's Iranian press). Critical public comments on the handling of the nuclear file were made by, among others, the former President and current head of the Expediency Council, Abkar Hashemi Rafsanjani, former chief nuclear negotiator and member of the Assembly of Experts, Hassan Rowhani, and Grand Ayatollah Hossein Ali Montazeri. Montazeri, for instance, reportedly used his Friday sermon to call Ahmadinejad's defiant stance toward the West unnecessarily provocative. Nazila Fathi, "Debate Grows in Iran Over Nuclear Program," *New York Times*, January 23, 2007. There was also a report that Rafsanjani might have "formed a committee overseeing the nuclear negotiations" and to assess whether the country's international standing is being damaged by Ahmadinejad's conduct. Robert Tait, "Old rival tests Ahmadinejad's nerve," *Guardian (UK)*, January 25, 2007.

166. "Political Problems Mount for Ahmadinejad," *BBC*, February 26, 2007.

167. Ian Black, "Iran Declared Nuclear Programme Irreversible," *Guardian (UK)*, February 27, 2007; and Robert Tait and Ian Black, "Ahmadinejad under Fire in Iran for Hardline Nuclear Stance," *Guardian (UK)*, February 27, 2007.

168. Anne Geran, "Diplomats Trying to Restart Iran Talks," *Associated Press*, February 22, 2007.

169. This comment was reported by CNN international correspondent, Christian Amanpour, in describing an extended 90-minute interview that she conducted with a "top Iranian official" calling for engagement with the United States. Christiane Amanpour, "Iranian Official Offers Glimpse From Within: A Desire for US Ally," *CNN* February 21, 2007.

170. Former President Mohammad Khatami spoke at Davos, calling for calm heads and dialog to resolve international concerns about the Iranian nuclear program, while former President Akbar Hashemi Rafsanjani spoke from Tehran about Iran's commitment to an exclusively peaceful nuclear program subject

to international law and IAEA inspections. Stella Dawson, "Khatami Calls for Cool Heads," *Reuters*, January 25, 2007; and "Rafsanjani: Iran Committed to Peaceful Use of Nuclear Energy," *IRNA*, January 24, 2007.

171. "Arab Leagues' Moussa Warns US against Iran Attack," *Reuters*, January 24, 2007.

172. Stella Dawson, "IAEA Chief Says Attack on Iran Would Be Catastrophe," *Reuters*, January 25, 2007.

173. For a description of ElBaradei's timeout proposal, see Mark Landler and David E. Sanger, "UN Atomic Chief Cites Iran Enrichment Plan," *New York Times*, January 27, 2007.

174. On Iranian openness to the timeout suggestion, see "Iran Wants Times to Review Plan That Delays UN Sanctions," *Associated Press*, January 29, 2007. On the American response to the proposal, see "U.S. Seems to Rule Out 'Timeout' Between Iran, West," *Reuters*, January 29, 2007.

175. For comments by Joseph Cirincione and Trita Parsi noting that all parties other than the U.S. administration remained concerned about the lack of negotiations and the apparent game of "nuclear chicken" being advanced by the United States, see Mark Heinrich, "ANALYSIS: Shunning 'Timeout Call,' Iran, West Face Conflict," *Reuters*, January 31, 2007. On the endorsement by EU officials of the timeout proposal, see Michael Adler, "EU Offers Olive Branch to Iran on Nuclear Issue," *AFP*, March 7, 2007; see also, Mark Heinrich and Karin Strohecker, "EU Powers at IAEA Urge Iran to Take Atom 'Timeout,'" *Reuters*, March 7, 2007.

176. IAEA, "Cooperation between the Islamic Republic of Iran and the Agency in the Light of United Nations Security Council Resolution 1737" (2006), February 9, 2007, GOV/2007/7 (derestricted March 8, 2007). For a list of all of the technical cooperation programs between the agency and Iran indicating the 22 that were suspended, see "Annex: Evaluation of Technical Cooperation Provided to Iran."

177. Michael Adler, "US Happy with IAEA's Reduction of Technical Assistance to Iran," *Agence France Presse*, February 12, 2007.

178. The IAEA issued a press release on January 22, announcing that it was discussing the matter with Iran and that those discussions were confidential but would not hamper with agency's ability to continue with inspections in accordance with Iran's Safeguards Agreement. "Statement by IAEA Spokesperson, Melissa Fleming on Iran," IAEA Press Releases, January 22, 207, Press Release 2007/01, *available at* http://www.iaea.org/NewsCenter/PressReleases/2007/prn200701.html.

179. Becky Anderson, "Interview with International Atomic Energy Agency Head Mohamed ElBaradei," *CNN*, January 26, 2007 (airtime 5.17 pm EST) (transcript on file with author).

180. For instance, one report quoted a diplomat in Vienna as saying that "Iran accused one senior expert of 'spying for his home country' in 2006 by using wiretapping equipment to collect information outside the purview of nuclear inspections." "UN Nuke Inspector Is Unsure about Iran," *Associated Press*, March 5, 2007.

181. According to reports, "Iran demanded Chris Charlier's removal last month in a letter to agency head Mohamed ElBaradei saying that Charlier leaked information about Iran's nuclear program." "IAEA Reassigns Senior Inspector," *Global Security Newswire,* February 13, 2007.

182. The full transcript of ElBaradei's interview with Daniel Dombey of the *Financial Times* is available on the IAEA Web site. "Transcript of the Director General's Interview on Iran and DPRK," February 19, 2007, *available at* http://www.iaea.org/NewsCenter/Transcripts/2007/ft190207.html. ElBaradei is very

specific throughout the interview about three principal claims: that there is no alternative to a negotiated resolution to the Iran nuclear dispute; that relying on sanctions alone will not succeed; and that "the Iranian issue will only be resolved when the US takes a decision to engage Iran directly…The US could be very helpful in providing the security assurances that obviously lie at the heart of some of the Iranian activities."

183. IAEA, "Implementation of the NPT Safeguards Agreement and Relevant Provisions of Security Council Resolution 1737 (2006) in the Islamic Republic of Iran: Report of the Director General," February 22, 2007, GOV/2007/8 (hereafter "IAEA February 2007 Report"). An additional finding cited in the report was the movement of nearly 9 tons of uranium hexafluoride feedstock from the Isfahan conversion facility to the Natanz commercial enrichment plant, presumably as a precursor to running the gas through the centrifuges being installed at the facility.

184. IAEA February 2007 Report, paras. 4, 7, 8, and 28.

185. Ibid., paras. 12–13.

186. Ibid., paras. 26 and 27.

187. Ibid., paras. 25–26.

188. Ibid., para. 14.

189. "Iran Urged to Open Nuke Program to UN," *Reuters*, March 6, 2007.

190. Greg Webb, "IAEA Governing Board Backs Nuclear Aid Cuts to Iran," *Global Security Newswire,* March 8, 2007.

191. These concerns were first raised in a letter from Oman to the IAEA Director General, on behalf of the Arab League, expressing concern about Israeli Prime Minister Ehud Olmert's comments in December that appeared to confirm the existence of a clandestine Israeli nuclear weapons program. The letter specifically referenced "double standards" in the enforcement of the nonproliferation norm, an issue that was then further debated during the IAEA meeting. "Arabs Protest Israeli Nuclear Hint," *Reuters*, March 6, 2007. The account of the debate at the board of governors meetings is based on comments by a senior Austrian diplomat (on file with author).

192. "UN Council to Consider Iran Sanctions," *Associated Press*, February 26, 2007.

193. On the various stumbling blocks in the negotiations for the new sanctions package, see "Six Powers Struggle on UN Sanctions Text for Iran," *Reuters*, March 8, 2007; "Flurry of Diplomatic Consultations as Iran Sanctions Talks Falter," *Agence France Presse*, March 8, 2007; and "No Deal on UN Sanctions for Iran," *BBC*, March 10, 2007.

194. Edith Lederer, "Deal Reached on UN Sanctions vs. Iran," *Associated Press*, March 15, 2007.

195. Ibid.

196. "Iran Sanctions Resolution Due for Saturday Vote," *Reuters*, March 23, 2007. While President Ahmadinejad had initially indicated that he would address the council in advance of a vote, his trip was cancelled on March 23, citing American "obstruction" in issuing visas to officials who would have traveled with him to the UN headquarters in New York. Alexandra Olson, "Iran's President Cancels UN Appearance," *Associated Press*, March 23, 2007.

197. The Russian nuclear agency, Rosatom, announced suspension of work on Bushehr in mid-February as a result of an Iranian payment shortfall. Iran's official explanation for the payment issue was that the switch from dollars to Euros had slowed work at the Iranian bank responsible for payments. The timing of the Russian announcement was viewed by some commentators as suggesting an effort to increase pressure on Iran in advance of the impending deadline for compliance

with Resolution 1737. In addition to the payment shortfall, however, Russia explained the suspension as a consequence of sanctions: "Atomstroiexport, the Russian state company in charge of Bushehr work, said UN sanctions against Iran were also contributing to the delays because of a trading ban on certain atomic equipment. 'There are certain obstacles affecting our work in Bushehr,' said Atomstroiexport spokeswoman Irina Yesipova. 'Because of the embargo a number of third countries declined to supply equipment (to Iran). That's why Russian producers have to provide all the equipment all of a sudden. It's a tough situation.'" "Russia Delays Work on Iran Nuclear Plant," *Reuters*, February 19, 2007. See also "Talks between Iran, Russia over Payment Delays at Bushehr Plan Yield No Result," *Associated Press/IHT*, March 8, 2007.

198. The Russian failure to meet the agreed schedule for the delivery of the first installment of nuclear fuel to Bushehr in March, prompted Iranian nuclear negotiator Ali Larijani to comment that the Russian delay validates the Iranian position that it can never rely entirely on an international fuel supply agreement. "UN Powers Could Reveal Iran Sanctions Today," *Global Security Newswire*, March 14, 2007 (reporting Larijani's comments).

199. For a report that Russia was deliberately withholding the fuel for political reasons, see Elaine Sciolino, "Russia Gives Iran Ultimatum on Enrichment," *New York Times*, March 20, 2007; and "Changing Course, Russia Links Progress on Iranian Reactor to Resolution of Broader Nuclear Crisis," *Global Security Newswire*, March 20, 2007.

200. In failing to make an anticipated announcement of nuclear advances at the time of the anniversary of the Islamic Revolution in February, President Ahmadinejad suggested that there would be advances in the Iranian program by April 9, 2007, close to the first anniversary of his April 11, 2006 announcement that Iran has enriched a small amount of uranium to a low level. "Ahmadinejad Defiant on Nuclear Program," *Associated Press*, February 11, 2007 (quoting Ahmadinejad as stating that "until April 9, 2007, you will witness the great advances of the Iranian nation…especially in the field of nuclear technology").

201. A report of a possible alternative channel to reach a compromise with Iran emerged in March 2007, in the form of discussions between Larijani and the Swiss deputy foreign minister, Michael Ambuehl, reportedly being coordinated with the IAEA. The proposal involved a suspension of Iranian enrichment activities that would permit the "dry-spinning" of centrifuges (without feeding uranium gas into the machines) while negotiating with the P5+1. Unfortunately, "key Western powers" were described in reports as "dismissive of the idea." Louis Charbonneau, "Swiss Discussed Compromise Idea in Iran: Diplomats," *Reuters*, March 21, 2007.

202. Daniel Dombey, "IAEA Chief Pessimistic over Iran Breakthrough," *Financial Times*, February 19, 2007.

203. For a detailed history of the spring 2003 proposal for comprehensive negotiation and rapprochement sent by the Iranian Foreign Ministry to the U.S. State Department and the Bush administration's decision to reject that offer, see Flynt Leverett, *Dealing with Tehran: Assessing U.S. Diplomatic Options toward Iran* (New York: Century Foundation, 2006), at pp. 11–16. A copy of the actual Iranian proposal to the United States in 2003 was made available by the *Washington Post* that first broke the story of the detailed proposal. Glenn Kessler, "2003 Memo Says Iranian Leaders Backed Talks," *Washington Post*, February 14, 2007, at p. A14. A PDF version of the proposal is available at http://www.washingtonpost.com/wp-srv/world/documents/us_iran_1roadmap. pdf. When the report of the Iranian proposal was released, Secretary Rice initially denied awareness of such a proposal, contradicting Leverett's account.

Anne Gearan, "Rice Disputes Claim of Iranian Overture," *Associated Press*, February 7, 2007. Leverett responded that Rice must have seen the memo and recounting that then Secretary of State Colin "Powell, in a discussion about the Iranian proposal, told him he 'couldn't sell it at the White House'" and this was the reason it was rejected. "Ex-Aide Says Rice Misled US Congress on Iran," *Reuters*, February 14, 2007. Larry Wilkerson, Colin Powell's chief of staff at the State Department confirmed Leverett's account. "Washington 'Snubbed Iran Offer,'" *BBC*, January 18, 2007.

204. The Bush administration's first envoy to Afghanistan in 2001, James Dobbins, gave a detailed account in a recent *Newsweek* article of Iranian assistance with the stabilization of Afghanistan in December 2001, focusing particularly on the efforts of Iranian representative Javad Zarif. The article notes that following the December 2001 Bonn conference, Iranian reformists then in power under President Khatami were hoping an opportunity had arisen to thaw relations with the United States. Instead, the reformists were undermined by the Axis of Evil speech, which confirmed the hardliners' position that the United States could not be trusted and would not forgo its goal of regime change with respect to Iran. Michael Hirsh and Maziar Bahari, "Blowup? America's Hidden War With Iran," *Newsweek*, February 19, 2007.

205. See, for example, Joshua Muravchik, "Bomb Iran," *LA Times*, November 19, 2006.

206. See *supra* notes 121–129 and accompanying text.

207. For examples of arguments by respected analysts illustrating why there can be no military solution to the Iranian nuclear dispute, see Dr. Frank Barnaby, *Would Air Strikes Work? Understanding Iran's Nuclear Programme and the Possible Consequences of a Military Strike*, Oxford Research Group (March 2007, with foreword by Dr. Hans Blix), *available at* http://www.oxfordresearchgroup.org.uk/publications/briefings/wouldairstriceswork.htm; and Joseph Cirincione, "No Military Options," Carnegie Endowment for International Peace, January 19, 2006, *available at* http://www.carnegieendowment.org/npp/publications/index.cfm?fa=view&id=17922.

208. See, for example, Yossi Mekelberg, "Israel and Iran: From War of Words to Words of War?" *Chatham House Middle East Programme*, March 2007 (MEP BP 07/01), *available at* http://www.chathamhouse.org.uk/pdf/research/mep/BPisraeliran.pdf; and Anthony Cordesman and Khalid al-Rodhan, "Iranian Nuclear Weapons? Options for Sanctions and Military Strikes," *Center for Strategic and International Studies*, October 2006.

209. "Annan Doubts Prompt Iran Decision," *BBC*, January 25, 2006, *available at* http://news.bbc.co.uk/go/pr/fr/-/2/hi/middle_east/4648276.stm. For a transcript of Hans Blix's comments, see Hans Blix, Address to the Arms Control Association: "Repairing the Nonproliferation System," January 25, 2006, *available at* http://www.armscontrol.org/events/20060125_transcript_blix.asp.

210. For instance, in an interview with Wolf Blitzer on CNN's "Late Edition," both former Secretary of State Madeleine Albright and former Secretary of State Henry Kissinger argued that there should be more tactical flexibility on the timing of an Iranian suspension as perhaps simultaneous with talks or within the first week, in order to create more "maneuvering room" on the question of pre-conditions. Similarly, former director of policy planning at the State Department and current president of the Council on Foreign Relations commented that the suspension precondition should not be allowed "to torpedo diplomacy" and should "be finessed, very easily and very quickly." "International Stance on Iran's Nuclear Program Criticized," *Associated Press/International Herald Tribune*, February 27, 2007. The same article cited comments by Hans Blix, former chief

UN weapons inspector, that were even more straightforward, calling for the United States to drop preconditions, engage with Iran and offer the country security guarantees.

211. One such proposal, rejected to date by the United States, but possibly worthy of consideration, is to permit the Iranians to "dry spin" centrifuges—that is to run them in a vacuum without feeding any uranium gas in for enrichment— which might allow the Iranians to gain a small margin of additional technical knowledge but without raising any direct proliferation concern. For a detailed discussion of different formulas by which Iran might suspend its enrichment activities without compromising its capacity to resume enrichment in the future, see Matthew Bunn, "Placing Iran's Enrichment Activities in Standby," Belfer Center for Science and International Affairs (June 2006), *available at* http://bcsia.ksg.harvard.edu/BCSIA_content/documents/bunn_2006_iran_standby.pdf.

212. For one report citing to such views among diplomats and analysts, see "Iran Sets Up 328 centrifuges at Big Atom Site: Sources," *Reuters*, February 1, 2007.

213. As noted above, the most recent estimate provided by the U.S. Director of National Intelligence suggested a timeline of 5–10 years before Iran would acquire a nuclear weapon capability. For the full transcript of the September 2006 interview in which then-Director of National Intelligence John Negroponte reiterated that Iran was estimated to be five to ten years from a nuclear weapons capacity by American intelligence officials, see, "Interview of Ambassador John D. Negroponte Director of National Intelligence with Robert Siegel," *National Public Radio*, September 1, 2006, *available at* http://www.dni.gov/interviews/20060901_interview.pdf. In a slightly more conservative estimate, the director general of the IAEA, emphasizing the existence of a window of opportunity to negotiate over the Iranian nuclear dispute, stated at the 2007 Davos meeting that the Iranians are at least 3–8 years from acquiring a nuclear weapons capability. "Status of Iranian Uranium Enrichment Activity Remains Unclear," *Global Security Newswire*, January 29, 2007. The Israelis also recently revised their estimate, with Mossad chief Meir Dagan testifying to the Israeli Knesset in December 2006 that the earliest date by which Iran could acquire a nuclear weapon was 2009. Aluf Benn and Gideon Alon, "Mossad Chief: Iran Will Not Get Nuclear Bomb Before 2009," *Haaretz (Israel)*, December 19, 2006. Other conservative estimates, such as a recent report issued by the International Institute for Strategic Studies, have also predicted that the earliest possible date for an Iranian nuclear weapons capability would be in a 2–3 year period. In its report, the IISS emphasized that this was a highly pessimistic projection requiring that the Iranians would face no technical obstacles in the their program, with a more realistic projection putting the date for a nuclear weapons capability out significantly further, with a timeline comparable to the U.S. estimate provided by Ambassador Negroponte. James Hackett, ed., *The Military Balance 2007* (London: International Institute for Strategic Studies), *available at* http://www.iiss.org/publications/the-military-balance.

214. For instance, former U.S. under secretary of state for Arms Control and International Security under the Bush administration and former U.S. ambassador to the UN under the Bush administration has repeatedly gone on the record, both in and out of office, stating that Iranian regime change is the only viable solution for the nuclear dispute. See, for example, Guy Dinmore and Daniel Dombey, "Bolton: Sanctions 'Help Regime Change,'" *Financial Times*, October 24, 2006; and "John Bolton calls for 'regime change' in Iran," *Bloomberg Newswire*, March 2, 2007.

215. See reports cited in notes 207–208.

216. For reports that have drawn the conclusion that deterrence is a preferable alternative to rollback, assuming Iran acquires a nuclear weapon capability or is adjudged to intend to do so, see Judith S. Yaphe and Charles D. Lutes, *Reassessing the Implications of a Nuclear Armed Iran*, (Washington, DC: Institute for National Strategic Studies, 2005); Michael Eisenstadt, "Deter and Contain: Dealing with a Nuclear Iran," in Henry Sokolski and Patrick Clawson, eds., *Getting Ready for a Nuclear-Ready Iran* (Carlisle, PA: Strategic Studies Institute, 2005); Jonathan Rauch, "Containing Iran," *Atlantic Monthly* (July/August 2006); Justin Logan, "The Bottom Line on Iran: The Costs and Benefits of Preventive War versus Deterrence," *Policy Analysis* (CATO Institute, 2006); and Barry Posen, "We Can Live with a Nuclear-Armed Iran," *New York Times*, February 27, 2006.

217. The closed-door discussions at the board meeting were described in comments by a senior diplomat, March 2007 (on file with author).

218. For a detailed discussion of one potential consortium arrangement on Iranian soil, see Sir John Thomson, "The Iranian Nuclear Crisis: A Risk Assessment," *BASIC* (Iran Discussion Paper No. 2, Mach 2007), at pp. 8–9, *available at* http://www.basicint.org/pubs/Papers/iran2.pdf.

219. Good faith negotiations, here, would be in contrast to a cosmetic American participations in negotiations to forge an international coalition for coercive action. There is reason to believe that the May 2006 American willingness to join in offering Iran a package was a result of the Bush administration's expectation that the suspension precondition would preclude Iranian participation and clear the path for Security Council action. See, for example, David E. Sanger, "For Bush, Talks with Iran Were a Last Resort," *New York Times*, June 1, 2006. This form of engagement, with the deliberate purpose of demonstrating the exhaustion of diplomatic options to facilitate coercion, will not yield a negotiated settlement since it suggests that at least one party enters talks without an interest in achieving a compromise.

220. On the degree of proliferation risk associated with a facility operating fewer than 6 cascades, see Thomson, "The Iranian Nuclear Crisis: A Risk Assessment," *supra* note 218.

221. On ElBaradei's comments regarding such a proposal, see David Holley, "Nuclear Chief Offers a Nonproliferation Plan: Promise Them Fuel," *L.A. Times*, October 6, 2005.

222. UN Secretary General Kofi Annan, "Address to United Nations Association of the United Kingdom," January 31, 2006, *available at* http://www.un.org/News/Press/docs/2006/sgsm10332.doc.htm.

223. This is particularly true when considered against the backdrop of revelations that the weapons inspections system in place for Iraq in the 1990s under UNSCOM was infiltrated by American and Israeli intelligence officials. See, for example, Scott Ritter, *Endgame: Solving the Iraq Crisis* (New York: Simon & Schuster, 1999). The author, a former weapons inspector with UNSCOM in Iraq alleges that the inspections were infiltrated by the CIA which used the intelligence gathered by the inspectors to pursue a policy of regime change in Iraq.

224. Mohamed ElBaradei, "Saving Ourselves from Self-Destruction," *New York Times*, February 12, 2004.

CHAPTER 10

Nuclear Dangers and Challenges to a New Nuclear Policy

David Krieger

It is worthwhile asking the question: What are nuclear weapons? In some respects the answer to this question may seem obvious, but this is not necessarily the case. To some, nuclear weapons are a scientific achievement that bestows prestige. This is the view that has been taken by each of the nuclear weapon states, with the exception of Israel. This perspective was on display when India and Pakistan conducted nuclear tests in 1998.

To others, nuclear weapons are a deterrent that protects a weaker state from a more powerful one. This is likely the view of North Korea and perhaps Iran, after having been designated by the U.S. president as part of the "axis of evil" and observing the United States attack Iraq, the third designated country in this axis. To still others, such as Israel, nuclear weapons represent a final response to an existential threat. To North Korea, nuclear weapons may represent a response to an existential threat and also a "bargaining chip" for security guarantees and development aid.

To others, nuclear weapons demonstrate a state's power in the international system. This likely reflects the view of the five original nuclear weapon states, the ones that also hold permanent seats on the United Nations Security Council—the United States, United Kingdom, Russia, China, and France—and quite possibly the rest of the nuclear weapon states as well.

Thus far, I have only given the probable views of states that possess nuclear weapons or may wish to do so. Let me now offer another view of nuclear weapons. They are weapons that kill massively and indiscriminately. As such, they are long-distance instruments of annihilation. Weapons that kill indiscriminately are illegal under international law. In this respect, any threat or use of nuclear weapons that failed to discriminate between civilians and combatants would be illegal. It is hard to imagine any threat or use of these weapons that would or even could discriminate.

The International Court of Justice (ICJ) has found that any threat or use of nuclear weapons would be generally illegal, allowing for the possible but uncertain exception under current international law of a circumstance in which the very survival of a state is at stake.[1] But even then, for such use to be legal it would have to meet the standards of international humanitarian law.[2] In other words, it would have to discriminate between soldiers and civilians, be proportionate, and not cause unnecessary suffering.

Nuclear weapons may also be viewed as cowardly and antidemocratic. More accurately, the weapons themselves may not be cowardly, but those who would threaten or use these long-distance killing machines are cowardly. Nearly all of the leading military figures of World War II recognized this and commented upon it. Admiral William Leahy, referring to the use of the atomic bombs at Hiroshima and Nagasaki, said, "[I]n being the first to use it, we had adopted an ethical standard common to the barbarians of the Dark Ages. I was not taught to make war in that fashion, and wars cannot be won by destroying women and children."[3]

Nuclear weapons are antidemocratic because they concentrate power in the hands of single individuals or a small cabal. They take away the most basic right of people everywhere—the right to survive. There will never be a democratic vote to use nuclear weapons. These weapons place in the hands of leaders the capacity to destroy cities, countries, and civilization, with the high likelihood that any use of nuclear weapons would lead to the destruction of the country that initiated a nuclear attack.

No Defense against Nuclear Attack

It is not possible to defend against a nuclear attack. Deterrence, which has been the main line of prevention, cannot provide physical defense against a nuclear attack. It is simply the threat of retaliation. This threat must be effectively communicated and believed by a potential attacker. It is, of course, not a meaningful threat against a nonstate extremist organization, which cannot be located. Deterrence theory is rooted in rationality. It posits leaders acting rationally to assure their survival, even in times of severe crisis. Basing protection against nuclear attack on rationality, unfortunately, is irrational.

This is what former commander-in-chief of the United States Strategic Command, General George Lee Butler, had to say about deterrence: "Deterrence serves the ends of evil as well as those of noble intent. It holds guilty the innocent as well as the culpable. It is a gamble no mortal should pretend to make. It invokes death on a scale rivaling the power of the Creator."[4]

Early in 2007, four former high-level U.S. officials—George Shultz, William Perry, Henry Kissinger, and Sam Nunn—published an article, "A World Free of Nuclear Weapons," in the *Wall Street Journal*. They addressed the issue of deterrence, arguing: "The end of the Cold War made the doctrine of mutual Soviet-American deterrence obsolete. Deterrence continues to be a relevant consideration for many states with regard to threats from other states. But reliance on nuclear weapons for this purpose is becoming increasingly hazardous and decreasingly effective."[5]

If deterrence is becoming more dangerous and less effective, what remains? U.S. leaders have put significant emphasis on missile defenses, but few knowledgeable scientists, other than those working on government contracts, believe that missile defenses would actually work under real-world conditions. There is a widespread understanding that missile defenses, in addition to being unreliable, can be easily overcome by offensive forces and the use of decoys. The U.S. push to deploy missile defenses has frayed relations between the United States and Russia and China, and led these countries to improve their offensive nuclear capabilities.

If neither deterrence nor missile defenses provide security against nuclear attack, what is left? Nothing is viable but diplomacy to eliminate nuclear arsenals. There is no reliable defense against nuclear attack. Major countries might consider returning to the "duck and cover" drills of the 1950s, although they might update the drills so that they took place in legislatures rather than in schools. These drills, of course, offer no protection to those who do them, but they might help awaken them to the dilemma and the need to take action to eliminate the threat by eliminating the weapons.

Nuclear Dangers

Since nuclear weapons continue to exist, nuclear dangers have not gone away, despite the ending of the Cold War and the break-up of the Soviet Union. What has largely ended is public concern for the dangers posed by nuclear weapons. The end of the Cold War has created a false sense of security, largely attributable to inertia and poor leadership. It is worthwhile reviewing current nuclear dangers.

1. The proliferation of nuclear weapons to other state actors. The more states in possession of nuclear weapons, the more likely they are to proliferate further and to be used. The spread of nuclear weapons dramatically increases problems of control, as was demonstrated by the case of Pakistan's A. Q. Khan.
2. The proliferation of nuclear weapons to extremist organizations. This is a danger that cannot be ruled out. Nuclear weapons in the hands of an extremist organization, such as al Qaeda, pose substantial danger to all countries, including the major nuclear weapon states.
3. The use of a nuclear weapon by an extremist organization against a state. The actual use of a nuclear weapon by an extremist organization against a state could result in destruction comparable to Hiroshima and Nagasaki, with added widespread security and economic implications. Questions would arise about the viability of the world economy, human rights, and democratic processes in the face of such an attack.
4. The use of a nuclear weapon by a nuclear weapon state against another state. Such use would be devastating and could trigger a nuclear war. It would end the taboo on the use of nuclear weapons that has existed since 1945.
5. An all-out nuclear war, initiated either intentionally or accidentally. The danger of an all-out nuclear war is always with us. It would be insane, but it could happen. Just as states stumbled into World War I, they could stumble again, by accident or miscalculation, into an all-out nuclear war.

These dangers are obviously not trivial, nor are they dangers with which anyone should feel comfortable. They are dangers that place civilization and even the human species at risk of annihilation.

Current nuclear dangers are fueled by the continued reliance of the nuclear weapon states on their nuclear arsenals for their security. Whereas these states once lived in a world of Mutually Assured Destruction, they now live in a world of *Mutually Assured Delusions*. Their greatest delusion is that they can continue to rely upon nuclear weapons for their own security and that of their friends, while preventing these weapons from spreading to others or being used again.

There have been repeated warnings over a long period of time that nuclear double standards cannot hold. In 1955, the Russell-Einstein Manifesto warned: "We have to learn to think in a new way. We have to learn to ask ourselves, not what steps can be taken to give military victory to whatever group we prefer, for there no longer are such steps; the question we have to ask ourselves is: what steps can be taken to prevent a military contest of which the issue must be disastrous to all parties?"[6]

In 1996, the Canberra Commission on the Elimination of Nuclear Weapons warned, "The proposition that nuclear weapons can be retained in perpetuity and never used—accidentally or by decision—defines credibility. The only complete defense is the elimination of nuclear weapons and assurance that they will never be produced again."[7]

This warning was repeated in 2006 by the Weapons of Mass Destruction Commission, chaired by Hans Blix. Their report, entitled *Weapons of Terror, Freeing the World of Nuclear, Biological and Chemical Arms*, stated: "So long as any state has such weapons—especially nuclear arms—others will want them. So long as any such weapons remain in any state's arsenal, there is a high risk that they will one day be used, by design or accident. Any such use would be catastrophic."[8]

A New Nuclear Policy

There have been many proposals for a new nuclear policy. The essence of such a policy is rooted in the following:

1. The obligation for good faith negotiations to achieve nuclear disarmament in Article VI of the 1970 Non-Proliferation Treaty (NPT);[9]
2. The 1996 Advisory Opinion of the ICJ, which stated, "There exists an obligation to pursue in good faith and bring to a conclusion negotiations leading to nuclear disarmament in all its aspects under strict and effective international control."[10]
3. The pledge in the 13 Practical Steps for Nuclear Disarmament agreed to by consensus at the 2000 NPT Review Conference: "An unequivocal undertaking by the nuclear-weapon States to accomplish the total elimination of their nuclear arsenals leading to nuclear disarmament to which all States parties are committed under Article VI."[11]

U.S. leadership will be necessary in order to move forward in implementing such a policy. Without U.S. leadership there will be little incentive for the other nuclear weapon states to act, and we are likely to remain frozen in the nuclear double standards of the status quo.

While U.S. leadership for a new nuclear policy has not been forthcoming, some hope exists in that the group of former U.S. officials—Shultz, Perry,

Kissinger, and Nunn—called for it in their January 2007 *Wall Street Journal* article. They endorsed "the goal of a world free of nuclear weapons and working energetically on the actions required to achieve that goal."[12] The four former officials argued, "Reassertion of the vision of a world free of nuclear weapons and practical measures toward achieving that goal would be, and would be perceived as, a bold initiative consistent with America's moral heritage. The effort could have a profoundly positive impact on the security of future generations."[13]

Once the political will for the goal of a world free of nuclear weapons exists, it will be possible to take the necessary actions to move from where we are to the goal. There have been many proposals for how to achieve the goal. A group of leading civil society organizations has drafted a Model Nuclear Weapons Convention that would lead to the elimination of nuclear weapons in a series of stages.[14] This Model Convention has been introduced to the United Nations by the Republic of Costa Rica. The 13 Practical Steps for Nuclear Disarmament agreed to at the 2000 NPT Review Conference sets forth another series of steps. The four former Cold Warriors set forth their own series of steps. What is most important in achieving the elimination of nuclear weapons, once there is sufficient political will, is that the disarmament be phased, transparent, verifiable, irreversible, and subject to strict and effective international control.

CHALLENGES TO A NEW NUCLEAR POLICY

There are many challenges to a new nuclear policy, but the greatest challenges lie in the orientation of the current leadership of the United States. In July 2007, the U.S. secretaries of state and defense and energy issued a joint statement: "National Security and Nuclear Weapons: Maintaining Deterrence in the 21st Century." This statement, contrary to the position taken by the four former U.S. officials, began by extolling "the essential role that nuclear weapons play in maintaining deterrence." It ended up by calling for replacing every nuclear weapon in the U.S. arsenal with a new type of thermonuclear weapon, the Reliable Replacement Warhead (RRW). They argued that "RRW is key to sustaining our security commitment to allies, and is fully consistent with U.S. obligations under the Nuclear Non-Proliferation Treaty—including Article VI." They also threatened that delays on RRW "raise the prospect of having to return to underground nuclear testing to certify existing weapons."[15]

The Bush administration is clearly not seeking to achieve a new nuclear policy, but a retrenchment of the status quo, one in which the United States remains the dominant nuclear weapon state. They seem unaware of the risks they are running, particularly the dangers that their nuclear policies create for the United States itself.

Further challenges to a new nuclear policy come from those states that want to defy the nuclear status quo of privileged nuclear "haves" maintaining their superiority over nuclear "have-nots." Israel, India, Pakistan, and North Korea were not content living in that two-tiered nuclear world, and pursued nuclear programs that led to the development of nuclear arsenals. South Africa had followed this path in earlier years, developed a small nuclear arsenal, and then reconsidered and dismantled its weapons. Without more concerted action to achieve nuclear disarmament, we can anticipate that more states will move toward a nuclear option in the future. Even today, some countries, like Japan, hold open the nuclear option as virtual nuclear weapon states, having both the technology and nuclear materials to develop nuclear arsenals in a very short time.

A general challenge to a new nuclear policy is the belief that a firewall can be drawn between nuclear energy and nuclear weapons. No such firewall is possible, and nuclear reactors, for power or research, have fueled the nuclear programs of Israel, India, and Pakistan. The designation of peaceful nuclear power as an "inalienable right" in the NPT is a contradiction that must be addressed if nuclear proliferation is to be controlled.

A Way Forward

In the end, the most important consideration may be that suggested by the *hibakusha*, the survivors of Hiroshima and Nagasaki, in their statement, "Nuclear weapons and human beings cannot co-exist." This is patently true. The two are now placed in an uneasy juxtaposition. One represents the technology of annihilation. The other represents the sum total of human achievement—past, present, and potential future. It should not be a difficult choice, but many of us on the planet seem to be voting against ourselves by our ignorance, apathy, and denial. An awakened populace may prove to be a potent force to achieve a nuclear weapon-free world.

Our challenge, as leaders in civil society, is to educate and advocate for a new nuclear policy that will move the world away from the nuclear precipice. In doing so, we may find many important partners, including the mayors of cities throughout the world who have joined Mayors for Peace led by Mayor Tadatoshi Akiba of Hiroshima; the network of parliamentarians in the Parliamentary Network for Nuclear Disarmament; and the governments of non-nuclear weapon states, such as those in the New Agenda Coalition, which have worked closely with the Middle Powers Initiative.

What has been accomplished thus far is not nearly enough. The world remains in peril. In Einstein's words, "we drift toward unparalleled catastrophe." Our challenge is to reverse that drift, to move back from the nuclear precipice, to prevent the catastrophe Einstein foresaw. To achieve a new and human-centric nuclear policy will require significant grassroots efforts within nuclear weapon states, and a major global campaign to bring pressure to bear upon these states from without. Already the southern hemisphere of the planet has organized itself into a series of Nuclear Weapon-Free Zones (NWFZ).

Europe could play an important role in the effort to achieve a nuclear weapon-free world by demanding that U.S. nuclear weapons be removed from Europe, by refusing to participate in missile defense programs, by stepping out from under the U.S. nuclear umbrella, and by convening a forum for the good faith negotiations for nuclear disarmament called for in the NPT. Now is the time to begin planning for a saner, more reasonable and law abiding U.S. administration that will replace the current one in early 2009.

Nuclear weapons currently divide humanity, but the recognition of their danger could be a force for uniting humanity for their elimination. This would be a great achievement not only for its expression of common human purpose, but also for the resources it would free for meeting basic human needs for food, health care, housing, education, the alleviation of poverty, and the protection of the environment. A new nuclear policy aimed at eliminating nuclear weapons should be the top priority on the global agenda.

NOTES

1. Advisory opinion of the International Court of Justice on the legality of the threat or use of nuclear weapons, United Nations General Assembly, A/51/218, 15 October 1996, p. 37.
2. Ibid., p. 36.
3. Leahy, William, *I Was There*, Whittlesey House, 1950, p. 441. This quote and others by World War II military and political leaders can be found at the Web site of Doug Long, Hiroshima: Was It Necessary?: http://www.doug-ong.com/quotes.htm
4. Butler, George Lee, "Ending the Nuclear Madness," Nuclear Age Peace Foundation, Waging Peace Series, 40 (September 1999), p. 17.
5. Shultz, George P., William J. Perry, Henry A. Kissinger, and Sam Nunn, "A World Free of Nuclear Weapons," *Wall Street Journal*, January 4, 2007.
6. The Russell-Einstein Manifesto, issued July 9, 1955, Web site of Pugwash Conferences on Science and World Affairs: http://www.pugwash.org/about/manifesto.htm.
7. Report of the Canberra Commission on the Elimination of Nuclear Weapons, Canberra: Commonwealth of Australia, August 1996, p. 9.
8. *Weapons of Terror, Freeing the World of Nuclear, Biological and Chemical Arms*, Stockholm: Weapons of Mass Destruction Commission, 2006, p. 17.
9. Treaty on the Non-Proliferation of Nuclear Weapons, signed at Washington, London, and Moscow on July 1, 1968, Web site of the Federation of American Scientists: http://www.un.org/events/npt2005/npttreaty.html Article VI of the treaty states: "Each of the Parties to the Treaty undertakes to pursue negotiations in good faith on effective measures relating to cessation of the nuclear arms race at an early date and to nuclear disarmament, and on a Treaty on general and complete disarmament under strict and effective international control."
10. Advisory Opinion of the ICJ on the legality of the threat or use of nuclear weapons, United Nations General Assembly, A/51/218, October 15, 1996, p. 37.
11. Final Document Issued by 2000 NPT Review Conference, May 20, 2000. Federation of American Scientists Web site: http://www.fas.org/nuke/control/npt/docs/finaldoc.htm.
12. Shultz et al., "A World Free of Nuclear Weapons."
13. Ibid.
14. For information on the Model Nuclear Weapons Convention see the Web site of the Lawyers' Committee on Nuclear Policy: http://www.lcnp.org/mnwc/index.htm.
15. *National Security and Nuclear Weapons: Maintaining Deterrence in the 21st Century* can be found at the Web site of the National Nuclear Security Agency: http://www.nnsa.doe.gov/docs/factsheets/2007/NA-07-FS-04.pdf.

PART IV

A New Direction

CHAPTER 11

Roadmaps to Disarmament: A Strategy for the Second Nuclear Era

Wade L. Huntley

INTRODUCTION

The 2005 Non-Proliferation Treaty (NPT) Review Conference ended in utter stalemate, producing no new ideas or proposals for strengthening the NPT regime or for confronting the crucial challenges of expanding nuclear dangers that the world today faces. The failure of the existing nuclear states to move genuinely toward their NPT nuclear disarmament commitments, combined with problematic compliance with NPT safeguards among many key non-nuclear states, have placed the NPT regime under unprecedented pressure. This paralysis highlights the present stagnation of global efforts to move meaningfully toward comprehensive nuclear disarmament.

This chapter examines how the world has reached this predicament and what actions could promote renewed progress:

- First, the chapter reviews the changed conditions and key challenges of the post–Cold War world, and discusses the continuing relevance and meaning of the goal of nuclear disarmament in this "second nuclear era."
- Second, the chapter proposes renewing progress toward nuclear disarmament by compelling all governments to generate and publish "roadmaps" to national nuclear disarmament that would then become the basis for constituting a single global "roadmap."

TODAY'S NUCLEAR CHALLENGES

In January 2007, a *Wall Street Journal* op-ed by four prominent U.S. ex-statesmen called on the United States to take the lead in rekindling "the vision of a world free of nuclear weapons" and in promoting "practical measures toward achieving that goal."[1] The debate instigated by that essay has helped restore appreciation that the quest for nuclear disarmament is as much a defining imperative in the twenty-first century as it was in the latter half of the twentieth century. However, the nature of that challenge has changed significantly with the end of the Cold War, marking the beginning of a "second nuclear era" whose novel elements the long-standing aspiration of nuclear disarmament needs to address meaningfully.

The Cold War Era

In the first nuclear era, a major focus was, rightly, on the two superpowers. The U.S.-Soviet arms race was piling up nuclear arsenals at a mind-numbing rate. At its peak, the U.S. nuclear stockpile contained nearly 32,000 warheads; for 40 years, that number never dipped below 20,000. The Soviet stockpile, at its peak, numbered over 40,000. That year, 1986, over 65,000 nuclear devices rested on the face of the planet. This arms race also saw escalating magnitudes in the sizes of these weapons. Testing of these increasingly large weapons was the "hot" edge of the "cold" war. During this period, the United States and Soviet Union together conducted over 1,700 nuclear tests. All told, there have been over 2,000 nuclear tests conducted worldwide.

Most dangerously, the superpower nuclear arsenals were coupled to strategic policies that put the use of these weapons in a hair-trigger state of readiness. In the United States these policies were expressed by the Single Integrated Operational Plan (SIOP) and through a multitude of deterrence commitments threatening first use of nuclear weapons in a fairly wide range of potential conventional conflicts. This razor's edge competition led to numerous situations where nuclear war was imminent, most famously during the Cuban Missile Crisis in 1962.

From Hope...

The end of the Cold War relieved some of these dangers, and so brought encouraging progress toward the end of nuclear disarmament. The United States and Russia acted bilaterally and unilaterally to significantly reduce their nuclear arsenals.[2] The U.S. arsenal is now down to about 10,000 warheads; Russia's is 15–20,000. Under the U.S.-Russia "Moscow Treaty," both sides will reduce "operationally deployed strategic warheads" to 1,700–2,200 by the end of 2012.[3] The United States and Russia also reached agreements to "detarget" their weapons, improving the strategic relationship, and to work together to secure fissile materials and technologies throughout the former Soviet Union.

There was also significant multilateral progress. Topping the list is the indefinite extension of the nuclear NPT in 1995. Equally important has been the extension of NPT membership to all countries in the world, except three already-nuclear countries (India, Pakistan, Israel), and agreement on a new protocol strengthening of the International Atomic Energy Agency (IAEA) safeguards securing the nuclear facilities in NPT countries.

Another major achievement was the successful negotiation of Comprehensive Test Ban Treaty (CTBT) in 1996, a long-standing milestone toward nuclear disarmament. There have been no nuclear tests since 1998, the longest hiatus ever. The incipient global norm against nuclear testing is a major step forward from the Cold War.

...To Frustration

But over the course of the 1990s, progress toward nuclear disarmament languished. Setbacks on old issues were accompanied by the emergence of new dangers. Despite achievement of the CTBT, the United States and other key states necessary to bring it into force have not ratified it. Negotiations on a companion treaty to end production of fissile materials is also stalled, most recently due to new U.S. claims that such a treaty cannot be verified.

The U.S.-Russia Moscow Treaty will go out of force the year target reductions are met, leaving those targets essentially nonbinding. Although U.S. and Russian nuclear forces have been "detargeted," thousands of warheads remain on hair-trigger, "launch on warning" alert status.

The United States, although reducing its total nuclear stockpile, has made plans to diversify and modernize its nuclear arsenal. The notorious "low-yield" and "bunker buster" devices are only some of the new designs under consideration. More dangerously, new U.S. nuclear war planning linking nuclear weapons intimately with conventional capabilities threatens to erode the "nuclear firebreak" long considered a key impediment to nuclear escalation. These plans are embedded in a strategic fabric including nuclear infrastructure modernization, which could eventually lead to new nuclear testing, and to strategic defenses, which expand offensive nuclear use options. Aggressive counterproliferation and preemptive strike doctrines pose perhaps a greater prospect of U.S. first use of nuclear weapons than Cold War era extended deterrence doctrines.[4]

The United States is not, however, the only source of new nuclear dangers. Russian nuclear arsenal reductions are dictated mainly by resource limitations, not disarmament commitment, and Russia has withdrawn its previous pledge of no first use of nuclear weapons. The United Kingdom and France are also sustaining their current arsenals and first-use doctrines, while China is embarked on a long-term modernization of its strategic nuclear forces that includes development of new solid-fueled intercontinental missiles that would reduce its launch time from hours to minutes.

Absent the shadow of superpower competition, many other states have felt both freer and more compelled to develop indigenous nuclear capabilities. The 1998 nuclear tests by non-NPT members India and Pakistan demonstrated the continuing appeal of nuclear weapons as both strategic tools and national symbols. North Korea became the first state to withdraw from the NPT in 2003, detonated a nuclear test explosion in 2006, and may now have assembled some 6–10 nuclear devices. North Korea's activities have increased fears of nuclear acquisition by Japan and South Korea, and have generated repercussions worldwide, as evidenced by recent developments in Iran.

Experiences with North Korea, Iran, and the A. Q. Khan network have spotlighted new proliferation dangers of civilian nuclear fuel technologies. According to the recent United Nations (UN) Secretary General's report, at least 40 countries now possess the industrial and scientific infrastructure to build nuclear weapons relatively quickly.[5] Vast quantities of nuclear materials, particularly in the former Soviet republics, remain unsecured and vulnerable to theft or surreptitious sale, posing perhaps the world's greatest proliferation threat.

Finally, in the aftermath of September 11, we are all keenly aware that the prospect of acquisition and use of a nuclear device by a nonstate organization is growing. Unlike state governments, many such groups would not hesitate to use such a device in a major city if they could obtain the means to do so. Even U.S. nuclear planners do not believe deterrence can work against terrorists.

Nuclear Threats and Nuclear Capabilities

Progress toward nuclear disarmament in the past decade has stalled in part because of political fecklessness, militaristic cultures, and the power of commercial arms interests. But these factors have long been present, and so cannot fully account for recent trends. Nor does the tenacious retention of nuclear weapons by those states that have them and the fervent desire to acquire them by the many parties that lack them derive from some abstract strategic logic. These ambitions have roots in specific circumstances in which the capacity to make nuclear threats provides political benefits. Nuclear disarmament efforts have stalled in part because we haven't caught up with how the post–Cold War international terrain has introduced a new nuclear era with reshaped nuclear dangers—dangers to which governments, by their nature, are less responsive.

During the Cold War, the fantastic numbers of nuclear weapons accumulated by the United States and the Soviet Union were rightly the focus of immediate arms control efforts. In the ideologically polarized climate of the Cold War confrontation, many regarded reducing nuclear arsenals as an imperative largely independent of politics. We can now see more clearly that nuclear dangers are not so independent of their political and social contexts. Indeed, it was the end of the superpower ideological competition, not reductions in their nuclear arsenals, that dissipated the palpable threat of massive nuclear war.

In the post–Cold War era, nuclear policies are even more deeply enmeshed in such broader contexts. The reduced perception of the prospect of global nuclear holocaust has increased perceptions by governments of the political value of making nuclear threats and increased the range of circumstances in which such threats can be effective.

Hence, the challenge of nuclear disarmament today is about more than just eliminating nuclear weapons themselves. Nuclear threat-making capacity is now as relevant as material capacity. New U.S. nuclear deterrence and counterproliferation strategies are more pernicious than the numerical size of the U.S. nuclear stockpile. China and India's resistance to joining multilateral arms control processes until U.S. and Russian arsenals are reduced to sizes comparable to their own are anachronistic.

Even states without nuclear weapons can leverage latent capabilities to make potent threats. As noted earlier, some 40 countries now possess the industrial and scientific infrastructure to build nuclear weapons relatively quickly. States whose potential nuclear weapons capabilities influence regional and global international relations (including disparate states such as Japan and Iran) are as responsible for promoting nuclear disarmament as is the United States.

Beyond the NPT

The utter stalemate of the 2005 NPT Review Conference in May 2005 demonstrates the unrelenting strain that the new pressures of the second nuclear era have placed on the core "bargain" that is the heart of the NPT regime.[6] This bargain pits the disarmament obligations of the NPT's nuclear-armed states (led by the United States) against the nonproliferation obligations of the NPT's non-nuclear-armed states (today most notably Iran).

Many consider these challenges to reveal that the NPT has failed, and that today's nuclear challenges are direr than any the world has yet faced. These viewpoints overlook how much more dangerous today's world would be had the NPT not prevented considerable proliferation since its inception in 1970. Indeed, paradoxically, the NPT is somewhat a victim of its own success. The world knows about the ambitions of North Korea and Iran that now challenge the NPT precisely because these countries have been subject to standards and verification activities created under the NPT's auspices. U.S. resistance to disarmament confronts the NPT only because the NPT is the only formal international U.S. commitment to achieve nuclear disarmament.

The NPT is at a crossroads today not because it has failed, but because nuclear dangers have changed. The increased value of nuclear threat-making, fueling perceptions of nuclear capabilities as a currency of power, has eroded the common obligation to pursue nuclear disarmament that all states share. Governments—both those with nuclear weapons and many of those without—are less motivated to pursue nuclear disarmament than previously. This ambivalence is a fundamental source of the paralysis of the NPT, which demonstrates the need for a new initiative, separate from the NPT, to rekindle substantive movement toward global nuclear disarmament.

ROADMAPS TO DISARMAMENT[7]

Today's wider scope of nuclear dangers, including the spreading reliance on nuclear threat-making and the insidious faith in nuclear weapons as a currency of international power, demand a new strategy for disarmament. This new disarmament strategy should focus on eliminating nuclear weapons coercion in all its forms, not just the weapons themselves. Such a strategy could engage all states equally, on a nondiscriminatory basis, sidestepping the conflicts between the nuclear "haves" and "have-nots" endemic to the NPT. This approach would also engage as equals the four non-NPT members.[8] Developing this kind of second track would rekindle consensual motivation for nuclear disarmament, begin the constitution of requisite global governance mechanisms, and ultimately transcend the current stalemate on capabilities reductions.

A New Nuclear Disarmament Strategy

Cold War era nuclear disarmament strategies tended to concentrate on elimination of the weapons themselves. A contemporary strategy needs to more inclusively aim to eliminate nuclear weapons coercion in all its forms. This is because many governments today—both with and without nuclear weapons—are seduced by misplaced faith in the power and prestige of nuclear capabilities.

Such governments have become increasingly ambivalent about the goal of nuclear disarmament.

Hence, nuclear disarmament cannot be achieved solely through intergovernmental mechanisms such as the NPT. Nuclear disarmament is now also very much about superseding the prerogatives of governments. This suggests the need to conceptualize the challenge of nuclear disarmament as a global public policy issue related to human security. It also suggests that a new disarmament initiative cannot be expected from governments—it must come from the people.

A new strategy to press governments to respond to the conditions of this new nuclear era must begin by reviving the global public's sense of the urgency to meet the considerable nuclear dangers the world still faces. Because governments have become so quiescent, this strategy would aim to mobilize popular power to compel governments to act meaningfully to achieve nuclear disarmament.

The United States bears a particular responsibility for leadership. Given today's global political realities, real progress toward nuclear disarmament requires the United States to take a leading role. Yet its government is among the most recalcitrant. Therefore, it is in the United States that popular power most requires mobilizing. Although opinion polls in the United States as much as elsewhere show broad public support for a world without nuclear weapons, few Americans consider nuclear abolition possible or realistic—the nuclear "status quo" has become an increasingly entrenched way of thinking. Hence, the U.S. public must be the primary focus of a new strategy to compel governments to action.

Drawing National Roadmaps

A new citizen-based initiative to revive global momentum toward nuclear disarmament could aim to compel all governments with extant or latent nuclear weapons capabilities to generate and publish "roadmaps" delineating how they would achieve disarmament. These roadmaps would then become the basis for transnational debate aimed at constituting a single public global roadmap. Roadmaps would overcome four principal obstacles to current disarmament efforts:

1. Roadmaps would dispel the impression that nuclear disarmament is utopian—too distant and indefinable ever to be achieved.
2. Roadmaps would be a constant reminder of the end to which all arms control and nonproliferation efforts are aimed.
3. Each country's individual roadmap would be a visible permanent metric of that state's progress.
4. The global roadmap would link all states in a sequential ordering, clearly identifying which are "next" to take defined steps, preventing paralysis.

Developing a national roadmap would not oblige any state to dismantle a single nuclear weapon. This is an advantage, because governments could not logically resist undertaking this small disarmament measure on grounds of national security, as happens with efforts to obtain other measures dealing with capabilities directly (such as de-alerting). The call to develop nothing more than a *plan* for disarmament would be nonthreatening in the short term to even the most ardent defender of nuclear weapons.

At the same time, disarmament roadmaps would act powerfully to reverse popular perceptions that nuclear disarmament, if desirable, is implausible or utopian. Nuclear arms advocates feed this perception by blithely dismissing nuclear disarmament as "unrealistic" in a dangerous world. Roadmaps, embodying a finite set of criteria and steps to achieve disarmament, would by their nature clear away the fog obscuring the path from today to a nuclear weapons-free world. Thus, demanding nuclear roadmaps would reinvigorate the idea of nuclear abolition in the public discourse. It would democratize the nuclear debate again, as was done during the nuclear freeze campaign of the 1980s—except now focusing on eliminating nuclear weapons rather than merely halting their buildup. Generating the roadmaps would begin the necessary process of national and international planning for nuclear disarmament, and create official government documents spelling out how to proceed.

Because the roadmaps would be compelled not just from the nine nuclear-armed states but also from states with latent nuclear capabilities, all countries would bear an equal responsibility to the obligation. In the United States, where the popular movement to compel these roadmaps should begin, the objective would be to achieve federal legislation requiring the U.S. government to prepare a disarmament roadmap and specifying the detailed criteria that roadmap would meet.

Roadmap Terms

Each state producing a roadmap would specify its material and political prerequisites for disarmament, and detail specific plans for verifiably eliminating all elements of its nuclear capabilities. This would include the irreversible dismantling of existing nuclear arms and verifiable restriction of all nuclear weapons development capacities of peaceful nuclear facilities.[9]

For states with nuclear weapons, issues to be addressed would include

- The technical facilities, capabilities, and procedures required to verifiably eliminate the nation's nuclear arsenal and securely dispose of the fissile materials contained in them.
- The timeline for phased dismantlement and disposition of these physical capabilities.
- The technologies and procedures necessary to allow international verification of nuclear disarmament while ensuring that the verification process itself does not risk proliferation of sensitive nuclear knowledge.

For both states with nuclear weapons and other states possessing latent nuclear weapons capabilities, issues to be addressed would include:

- The national capacity to prepare a complete accounting for all fissile materials in the nation's territory.

- The procedures or policies to provide high confidence that no state is hiding nuclear material or weapons, while claiming either to have eliminated its nuclear arsenal or to have never possessed one in the first place.
- The level of confidence the state would require in disarmament verification before it could verifiably dismantle the last nuclear weapon or put the last kilogram of fissile material under IAEA safeguards.
- The national security conditions required to eliminate all national need for reliance on nuclear weapons and nuclear deterrence, through security assurances under irreversible international agreement where possible or through conventional force substitutes where necessary.
- Economic conversion mechanisms to provide adjustment assistance, alternative employment opportunities, and income security for the people and communities that now depend on nuclear weapons systems for their livelihood.

Publication of these national reports would create a matrix of conditions for global nuclear disarmament. The cumulative list would no doubt be daunting. But it would also be finite.

The existence of the concrete roadmaps would curb extremes of the current debate over the prospect of global nuclear disarmament. Nuclear arms advocates, faced with a finite set of criteria for disarmament, would no longer be able to blithely dismiss nuclear disarmament as a utopian aspiration without real meaning in the practical world. At the same time, proponents of disarmament would face directly the difficult technical and political security challenges that would have to be overcome to achieve nuclear abolition.

The existence of these national roadmaps would also initiate global dialogue and debate toward combining them into a single global roadmap to disarmament. After a suitable period of dialogue, an international conference would be convened to knit together the roadmaps into a comprehensive plan for nuclear disarmament capable of receiving universal support. This conference would be convened under the authority of the UN Security Council, either under the auspices of the UN Conference on Disarmament, the IAEA, or as an independent process. The conference would meet without an expiration date until the global roadmap is achieved. This roadmap would provide the backbone for the oft-advocated nuclear weapons convention.

Alternatively, the roadmap plans could be framed in the context of existing international responsibilities, such as the disarmament obligations of all NPT members under Article VI of that treaty[10] and the International Court of Justice (ICJ) ruling that there exists a duty to pursue and conclusively achieve nuclear disarmament. The roadmap plans could also be implemented as a series of reciprocal independent initiatives, following the model of the 1991 U.S.-Soviet reductions; such initiatives could complement more multilateral processes by sustaining momentum of practical disarmament steps.

The resulting roadmap will be complex, and its timeline for achievement would likely be extended. Implementation of the roadmap would be fraught with challenges as international conditions continue to evolve in unpredictable ways. But with a roadmap in hand specifying reciprocal steps by all states, progress could be carefully metered and monitored, and accountability for setbacks fairly allocated.

A Civil Society Strategy

Building momentum for nuclear roadmaps would require a sustained commitment of citizen involvement. Civil society mobilization should begin in the United States, but would ultimately be initiated in all countries with existing or latent nuclear weapons capabilities. In the United States, the strategy would focus on insisting that the U.S. government develop a disarmament roadmap. The ultimate aim would be to have a congressional mandate requiring the government to produce a detailed roadmap according to a fixed timeline (perhaps attached as a binding amendment to defense authorization legislation).

The civil society strategy could follow two simultaneous tracks.

Model Resolution. In the United States, the strategy would focus on developing a model resolution: a simple statement describing the purpose of the disarmament roadmap, obliging the government to produce a meaningful roadmap and outlining what the criteria of the roadmap should be. The campaign would encourage adoption of the model resolution by citizens' groups, religious bodies, governmental councils and agencies, professional associations, trade unions, business groups, service organizations, and other civil society groups. The goal would be to gain the endorsement of thousands of such groups, so that virtually the entire society expresses support for the roadmaps.

A further stage of this strategy would involve presenting the resolution to voters in nonbinding ballot measures. This second phase could begin after the first is already under way and could be tested in a pilot project in a few localities.

Independent Roadmaps. In addition to demanding that governments develop disarmament roadmaps, citizens' groups could develop their own roadmaps. They could publicize or update the best of the existing plans for disarmament, such as the 1996 Canberra Commission report. They could hold citizen hearings and invite expert testimony on why and how governments should proceed toward the elimination of nuclear weapons. People could be encouraged to learn about and develop proposals for nuclear disarmament. To demonstrate the viability of renouncing nuclear weapons, the campaign could produce reports and analyses examining the experiences of countries such as South Africa and Ukraine that gave up nuclear weapons after acquiring or developing them.

This activity would serve several purposes:

- Educate millions of people on both the need for and practicality of nuclear disarmament.
- Invest in these people the commitment to work for the elimination of nuclear weapons.
- Demonstrate the viability of governmental roadmaps, further underscoring the plausibility of nuclear disarmament.
- Increase popular pressure for governments to adopt roadmaps.

Questions and Challenges

Several questions and challenges remain to be addressed. It is quite conceivable that the U.S. government and other nuclear weapon states will simply refuse to develop the required nuclear roadmaps, or will produce documents asserting that disarmament is impossible. These governments are, after all, more ambivalent about disarmament than ever before.

The campaign can anticipate this resistance by assuring that the requirement to develop roadmaps is established in binding law, and that the requirements for the roadmaps are highly specific. More importantly, the campaign must develop sufficiently strong levels of political support to mobilize pressure for the government to fulfill its obligation to plan for disarmament. This depth of support may require years to generate, and the campaign should attempt to require a legally binding disarmament roadmap from Congress only after it has already developed a very broad base of public support.

The next challenge would be to ensure that governments producing roadmaps actually implement them. There are many progressive plans that are never implemented because of political resistance from entrenched vested interests. The response to this resistance would be to refocus the campaign on the new goal to "start the plan" by focusing on implementation of the first steps provided in the plan, whatever they may be. At this stage the campaign would direct its momentum toward ensuring that elected officials remain accountable for seeing that implementation of the roadmap is fulfilled.

It is important to remember that the very process of building the campaign for nuclear roadmaps will change the public debate and prompt a range of responses from political adversaries and third parties. Typically, as such campaigns generate momentum, efforts emerge to undercut them through compromise. During the nuclear freeze campaign, for example, congressional moderates responded by generating pressure on the Reagan administration to adopt a more flexible arms control negotiating policy toward the Soviet Union. A disarmament roadmaps campaign must be prepared for similar responses.

An intricate problem will emerge if a transformation of the U.S. position is achieved, but governments of other nuclear-armed or nuclear-capable states fail to reciprocate. Each state's roadmap, including that of the United States, will likely be tied to conditions requiring other states to act as well. No state will be able to fully implement its roadmap without reciprocity.

This problem is the reason for international coordination of the roadmaps, either through an international conference or other means, to link the roadmaps to one another, spelling out the sequencing of reciprocal implementation. The integrated global plan will in itself provide a powerful political instrument to pressure governments to follow through with commitments, because each stage of implementation of the global plan would be universally known and the state(s) responsible for the next steps evident to all. No state could deny, as they can today, that it is "their turn" to act.

But the United States, as the world's preeminent power, has an assurance of security exceeding all other states. This provides it with latitude of action enabling it to "go first." Moreover, U.S. preeminence today sets the tone for global politics. Current policies entrenching U.S. commitment to retaining its nuclear capabilities endorse and embolden proliferation ambitions worldwide. A reversed U.S. posture firmly forswearing any reliance on nuclear threats would dramatically deflate the image of nuclear weapons as a useful currency of world power. Increased U.S. support for existing international institutions aiming to curb nuclear proliferation would further impinge the abilities of smaller countries to resist global pressures to adopt and follow their own disarmament roadmaps.

Ultimately, if other states fail to reciprocate, the disarmament process will stall. But if the United States is fulfilling a genuine leadership role, mobilizing global civil society to begin pressuring other states to follow through will be a much more achievable objective than at present.

Perhaps the most important challenge will be sustaining the required level of citizen commitment and involvement over the several years that will be necessary to achieve the objective of an integrated global roadmap. This problem cannot be "solved," but it can be managed by establishing a series of achievable interim goals and objectives that will give citizens a sense of empowerment energizing them to continue the campaign toward the longer range objective. Gaining approval for roadmap resolutions will provide opportunities for achieving interim objectives. Each church body or professional organization that adopts the civil society resolution will provide a victory for those who organize for it. Winning voter referendum campaigns on behalf of the resolution will provide an even greater sense of empowerment. These victories will build upon one another as the campaign gradually acquires momentum for the challenge of pressuring Congress and the federal government.

Interim victories also can be achieved by linking the long-range effort to short-term campaigns against, for example, the development of new nuclear weapons. The recent effort to block the bunker buster (successful for the moment) advances the longer range goal. The campaign will also address other interim challenges and opportunities as they arise, constantly linking short-term efforts to the long-range objectives. This linkage, in turn, will help cement the shorter-term gains. By combining short and long-term efforts in this manner, the campaign can empower its supporters with interim successes while building momentum over the long term to abolish nuclear weapons.

CONCLUSION

Nuclear disarmament has always been not only an ultimate goal, but also a vision with practical consequences for nearer-term arms control and nonproliferation practices. The vision reminds us that arms control and nonproliferation are means to a greater end, not simply instruments to curb the greatest dangers of a nuclear status quo. Sustaining global nuclear disarmament as the ultimate objective is a prerequisite for any arms control and nonproliferation achievements to be sustainable. In other words, to be realistic, solutions even to immediate nuclear challenges must aim to advance nuclear disarmament.

But today, we face a cruel paradox: success in mitigating the greatest nuclear dangers of the Cold War era has made it easier for governments to disassociate the nearer-term means from the ultimate end. Some nuclear dangers of the emerging second nuclear era are more potent than those of the first. But these nuclear dangers are also different in kind, and not strictly comparable. Now more than ever, these dangers are tied to threats to use nuclear weapons to instill fear and seek gain in specific social and political contexts.

Here emerges a second paradox: although the responsibility of states to pursue disarmament is broader, the diminution of the prospect of massive nuclear war has made the world appear to be "safer" for governments to embrace nuclear capabilities (extant or latent) as currencies of power and prestige. Governments of states possessing nuclear weapons increasingly regard arms control not as a means to disarmament but as an instrument only to curb the greatest dangers of a nuclear status quo. Governments of incipient nuclear weapon states increasingly regard nonproliferation not as a means to disarmament but as an instrument only to prevent new entrants into the nuclear "club." Both sets of governments, grasping the short-term "fix" nuclear weapons seem to offer, have abandoned the long-term imperative of nuclear disarmament.

For this reason, civil society efforts to rekindle a global movement toward nuclear disarmament are as vital as ever. More than before, such efforts must now also recognize the depths to which nuclear weapons and nuclear threat-making are enmeshed in global security structures, and must therefore also offer progressive new forms of global governance that create security structures sustainable in a non-nuclear world. The imperative of nuclear disarmament is today inseparable from the need to establish new forms of global governance independent of the sovereign state system and based on principles of law and democratic accountability.[11]

Realizing practical progress toward nuclear disarmament, however incremental, sustains the viability of this vision. Such progress further constitutes that vision by adding depth and substance to it, and transmits to future generations the requisite knowledge and skills, and imagination, to carry forth that imperative.

We know that, with wisdom and conviction, real near-term progress can be made. The experiences of the early 1990s, among others, have proven that. We also know that the ultimate goals, if distant, are not utopian. In the words of William Arthur Ward, "If you can imagine it, you can achieve it. If you can dream it, you can become it."[12]

NOTES

1. George P. Shultz, William J. Perry, Henry A. Kissinger, and Sam Nunn, "A World Free of Nuclear Weapons," *Wall Street Journal,* January 4, 2007.
2. The 1987 Intermediate-Range Nuclear Forces (INF) Treaty eliminated the entire category of ground-launched mid-range nuclear missiles in Europe. In 1991, Bush the First removed nuclear weapons from all naval deployments, except strategic submarines, and all overseas deployments, except in Europe under NATO auspices.
3. Although the U.S. total stockpile will remain around 10,000, by 2012 Russia may have as few as 2,000.
4. For an elaboration of this analysis, see Wade L. Huntley, "Threats All the Way Down: U.S. Strategic Initiatives in a Unipolar World," *Review of International Studies* (January, 2006).
5. *A More Secure World: Our Shared Responsibility*, Report of the UN Secretary General's High-Level Panel on Threats, Challenges and Change, United Nations, 2004, p. 39.
6. See Wade L. Huntley, "The NPT at a Crossroads," *Foreign Policy in Focus* (Silver City, NM and Washington, DC), July 1, 2005 (http://www.fpif.org/fpiftxt/144).
7. This section benefits from the insights of David Cortright, Fourth Freedom Forum.

8. India, Pakistan, and Israel are the only three countries in the world that have not joined the NPT. All have nuclear weapons. North Korea joined the NPT in 1987 but withdrew in 2003 and has now demonstrated nuclear weapons capability. The 2005 NPT Review Conference did not acknowledge North Korea's withdrawal.

9. Some of the subsequent criteria are drawn from George Perkovich, Jessica Tuchman Mathews, Joseph Cirincione, Rose Gottemoeller, and Jon Wolfsthal, *Universal Compliance: A Strategy for Nuclear Security*, Report by the Carnegie Endowment for International Peace, March 2005, pp. 145–57. The present proposal broadens the disarmament concept of *Universal Compliance* by calling for participation by all countries with potential nuclear weapons capabilities, not just with fissile material stocks, and by including in the roadmaps each country's security and political as well as material prerequisites.

10. Note that the nonuniversality and discriminatory basis of NPT membership may limit its applicability as a legal framework to which roadmap-based disarmament obligations could be attached.

11. States are unlikely to go away any time soon, and will remain the loci of decisions to develop nuclear weapons and utilize nuclear threats. But globalization is already producing new forms of transnational nongovernmental communication and action that impinges state sovereignty and constitutes incipient alternative global governance mechanisms. These mechanisms can be nurtured and grown to supplement domestic efforts and effectively increase all states' accountability for nuclear weapons decision making.

12. *Thoughts of a Christian Optimist: The Words of William Arthur Ward*, Vol. 2, 1977, The Good Book Publishing Company.

CHAPTER 12

Strengthening International Security through International Law

Jürgen Scheffran

The Link between International Security and International Law

Many of the dangers that the world faces today, including risks of proliferation and nuclear war, violent regional conflicts and the threat from terrorist attacks, or climate change and environmental disasters, cannot be resolved or prevented by a single nation, even not the most powerful one. Thus, collaboration and agreement of the international community is required to tackle these challenges, codified by international law to provide mutual assurance that policies are pursued in an integrated, coordinated, and effective way. Without international law, states are not bound and can act freely, pursuing national security interests and threat perceptions. International law defines the rules of the game to diminish conflict and enhance cooperation.

How important these rules are is well demonstrated by the prisoner's dilemma in game theory. Here two actors are in a better situation if they both cooperate rather than not cooperate. However, by individually defecting from cooperation they could aim for individual gains as long as the other actor continues to cooperate. If both sides individually give up cooperation for these benefits, they end up in a situation that is worse for both. To prevent both actors from noncooperation for the mutual benefit requires agreement based on communication, verification, and control to enforce the agreement. To discourage violations of an agreement they need to be detected and the expected benefits from violation to be denied. It is important that a violation has to be reliably verified and the response is credible. While both requirements could be realized by the actors themselves according to their capabilities and interests, it is more efficient to transfer these tasks to an authority that is not bound by individual capabilities and interests. To verify and enforce compliance with an agreement it needs to be prescribed in the clearest possible way within a framework of accepted legal terms.

The consequences of unregulated warfare and arms races have been demonstrated throughout military history where actors were caught in prisoner's dilemma situations or, even worse, in zero-sum games where the gain by one actor could only be achieved by the losses of another actor and, thus, no common ground for cooperation could be found. Under such circumstances it is hard for actors to preserve their security, that is, to avoid threats to their very existence and identity. Events that could cause intolerable damage and have a significant likelihood lead to insecurity for vulnerable actors. If the existence or identity of actors is at stake in such conflicts, they mobilize their resources to survive. Strategic thinking, power plays, and mutual threat perceptions have increased military capabilities that exacerbated rather than reduced the security dilemma. An unregulated interaction often supports worst case scenarios resulting in arms races and wars, which were only restrained by the capabilities and resources of the actors involved.

In international relations the key actors are nation-states, which seek to preserve their existence and identity in interaction against potential risks, in particular against threats from other nations' use of force. International law regulates interactions by restraining the actions of states and providing rules that everyone can rely on. Restraining the threatening capabilities is thus an important incentive for arms control, disarmament, and nonproliferation agreements that seek to enhance stability and reduce the risks and costs of conflict. Reducing capabilities, however, is not enough and often not possible as long as motivations are driving these capabilities. It is therefore essential to also deal with these motives through security policies that diminish strategic incentives and threat perceptions.

While international law can contribute to international security in different ways, multilateral treaties alone cannot ensure security, but they offer a framework to address today's security challenges. Multilateral treaties and the regimes they establish "contribute to national and global security by articulating norms, creating monitoring and enforcement mechanisms, and providing benchmarks for progress."[1] A key issue is whether the verification and enforcement mechanisms work and are sufficient to detect and deter violations. A respected authority that could provide these tasks effectively does not yet exist in the international system. The United Nations (UN) Security Council is still bound by the veto power of its permanent members that are the nuclear weapon states.

While the benefits of cooperation and international law appear to be obvious, the distribution of these benefits can be uneven. Some states may not see the benefits to be worth the costs, in particular the restraints on their sovereignty. The situation is particularly difficult with a hegemon that pursues unlimited power projections. This is most vividly demonstrated by the tendency of the Bush administration to move away from binding international law and multilaterally agreed arms control to rely on its own (military) strength. A doctrine of superiority that rests on nuclear weapons, missile defenses, and dominance in space could create enormous uncertainties, instabilities, and risks for international security that could also undermine the national security of the United States.

Even though the prospects for international law and arms control based on multilateral agreements currently may seem remote, this should not exclude conceptual thinking about and broadening of political support for alternatives. Conceptual thinking is important, even more under the current circumstances when even incremental steps seem to be excluded. The quest for strengthening of international law in general and of arms control and disarmament in particular should not only be based on political opportunities, in particular not on the preferences, interests, and power structures of current administrations. It is essential to conceptualize and design long-term alternatives beyond day-to-day power games in order to create conditions for long-term change.

In this chapter some alternative concepts are presented, based on previous work on the control of nuclear weapons, ballistic missiles, missile defenses, and space weapons, all of which have shaped the security landscape after World War II. While military arms races before the war were often driven by offense-defense interactions and the technological dynamics, the strategic situation drastically changed with the advent of nuclear weapons and ballistic missiles, which enormously increased the damage potential compared to conventional weaponry. Nuclear weapons not only threaten the existence of nation-states but of mankind. With ballistic missiles large distances can be crossed with a speed unknown before. While bullets from guns cross distances at several hundred meters per second (making reactions at close distance impossible), ballistic missiles reach 10 times that speed, practically excluding reactions over continental and even intercontinental distances. The combination of vast destructive power and high speed over large distances created an irresistible weapon: the nuclear-armed Intercontinental Ballistic Missile (ICBM). With these weapons, it became possible to leave the Earth's atmosphere and fly through outer space, which not only transformed global warfare but also opened the possibility of space warfare. Ballistic missiles became vehicles to launch objects into Earth orbit for an extended period. Because of the high speed of ballistic missiles and the large range of their trajectory, attempts to counter this threat by missile defense systems have failed to date. However, missile defenses open a Pandora's box of weapons to intercept objects in space. The need for a physical mechanism that is faster than the movement of masses spurred the development of directed energy weapons, such as laser weapons, that work at the speed of light. The control of these weapons is discussed in the following, with a focus on a Nuclear Weapons Convention, international control of ballistic missiles and other delivery systems, and the strengthening of international space law by concepts of space security and a space weapons ban. At the end, the role of verification and enforcement is discussed.

Nuclear Disarmament and the Nuclear Weapons Convention[2]

The Political Context

After the end of the Cold War the demand for a Nuclear Weapon-Free World (NWFW) found increasing support among governments and Non-Governmental Organizations (NGOs). From the beginning, the debate focused on both the desirability and the feasibility of this goal.[3] After the 1995 Review and Extension Conference of the Non-Proliferation Treaty (NPT), a political chain of actions for the abolition of nuclear weapons emerged, including the protest against nuclear testing; the Hiroshima and Nagasaki anniversaries; the Nobel Peace Prize for Joseph Rotblat and the Pugwash movement; the foundation of the Abolition 2000 Global Network and of the Canberra Commission on the Elimination of Nuclear Weapons; the Advisory Opinion of the International Court of Justice (ICJ) on the legality of the threat or use of nuclear weapons; and a statement by 60 military leaders, calling for the elimination of nuclear weapons.

One of the ideas of how to achieve a NWFW is the concept of a Nuclear Weapons Convention (NWC). Such a comprehensive convention would effectively prohibit and eliminate all nuclear weapons and their infrastructure. It would supplement a Biological Weapons Convention and a Chemical Weapons Convention, completing the ban on all Weapons of Mass Destruction (WMD). The NWC concept has been suggested since its foundation in 1993 by INESAP and was supported by the International Coalition for Nuclear Non-Proliferation and Disarmament, including NGOs such as IPPNW, IPB, IALANA, INES, and INESAP[4] as founding members.[5] An INESAP Study Group, comprising of more than 50 experts from 17 countries, presented its report "Beyond the NPT: A Nuclear Weapon-Free World" during the NPT Review and Extension Conference in New York in April 1995, which outlines the transformation process of the traditional nonproliferation regime into a NWFW regime, represented by a Nuclear Weapons Convention. The substance of the NWC is summarized as follows:[6]

> The NWC would have to ban not only the possession and production of nuclear weapons; it would also prohibit all kinds of acquisition (including research), transfer, deployment (or any preparations for re-deployment), use and threat of use. The convention would call for the elimination of the whole infrastructure serving the manufacture and possession of nuclear warheads and their means of delivery. It would provide a system of international control for guarding and accounting for all remaining weapon-usable fissile material. The convention would incorporate, and thus replace, other existing relevant treaties as bans on nuclear weapon tests, and on the production of weapon-grade fissile material—it would make these bans universal. The convention would replace the NPT itself.

On the same occasion, a statement was signed by more than 200 NGOs, which became the founding document for the Abolition 2000 Global Network. In the first of 11 demands, it calls for "negotiations on a nuclear weapons abolition convention that requires the phased elimination of all nuclear weapons within a timebound framework, with provisions for effective verification and enforcement."

In its August 1996 report, the Canberra Commission on the Elimination of Nuclear Weapons identified two options to achieve a NWFW through an "incremental approach of a number of separate instruments or through a comprehensive approach which would combine all relevant instruments into a single legal instrument, a nuclear weapons convention." The comprehensive approach would entail "the negotiation of a new treaty prohibiting the development and possession of nuclear weapons to replace the NPT and possibly other treaties such as a CTBT and possible future conventions on the cessation of the production of fissile materials for nuclear explosive purposes and on the non–first use of nuclear weapons."[7]

In its 1998 report on *The Future of U.S. Nuclear Weapons Policy* the U.S. National Academy of Sciences' Committee on International Security and Arms Control mentioned as one of four possible disarmament approaches,

> an international conference charged with creating a new treaty to prohibit the possession of nuclear weapons. This new treaty would replace the NPT and possibly other treaties such as the Comprehensive Test Ban Treaty. The negotiations leading to the Biological and Chemical Weapons Conventions are examples of an international process to outlaw an entire class of weapons.[8]

The demand for NWC negotiations reached the government level with three resolutions adopted by the United Nations General Assembly (UNGA) on December 10, 1996.[9] The UNGA readopted the 1995 timebound framework resolution 51/45 O and also readopted the resolution 51/46 D introduced by India, which calls for negotiations on a Convention on the Prohibition of the Use of Nuclear Weapons, both with the additional reference to concluding a NWC. These additions were inspired by the resolution 51/45 M that was newly introduced by Malaysia. This resolution welcomed the unanimous conclusion of the ICJ that "there exists an obligation to pursue in good faith and bring to a conclusion negotiations leading to nuclear disarmament in all its aspects under strict and effective international control," and called upon "all states to fulfill that obligation immediately by commencing multilateral negotiations in 1997 leading to an early conclusion of a nuclear weapons convention prohibiting the development, production, testing, deployment, transfer, threat or use of nuclear weapons and providing for their elimination." The Malaysian resolution, with the lobbying power of the Abolition 2000 Global Network, gained more cosponsors and positive votes (two-thirds of the voting states) than the other two resolutions, including a number of Western countries and China as a nuclear weapon state.[10] In March 1997, a majority of the European Parliament supported the central demand for NWC negotiations.

Negotiations on a NWC could serve as a framework for the elimination of nuclear weapons, focusing, harmonizing, and joining together future nonproliferation and disarmament measures into an integrated concept. Within an incremental-comprehensive approach, unilateral measures and declarations could be combined with bilateral negotiations between the United States and Russia, negotiations among the five permanent members of the Security Council (P-5) and multilateral negotiations in the Conference on Disarmament (CD) or other bodies. Incremental and comprehensive approaches to a NWFW would complement and reinforce one another. Single measures could serve as building blocks of a comprehensive convention that could be realized step by step. Such steps include the no first use of nuclear weapons and further security guarantees, new nuclear weapon-free zones (NWFZ), a deep reduction of the nuclear arsenals and delivery systems, a ban on nuclear weapons materials, further restrictions on nuclear weapons development as well as the closure and conversion of nuclear weapons facilities. Concerns of states about asymmetries and disadvantages inherent in single steps need to be balanced.

To demonstrate the feasibility of a comprehensive phased plan for nuclear disarmament and to promote negotiations toward this goal, the Lawyers' Committee on Nuclear Policy (LCNP), in collaboration with INESAP and

IPPNW and with support by the Abolition 2000 network, initiated the drafting of a Model NWC. In February 1996, a drafting committee of lawyers, academics, scientists, disarmament experts, and diplomats was established that held meetings in New York and Darmstadt, Germany. One principle for the drafting has been the "search for a regime sufficiently restrictive to ensure the highest level of confidence in compliance, but also sufficiently permissive to allow states to join without jeopardizing their legitimate security interests and commercial activities."[11] Drawing on existing treaties and documents (Strategic Arms Reduction Treaty [START] and Intermediate-Range Nuclear Forces [INF] Treaty, Chemical Weapons Convention, regional NWFZ, Comprehensive Test Ban Treaty, Security Council resolutions, IAEA safeguard agreements), the essential elements of a comprehensive convention to prohibit and eliminate nuclear weapons were identified. The drafting committee was able to complete the first discussion draft in a relatively short period of time and presented it to the public during the NPT PrepCom in April 1997. With support by the Republic of Costa Rica, the Model NWC became a UN document in the same year and was published as a book in 1999 with explanations and comments.[12]

Although the Middle Powers Initiative and the New Agenda Coalition opened new opportunities for action, after 1997 the political conditions for nuclear disarmament dramatically declined. Nuclear and missile testing by India and Pakistan in 1998 as well as missile testing by Iran and North Korea played into the hands of those in the United States who shifted the coordinates toward missile defense and a "conservative revolution." In addition to these and other factors, the terrorist attacks of 9/11 in 2001 and the war in Iraq in 2003 induced a chain of violent events that made the prospects for disarmament remote. An obvious indicator is the stalemate at the Geneva-based Conference on Disarmament since 1997.

The crisis has renewed interest in concepts of nuclear abolition, as can be seen from the *Wall Street Journal* article of January 4, 2007 by Henry Kissinger, George Shultz, William Perry, and Sam Nunn on the need to achieve a nuclear weapon-free world. Along these lines, former UK Foreign Secretary Margaret Beckett in a key note speech at the 2007 Carnegie International Nonproliferation Conference, promoted the vision of nuclear abolition and the development of technical and political instruments to achieve complete nuclear disarmament. A revised Model Nuclear Weapons Convention was prepared by a drafting committee as part of a book launch at the 2007 NPT PrepCom.[13] In the same year, the Australian Senate, New Zealand Parliament, and European Parliament adopted draft resolutions, calling for nuclear abolition and/or the achievement of a NWC. Further initiatives were launched in the UK House of Commons and U.S. Congress.[14]

STRUCTURE AND CONTENT OF THE
MODEL NUCLEAR WEAPONS CONVENTION

The Model Nuclear Weapons Convention comprises 19 Articles on 60 pages, 8 preliminary annexes/protocols plus a commentary, a summary, and statement of purpose. The preamble refers to previous agreements and to guiding principles of the convention. Article I contains general obligations not to "research, develop, test, produce, otherwise acquire, deploy, stockpile, maintain, retain or transfer nuclear weapons" as well as related nuclear materials, delivery systems, and components, and not to use or threaten to use nuclear weapons. All existing nuclear weapons, their development, and production facilities as well as delivery systems, command, and control facilities are to be destroyed or converted. The prohibitions also cover special nuclear materials, that is, fissionable or fusionable materials that can be used to build a nuclear weapon (especially highly enriched uranium [HEU], uranium-233, plutonium, tritium). The obligation to place special nuclear materials under international control until a safe method of disposition is found would make diversion of such materials more difficult.

In Article II, 81 definitions are given that are an integral part of the Model NWC. They are important to avoid ambiguity and potential loopholes that facilitate circumvention. For the definition of nuclear weapons, different alternatives are offered. According to the first definition, drawn from the Treaty of Tlatelolco, they comprise "any device which is capable of releasing nuclear energy in an uncontrolled manner and which has a group of characteristics that are appropriate for use for warlike purposes." The phrase "group of characteristics" is not specified. The second definition is more comprehensive and includes radiological weapons and weapons with nuclear triggers, such as particle beam and high energy laser weapons. It includes explosive devices "in assembled or disassembled form" in order to prevent attempts to circumvent the provisions of the convention by removing a key component and rendering an otherwise functional nuclear weapon temporarily inoperable. The language "designed for or capable of" allows the definition to cover devices that might not have been originally designed as nuclear weapons but could be used as such (close to the War Weapons Control Act of Germany). The current Model NWC includes separate provisions on warheads and delivery vehicles.

A third approach to the definition of nuclear weapons would be to follow the pattern of the Chemical Weapons Convention. The premise would be that any radioactive isotope (beyond a specified quantity or concentration) that might be used in a weapon to cause death, harm, or incapacitation to life forms or their genetic structures, must be destroyed, prohibited, or carefully controlled. This definition is complicated by the fact that basically all materials undergo a radioactive decay within a certain half-life. Many chemicals can be also toxic at certain concentration (e.g., alcohol, medicaments, etc.) but they would not be called "weapons." The potential degree of harm and the practical usability as a weapon is important. The degree to which nuclear materials are harmful is left to future research.

In Article IV, the Model NWC proposes a flexible series of coordinated phases for implementation. The suggested deadlines are offered as recommendations and are based on evaluations of technical feasibility, with the understanding that states would negotiate the actual deadlines. Moreover, the NWC allows for extension of deadlines if a state party is unable to complete obligations within the time allotted.

The International Control of Delivery Systems[15]

While many countries have agreed to eliminate biological and chemical weapons and also pledged in the NPT to forgo or eliminate nuclear weapons, there is still no multinational treaty restricting the development and use of delivery systems. Although the NPT preamble emphasizes "the elimination from national arsenals of nuclear weapons and the means of their delivery pursuant to a Treaty on general and complete disarmament under strict and effective international control," the NPT does not further specify how this ultimate goal could be achieved for delivery systems. Until recently, ballistic missiles and other delivery systems have been largely ignored in international arms control and disarmament negotiations. This deficit was pointed out by Jayantha Dhanapala, the former UN under secretary general for Disarmament Affairs: "Why is public debate mired today in a duel between deterrence and defense, with scant attention to missile disarmament?"[16]

The proliferation of delivery systems is one of the critically important issues in the overall disarmament agenda. Delivery systems are an important part of WMD, in particular, nuclear weapons. Appropriate means of delivery are required to transport a nuclear weapon from its storage or deployment area to its target in a "militarily useful" way. Sophisticated delivery systems are costly and difficult to produce and, in many cases, are the most visible part of a nuclear weapon. Therefore, the control of nuclear-capable delivery systems would be an important step to make nuclear weapons useless and reduce the threat of their use. This is especially true for ballistic missiles, which represent effective and powerful means to deploy nuclear weapons.

The new world situation has rendered the huge missile arsenals of the Cold War obsolete and improved the conditions for effective missile controls. To reduce the missile threat and prevent destabilizing military reactions to missile proliferation such as ballistic missile defense, adequate control measures are needed. Restricting the means for delivery of WMD is essential to reduce the threat posed by such weapons. Effective control is complicated by the fact that a variety of delivery systems could potentially be used. This includes rather sophisticated delivery systems like ballistic missiles, airplanes, cruise missiles, drones, and artillery, as well as a wide range of "low-technology" delivery systems—such as civilian cars, aircraft, ships, or even suitcases—that can transport nuclear or other payloads. While control in the first category could effectively restrict the military value of WMD, control in the second category would have only a minor effect compared to the enormous efforts necessary. Therefore, it is reasonable to focus control on delivery systems that are explicitly designed for their military purpose and deal with the residual risk of low-tech means of delivery by other measures.

In the first category of specially designed delivery systems, experts emphasize the priority for control of the various delivery systems differently. Most attention has been focused so far on ballistic missiles, but for some observers the military effectiveness of ballistic missiles has been exaggerated compared to aircraft. According to a 1991 study of the Center for International Security and Arms Control (CISAC), "modern aircraft are, indeed, very capable and cost-effective alternatives for ground-missions." Compared to ballistic missiles, combat aircraft with equivalent capabilities are widely distributed across the globe. There are only a few hundred ballistic missiles with ranges beyond 300 km in the hands of developing countries, compared with many thousand military aircraft beyond this range. A growing number of countries have indigenous design and production capabilities, and a range of first-rate aircraft are for sale in the international marketplace.

Although the proliferation of land-attack cruise missiles is still at an early stage, cruise missiles potentially pose a proliferation threat comparable to that of ballistic missiles and attack aircraft, and are deserving of more nonproliferation efforts. Cruise missiles could be easier to build than advanced attack aircraft or ballistic missiles, do not require highly trained pilots nor do they place pilots at risk, could be less vulnerable than airplanes to preemptive or suppressive attacks, and are potentially inexpensive compared to both ballistic missiles and attack aircraft. Using Global Positioning System (GPS) guidance information, cruise missiles are potentially highly accurate (dozens of meters) and, thus, could be more destructive as conventional weapons than current ballistic missiles.

Compared to other nuclear-capable delivery platforms, submarines can operate covertly, so that it is difficult to monitor their location continuously. Due to stealth technology, long range (more than 10,000 miles), and the ability to operate submerged for extended periods, submarines are potentially able to launch strategic or tactical nuclear weapons from close to the territory of an adversary. During the Cold War, nuclear weapons were widely deployed on nuclear-powered submarines. Although non-nuclear weapon states and "threshold" states do not possess such nuclear-powered submarines, it is possible that modern conventional-powered submarines could play a decisive role in future military conflicts.

Compared to the variety of potential delivery systems for WMD, the present control regime is insufficient. The dominant approaches have been bilateral arms control and disarmament between the United States and Russia:

- The INF Treaty of 1987 removed the land-based intermediate-range nuclear forces of the United States and Russia (including Cruise Missiles) with a 500–5,500 km range.
- The Strategic Arms Reduction Treaties (START) include a limitation of long-range missiles and bombers to 1,600 km and a reduction of strategic warheads to 3,000–3,500 km.
- The Moscow Treaty (Strategic Offensive Reductions Treaty) of 2002 does not explicitly mention missiles but seeks to reduce the strategic warheads to 1,700–2,200 by the end of 2012.

A few other agreements were designed to further restrain delivery systems:

- The 1972 Anti-Ballistic Missile (ABM) Treaty, which was abrogated by the Bush administration in 2002, banned strategic missile defense systems for both superpowers, including development, testing and deployment of rocket-based components for that purpose.
- The Outer Space Treaty of 1967 bans the deployment of objects in orbit that carry WMD.
- The conventions for the elimination of chemical and biological weapons also ban delivery systems designed for the use of these weapons.
- The UN Weapons Register of 1992 determines those weapons for which information has to be provided, including launchers and missiles with more than 25 km range.
- The agreements for NWFZ in Latin America, South Pacific, Southeast Asia, and Africa do not explicitly cover delivery systems if they are not an inseparable part of a nuclear weapon.

The current approach to curbing missile proliferation is the Missile Technology Control Regime (MTCR), which was initiated in 1987 with seven members. MTCR membership has grown to 34 countries.[17] Although the MTCR has been successful in creating an international norm against missile exports and has delayed some missile programs, more significant accomplishments are impeded by problems and shortcomings. The MTCR is not a binding treaty; there are no specific verification or enforcement mechanisms, and membership is essentially restricted to the suppliers. Existing ballistic missile arsenals are not addressed, the asymmetry between "haves" and "have nots" is ignored, and various shorter-range missiles have been deployed in a number of developing countries.[18] Strict export controls for dual-use goods undermine the civilian technology cooperation and economic interests in civilian space flight.

Because of these major deficiencies, supply-side controls need to be complemented or replaced by more cooperative demand-side solutions that go beyond the MTCR. The most effective strategy against proliferation is to create an international norm by convincing all states to forgo the option of having WMD and related delivery systems. Appropriate measures include not only barriers such as export controls but global and regional disarmament, arms control, and conflict resolution measures, security incentives as well as international economic and technology cooperation in exchange for giving up WMD.

Regional approaches for arms control could include CBMs like launch notification and exchanges of information, including establishment of data centers, conversion programs, common seminars on military forces and strategy, regional flight test bans, a freeze of R&D on missile technologies for military purposes. The importance of regional approaches to disarmament and confidence-building was demonstrated in South America (Argentina and Brazil) and South Asia (India and Pakistan).

Since the different types of delivery systems are closely interrelated, it is insufficient to restrict control only to one means of delivery. As has been outlined in the 1995 INESAP Study "Beyond the NPT," an integrated approach is necessary that goes beyond the present regime. According to this study, a number of possible measures for limiting systems that could be used for nuclear delivery could complement and facilitate the elimination of nuclear weapons (for ballistic missiles see the following section):

- *Cruise missile* nonproliferation efforts, such as the MTCR, should be continued and, if possible, expanded. However, it may be necessary to adopt arms control approaches that deal with the similarities between attack aircraft and cruise missiles, and between their underlying technology bases. Verification is difficult but not an insurmountable problem, as the INF Treaty proved.
- To prevent *military aircraft* proliferation, states could include limits on the numbers and capabilities of military aircraft in their regional arms control regimes. Even though currently unrealistic, a global ban on new types of combat aircraft would prevent both vertical and horizontal proliferation in a nondiscriminatory way.
- To address the possibility that nuclear weapons could be deployed much more widely on *submarines*, a first step would be the creation of an international control regime, similar to the MTCR, focusing on technologies

critical for advanced submarines. Joint naval task groups operated by the UN could monitor and, if necessary, control the operation of diesel submarines during crises.

Building an International Norm against Ballistic Missiles[19]

The most immediate candidate for control of delivery systems are ballistic missiles, which are perceived as especially threatening and provoking the development of ballistic missile defense systems. In the light of technical difficulties and the lengthy development periods for both ballistic missiles and missile defenses, there is a chance for political initiatives to contain the emerging missile race. A global missile threat from states such as North Korea or Iran does not yet exist, and will not materialize in the near term; nor will the United States have a working missile defense to deploy soon. Instead of rushing to join or counter a nonexistent missile shield against a nonexistent missile threat, the international community would be better advised to take joint action and collaborate on preventing a missile race on earth and in outer space, and promoting the disarmament of nuclear weapons and delivery systems. Diplomatic initiatives are required to reduce the role of ballistic missiles in critical regions (Northeast Asia, South Asia, Middle East) and to develop an international norm against ballistic missiles. As the dangers of an offense-defense missile race become imminent, the need for an international initiative to control ballistic missiles becomes more urgent. In recent years a number of initiatives on missile control have been launched:

- Russia and the United States have operated a system for the monitoring of missile tests for more than three decades. With the 1971 *Accidents Measures Agreement*, both sides were required to notify certain missile tests in advance, which has been specified by additional agreements (*Incidents at Sea Agreement*, SALT-II). In 1988, a more comprehensive system for ballistic missile launches was established that required notification of launch time and location for ICBMs as well as the intended target area. These data were transmitted to the newly established crisis response center. Missile launches were monitored by radar facilities on the ground (such as the U.S. Ballistic Missile Early Warning System), at sea and in the air. In the early 1990s, the idea of a multilateral missile monitoring system was discussed, in the context of the proposal for a Global Protection Against Limited Strikes (GPALS) system. During the millennium fever in 1999, both sides established a joint early warning center, and in the following year Presidents Clinton and Yeltsin established the Joint Data Exchange Centre (JDEC) in Moscow to facilitate transparency and data exchange about launches of ballistic missiles with more than 500 km range, including those from other countries. Signed on December 16, 2000, the U.S.-Russian Memorandum of *Understanding on Notification of Missile Launches* provides for pre- and postlaunch notification of all ballistic missile tests and space launches, as well as notification of failed satellite launches. Other countries could join the agreement.[20] Even though this memorandum did not find the support of the Bush administration, the JDEC in Moscow was continued.

- A related initiative has been the Russian proposal for a Global Control System (GCS) for the nonproliferation of missiles and missile technology. A Global Monitoring System (GMS) would increase transparency with regard to missile launches and reduce the risk of miscalculation or misunderstanding. Such a regime could include controls on missile and missile technology transfers to third countries and provide prior notification of test launches of ballistic missiles and space launch vehicles. In order to discourage proliferation, the GCS would offer security incentives to abstain from missile development and assistance in the peaceful uses of space for states that completely give up and convert their missile programs and capabilities.[21] Launched in 1999 and further explored at several expert level meetings in Moscow,[22] the proposal acknowledges the security concerns raised by missile programs and the need for security assurances. Despite the participation of 71 countries, including North Korea, the initiative did not lead to concrete results in face of opposition from the U.S. government that saw GCS as a vehicle against the missile defense plans.

- There is an evident need to strengthen the MTCR by developing and enhancing confidence-building measures (CBMs) among states with missile capabilities. During the 1999 MTCR Plenary in Noordwijk, the Netherlands, the missile suppliers discussed voluntary commitments to "responsible missile behavior," without publicly explaining their meaning. At the conference in The Hague in November 2002, states agreed on an International Code of Conduct (ICoC) against Missile Proliferation, including a set of principles, commitments, CBMs, and incentives to contain and delegitimize missile proliferation.[23] The *Hague Code of Conduct* (HCoC) remained below expectations and comprises various general principles, moderate obligations, and limited CBMs such as the annual statements on missile policy and the notification of missile launches, which should include information on the general class of ballistic missiles or space launchers, the time and area of location and the planned flight direction. This can be complemented by voluntary information on the type and purpose of a launch and the target area. The possession of missiles is not prohibited and the intended reduction of national missile arsenals remained vague. Not much was left of the originally planned "responsible missile behavior," which raised the concern that the main purpose was to stop proliferation but not question the existing missile arsenals that would discriminate newcomers. There is neither a formal secretariat nor an implementing organization. By January 2004, HCoC was supported by 111 states, including the United States.

- In October 2000, Iran introduced a resolution on missiles to the fifty-fifth session of the UN First Committee, which was adopted (A/C.1/55/L.1/Rev.1). The resolution emphasizes the "need for a comprehensive approach towards missiles, in a balanced and non-discriminatory manner, as a contribution to international peace and security." It requests the secretary general, with the assistance of a panel of governmental experts, to prepare a report on missiles in all its aspects. After three meetings of the UN Panel of Governmental Experts (UNPGE) on Missiles it presented its final report in 2002.[24] The report summarized basic aspects of missile development and listed the existing agreements in these fields, but because of

large divergences in the panel over the threat assessment no recommendations were made. This definition is useful: "A missile is an unmanned,
self-propelled, self-contained, unrecallable, guided, or unguided vehicle
designed to deliver a weapon or other payload. A ballistic missile is a
weapon-delivery vehicle that has a ballistic trajectory over most of its flight
path." The report emphasizes the large diversity of missiles and estimates
the total number of missiles worldwide as 120,000, compared to 35,000 at
the end of World War II. In September 2002, the establishment of a second
working group was adopted that did not find a consensus document.[25]

All these initiatives fell short of the initial promises and expectations.
Conflicting interests of the missile powers and, in particular, the lack of interest
of the Bush administration in multilateral arms control led to minimal consensus, which watered down the original intentions and did not restrain missile
programs. The link between ballistic missiles and space launchers was recognized as a problem. In none of the initiatives was the disarmament or elimination of ballistic missiles seriously considered. Countries like Canada, which in
2000 pushed for strengthened missile controls, gave in to the pressure from
Washington.[26]

While progress among governments remains slow, it is important to think
ahead toward a more comprehensive international missile control regime that
takes into account the various stages of missile development, and the asymmetries among missile owners. As missile development advances, the potential
threat increases. Once a missile has been tested, bans on deployment will be more
difficult—since rapid breakout from an agreement remains possible—and will
require stricter controls. Strengthening international ballistic missile controls
will be a long-term process necessarily involving the adoption and evolution of
a wide range of measures, from comparatively modest measures (i.e., a code of
conduct, bolstered export controls, and missile monitoring, and launch notification agreements) to far-reaching disarmament treaties establishing global missile
disarmament. Intermediate options would include restrictions on missile testing
and the creation of missile-free zones. Obvious candidates for such areas would
be Latin America and Africa, both of which have established NWFZ.

A missile nonproliferation regime, allowing missile owners to keep their
arsenals, would have limited efficiency compared to nondiscriminatory missile
disarmament. The only way to deal with asymmetries between countries would
be to set up an international norm against ballistic missiles that entitles all
countries to equal rights. To build momentum for a comprehensive alternative,
a step-by-step approach is appropriate that keeps the long-term goal in mind.
Initial steps could be risk reduction and confidence-building measures, such
as dealerting, improved ballistic missile early warning, and launch notification.
The monitoring and surveillance of missile and space-related activities and the
exchange of technical data would support an effective missile control verification
system.

Test restrictions would effectively prevent new missile designs and limit
modification of traditional technology, although unsophisticated indigenous
missile systems could still be developed and deployed with minimal testing. A
ballistic missile flight test ban would preclude the testing of new missiles and
reduce the chance of accidental or intentional war. In order to prevent a missile

race and buy more time for political initiatives, it would be helpful to institute a moratorium on the further development, testing and deployment of ballistic missiles. To address concerns about asymmetries and discrimination, a "missile freeze" could cover offensive and defensive missiles and be designed as a temporary measure while countries negotiate disarmament steps for missiles and other delivery systems. Simultaneous regional security initiatives would be crucial to diminish incentives for missile development.

When planning next steps, long-term perspectives should be taken into account. In 1992, expanding the proposal discussed between Ronald Reagan and Mikhail Gorbachev at the 1986 Reykjavik Summit, the Federation of American Scientists (FAS) developed a model for the elimination of ballistic missiles: Zero Ballistic Missiles (ZBM).[27] Such a regime would aim at the complete elimination of offensive ballistic missiles and combine unilateral declarations with regional and global multilateral agreements. The ZBM proposal—which the FAS backed up with a complete draft treaty—combined a comprehensive framework with a stepwise approach, including bilateral cuts between the United States and Russia, ballistic missile-free zones, an international missile conference, the creation of an International Agency for Ballistic Missile Disarmament, and, finally, agreement on the varying schedules necessary to reach zero ballistic missile capability.

The case for a regime to control and monitor space launchers is greatly strengthened when considered in the context of preventing an arms race in outer space. Since man-made objects in orbit would enter space through space rockets, a monitoring system at space launch facilities could not only search for indications of ballistic missile use, but also for the space weapon usability of the payload. This would provide increased transparency concerning space activities in general, and would effectively exclude the deployment and testing of space weapons using ground-based space launchers. A control regime on ballistic missiles and space weapons could be extended also to the international control of ballistic missile defenses, reversing the abrogation of the Bush administration from the ABM Treaty in 2002. The terms of a new treaty could be made more precise and verifiable and/or be internationalized. Such limits would relate to the altitude, relative distance, and velocity of interceptor tests, and to limits on laser brightness or to the aperture of sensors and mirrors.[28]

INTERNATIONAL SPACE LAW AND SPACE SECURITY[29]

Outer Space: Heritage of Mankind or New War Zone?

Space is increasingly used for a variety of purposes, including the military use of satellites for information gathering and transmission, which leads to a growing dependence on space objects.[30] Contrary to the factual military use of space, the international community has always expressed a strong desire to preserve space for peaceful purposes, and in the beginning this included the United States. In 1957, U.S. Ambassador John Cabot Lodge submitted a memorandum on arms control in space to the UN, which proposed the establishment of a multilateral disarmament control system with international inspections and participation of all states to ensure that future developments in outer space are directed exclusively toward peaceful and scientific purposes. In 1958, the "National Aeronautics and

Space Act (NASA Act)" explicitly states, "The Congress hereby declares that it is the policy of the United States that activities in space should be devoted to peaceful purposes for the benefit of all mankind."[31]

Despite fierce competition in the Cold War, which extended to outer space, the large majority of states agreed to the cornerstone of international space law, the 1967 "Outer Space Treaty" (OST),[32] with additional agreements on outer space negotiated subsequently. The countries that signed the OST agreed to use space for peaceful purposes, as a heritage of mankind. The establishment of military bases, installations, and fortifications on the moon and other celestial bodies is prohibited, as are weapons of mass destruction in Earth orbit, but not the deployment of weapons in outer space. The essential legal term "peaceful" has not been defined, leaving room for a wide range of interpretations, from "nonmilitary" to "nonaggressive,"[33] and now even "offensive," stretching the meaning of "peaceful" beyond recognition.

The military use of space has become even more relevant in the course of time, but the weaponization of space can still be prevented. In addition to being reserved "exclusively for peaceful purposes," outer space is an essential and vulnerable part of Earth's environment and needs to be protected against activities that spoil or exploit it, such as creating space debris by military activities and weapons tests. Connected to this is the right of the international community to space security, that is, protection against threats in space and from space. International legal norms support a cooperative approach toward space security, jointly preventing threats and associated risks. The effectiveness of an international legal norm is measured by the degree of risk reduction it provides as compared to an unregulated situation in which countries take unilateral military action. There are good arguments why an unregulated situation creates more security risks for all states, including the United States. The imperative of power projections toward space dominance is contrary to the principle of space as a "common heritage of mankind," which should not be subject to conflict, private ownership, or national appropriation.[34] These principles are enshrined in the OST, according to which the use of space "shall be carried out for the benefit and in the interests of all countries, irrespective of their degree of economic or scientific development, and shall be the province of all mankind."

As outer space has been widely acknowledged as a common heritage of mankind, which should be used for the benefit of *all* countries, the international community has long been calling for the prevention of an arms race in outer space, seeking to strengthen international space law and arms control in space by introducing provisions against the weaponization of space. For more than two decades, the UN General Assembly has adopted resolutions on the "Prevention of an Arms Race in Outer Space" (PAROS) with overwhelming majority, with only the United States and one or two small states abstaining.[35] The desire for peaceful space use has been a main motive of the work of the UN Committee on the Peaceful Uses of Outer Space (UNCOPUOS), where international space law has been developed. Dealing with the military use of space remains the responsibility of the CD in Geneva but the permanent stalemate at the CD on this issue has hampered any progress on arms control in space.[36] International civil society has also actively participated in discussions and projects on the prevention of a space weapons race.

A key question is whether the transition from the *militarization* to the *weaponization* of space can be prevented, opening the "high frontier" for "space warfare," to the point of calling for weapons to project force "to, from, in and through" space. As yet, the efforts to research, develop, and test various kinds of space weapons have not led to operational systems. One of the main reasons for the slow "progress" in weaponizing space is the difficulty in carrying out the ensuing tasks. Development of the required technologies is very costly and turns out to take much longer than anticipated. Space weapons can be defined as "systems based either terrestrially or in space for anti-satellite missions; or systems based in space designed to attack terrestrial targets."[37] Dual use—exemplified not only in space weapons capabilities of missile defense components but also in the inherent civil-military ambivalence of space technology such as rockets and satellites—blurs the boundary to space weapons to some degree.

From Risk Reduction to a Space Weapons Ban

Space objects are designed for a hostile space environment that is characterized by vacuum, radiation, temperature extremes, and a limited energy supply. They also must survive the strains of launch and sometimes the stress of reentry. Space systems can fail as a result of a variety of reasons: component failure and degradation; design, development, production, programming, or mission errors; interruption of ground communication caused by accidents, jamming, or ground attacks; collision with space debris; physical attack; blinding of sensors; hacking; deception; or hijacking. In a concrete case, it might be difficult to trace a system failure back to a specific cause, which in many cases could be space debris. Vulnerabilities and threats would be considerably increased with advanced space weapons, such as maneuverable satellites, space mines, microsatellites, kinetic kill vehicles, chemical and nuclear explosives, or particle, microwave, and laser beams. They would contribute significantly to the complexity and instability of the strategic situation, which ultimately would not serve the security interests of any country, including the United States.

To some degree, the survivability of space objects against some of the potential attacks can be increased by passive or active protection measures. Some of these measures are costly and do not provide security against all kinds of attacks and technologies. For the most important satellites of the United States, some or all of these measures have already been implemented. Within the existing framework of international space law, confidence-building measures can contribute to stabilizing international security including

- advanced notification and more detailed information about space launches and experiments (e.g., with lasers);
- establishment of a crisis hotline between major missile and space powers;
- a code of conduct for responsible space behavior, learning from the ongoing process of the MTCR;[38]
- improved international monitoring system and information exchange; and
- strengthened international space cooperation that improves transparency and reduces incentives for indigenous space development.

In addition, rules of the road could be agreed for outer space:

- keep-out zones, minimum flyby distances, and speed limits around satellites to increase warning time against attack and reduce efficiency of attack;
- satellite immunity and noninterference with satellites; and
- reduction of space debris.

A combination of satellite hardening, confidence-building, and rules of the road might better protect satellites against existing residual (nondedicated) space threats such as attacks with ICBMs and maneuverable satellites, with radio or laser beams not explicitly developed for weapon purposes. High-altitude nuclear explosions are a severe risk for all electronic components in space, not just from direct impact but even more so from captured radiation in the Van Allen radiation belt.

If dedicated space weapons based on new technologies are developed, the existing regime would not be sufficient to substantially diminish the emerging threats. Additional risk reduction could be achieved by partial arms control measures, which by agreement would restrict or ban certain kinds of weapons or weapon uses. These could include the following:

- A ban on testing, deployment, and use of weapons above a specific altitude would relegate weaponization to low-Earth orbits and keep the remaining outer space a weapon-free zone. Possible altitudes could range from 500 km to 5,000 km in order to protect space objects beyond that range. Protecting high-orbit navigation satellites and geostationary communication and early warning satellites is of greatest importance to military and commercial interests. However, allowing weapons development in low-Earth orbits could open the door to space weaponization, and it would not preclude the development of sophisticated low-Earth orbit weapon systems that could later be extended to higher orbits.
- The legal and physical protection of manned missions and the prohibition of manned military space operations could prevent people from being involved in space warfare. Most important, it would protect manned space stations by maintaining keep-out zones and shielding them against space debris and some forms of attack.
- Certain types or deployment modes of space weapon systems and technologies could be banned—in particular, ASAT or BMD systems, or weapons with a predominantly offensive role. Laser and other kinds of beam weapons could be excluded, whether ground-based or space-based. Small satellites below a specific size limit (e.g., 10 cm) or weight limit (e.g., 10 kg) could be restricted.
- States could restrict particular stages in the life cycle of a weapon such as research, development, testing, production, deployment, or use. For example, an ASAT testing moratorium was established in the mid-1980s between the United States and the Soviet Union. A ballistic missile flight test ban was also discussed at that time.
- Specific limits on interception speeds and altitudes or the size of mirrors and power levels could be agreed upon.

- Partial arms control measures could be embedded into more comprehensive arms control regimes in space, including a global ban on weapons against objects in space and from objects in space against any target.

Comprehensive space arms control would seek to ban certain kinds of weapon systems completely at an early stage to effectively prevent an arms race in space before these weapons are tested or become operational. A comprehensive arms control regime has the advantage of being politically comprehensible and attractive to the general public. Such regimes require an unprecedented degree of cooperation and, given the current political circumstances, would be resisted by the Bush administration.

A global ban on weapons against objects in space and from objects in space against any target would prohibit development, testing, and deployment of such systems. In the past two decades, various proposals, both from governments and NGOs, have been suggested and discussed. Of particular interest are the Soviet proposal of 1983; an ASAT ban proposal of the Union of Concerned Scientists in the same year; and the Draft Treaty on the Limitation of the Military Use of Outer Space proposed by German scientists in 1984.[39] More recent is a proposal for a space weapons ban introduced to the Conference on Disarmament by China and Russia in 2002 and the Space Preservation Act introduced by U.S. Congressman Dennis Kucinich in 2002 (and since re-introduced several times including in May 2005).[40]

Banning space weapons would focus on those systems that are "specially designed" to destroy space objects (including ASATs on the ground, on the sea, or in the air), and on space objects themselves that are specifically designed to destroy other targets regardless of their basing mode. While this does not resolve the problem of dual use–capable systems, it would exclude a large class of the most threatening systems and activities. A residual risk from nondedicated systems (such as maneuverable satellites or rockets) remains, but this problem needs to be dealt with by a set of measures to reduce these residual risks (including satellite hardening, improved monitoring, security concepts, etc.). A comprehensive approach could integrate risk reduction measures and partial agreements in a phased step-by-step approach, as has been discussed in incremental-comprehensive approaches to nuclear disarmament. For each step, efforts and benefits must be balanced. The overall concept has to be chosen in a way that best serves space security.

As pointed out by Detlev Wolter, the peaceful use of space is an essential cornerstone in the concept of "common security" in outer space, which includes the following measures:[41] "the prohibition of active military uses of a destructive nature in the common space; a comprehensive package of confidence-building measures with multilateral satellite monitoring and verification systems as well as a protective regime for peaceful space objects based on immunity rules for satellites, such as a 'rules of the road' and a 'code of conduct.'" He suggests negotiation of a multilateral Treaty on Common Security in Outer Space (CSO Treaty) as the adequate mechanism to implement the Outer Space Treaty. This should be accompanied by the establishment of an International Organisation for Common Security in Outer Space, which will be tasked with monitoring the implementation of the agreement.

Principles and Means of Verification and Enforcement[42]

An arms control treaty will be effective only if it can be adequately verified and enforced, both in political and technical terms. Verification policies should be designed to assure early detection and interpretation of information necessary for the prevention of prohibited activities and permit timely response. Verifiability of a treaty is not an absolute issue, but a matter of degree depending on political assumptions and requirements as well as the available resources and capabilities for verification.[43] Most crucial is the question of "tolerable" degrees of verifiability and their associated residual risks. For the Reagan administration, for instance, nothing short of 100 percent certainty that the Soviets were not cheating was tolerable. Since this was impossible to achieve with limited verification efforts, the requirement prevented any progress on disarmament. With Gorbachev, however, confidence and trust increased between the superpowers, and finally even Reagan accepted much lower verification standards in order to conclude the INF and START treaties. More verification was seen as too costly, and the residual risks were accepted because the potential security implications were perceived as manageable. Thus, between friendly nations even the lowest standards of verification could be tolerable because the incentive and probability of cheating seem negligible. In consequence, with increasing trust and cooperation between nations the need and costs for verification become more and more irrelevant.

The tasks of verifying legal obligations can be divided into the following three main stages:

1. Baseline information exchange and data gathering: Identify the current status of the weapons complex with reasonable accuracy without proliferating sensitive information.
2. Disarmament: Monitor the agreed path of reducing arms and eliminating the associated weapons complex within tolerable limits of uncertainty and sufficient confidence.
3. Prevent rearmament: During the disarmament process, observe any objects and detect any activities that might indicate a weapons capability.

Verification in all three stages would need to focus on monitoring a complex range of treaty-limited items (objects), treaty-limited states and processes (activities), and their combination. What actually needs to be verified is the combination of required/prohibited objects and activities. For the Nuclear Weapons Convention, for instance, these include dismantlement of nuclear weapons; disposition of nuclear material; conversion or destruction of certain nuclear facilities; monitoring the location and status of nuclear weapons, nuclear materials, nuclear facilities, delivery systems, command, and control systems to ensure that they are not used for research, development, testing, production, transport, deployment, or use of nuclear weapons. Other activities would include storage, transfer, and handling of nuclear weapons and fissile material.

According to Steve Fetter, the disarmament and verification process is iterative: "Parties agree to reductions on the assumption of shared goals; the verification of these reductions builds confidence between the parties in that assumption, making increased transparency and deeper reductions possible."[44] Thus, verification is a dynamic process with the four phases of declaration, monitoring, inspection, and enforcement being repeated successively, but also in parallel. All four steps would be required to assure adequate verification. In the past, the process was incomplete and could, therefore, not be iterated, because either declarations were not given, monitoring was technically incomplete, inspections were politically unfeasible, or enforcement was lacking power.

To assure that the obligations are realized within tolerable limits of deviation, a variety of verification means and procedures can be applied: *Monitoring technologies* (remote sensing in the visible, infrared or radar spectra; seismological, radionuclide, hydroacoustic, and infrasound monitoring; on-site sensors); *cooperative procedures* (information exchange; inspections; preventive controls; nuclear archaeology; item counting; confidence-building measures; joint overflights); *institutional verification* (international agency; consultation; dispute settlement). Some technical possibilities are principally available; others require additional research and development.

The Role of Citizens, Scientists, and the Public

Citizens and NGOs can play an important role in promoting and implementing arms control and disarmament. In order to increase public awareness, a greater public discourse on the proliferation problem and its resolution is required. By building a network of information exchange and debate, experts, civil society, and officials could be jointly engaged in this process. Although comprehensive proposals may currently seem utopian, they may become more, not less, important as a means of preserving stability and reducing uncertainty in a world of dangerous and costly arms races. If the arms race on earth and in space is not prevented, the situation could become more unstable, complex, and out of control. Even the United States may wish to take international measures to reduce uncertainty and prevent damage to its own security interests once ICBMs, ASATs, nuclear, and laser weapons of other countries are fully developed. Whether a control system will work in a hostile environment is questionable.

Notes

1. N. Deller, A. Makhijani, and J. Burroughs, eds., *Rule of Power or Rule of Law? An Assessment of U.S. Policies and Actions Regarding Security-Related Treaties* (Apex Press, 2003). For surveys on international law, see B. H. Weston, R. A. Falk, H. Charlesworth, *International Law and World Order*, 3rd ed. (West Group, 1997); M. N. Shaw, *International Law*, 5th ed. (Cambridge University Press, 2003); A. Cassese, *International Law* (Oxford University Press, 2001); C. Ku and P. Diehl, eds., *International Law: Classic and Contemporary Readings* (Lynne Rienne, 1998).

2. This section is based on J. Scheffran, "Content and Verification of a Nuclear Weapons Convention," in J. Rotblat, ed., *Remember Your Humanity* (Singapore: World Scientific, 1999), pp. 318–334.

3. J. Rotblat, J. Steinberger, and B. Udgaonkar, eds., *A Nuclear-Weapon-Free World: Desirable? Feasible?* (Boulder, CO: Westview Press, 1993). Considerations on a comprehensive nuclear disarmament treaty are made in this book by M. Bruce,

H. Fischer, and T. Mensah, *A NWFW Regime: Treaty for the Abolition of Nuclear Weapons*, pp. 119–131.

4. International Physicians for the Prevention of Nuclear War, International Peace Bureau, International Association of Lawyers against Nuclear Arms, International Network of Engineers and Scientists for Global Responsibility, International Network of Engineers and Scientists against Proliferation.

5. See documents in *INESAP Information Bulletin*, No. 1, April 1994. For a more recent update see J. Scheffran, W. Liebert, and M. Kalinowski, "Beyond the NPT: The Nuclear-Weapons-Free World," *INESAP Information Bulletin*, 25 (April 2005), pp. 4–9.

6. *Beyond the NPT—A Nuclear-Weapon-Free World, INESAP Study Group Report* (Darmstadt/New York, 1995), p. 9. The Executive Summary has been published as a supplement in *INESAP Bulletin*, 6 (July 1995).

7. *Report of the Canberra Commission on the Elimination of Nuclear Weapons, Canberra*, August 1996.

8. The other three options are a convention limited to the five nuclear weapon states; supplementing the NPT; an NPT amendment process; and an expansion of the NWFZ. See *The Future of U.S. Nuclear Weapons Policy*, Report by the Committee on International Security and Arms Control, National Academy of Sciences (Washington, DC: July 1997).

9. The UN has, from its very first resolution Res. 1, 1(1) in 1946, supported the goal of the elimination of nuclear weapons, however, without specific plans of how to reach such a goal until the 1995 resolution (Res. 50/70 P), calling for a timebound framework for nuclear disarmament.

10. See M. Datan, A. Ware, J. Scheffran, Nuclear Weapons Convention on Track, *INESAP Bulletin*, 11 (December 1996), pp. 4–6. The link between the ICJ judgment and the NWC has been analyzed in W. Liebert, J. Scheffran, and M. Kalinowski, "Vom Urteil des Weltgerichtshofs zur Nuklearwaffenkonvention," in: IALANA, ed., *Atomwaffen vor dem Internationalen Gerichtshof* (Münster: LIT-Verlag, 1997), pp. 367–385.

11. *Commentary on the Model Nuclear Weapons Convention* (New York: LCNP, April 1997), p. 1.

12. M. Datan, A. Ware, M. Kalinowski, J. Scheffran, V. Sidel, and J. Burroughs, *Security and Survival. The Case for a Nuclear Weapons Convention*, IPPNW/ IALANA/INESAP, Cambridge, 1999.

13. M. Datan, F. Hill, J. Scheffran, and A. Ware, *Securing Our Survival—The Case for a Nuclear Weapons Convention*. IPPNW, IALANA, INESAP, Cambridge 2007; www.icanw.org/publications, www.inesap.org/books/securing_our_survival.htm.

14. PNND, Parliamentarians for Nuclear Nonproliferation and Disarmament, Update 18, July-August 2007.

15. The following is based on J. Scheffran, "Nuclear Disarmament and the International Control of Delivery Systems," *NWC Monitor*, 3 (2002); J. Scheffran, "Elimination of Ballistic Missiles," in J. Rotblat and M. Konuma, eds., *Towards a Nuclear-Weapon-Free World* (World Scientific, 1997), pp. 310–326.

16. "Eliminating Nuclear Arsenals: The NPT Pledge and What It Means," speech by Jayantha Dhanapala to the All-Party Group on Global Security and Non-Proliferation, House of Commons, London, July 3, 2000. For full text, see *Disarmament Diplomacy*, 47 (June 2000).

17. Siehe www.mtcr.info, projects.sipri.se/expcon/mtcr_documents.html.

18. See J. Scheffran and A. Karp, "The National Implementation of the Missile Technology Control Regime: U.S. and German Experiences," in H. G. Brauch, H. J. v.d. Graaf, J. Grin, and W. Smit, eds., *Controlling the Development*

and Spread of Military Technology (Amsterdam: VU University Press, 1992), pp. 235–255; D. Ozga, "A Chronology of the Missile Technology Control Regime," *The Nonproliferation Review* (Winter 1994), pp. S. 66–93; M. Smith, "Efficiency and Inefficiency of the MTCR," *INESAP Information Bulletin,* 19 (March 2002), pp. S. 64–65.

19. This section builds on J. Scheffran, "Moving Beyond Missile Defense: The Search for Alternatives to the Missile Race," *Disarmament Diplomacy,* 55 (March 2001), pp. 21–26. A. Lichterman, Z. Mian, M.V. Ramana, and J. Scheffran, "Beyond Missile Defense," *INESAP Briefing Paper,* 8 (March 2002); also published by Global Resource Action Center for the Environment (New York, October, 2002). J. Scheffran, "Rüstungskontrolle bei Trägersystemen," in G. Neuneck and C. Mölling, eds., *Die Zukunft der Rüstungskontrolle* (Nomos, 2005), pp. 354–366; J. Scheffran, *Missiles in Conflict,* UNIDIR Disarmament Forum (1/2007), pp. 11–22.

20. J. Steinbruner, *The Significance of Joint Missile Surveillance,* An Occasional Paper of the Committee on International Security Studies, Boston: American Academy of Arts and Sciences, July 2001; *Memorandum of Agreement between the United States of America and the Russian Federation on the Establishment of a Joint Center for the Exchange of Data from Early Warning Systems and Notifications of Missile Launches,* June 4, 2000, www.state.gov/t/ac/trt/4799.htm; *Memorandum of Understanding on Notification of Missile Launches,* Bureau of Arms Control, Dept. of State, December 16, 2000, www.state.gov/t/ac/trt/4954.htm.

21. Global Control System for Non-Proliferation of Missiles and Missile Technologies. Concept, Discussion Review and Follow-Up Steps, February 15, 2001. See also V. Abrosimov, "Preventing Missile Proliferation: Incentives and Security Guarantees," *Disarmament Diplomacy,* 57 (Mai 2001), pp. 4–8.

22. For details of the first experts-level meeting, see M. Rice, Russia Proposes Global Regime On Missile Proliferation, *Arms Control Today,* May 2000; for the second meeting, see *Disarmament Diplomacy,* 54 (February 2001). An unofficial collection of documents can be found on the website of the Federation of American Scientists, www.fas.org/nuke/control/mtcr/news/GSC_content.htm.

23. The HCoC text can be found at www.acronym.org.uk/docs/0211/doc13.htm together with other documents. See also M. Smith, "Stuck on the Launch Pad? The Ballistic Missile Code of Conduct Opens for Business," *Disarmament Diplomacy,* 68 (December 2002/January 2003), pp. S. 2–6; M. Smith, "On Thin Ice: First Steps for the Ballistic Missile Code of Conduct," *Arms Control Today* (July/August 2002), pp. 9–13.

24. The issue of missiles in all its aspects, UNGA A/57/229, July 23, 2002. On the work of the expert group, see Lee Ho Jin, "Observations and lessons from the work of the Panel of Governmental Experts on Missiles," in *UNIDIR Disarmament Forum,* 3 (2003), pp. S. 67–70; W. Pal S. Sidhu and C. Carle, "Managing Missiles: Blind Spot or Blind Alley?" in *Disarmament Diplomacy,* 72 (August–September 2003).

25. On the status of the Study Group see The issue of missiles in all its aspects, Report of the Secretary-General, UN General Assembly A/61/168, New York, July 20, 2006.

26. *Ballistic Missiles Foreign Experts Roundtable Report,* March 30–31, 2000, Canadian Centre for Foreign Policy Development, April 7, 2000; *The Missile Defense Debate: Guiding Canada's Role,* Liu Centre for the Study of Global Issues, 2001. For a report on the consultation, see www.liucentre.ubc.ca/report/Defensereport.html.

27. Revisiting Zero Ballistic Missiles—Reagan's Forgotten Dream, *FAS Public Interest Report,* May/June 1992; L. Lumpe, Zero Ballistic Missiles and the Third

World, *Arms Control*, 14.1 (April 1993), pp. 218–223; A. Frye, Zero Ballistic Missiles, *Foreign Policy*, 88 (Fall 1992), pp. 12–17.

28. J. Pike, *Quantitative Limits on Anti-Missile Systems—A Preliminary Assessment* (Washington, DC: FAS), May 22, 1987; a shorter version can be found in *Scientific Aspects of the Verification of Arms Control Treaties, part II*, pp. 137–198, Hamburger Beiträge zur Friedensforschung und Sicherheitspolitik, June 1987.

29. This section relies on R. Hagen, J. Scheffran, International Space Law and Space Security, in M. Benkö, and K.-U. Schrogl, eds., *Space Law: Current Problems and Perspectives for Future Regulation* (Eleven International Publishing, 2005), pp. 273–301; J. Scheffran, Risk reduction and monitoring in outer space, in *Safeguarding Space for All: Security & Peaceful Use* (UNIDIR Geneva, UN Press, 2005); J. Scheffran, Options for Rules in Outer Space, *INESAP Information Bulletin*, 20 (August 2002), pp. 9–14.

30. G. Neuneck and A. Rothkirch, *The Possible Weaponization of Space and Options for Preventive Arms Control*, German Journal of Air and Space Law, 55 (Winter 2006), pp. 501–517.

31. Section 102(a) National Aeronautics and Space Act (NASA Act), Public Law 85-568, 85th Congress, First Session, H.R. 12575, July 29, 1958; www.hq.nasa.gov/ogc/spaceact.html as amended.

32. www.oosa.unvienna.org/SpaceLaw/outersptxt.html.

33. For more details, see H.-J. Heintze, "Peaceful Uses of Outer Space and International Law," in W. Bender, R. Hagen, M. Kalinowski, and J. Scheffran, eds., *Space Use and Ethics* (Münster: Agenda, 2001), pp. 243–250.

34. K.-U. Schrogl, "Space Law and the Principle of Non-Appropriation," in Bender et al., pp. 251–253. On space privatization see J. Scheffran, "Privatization in Outer Space," in E. U. von Weizsäcker, O. R. Young, and M. Finger, eds., *Limits To Privatization, A Report to the Club of Rome* (London/Sterling, VA: Earthscan, 2005), pp. 79–83.

35. See www.oosa.unvienna.org/SpaceLaw/gares/index.html for access to all UNGA resolutions on outer space.

36. C. Singer, Space Weapons and the Conference on Disarmament, *INESAP Information Bulletin*, 20 (August 2002), pp. 25–26.

37. T. Hitchens, *Update on U.S. Military Space Policy and Strategy*, June 8, 2005; www.cdi.org.

38. In 2004 the Stimson Center, with U.S. NGO experts, drafted a Model Code of Conduct for Responsible Space Faring Nations. The full text of the Model Code of Conduct can be found at www.stimson.org/space.

39. See H. Fischer, R. Labusch, E. Maus, and J. Scheffran, "Entwurf eines Vertrages zur Begrenzung der militärischen Nutzung des Weltraums," in R. Labusch, E. Maus, and W. Send, eds., *Weltraum ohne Waffen* (München, 1984), pp. 175–187. For the English version, see "Treaty on the Limitation of the Military Use of Outer Space," in J. Holdre and J. Rotblat, eds., *Strategic Defences and the Future of the Arms Race* (New York, 1987); J. Scheffran, "The Göttingen Proposal for a Space Treaty," *INESAP Information Bulletin*, 20 (August 2002). The Draft Treaty was debated in autumn 1984 in the German Parliament and found support from the SPD and Green Party but was opposed by CDU/CSU and FDP.

40. Several of these treaty proposals have been documented in *INESAP Information Bulletin*, 20 (August 2002); www.inesap.org/bulletin20.htm.

41. D. Wolter, *Common Security in Outer Space and International Law*, United Nations Institute for Disarmament Research (UNIDIR), Geneva, 2006.

42. This section builds on J. Scheffran, "Content and Verification of a Nuclear Weapons Convention," in J. Rotblat, ed., *Remember Your Humanity*

(Singapore: World Scientific, 1999), pp. 318–334. Further aspects of verification, including those for nuclear, missile, and space arms control, are discussed in J. Scheffran, "Verification and Stability—The Strategic Impact of Uncertainties and Perceptions," in H.-G. Brauch, ed., *Verification and Arms Control Implications for European Security, Part II* (Mosbach: AFES-PRESS, 1990), pp. 191–196; J. Scheffran, "Verification of Ballistic Missile Bans and Monitoring of Space Launches," in W. Liebert and J. Scheffran, eds., *Against Proliferation towards General Disarmament* (Agenda 1995), pp. 156–164; M. Datan and J. Scheffran, "Principles and Means for Verification of a Nuclear Weapons Convention," *INESAP Information Bulletin*, 14 (November 1997), 21–24; M. B. Kalinowski, W. Liebert, and J. Scheffran, "Beyond Technical Verification. Transparency, Verification, and Preventive Control for the Nuclear Weapons Convention," in M. B. Kalinowski, *Global Elimination of Nuclear Weapons* (Baden-Baden: Nomos, 2000), pp. 61–68; R. Hagen and J. Scheffran, "Is a Space Weapons Ban Feasible? Thoughts on Technology and Verification of Arms Control in Space," *UNIDIR Disarmament Forum* 1 (2003), pp. 42–51.

43. Such principles have been outlined in J. Scheffran, "Verification and Risk for an Anti-Satellite-Weapons Ban," *Bulletin of Peace Proposals*, 17.2 (1986), pp. 165–174.

44. S. Fetter, *Verifying Nuclear Disarmament* (Washington, DC: Henry L. Stimson Center), Occasional Paper No. 29, October 1996.

CHAPTER 13

Preventing Nuclear Catastrophe: Where Do We Go from Here?

Mohamed ElBaradei

Four American *éminences grises*—Henry Kissinger, William Perry, George Shultz, and Sam Nunn—representing a wealth of experience in defense and security strategies—declared that reliance on nuclear weapons as a deterrent is becoming "increasingly hazardous and decreasingly effective." They called for urgent international cooperation to move toward a world free from nuclear weapons.

The following week, the *Bulletin of the Atomic Scientists* announced that they were moving the hands of their famous Doomsday Clock two minutes closer to midnight. "Not since the first atomic bombs were dropped on Hiroshima and Nagasaki," they reported, "has the world faced such perilous choices."

THE EVOLVING NUCLEAR THREATS

In recent years, it is clear that nuclear threats have become more dangerous and more complex. A new phenomenon of illicit trade in nuclear technology has emerged. Countries have managed to develop clandestine nuclear programs. Sophisticated extremist groups have shown keen interest in acquiring nuclear weapons.

In parallel, nuclear material and nuclear material production have become more difficult to control. Energy security and climate change are driving many countries to revisit the nuclear power option. But with that, there is also an increasing interest in mastering the nuclear fuel cycle to ensure a supply of the necessary nuclear fuel. The concern is that by mastering the fuel cycle, countries move dangerously close to nuclear weapons capability.

Add to that the threat of the nuclear weapons that already exist. Roughly 27,000 nuclear warheads remain in the arsenals of nine countries. Strategic reliance on these weapons by these countries and their allies undoubtedly motivates others to emulate them. And of course, plans to replenish and modernize these weapons creates a pervasive sense of cynicism among many non-nuclear weapon states—who perceive a "do as I say, not as I do" attitude. I would like to share with you some ideas that may help to prevent nuclear catastrophe.

STRENGTHENING THE NUCLEAR NONPROLIFERATION REGIME: FOUR CRITICAL ASPECTS

First, we must *secure existing nuclear material stockpiles* and *tighten controls over the transfer and production of nuclear material*. Effective control of nuclear material is the "choke point" for preventing the production of additional nuclear weapons.

There are currently over 1,800 tonnes of plutonium and High-Enriched Uranium (HEU) in civil stocks. Many initiatives are in progress to help countries improve *physical protection* of this nuclear material. Good progress has been made in the past few years, but hard work still lies ahead. Efforts in that direction should be redoubled.

Controlling the *export* of nuclear materials and technology has, in the past, proven a weak link in the nonproliferation chain. Information on exports should be systematically shared with the International Atomic Energy Agency (IAEA), to assist in verifying their end use. In addition, to increase their effectiveness, export control mechanisms should be expanded to include all nuclear suppliers.

We should also work to minimize and eventually eliminate the civilian use of HEU—particularly uranium enriched to 90 percent or greater. Nearly 100 civilian facilities around the world, mainly research reactors, operate with small amounts of HEU. But most of their functions could be achieved using Low-Enriched Uranium (LEU). Research should continue to address the remaining technical hurdles in order to enable research reactors to perform all required functions using LEU.

It is also crucial that we improve control over nuclear material production: that is, uranium enrichment and plutonium separation activities. More than three years ago, I raised this issue in an article in *The Economist*. I am encouraged by the range of ideas and proposals that continue to come forth as a result. Some have proposed the creation of an actual or virtual reserve fuel bank of last resort, under IAEA auspices, for the assurance of supply of nuclear fuel. This bank would operate on the basis of apolitical and nondiscriminatory nonproliferation criteria. Russia has proposed converting a national facility into an international enrichment center. And Germany has recently proposed the construction of a new, multinational enrichment facility under IAEA control.

At the IAEA, we have been examining these and other ideas and their associated legal, technical, financial, and institutional aspects, with a view to presenting a progress report to our member states in the next few weeks. Controlling nuclear material is quite a complex process; yet if we fail to act, it could be the Achilles' Heel of the nuclear nonproliferation regime. And it is clear that an incremental approach, with multiple assurances in place, is the way to move forward. The ultimate goal, in my view, should be to bring all such operations under multinational control, so that no one country has the exclusive capability to produce the material for nuclear weapons.

Technological innovation is also essential. We should support R&D on proliferation resistant fuel cycles—as well as technological innovation to enhance nuclear safety, security, and waste management.

Second, we must *strengthen the verification authority and capability of the IAEA*. Effective verification has four elements: adequate legal authority; state-of-the-art technology; access to all relevant information; and sufficient human and financial resources. The additional protocol to comprehensive safeguards agreements has proven its value since its adoption in 1997. With better access to relevant information and locations, the IAEA provides better assurance. Without the additional protocol, we cannot credibly verify the absence of undeclared nuclear material or activity. But regrettably, we have this mechanism in force in less than half the countries party to the Non-Proliferation Treaty (NPT). In fact, we have more than 30 NPT member countries that have not even concluded a safeguards agreement—and for which we cannot perform any verification activities. For a credible verification system, a safeguards agreement and an additional protocol should be the universal standard.

In 2004, a United Nations (UN) High Level Panel singled out the IAEA's work as "an extraordinary bargain." For $130 million per year, we verify the nuclear programs of all non-nuclear weapon states—which amounts to more than 900 declared nuclear facilities in 70 countries. Our presence on the ground, combined with our technical expertise, provides unique information and assurance. We are the eyes and ears of the international community.

Yet the agency constantly risks lagging behind in the technology race, because we are forced to make do on a shoestring budget. As new facilities and countries come under safeguards, our portfolio is constantly expanding, without corresponding increases in funding or personnel. Even now, with every other world leader highlighting nuclear proliferation and nuclear terrorism as the number one global security threat, we continue to struggle to achieve a modest budget supplement of $15–20 million dollars.

Given the threats we face, given that IAEA verification, as we have learned, can be crucial for decisions on war and peace, it is obvious that support for the agency is key to a viable system of nonproliferation and of international security.

Third, the *nuclear nonproliferation regime must develop a more effective approach for dealing with proliferation threats*. The NPT and the IAEA statute make clear our reliance on the United Nations Security Council to ensure compliance with nonproliferation obligations. The present system offers an array of measures ranging from dialogue to sanctions to enforcement actions. But judging by our record in recent years, these measures—rather than being applied in a systematic manner to deal effectively with proliferation issues—are employed haphazardly, and too often with political overtones.

Dialogue is withheld as a reward for good behavior, rather than as a means to change behavior and reconcile differences. Public rhetoric substitutes for effective diplomacy. The lesson should be obvious by now: we cannot bomb our way to security. Rather, we should focus on addressing the underlying causes of insecurity.

For nuclear nonproliferation to be enforced effectively, we need a more agile and more systematic approach for responding to cases of proliferation. Dialogue, incentives, and sanctions—and, in extreme cases, enforcement measures—all have their place in such a system; but the system itself must be drastically reformed. The Security Council will have clear moral authority and full public acceptance if the nonproliferation and arms control regime it is aiming to enforce is universal, with one clear commitment by all parties, including the nuclear weapon states: the establishment of a nuclear weapon-free world. Short of this, the council's ability to deal with proliferation issues will continue to be of limited effectiveness—as past experiences have clearly shown.

Equally important, for the Security Council to be effective in dealing with proliferation threats, it must recognize the inextricable linkage between different threats to our security. Poverty in many cases leads to human rights abuses and lack of good governance. This in turn results in a deep sense of disempowerment and humiliation, which creates the ideal breeding ground for extremism and violence. And it is in regions of long-standing conflicts that countries are most frequently driven to pursue nuclear weapons and other weapons of mass destruction. The council, therefore, must operate in a framework that recognizes the indivisible nature of security, and the symbiotic relation of all its aspects.

This brings me to the urgent need to revive disarmament efforts. *We must find a way for disarmament to be taken seriously.* Article VI of the NPT requires parties to the treaty to pursue disarmament negotiations in good faith, as well as negotiations "on effective measures relating to cessation of the nuclear arms race at an early date." Thirty-seven years after the *treaty* entered into force, we are well past the date when states party should be developing new nuclear weapons.

Yet that is precisely what is happening. Virtually all nuclear weapon states are extending and modernizing their nuclear weapon arsenals well into the twenty-first century, with some making statements about the possible use of nuclear weapons, or the development of more "usable" nuclear weapons. Some have even started to question their legal obligation to disarm under the nuclear NPT—despite the agreed interpretation by all NPT Parties, including the nuclear weapon states, at the 2000 NPT Review Conference, of the "unequivocal undertaking by the nuclear-weapon States to accomplish the total elimination of their nuclear arsenals." It should be no surprise that many states have started to question the credibility of the commitment of the weapon states to disarm.

And consider some of the justifications that have been recently put forward by some of the nuclear weapon states. *No major power is getting rid of their nuclear weapons, so why should we?...Despite the current lack of a nuclear threat, we cannot be sure that one will not reemerge over the next 50 years....Our country (or region) must be protected by a nuclear deterrence capability....We can be trusted to use restraint with our nuclear weapons.*

The flaws in these arguments are painfully obvious. The very same logic could be used by every country to justify developing its own nuclear deterrent. Why, some ask, should the nuclear weapon states be trusted, but not others— and who is qualified to make that judgment? Why, others ask, is it okay for some to live under a nuclear threat, but not others, who continue to be protected by a "nuclear umbrella"?

What the weapon states consistently fail to take into account is the impact of their actions. Whether they choose to continue their reliance on nuclear weapons, as the centerpiece of their security strategy, or to abandon that reliance, their choice will undoubtedly influence the actions of others.

A New Security Paradigm

It is therefore clear that a security strategy rooted in "Us versus Them" is no longer sustainable. Every country, irrespective of its ideology or orientation, will do what it takes to feel secure, including through seeking to acquire nuclear weapons. This is the stark reality, moral equivalence aside. What makes this more dangerous is that, in an era of globalization and interdependence, the insecurity of some will inevitably lead to the insecurity of all. The solution, therefore, in my view, lies in creating an environment in which nuclear weapons are universally banned, morally abhorred, and their futility unmasked.

The prospects for progress in preventing nuclear catastrophe will remain grim unless we begin working on a new security paradigm. A security paradigm in which no country relies on nuclear weapons for its security. A system with effective mechanisms for resolving conflicts. A system in which long-standing regional tensions, like those in the Middle East, are given the priority and attention they deserve. A system that is equitable, inclusive, and effective.

In April 2007, the International Campaign to Abolish Nuclear Weapons was launched in Melbourne, Australia. The campaign calls for a Nuclear Weapons Convention—a convention to outlaw nuclear weapons worldwide, much like the conventions on biological and chemical weapons.

In July 1996, the International Court of Justice (ICJ) declared that "the threat or use of nuclear weapons would generally be contrary to the rules of international law applicable in armed conflict, and in particular the principles and rules of humanitarian law."

As with the convention on antipersonnel landmines, public involvement could provide the momentum to make the Nuclear Weapons Convention a reality. Christopher Weeramantry, a former judge of the ICJ who took part in its landmark 1996 Advisory Opinion on nuclear weapons, has written that, "if we want more than the kind of snail's pace action of the past 50 years, we need a public campaign worldwide that is vocal enough to force swift action."

We are at a crucial juncture. The system is faltering. We need serious commitments on nuclear disarmament, with clear milestones and accountability. We need an effective approach for dealing with proliferation threats. We need to develop a multinational approach to the nuclear fuel cycle. We need a universally robust verification system. We need an effective system for the security of nuclear material. And above all, we need to start serious work toward a new collective security paradigm. If we want to prevent a nuclear catastrophe, the deadline for action is now.

PART V

Stepping Back from the Precipice

CHAPTER 14

Turning Away from the Nuclear Precipice

David Krieger

Is elimination of nuclear weapons, so naïve, so simplistic, and so idealistic as to be quixotic? Some may think so. But as human beings, citizens of nations with power to influence events in the world, can we be at peace with ourselves if we strive for less? I think not.

—Robert S. McNamara, former U.S. secretary of defense

I believe that despite the enormous odds which exist, unflinching, unswerving, fierce intellectual determination, as citizens, to define the real truth of our lives and our societies is a crucial obligation which devolves upon us all. It is in fact mandatory.

If such a determination is not embodied in our political vision we have no hope of restoring what is so nearly lost to us—the dignity of man.

—Harold Pinter, 2005 Nobel Lecture

The world has been on a sure and steady path toward the nuclear precipice. It is being led in this direction not so much by small rogue states as by the most powerful of all states, the United States. U.S. nuclear policies are placing the world on a collision course with disaster. The United States seeks to deter and inhibit states deemed to be unfriendly to U.S. interests from developing nuclear arsenals, while at the same time turning a blind eye to the nuclear programs of states deemed to be friendly to U.S. interests. Moreover, U.S. policies assume an unquestioned right for the United States and other established nuclear weapon states to maintain this status. Such continued and blatant double standards cannot hold.

The United States initiated a war against Iraq on the false premise that it had programs to create nuclear and other weapons of mass destruction. Further, the United States has developed contingency plans for the use of nuclear weapons against Russia, China, Iraq, Iran, North Korea, Syria, and Libya.[1] At the same time the United States protects Israel's nuclear program from international censure, and seeks to change U.S. nonproliferation laws in order to provide nuclear materials (NMs) and technology to India, a country that developed nuclear weapons outside the Non-Proliferation Treaty (NPT).

The only real hope to avoid falling from the nuclear precipice into the abyss below is for people throughout the world, and particularly those in the United States, to demand that these weapons be abolished before they abolish us. It is a daunting task, but one that is necessary if we are to save civilization and life on earth. In light of the modest gains that have been achieved to date in relation to the enormity of the challenge presented by nuclear weapons, the task is all the more essential.

Deterrence Is a Failed Strategy

For most of the Nuclear Age, the security of powerful nations has rested upon a theoretical construct known as deterrence. Deterrence theory posits that nuclear attacks can be prevented by the threat of nuclear retaliation. For the most powerful nations, the theory has spawned threats of massive nuclear retaliation, sufficient to destroy not only the attacking nation, but likely civilization and much if not all life on Earth.

One of the great fallacies of strategic thinking in the Nuclear Age stems from deterrence theory being based upon presumptions of rationality. The theory holds that a rational actor will not attack an enemy that could massively retaliate against one's own country. But what would happen if there were irrational actors in the system? What would happen, for example, if the leader of a small nation in possession of nuclear weapons believed irrationally that he could attack a more powerful country with impunity? What would happen if a leader was suicidal and didn't care about the prospects of retaliation? In such cases, deterrence would fail and the nuclear threshold would again be crossed with devastating consequences that cannot be fully foreseeable.

In addition to being a theory based upon the flawed premise that there will be only rational actors, deterrence theory requires that it must be physically possible to retaliate against an attacker and that a potential attacker must understand this. Thus, deterrence theory has no validity against a nonstate terrorist organization such as al Qaeda. Should such an organization obtain nuclear weapons, deterrence would be of no avail. The only security against a terrorist nuclear attack is prevention—preventing nuclear weapons or the materials to make them from falling into the hands of terrorists. There is no tolerance for error.

In the case of nonstate extremism, security cannot rest upon deterrence. This means that a powerful country does not increase its security by adding to the quality or quantity of its nuclear arsenal. Rather, the opposite is the case. The fewer nuclear weapons there are in the world, the less possibility there would be for one or more of these weapons to fall into the hands of an extremist organization. The same is true of weapons-grade NMs.

Nuclear Weapons and Power

The advent of nuclear weapons represented an enormous leap in the power of weaponry. The development of these weapons by elite scientists during World

War II successfully tapped the potentially vast power inherent in Einstein's theory, $E = mc^2$, for destructive purposes. While humans have always devised destructive weapons, nuclear weapons moved the bar of destructiveness to new heights. With nuclear weapons, a single weapon could destroy a city, as demonstrated at Hiroshima and Nagasaki. Those who created or obtained these weapons seemed to possess a unique and special power of death over life. In the aftermath of World War II, this power was possessed at first only by the United States, but over the next decades other countries would join the nuclear club: the Soviet Union, United Kingdom, France, China, Israel, India, Pakistan and, most recently, North Korea.

But the power conferred by nuclear weapons is ghostly and illusory, for it cannot be used without causing death and destruction on such a massive scale that the attacker would be branded by all the world as cowardly and inhuman. In the case of the use of nuclear weapons at Hiroshima and Nagasaki, the United States justified its attacks both to its own people and to the world as necessary to end a long and brutal war in which it had been the victim of an unprovoked attack. Since then, nuclear weapons have dramatically increased in power, but the ability to use the weapons has been curtailed by moral constraints against such massive killing. This has been true even when a nuclear-armed country is losing a war, as was the case with the United States in Vietnam or the Soviet Union in Afghanistan.

Nuclear weapons are more useful to relatively weak actors than to those who are already powerful in other ways. For example, they may give North Korea the ability to deter the United States, and Pakistan the ability to deter India. Beyond the possibility of deterrence, nuclear weapons in the hands of an extremist organization would provide the potential to bring even the most powerful countries to their knees by destroying their cities.

The Logic of Self-Interest

A further negative consequence of reliance upon nuclear weapons is that a nuclear weapon state must not only be concerned with safeguarding its own nuclear arsenal and weapons-grade NMs, but also with the capacity of all other nuclear weapon states to protect their arsenals and NMs. It must be assumed that extremist groups would seek to prey upon the weakest links among the states in possession of nuclear weapons.

It is in the self-interest of the most powerful states to lead the way to nuclear disarmament. The logic for this position can be set forth as follows:

1. Large nuclear arsenals are like dinosaurs in having little adaptability to changing strategic circumstances.
2. The more powerful the nation in conventional terms, the less utility for security is provided by a nuclear arsenal.
3. Weaker countries, particularly those threatened by more powerful adversaries, have the greatest incentive to develop nuclear arsenals for purposes of deterring a nuclear-armed adversary.
4. The more states that develop nuclear arsenals, the greater the danger will be that these weapons or the materials to make them will fall into the hands of nonstate extremists.

5. Nonstate extremists need not hesitate to use these weapons against far more powerful states for fear of retaliation (because they *believe* that they cannot be located).

6. It is strongly in the security interests of powerful states to minimize the possibility of nuclear weapons falling into the hands of extremist groups.

7. The nuclear policies of the most powerful nuclear weapon states must have zero tolerance for nuclear weapons or materials from any state falling into the hands of extremist groups.

8. Preventing extremist groups from obtaining nuclear weapons can only be achieved by dramatically reducing the number of nuclear warheads in the world and bringing the remaining weapons and materials to make them under strict and effective international control.

9. To achieve this will require a high degree of international cooperation, with leadership from the principal nuclear weapon states.

10. Only the United States, as the world's most militarily powerful state, can effectively initiate such cooperative action, and it is strongly in U.S. security interests to do so.

A Failure to Heed Warnings

From the very beginning of the Nuclear Age, clear thinking individuals have warned of the dangers to humanity. The warnings have been passionate and numerous. They have come from individuals in all walks of life—scientists, physicians, literary figures, philosophers, and generals. Albert Einstein, for example, warned, "The unleashed power of the atom has changed everything save our modes of thinking, and thus we drift toward unparalleled catastrophe."[2] General George Lee Butler, the former commander in chief of the U.S. Strategic Command, has argued, "We cannot at once keep sacred the miracle of existence and hold sacrosanct the capacity to destroy it. It is time to reassert the primacy of individual conscience, the voice of reason and the rightful interests of humanity."[3]

But such warnings seem to have fallen on deaf ears among political leaders. Despite the end of the Cold War, reliance on nuclear weapons for the security of powerful nations has not diminished. The Bush administration is promoting the development of a Reliable Replacement Warhead (RRW) to replace every thermonuclear weapon in the U.S. arsenal, a move that would do more to assure the continuation than the reliability of the U.S. nuclear arsenal for many decades into the future. In doing so, the United States is sending a message to other nuclear and potential nuclear weapon states that these weapons are useful. With the U.S. abandonment of the Anti-Ballistic Missile (ABM) Treaty, Russia has improved the capabilities of its missile delivery system to assure that its nuclear-armed missiles would not be intercepted by the U.S. missile defense system. China has responded by modernizing and expanding its nuclear arsenal.

In the more than 60 years of the Nuclear Age, there has been no fundamental shift in thinking among those in possession of nuclear weapons. The weapons are deemed necessary to prevent others from initiating a nuclear attack, even in post–Cold War circumstances in which nuclear weapon states do not view each other as enemies, with the exception of India and Pakistan. Rather than seize the opportunity to dramatically reduce and dismantle their nuclear arsenals, the principal nuclear weapon states seek to assure the reliability of the weapons and their delivery systems. In doing so, they fail to close the door on nuclear proliferation to other states and extremist organizations. They leave open the possibility of future nuclear attacks.

A Unique Responsibility

On the fifth anniversary of the United Nations Millennium Summit, Kofi Annan, the then secretary general of the UN, issued a report, *In Larger Freedom: Towards Development, Security and Human Rights for All.* In this report, the secretary general stated,

> the unique status of nuclear-weapon States also entails a unique responsibility, and they must do more, including but not limited to further reductions in their arsenals of non-strategic nuclear weapons and pursuing arms control agreements that entail not just dismantlement but irreversibility. They should also reaffirm their commitment to negative security assurances. Swift negotiation of a fissile material cut-off treaty is essential. The moratorium on nuclear test explosions must also be upheld until we can achieve the entry into force of the Comprehensive Nuclear Test-Ban Treaty.[4]

The secretary general urged the parties to the NPT to endorse these measures at the 2005 NPT Review Conference, but unfortunately the nuclear weapon states, led by the United States, exercised their power in such a way as to assure that the Review Conference ended without agreement and in failure.

The "unique responsibility" of the nuclear weapon states falls to them both because of their power and because of their obligations. The NPT itself lays out the basic responsibility of the nuclear weapon states: "to pursue negotiations in good faith on effective measures relating to cessation of the nuclear arms race at an early date and to nuclear disarmament."[5] Following the entry into force of the NPT in 1970, the United States and the USSR continued to improve their nuclear arsenals for the next three decades. But at the 2000 NPT Review Conference, they agreed to 13 Practical Steps for Nuclear Disarmament, including an "unequivocal undertaking . . . to accomplish the total elimination of their nuclear arsenals."[6] This promise, like others made over the years, proved to be little more than words, as the United States worked against achieving progress on nuclear disarmament in the Geneva-based Conference on Disarmament and at the 2005 NPT Review Conference.

The International Court of Justice (ICJ) Opinion

In 1996, the ICJ issued an Advisory Opinion on the illegality of the threat or use of nuclear weapons. The court found that "the threat or use of nuclear weapons would generally be contrary to the rules of international law applicable in armed conflict, and in particular the principles and rules of humanitarian law."[7] The court went on to indicate its inability to determine the law in the particular instance in which the very survival of a state was at stake. It found that "in view of the current state of international law, and of the elements of fact at its disposal, the Court cannot conclude definitively whether the threat or use of nuclear weapons would be lawful or unlawful in an extreme circumstance of self-defense, in which the very survival of a State would be at stake."[8] It is important to note that the court was *not* saying that under such circumstances the threat or use would be lawful, but only that it could not make that determination.

The court then took the unusual step of going further than asked and unanimously concluded, "There exists an obligation to pursue in good faith and bring to a conclusion negotiations leading to nuclear disarmament in all its aspects under strict and effective international control."[9] The court left no doubt that the nuclear disarmament commitment set forth in Article VI of the NPT was a legal commitment binding upon the nuclear weapon states.

Barriers Along the Path

There have been legal and moral barriers, as well as those of practicality and security, along the twisted path leading to the nuclear precipice. But despite promises, obligations, and apocalyptic warnings, the nuclear weapon states continue to move surely and steadily down this deadly path. Legal, moral, and practical barriers have not been sufficient to move the leaders of nuclear weapon states to step away from this path. It is worth contemplating what might lead to a change in direction.

Changing Direction

Determining what needs to be done is not the difficult part of the task. Many important proposals have been put forward for changing direction and moving away from the nuclear precipice. One important agreement is the 13 Practical Steps for Nuclear Disarmament that was unanimously supported at the 2000 NPT Review Conference.[10] Another example is the proposal by Mohamed ElBaradei, the director general of the International Atomic Energy Agency (IAEA) and the 2005 Nobel Peace Laureate. He called for the international community to take the following seven steps:

1. A five-year hold on additional facilities for uranium enrichment and plutonium separation.
2. Speeding up existing efforts to modify the research reactors worldwide operating with highly enriched uranium (HEU) and converting them to use low-enriched uranium (LEU), not suitable for making bombs.
3. Raising the bar for inspection standards to verify compliance with NPT obligations.
4. Calling upon the UN Security Council to act swiftly and decisively in the case of any country withdrawing from the NPT.
5. Urging states to pursue and prosecute any illicit trading in NM and technology.

6. Calling upon the five nuclear weapon states that are parties to the NPT to accelerate implementation of their "unequivocal commitment" to nuclear disarmament.
7. Acknowledging the volatility of long-standing tensions that give rise to proliferation, in regions such as the Middle East and the Korean peninsula, and take action to resolve existing security problems and, where needed, provide security assurances.[11]

ElBaradei emphasized that all steps required a concession from someone, and that none would work in isolation. As ElBaradei stressed, concessions must come from all, including the nuclear weapon states, which must change their policies. At present, the nuclear weapon states seek to prevent proliferation, but are failing to fulfill their disarmament obligations. They seem content to live indefinitely in a world of nuclear "haves" and "have-nots." This is a short-sighted perspective, one that is not sustainable. Until this is recognized by the leaders of the nuclear weapon states, there is not much hope to achieve a balanced approach to preventing nuclear proliferation and achieving nuclear disarmament.

The Need for Leadership

If the world is going to move in a new direction, away from the nuclear precipice, certain qualities of leadership will be needed. These include

- *Imagination*: the ability to imagine the catastrophic consequences of remaining on the path we are on.
- *Respect for human dignity*: the recognition that nuclear weapons and human dignity are incompatible.
- *Vision*: the ability to see another way forward, a world in which security can be obtained without reliance on nuclear weapons.
- *Courage*: the willingness to challenge the business-as-usual ingrained attitudes of the defense establishment and its so-called security experts.

One notable former leader of a nuclear weapon state, Mikhail Gorbachev, came to office with these qualities. He proposed in the mid-1980s that nuclear weapons be abolished by the year 2000. Unfortunately, he was not in a position to act alone, but needed the support of the United States. He came close to achieving this when he met with U.S. President Ronald Reagan at the Reykjavik Summit in 1986. The two leaders talked seriously about eliminating all nuclear weapons, but their agreement faltered on the issue of missile defenses, which Reagan was committed to implementing and Gorbachev feared.

We cannot count on another political leader to emerge with these qualities. Rather than waiting for such a leader to come along and save humanity, ordinary people must become leaders and create the necessary political will that leaders of nuclear weapon states will have no choice but to act in the interests of all humanity. Awakening the people of the world to accept this responsibility is the work of civil society organizations committed to these issues. It is certainly the greatest challenge of our time.

NOTES

1. Excerpts from the Nuclear Posture Review, submitted to the Congress on December 31, 2001, can be found at: http://www.globalsecurity.org/wmd/library/policy/dod/npr.htm.

2. This warning by Einstein is widely quoted and thought to have originated in a 1946 fundraising letter for the *Bulletin of the Atomic Scientists*. See, for example, Krieger, David, ed., *Speaking of Peace*, Nuclear Age Peace Foundation Web site, www.wagingpeace.org/menu/issues/peace-&-war/start/speaking-of-peace.pdf.

3. Butler, George Lee, "Death by Deterrence," *Resurgence*, 193, http://www.resurgence.org/resurgence/issues/butle193.htm.

4. *In Larger Freedom: Towards Development, Security and Human Rights for All*, Report of the Secretary General, United Nations General Assembly, A/59/2005, March 21, 2005, p. 28.

5. Treaty on the Non-Proliferation of Nuclear Weapons, entered into force March 5, 1970.

6. Final Document Issued by 2000 NPT Review Conference, May 20, 2000. Federation of American Scientists Web site: http://www.fas.org/nuke/control/npt/docs/finaldoc.htm.

7. Advisory Opinion of the ICJ on the legality of the threat or use of nuclear weapons, United Nations General Assembly, A/51/218, October 15, 1996, p. 36.

8. Ibid., p. 37.

9. Ibid.

10. Final Document Issued by 2000 NPT Review Conference, May 20, 2000. Op. cit.

11. ElBaradei, Mohamed, "Seven Steps to Raise World Security," *Financial Times*, February 2, 2005.

CHAPTER 15

Nuclear Weapons, War, and the Discipline of International Law

Richard Falk

The deepest challenge confronting those who seek the abolition of nuclear weapons arsenals and unconditional prohibition of future acquisition cannot be met by relying on the pious rhetoric about the legal prohibitions applicable to nuclear weaponry. International law certainly affects the aura of illegitimacy that surrounds any discussion of nuclear weaponry, but its clear pronounce-ments and authoritative arrangements have not demonstrated any capacity to influence behavior, especially of the nuclear weapon states. Most international law experts would agree that any threat or use of nuclear weapons, except pos-sibly in retaliation against a prior nuclear weapons strike or when the survival of a state was at stake, is unlawful, yet the doctrines and policies of states have involved threats without adverse consequences. The highest judicial body in the United Nations (UN) system endorsed this general assessment in its Advisory Opinion on the Legality of the Threat or Use of Nuclear Weapons delivered in 1996. Beyond this, the most comprehensive international treaty on the subject, the Non-Proliferation of Nuclear Weapons (1968), commits nuclear weapon states in Article VI to end "the nuclear arms race at an early date" and "pursue negotiations in good faith" to achieve "nuclear disarmament." Such clear legal admonitions have been ignored by nuclear weapon states, most pointedly by the United States, without causing any notable criticism either in diplomatic circles or within domestic politics.

The reality of the situation is this. International law is clear that there exist strong rules prohibiting threat or use of nuclear weapons and an even clearer obligation to negotiate a treaty obligating their elimination. This clarity in international law has for more than six decades seemed irrelevant to the policies pursued by nuclear weapon states, and there seems to be no political will among foreign governments or even world public opinion to insist on implementing these legal obligations. In this sense, the task for those advocating abolition is to arouse public and governmental opinion to the point where the politi-cal will exists to press for enforcement. There have been moments, especially caused by public anxiety, when civil society movements have called for nuclear disarmament. Such moments followed the Cuban Missile Crisis that demon-strated to the public how close the world had come to a nuclear war in 1962 or upon efforts by the Reagan presidency to deploy nuclear weapons in Europe that gave rise to the fear that maybe the superpowers would have a nuclear exchange in Europe while sparing their own countries. A more ambivalent effort occurred around the "nuclear freeze" movement that did not challenge the possession of nuclear weapons, but tried to stop the expansion of existing arsenals and the development of new kinds of nuclear weapons. Such movements of concern had strong momentary impacts, but were not sustained very long after the crisis mood receded from political consciousness.

At this point, where nuclear fears are concentrated in the West on the prospects that such weaponry may fall into the hands of terrorists and the sense that proliferation has already gone too far for geopolitical safety, there is a climate of opinion that seems more favorable than during the Cold War for the establishment of a nuclear disarmament regime established through a phased treaty. The Shultz/Perry/Kissinger/Nunn statement, the tensions associated with the confrontation with Iran over its nuclear program, and the worries about the Pakistan stockpile of nuclear weapons are indicative of a political mood dis-posed to rethink the security role of nuclear weapons for the states that currently possess the weaponry. Whether this mood is expanded, and a global movement mobilized to exert pressure on nuclear weapon states, remains to be seen, but more so than at any point since the end of the Cold War, the issue is discussable in the mainstream and is being discussed.

To encourage this more activist antinuclear outlook it is important to enlist the moral and political imagination. This gives a critical perspective to the nuclear past that may encourage a more critical attitude toward the present and a more hopeful approach to the future. As with any deeply rooted set of practices, we cannot understand the difficulty of changing fundamental attitudes toward nuclear weaponry unless we consult the historical background, and do so by way of the political and moral imagination. This is not mainly a matter of reminding ourselves of the massive, acute, and prolonged suffering associated with the use of atom bombs against the cities of Hiroshima and Nagasaki. It is more an inter-pretation of the context of the use of such weapons, and why the horrifying spec-tacle that was caused did not produce more of an effort to make sure that such weapons were never, never used again. It is true that in the immediate aftermath of World War II, leaders including Harry Truman and Winston Churchill talked of the urgent need to move toward a much more secure form of world order to avoid any recurrence of large-scale warfare. But this temporary sense of shock was quickly overcome by a return to normalcy: the thirst for the most powerful weaponry that could be produced by existing technology, the emerging sense of a geopolitical struggle for global ascendancy with the Soviet Union in which this weaponry was supposed to give the West a strategic edge, and the claim by war thinkers, most notably Herman Kahn, that the apocalyptic imagery associated with nuclear war was greatly exaggerated, and that it would be entirely possible to recover fully from a nuclear attack in a matter of months.

This pronuclear outlook was solidified into a political consensus in the United States as Cold War goals gained priority in policy circles, and reinforced by a variety of special interests eventually identified by President Eisenhower in his celebrated Farewell Address as "the military-industrial complex."

My intention in this chapter is look below the surface of this historical unfolding of the Nuclear Age and consider what might have been the status of nuclear weapons if the development of the bomb had proceeded on a somewhat different course. Let us consider that in the last stages of World War II, Germany had developed nuclear weapons prior to the United States and went on to use their two or more bombs against Allied cities of Manchester and Liverpool in Great Britain, chosen at random for illustrative purposes. Yet, as seems likely, despite these devastating strikes, Germany had nevertheless gone on to lose the war. If this had happened, two very different consequences for the Nuclear Age would have in all probability have resulted. First, it seems almost certain that the attacks would have been treated by the victorious side as definitive proof of Nazi barbarism, and would in all likelihood have been publicized at the time in as much grim detail as possible to intensify Allied support for the war effort. After such a campaign of outrage and war propaganda it seems highly unlikely, that having witnessed and experienced the horror of nuclear devastation of our closest ally, that the United States, assuming their later development, would have dared use these same weapons against Japan. It would have been almost unimaginable to suppose that having shown the world for purposes of wartime propaganda what these weapons do to human beings and to cities that these weapons would ever have been used again by the United States even against Germany except possibly under the exceptional circumstance where national survival was genuinely at risk. I doubt that the United States would have used atomic bombs against Germany if it were already on the verge of victory in World War II. In this hypothetical situation, then, Germany would remain responsible for initiating the Nuclear Age.

An American atomic attack against Japan also would have likely seemed unacceptable at the time, despite the deep resentment directed at Japan due to its attack on Pearl Harbor and its cruel wartime tactics. In fact, the war against Japan was virtually won in any event by August 1945 when Hiroshima and Nagasaki were attacked, and an invasion of the Japanese mainland could have in all probability been avoided through a negotiated surrender, although historians continue to debate this point. It needs to be admitted that the same arguments used by advocates of the atomic attacks would have been available despite the prior use by Germany: saving American lives, ending the war more rapidly, intimidating the Russians, and convincing ourselves that the American weapons really worked. Taking these factors into account requires an acknowledgment that this portrayal of probable American nonuse was by no means a sure thing even beneath the shadow of a condemned German use, but it does seem far more likely that the voices of restraint would have prevailed within American decision-making circles at the time. Part of what encouraged this initiating use was the unavailability of any landscapes of atomic horror, enabling the policy debate to remain focused on abstract strategic and military goals, raising issues of tactics not essentially different from the earlier discussions that led up to the authorization of indiscriminate bombing campaigns carried out against German and Japanese cities with the avowed intention of spreading terror among the civilian population.

Second, if we grant for the sake of speculation that nuclear weapons had not been used by the United States in World War II along the lines of the reasoning presented, then it is almost certain that the threat, use, and possession of nuclear weapons would have been criminalized at the war crimes trials of German leaders at Nuremberg. As a result, the world would have entered the Nuclear Age with a strongly and formally established legal, moral, and political consensus that the threat or use of weapons of mass destruction by any government is unconditionally prohibited and criminalized as an instrument for the conduct of conflict or the pursuit of national interests. The United States could have strengthened its case for postwar global leadership due to its decision to refrain from using its atom bombs despite the political pressures and temptations to do so.

There are other consequences to be taken into account in analyzing the present set of circumstances that imperils the human future by persisting risks that at some future time nuclear weapons will indeed be used. The encouraging fact that they have not been used in the more than 60 years since Hiroshima provides little comfort as we know that there were several occasions of near use, and the present possessors of these weapons have attitudes and conflicts that could easily result in use. Again, the failure to get rid of the weaponry after 1945 calls to our attention another characteristic of the operation of law in the context of war. We need to understand that one of the greatest weaknesses of international law is that the winners in major wars tend to delimit both zones of prohibition and of criminality for the future. The deep historical irony here is that had Germany succeeded first with their crash program to produce the atomic bomb, the world is quite likely to have been in a much more favorable situation than was the case resulting from the American-led victory. International law is subject to very powerful influences, either constructive or destructive, that reflect the tactics and ideas of those who come out on top in major historical struggles, especially those with ideological stakes. The winners in a war such as World War II, which was, in the deepest sense, widely regarded a just war exerting a strong influence in determining which practices in war are to be tolerated in the future. The war was a necessity from the perspective of liberal values and democratic constitutionalism. It defeated a Fascist plan to control and shape world order, destroyed the Nazi system of genocidal rule, and ended an epoch of brutal Japanese imperialism in Asia. It was inevitable under these conditions, combined with the sacrifice in lives and resources, that the Allied victory would be uncritically celebrated as a moral vindication. Unfortunately, as argued here, this welcome outcome of World War II had the serious paradoxical consequence of leaving us with a far more dangerous nuclear weapons legacy than might otherwise have been bequeathed to future generations.

Despite the general approval of the outcome of World War II throughout the world, the name "Hiroshima" is viewed outside the United States with the same sort of horror at the capacity of governments to do terrible things to their human and political enemies as is Auschwitz. A sense of moral equivalency between such atrocities exists at the level of world public opinion and, in some respects, the shadow of Hiroshima is somewhat darker than that cast by Auschwitz because the entire world has been living with the risk of nuclear annihilation ever since 1945. One essential difference between these two epochal challenges to our humanity is that Auschwitz was perpetuated by the losers and almost universally proscribed, while the bombing of Hiroshima was the work of the winners and treated by most of the world as exempt from condemnatory criticism.

Most of us realize that history is mainly written by the winners, but we are much less conscious of the equally troubling reality that international law often develops to repudiate losers and validate winners. In light of our preceding discussion, it is fully understandable and not surprising that the crime of geno-cide was outlawed in the Genocide Convention shortly after World War II. A treaty was successfully negotiated, despite global tensions, and over the years has been almost universally ratified by the governments of the world. In contrast, even the first use of nuclear weapons has not produced a weak commitment in the form of a nonbinding joint declaration by nuclear weapon states. More generally, nuclear weapons have been developed and deployed as almost normal weapons of war, initially relying in public mostly on a deterrence rationale when the Soviet Union and the United States were superpower rivals. Since 1992 when the Soviet Union collapsed, and Russia was no longer considered an adversary, there has been no push toward nuclear disarmament and, quite incredibly, there has not even been a willingness to de-alert nuclear weapons so that their launch would be delayed till a considered political decision could be made free from the inclination to act without assessing the consequences. International law can be a positive force for change with respect to global behavior of states, but not if the geopolitical winners are opposed. Without taking account of this disturbing assessment of the content and authority of international law our expectations will be too high, and tempt us to believe that international law consistently mir-rors the best interests or the shared moral sentiments of humanity. The more sober truth is that international law must mediate between idealistic goals and the more mundane geopolitical ambitions of leading states that are often amoral and militarist, as well as being indifferent to the aspirations of global civil society to achieve a more peaceful, sustainable, and just world order.

The Greatest Mind-Game of Our Era

Against such a background, the greatest mind-game of our era is the degree to which the nuclear weapon states have convinced the media and most of the world that the danger of these weapons arises from the countries that *don't* possess them rather than from the countries that *do*. It is an incredible intellectual and political feat to have shifted the burden away from those countries that have developed and possess these weapons—and in one case actually used them—and continue to insist that they have the right to retain and develop them, refusing to take off the table of diplomatic options their possible future use, or even their first use. It's an extraordinary mind-game that works with most of us, including many people in the peace movement. Most have quietly accepted these distort-ing assumptions, settling for, saying, "let's do our best to slow down the nuclear arms race" or "let's stabilize at a lower-level existing arsenals of nuclear weapons, and let's devote our reformist energies to the perils of nuclear proliferation." Or even worse, "we need these weapons to defend against terrorism or to frighten governments that might be tempted to help extremist groups acquire weapons of mass destruction, but only we in the West are responsible and civilized enough to carry out such a mission."

This blindsiding of the true risks of nuclear war is a dangerous course to take. It is also a politically futile and morally sterile approach to what should be our main preoccupation—preventing the threat or use of these weapons by anyone ever and thereby contributing to the establishment of a safer and fairer world. This latter way of thinking about the risks would return the focus to where it

belongs; namely, on the nuclear weapon states. It would return our attention to
nuclear disarmament, partial arrangements based on the regional elimination of
all weapons of mass destruction, and on the criminalization of threats or uses of
nuclear and other weapons of mass destruction. To be sure, a regime of prohibition accompanied by disarmament would need to have safeguards against the
stealth development of these weapons by states and nonstate political actors,
including those that never possessed such weapons in the past. But such an effort
would be incidental to the main problem of renouncing and eliminating existing
stockpiles, and taking steps to reassure others that no cheating was taking place
by keeping a cache of hidden weapons or through the retention of secret facilities
with the materials and know how to bring nuclear weapons quickly into being
in the future.

This mind-game of nonproliferation has recently morphed in sinister direc-
tions. In recent years, quite incredibly, the most powerful pretext for aggressive
war has come to be associated with alleged efforts to prevent certain additional
states from acquiring these weapons. Recourse to war against Iraq in 2003 and
the persisting buildup of tensions in relation to Iran are both aggressive undertakings predicated on the notion that the existing nuclear weapon states, led by
the United States, have some kind of global mandate to wage aggressive war in
order to prevent others from possessing these weapons, or even from acquiring
the knowledge, materials, and technology that might at some future time be
dedicated to the production of such weaponry. As we know with respect to Iraq,
it was a fictitious and duplicitous scenario concocted by American intelligence
agencies or extremist political leaders to validate recourse to a nondefensive war:
there were no weapons of mass destruction to be found in Iraq and no serious prospect of an Iraqi nuclear weapons capability for many years even if that
had been Baghdad's intention, which has never been established. Back in 2002
and early 2003, feverish American diplomacy was relied upon to persuade other
governments, the UN, and public opinion that it was necessary for the United
States (and Britain) to wage a war in defiance of international law, in defiance
of the UN, because our country, itself a nuclear weapons superpower, believed
it was entitled to wage war to prevent another country from acting to acquire
these weapons. Even if the factual allegations had turned out to be true, which
they were not, it would still not have provided an acceptable basis for recourse
to war.

Not only did this American diplomacy provide the pretext for the Iraq War,
but it also served to obscure what seem to have been the real motivations for
the war. We all know by now, or should know, that oil, control of the Middle
East, the security of Israel, and a whole series of other things were the dominant
motivations for this war, although not acknowledged to this day. Yet, beneath
the banner of counterproliferation, as fused and confused with counterterrorism
since 9/11, an aggressive war was launched against a helpless sovereign state that
had been previously decisively weakened by devastating air attacks during the
First Gulf War of 1991 followed by 12 years of crippling sanctions. As Americans
we need to remember at this time that aggressive war was viewed at Nuremberg
as the greatest possible international crime, and Germans found guilty of its
commission (and in Toyko, Japanese) were executed or sentenced to long prison
terms. It should also be appreciated, especially by young Americans, that it was
the U.S. government that pushed hardest for this criminalization of aggressive

war in the period following the end of World War II. It was part of the effort at the time to validate its defensive war against Germany and Japan and to deter future aggressive wars. In contrast, recently, the United States has been opposed to treating "aggression" as an international crime, evidently seeking to avoid any constraints on its geopolitical discretion to use force and wage war. The U.S. government used its diplomatic muscle to prevent the inclusion of aggression as an international crime in the Rome Treaty that led to the establishment of the International Criminal Court. In 2006, the House of Lords issued a decision (*Jones and Others v. Regina*) through a panel of Law Lords (the highest tribunal in the British legal system) affirming the continued existence of the international crime of aggression, rejecting prosecution arguments that the concept of aggression was too vague to be capable of legal definition.

Thus, the mind-game of nonproliferation both distracts us from the real challenges of nuclearism and provides nuclear weapon states with a geopolitical justification for launching an aggressive war. To make progress toward denuclearization and world peace requires us to expose and reject the game, and recognize that disarmament, not nonproliferation, is the proper goal of national security policy.

The Non-Proliferation Treaty (NPT) Has Been Materially Breached

In the present setting this American crime of aggressive war has been waged to keep other countries from acquiring the weapons that we continue to possess and develop. Actually, the treaty itself gives any country an escape route via Article X that allows a party to withdraw for reasons of its national security provided it gives three months notice. It is only by means of a geopolitical override of this treaty right that countries such as North Korea and Iran can be kept accountable within the bounds of the treaty itself.

Further, the NPT, to the extent that it represents the present embodiment of international law in this area, has been materially and flagrantly breached by the nuclear weapon states. According to the law of treaties, when one side breaches a treaty in a material, that is, an important manner, then all parties enjoy a right to withdraw, denounce the treaty, or to suspend its operation with respect to itself. Every party to the treaty would under these circumstances be entitled to treat the whole agreement as void. The nuclear weapon states are obliged in Article VI to commit themselves to end the nuclear arms race, seek nuclear disarmament in good faith, and to go on and attempt to negotiate general and complete disarmament. This commitment was undertaken by the nuclear weapon states in exchange for the agreement of non-nuclear weapon states to forego their own weapons option, and to encourage their participation in a legal arrangement that was negotiated to be balanced and fair to both categories of states. In this regard, the Article VI commitment was treated during negotiations as a fundamental premise of the NPT, being affirmed unanimously by the International Court of Justice (ICJ) in its seminal Advisory Opinion of 1996, an interpretation of legal obligations that was supported even by the U.S. judge on the court who on substantive grounds refused to regard nuclear weapons as illegal under all circumstances. For reasons of law and fairness, this refusal of the nuclear weapon states to implement their nuclear disarmament commitment undermines any insistence that the non-nuclear states continue to be bound by the treaty. The NPT, regardless of whatever good intentions guided its original establishment and independent of later claims by its proponents that it has slowed proliferation, is a casualty of the unwillingness of the nuclear weapon states, led by the United States to move genuinely toward nuclear disarmament.

The second difficulty is the extremely discriminatory manner in which this treaty has been interpreted and applied over the years to advance geopolitical, not legal, goals. Germany and Japan developed a complete nuclear fuel cycle without encountering the slightest opposition, while Iran is being threatened with war because Iran is seeking to possess the kind of peaceful nuclear energy technology that is promised by Article IV of the NPT. It is true that such technology has the potential to be diverted for weapons use, but until such a violation occurs, it is inappropriate to deny a country access to a technology that it is entitled to use for peaceful purposes, and that other non-nuclear states have been allowed to develop even as we assume for the present purposes of analysis, that the NPT continues to be an operative legal regime despite violations by nuclear weapon states and the discriminatory implementation of its central provisions in relation to nonweapons states. To covert the possible future violation of the NPT by Iran into a pretext for aggressive war is a grotesque and dangerous tactic now being employed by the United States, and aggravated by the refusal of the U.S. government to give assurances that it will not itself use nuclear weapons in some future attack on Iran's nuclear facilities.

Israel has refused to become a party to the NPT, possesses a documented arsenal of nuclear weapons that its officials implicitly brandish from time to time, including in relation to Iran, and exists in a region of unresolved conflict where its neighbors have all been adversaries in recent wars. Despite these worrisome factors, Israel has never been publicly criticized by the United States for its secret program to develop and acquire nuclear weapons, and by most reliable accounts was actually assisted by several nuclear weapon states in violation of their legal obligations. The geopolitical regime of counterproliferation administered by the United States does not even comment upon the Israeli policy or arsenal, which discredits the claim that it is intended to supplement the legal regime of non-proliferation by its own disciplinary authority. Since this counterproliferation policy pursued unilaterally by the United States is applied only selectively (that is, against enemies, but not friends), it lacks any legitimacy even as a proposed rule of order, much less law.

CONCLUSION

This chapter reaches three conclusions. First, the policies of the Bush presidency on these issues of nuclear weapons are only worse by a matter of degree than those of earlier U.S. administration. Every American president since 1945 has essentially endorsed a nuclearist geopolitics based on the idea that the United States gains strategic advantages from maintaining its nuclear weapons arsenal and taking whatever steps are necessary to retain U.S. superiority with respect to this weaponry. Second, it is time that antinuclearists take explicit account of the deficiencies associated with the operation of the NPT, and either regard the treaty as void or insist on its revival on the basis of nondiscrimination, mutuality and fulfillment of the commitment to achieve complete nuclear disarmament. Third, and finally, that the leaders of this country, the most militarily powerful state in the world, should accept the guidelines of international law with regard to the use of force and the initiation and conduct of wars.

There persists a form of crackpot wisdom that assumes that a powerful country is better off if it has the discretion to use force without exhibiting respect for the restraining discipline of international law. But if you look back at recent controversial moments in American foreign policy there would have been notable benefits associated with respecting international law. Taking such a legalist outlook seriously would have meant that the U.S. government would never have bombed Hiroshima and Nagasaki, nor intervened in Vietnam, nor invaded Iraq, or threatened Iran. Geopolitical benefits would have resulted for the United States in most of these situations if it had adhered to the minimum and core principles of international law. If it had done so, today this country would be better, prouder, more hopeful, and, of course, more respected around the world and, hence, more effective and appreciated as a responsible global leader.

It is toward such ends that citizens in the United States and elsewhere should work, including by our insistence that we wish to live under a government that acts on the basis of the Rule of Law in world affairs as well as in domestic life. In this spirit it is desirable for citizens with these values to do what it takes to achieve a world without weapons of mass destruction and, more idealistically, to devote their energies and resources on behalf of a world without weapons of any kind. Engaging seriously with the vision of a warless world also entails being dedicated to the eradication of poverty, disease, and other avoidable forms of human suffering. The argument of this chapter is that there exists a specific, unmet, and urgent responsibility here in the United States to address the panoply of dangers associated with nuclear weaponry, and to abandon a self-serving approach that pretends that the major risks of the weapons are due to the behavior of several non-nuclear states that must be made to bear the burdens of adjustment.

CHAPTER 16

Where We Stand: A Dialogue

David Krieger and Richard Falk

Krieger: We are standing at a very dangerous precipice in the Nuclear Age. Many people thought that the issue of nuclear weapons, the danger of nuclear weapons, went away at the time that the Cold War ended and the Soviet Union broke apart. The issue went off the radar screens of many, many people. Nuclear weapons today pose very serious dangers both to their possessors and to the rest of humanity. The problem of nuclear weapons needs to be grappled with in a very urgent manner.

Falk: My sense is that there is no question that we are at a point of great danger—nuclear danger—associated with this post–Cold War complacency on the one side, and the lack of control over the spread of weapons and the control over the nuclear materials (NMs), more generally. But at the same time the situation—the very loss of this kind of illusion of control that existed during the Cold War—has made some very influential policymakers rethink the wisdom of retaining nuclear weapons as an integral dimension of American security. Hence, it is a time both of danger, but in a certain sense a time of unprecedented potential opportunity to challenge the assumptions of nuclearism that have existed ever since the end of World War II.

Krieger: In early 2007, Henry Kissinger, George Shultz, William Perry, and Sam Nunn published an article in which they said some of the things that many of us have been saying for a long time—that nuclear weapons pose a great danger to the United States, that it is time to rethink our approach to nuclear weapons in terms of our own security, and that the United States needs to lead the way out. That was a very promising statement coming from individuals who are well positioned within the foreign policy establishment of the United States, but it didn't really appear that their statement had a lot of traction. It was a hopeful statement for the possibility of transformation, but then it didn't appear that there was much activity that followed it from the foreign policy and military establishments in the United States.

Falk: I certainly agree with that. But I think it's important to emphasize that these are not just four members of the foreign policy establishment. They are four stalwart figures who speak as authoritatively as any person in America on this kind of issue of national security. They include two former secretaries of state and a secretary of defense as well as the former chairman of the Senate Arms Forces Committee. It's important to understand that even though their argument converges in a certain way with the kinds of things that antinuclear people have been saying for decades, they come to this conclusion without in any way departing from their realist perspectives on world issues. So this is a rethinking of realism by these important figures.

You have two things at stake here. One is: are they accurate in their assessment of what this sort of new realism implies for nuclear weapons? And, if they are, or even if they are not, how come others who either agree or disagree have basically ignored a statement of such prominent individuals?

Krieger: There is no doubt that they are accurate in their assessment that a continuation of the status quo viewed only in realist security terms poses an enormous threat to the United States itself, actually probably an existential threat to the United States. From my perspective, we could conclude that they have been slow to reach that position. Coming to it in early 2007 is fairly late in the game, but perhaps not too late. The threat is that as long as we continue to behave as though nuclear weapons enhance our security, others will do the same. And it increases the possibility that these weapons will end up in the hands of people for whom deterrence is not a possibility because they can't be located and, therefore, they can't be deterred. So, on your first question, Richard, they're certainly accurate in their assessment of a nuclear danger to the United States. Your second question is much harder: why there hasn't been more resonance in the foreign policy establishment? I don't know the answer to that.

Falk: We might have at least expected either agreement or disagreement. It surely is an important enough statement by important enough people on an important enough issue that this virtual silence that has followed is significant evidence that the nuclear weapons establishment is so deeply entrenched in the bureaucracy of our government that it doesn't care what private citizens say, whoever they are, however important they are. And that's a very discouraging but revealing kind of conclusion. It may help think to back to Eisenhower's famous warning about the military-industrial complex, and how that warning from the most credible possible source has gone unheeded for almost 50 years. And if it was a problem when Eisenhower made that statement in his farewell speech, one can only imagine how much more serious it is 50 years or so later. I think we have to grasp the significance of this kind of nuclearism being locked into the American policy establishment in such a way as to make it unaccountable to any kind of pubic scrutiny. That's the way I read this most disturbing silence.

Krieger: Another explanation for the silence may be that nuclear weapons have been so deeply entrenched in our military policy that they have come to think of these weapons and strategies concerning their use to be technical issues and not really policy issues to be challenged. There never was the debate at the end of the Cold War about what to do now that the world had changed so dramatically. The relationship between the United States and Soviet Union was transformed, but the Cold War mentality that drove the nuclear arms race was never effectively transformed at the same time.

Falk: I would argue though that it was less a Cold War mentality than a hegemonic mentality—that nuclear weapons from their initial use at Hiroshima and Nagasaki imparted the sense of American geopolitical dominance. And this attitude, it seems to me, helps us understand why there was no disposition after the Soviet threat disappeared, which had been relied upon for decades to justify the buildup of nuclear weapons and retention of the nuclear weapons arsenal. Why that change in the geopolitical landscape didn't produce an instant impulse to seize the opportunity to get rid of these weapons once and for all. It was such an opportune moment. It is my understanding, and you may know more about this than I do, that not only was there no expression of even a rhetorical interest in nuclear disarmament, but there were private communications made to Yeltsin in Russia by the U.S. government *not* to get rid of his nuclear weapons. We didn't want the pressure to emerge to have to do something about our nuclear weapons arsenal, if Yeltsin, for instance, proposed nuclear disarmament or started in a dramatic way to dismantle the Russian nuclear weapons establishment.

Krieger: The Russians have always been ahead of us in wanting to take nuclear weapons to a lower level. And the general explanation for that has been that they can't afford to retain the large nuclear arsenal that they had during the Cold War. And so as their weapons were becoming less useful to them, and in fact something of a burden, they have tried to get the United States to come with them to lower levels. Even now there has been an offer on the table, for some time, from Mr. Putin, that the next step should be to take deployed strategic nuclear weapons down to 1,500 on each side, and he has even proposed the number 1,000, which the United States has not been willing to do. So I think your hegemonic concept of why the United States has held so tightly to its nuclear weapons appears to be confirmed by our reluctance to go lower at this point.

This seems like a very short-sighted policy to me because nuclear weapons would appear to be the only weapons system that is capable of destroying the United States as a nation. And it wouldn't take that many nuclear weapons to do that. It strikes me that the United States would be infinitely better off in a world without nuclear weapons, and I think that realization must also have occurred to Mr. Kissinger and the others in putting forward their proposal.

Falk: In my view, this question of evaluating the utility of nuclear weapons is not a relevant policy question, because of the degree to which the retention and further development of nuclear weapons is controlled by an unaccountable bureaucracy linked to the private sector companies that produce the weapons and the laboratories that develop ever new weapons. Skepticism about nuclear weaponry is swept aside or just ignored because of these strong vested interests in sustaining the nuclear establishment and its supportive bureaucracy. Such a conclusion is powerfully reinforced for me by this inability of even the Kissinger group to provoke a reaction. This nonreaction confirms my fear that nuclear-ism remains so deeply part of the governmental consensus that it's essentially undiscussable.

Krieger: It seems that the nuclear heart resides in the nuclear weapons laboratories.

Falk: You think it has a heart?

Krieger: I think it's a steel heart.

Falk: That's a confession I never expected to hear.

Krieger: It's a steel-hearted weapon. But I think the steel heart resides in the nuclear weapons laboratories—the place where they conceive of nuclear weapons, the place where they develop nuclear weapons, the place where the technology is the dominant aspect of the weapons. It seems strange that the policymakers would come to the point of deferring to the technologists.

Falk: I wonder if that's right? I mean I think the labs are obviously important, and the technology people, but as, I think, has been pointed out in the past, these labs would remain equally relevant, if not more so, in monitoring, verification, and in the sophisticated technologies that would be associated with a serious disarmament process. So again, I would come back to the essential feature of nuclear weapons as having endowed our governmental elites with this sense of hegemonic superiority that cannot be compromised without in some way weakening the stature of the United States as a global actor.

Krieger: Obviously it is a foolish proposition to think that you can maintain your hegemonic status with a weapon that a number of others equally possess, and some others less equally possess. But it could be destructive to the very existence of the United States since it is a weapon that by its very nature provokes others to threaten to respond in kind and thus puts every American citizen in jeopardy of nuclear annihilation. You may be correct that that's the thinking of U.S. government elites, but if that is their thinking it's a rather strange and bizarre psychological position to think that we are going to maintain dominance with weapons that are as likely to lead to our annihilation.

Falk: But couldn't you say, David, that this was true ever since the Soviet Union first developed its own capability, and that at every point this nuclear weapons establishment has insisted on exempting the retention of nuclear weapons from their own realist way of viewing the world. This retention and development of nuclear weapons has always posed a grave threat to American and world survival and well-being, and yet since the very earliest period, after a brief interlude of anxiety following Hiroshima and Nagasaki, these issues have been off the effective table of discussable questions. And why I attach so much significance to the Kissinger group's statement is that it's the first time that any public figures of this stature have tried to put the issue again in the public domain of discussable security issues.

Krieger: During the Cold War it was easier for these elites to argue that nuclear weapons were necessary for purposes of deterring the Soviet Union, and I don't think the kind of statement that Kissinger and others have now made could have come about during the Cold War. There was an orthodoxy then, that deterrence in a sense was God...or deterrence was necessary and, therefore, the weapons were necessary. But it seems much more obvious, in the aftermath of the Cold War, that that argument has broken down, and that nuclear weapons are, in fact, a more potent tool in the hands of the weak than they are in the hands of the strong, and the United States certainly fits into the equation of the side of the strong.

Falk: Let me raise a question. I think deterrence was never the only or even perhaps the primary reason why there was so much resistance to considering nuclear disarmament during the Cold War. If you remember, Kissinger himself made his reputation by discussing the usability of nuclear weapons in limited war situations, and part of this strategic argument, especially in the early phases of the Cold War, in the 1950s and 1960s, was that the United States needed nuclear weapons to offset the supposed conventional advantages of Soviet military manpower and their physical location or their geographic location in the strategic areas of the world, particularly in Euro-Asia. Therefore, I think that it is still surprising that from a realist policy perspective there wasn't more of a challenge to this idea that nuclear weapons were a usable part of one's security capabilities. People like George Kennan did his best from a realist perspective to raise this issue, but even he, as influential as he was at that time, was ignored pretty much.

Krieger: There has always been a subtext to nuclear weapons, which is that they can force other countries to take steps or not take steps based on threat alone, what Dan Ellsberg refers to as putting a loaded gun to someone's head, and telling them to do something. You don't need to pull the trigger; you only need to threaten. Again, for whatever utility that has had, it would seem to me that the utility would at this point in time be outweighed by the countervailing threat to the United States itself, either current or potential, and that's essentially what was being recognized by Shultz, Kissinger, Perry, and Nunn.

Falk: But if the disutility of these weapons is so obvious, even to these leading figures who have long been part of this nuclear weapon establishment, why hasn't their public expression of urgent concern stirred some kind of response?

Krieger: I don't know the answer to that. There has been a deafening silence that has surrounded their statement; in fact, the only resonance it seems to have had is with civil society—with civil society organizations like ours, picking it up and trying to give it more resonance.

Falk: The antinuclear community was clearly not the audience that the Kissinger group had in mind. You don't publish in the *Wall Street Journal* on these issues with this kind of grouping of prominent policymaking figures unless you are trying to reach the elites of the country.

Krieger: This also raises the question of why business and corporate concerns haven't reacted to the statement more strongly. They have a lot to lose, as do all of us.

Falk: Yes.

Krieger: We might shift the discussion slightly and talk about the nuclear Non-Proliferation Treaty, which came into effect in 1970, and called in Article VI for the nuclear weapon states to engage in good faith negotiations for nuclear disarmament. And, as you well know, that part of the treaty, that very essential part of the treaty, seems to have largely been ignored by the nuclear weapon states. Again, looking at the international community, you wonder why there hasn't been more outcry and outrage at the failure of the nuclear weapon states to fulfill their legal responsibilities under that treaty.

Falk: Yes, it certainly appears to me to be an essential provision of the treaty and part of the bargain by which the nuclear weapon states were allowed to temporarily retain their weapons in exchange for the non-nuclear weapon states foregoing a weapons option. I should point out that the obligatory character of this commitment to good faith negotiations was unanimously endorsed by the

International Court of Justice in its 1996 Advisory Opinion on the Legality of the Threat or Use of Nuclear Weapons. It should be recalled that this provision in the NPT goes beyond nuclear weapons, obligating countries to seek general and complete disarmament through international negotiations.

Krieger: That's correct.

Falk: And I think that's an important issue that has been more or less forgotten even by people like ourselves who have been concerned with nuclear weapons—because it raises this whole question as to what is the connection to global militarism and the existence of these particular weapons of mass destruction that are especially troubling, but also the wider embrace of a militarist approach to security and conflict resolution in the world.

Krieger: Actually, Article VI of the Non-Proliferation Treaty has three points: the first is that there would be a cessation of the nuclear arms race at an early date; the second is good faith negotiations for nuclear disarmament; and the third is similar negotiations for general and complete disarmament. So all three are there. I think what the International Court of Justice was saying in its Advisory Opinion was that nuclear disarmament is an obligation in and of itself and doesn't have to wait for general and complete disarmament.

I think that is an important consideration, but you're right that the Non-Proliferation Treaty went even further in calling for general and complete disarmament. Up to this point, I would say that this portion of Article VI has been treated as a reason for not accomplishing the nuclear disarmament portion, and following the court's decision in 1996, I think that this could no longer stand as an excuse for not proceeding with nuclear disarmament. General and complete disarmament remains a requirement of the treaty, but one that, in light of the fact that there has been so little progress on nuclear disarmament, has not been given the prominence that it deserves.

Falk: Shouldn't we at least entertain the possibility that emphasizing a critique of militarism more generally—arm sales, the waste of resources that goes into the construction of this enormous military machine that the United States has assembled now, that costs as much to maintain as what all the other countries in the world put together spend on their national security—that maybe it's time that we do take seriously the whole gamut of militarism as a focus of urgent concern. Possibly this broadened concern would make it easier for political leaders to say, "Well at least we can get rid of the nuclear weapons so that we can keep the big military machine functioning." It would be in a sense a fallback, providing the political leadership of the nuclear weapon states with a way of avoiding the impact of a more frontal attack on militarism by doing something that would contribute to overall global security.

Krieger: One of the reasons why nuclear disarmament has been so difficult in the United States is that nuclearism is so deeply imbedded in militarism, and militarism so deeply imbedded in corporatism. There are a lot of profits being wrung from our militarist approach to policy by corporations. And embedded within militarism are the policies related to nuclear weapons. I wonder if it's not possible that one of the reasons for the resistance among the foreign policy elites to doing more to disarm nuclear weapons isn't perhaps the unspoken understanding that if you pull the nuclear string, this military cash cow will begin to unravel. I don't know exactly who is profiting, but I do know that since the end of the Cold War the United States has been spending about $40 billion a year, or a third more than during the Cold War, on maintaining nuclear weapons and their delivery systems. So there is a large amount of money involved.

Falk: Yes, but I think there is an even larger amount of money that's involved with this absolutely dysfunctional global military machine that at best is wasted money. We see what happens when the military machine is actually used as in Iraq or earlier in Vietnam. It has very little utility even from a strictly realist perspective of power politics. The same realistic critique that makes nuclear weapons appear to be a dangerous and superfluous commitment of resources also applies to most of this global military machine. What is the benefit of 700 American military bases that are maintained all over the world? What is the need for a separate regional navy in every ocean? Or, what is the need for the militarization of space? All of these kinds of unexamined major dimensions of this military machine, this megamachine, need to be subjected to critical examination.

Krieger: I agree with you entirely. I doubt very much that the Kissinger group would be willing to go that far. One principle for examining the entire military establishment of the United States would be: What is necessary for *defense*? I would pose these questions: Does this base or this weapon provide the country with defense, or is it offensive? Does it have an aggressive component? The government has tried to position nuclear weapons, through the language of deterrence, as having some defensive capabilities, but in fact I think it is very mistaken to conceptualize nuclear weapons as a defensive element of a military posture. They are entirely an offensive weapon and one that is incapable of operating within the bounds of international law. They kill indiscriminately. You use a nuclear weapon and you have committed a crime under international law. You threaten to use a nuclear weapon and you have committed a crime under international law. So we are living in this state of perpetual criminality, and are standing on the precipice of even greater criminality.

Falk: We have been living on that precipice for a very long time and it goes back to the prenuclear reliance on strategic bombing during World War II, where whole cities were incinerated. The whole objective of the use of strategic air power was terroristic in the sense that it was trying to inflict as much damage on civilian society as possible, to demoralize civil society from continuing to support the war. This reliance on indiscriminate wartime violence against civilian society has, it seems to me, very deep roots in the political consciousness of even the most liberal and democratic—so much so that it has been basically unchallenged even in the United States. Such tactics treat indiscriminate warfare as a legitimate part of American national security strategy. We find the same argument surfacing these days about saving American lives in relation to the reliance on torture as a tactic used against detainees in Guantanamo or Abu Ghraib. The identical argument was used to justify the Hiroshima and Nagasaki bombings.

That argument was repeated in the torture context very recently by George Tenet, the former director of the CIA, when he was questioned about the so-called unorthodox interrogation practices that President Bush endorsed in his

September 6, 2006 speech. Tenet said that if the American people understood that these techniques saved American lives they would have no problem giving their backing to government policy. What I am saying is that we are dealing with a whole constellation of attitudes and deep-seated beliefs and practices that have been engaged in by our government and have been acquiesced in by the citizenry of this country.

Krieger: The Tenet approach to torture that you mention could have been taken from the television show *24*, which seems to present the same viewpoint to the American people.

Falk: And it's frightenly popular with the viewing public.

Krieger: That's true. What strikes me about what you just said is that when you use strategic bombing you terrify the population—you kill many innocent people and you terrify the population. When you have the threat or the use of nuclear weapons, you have a combination of ignorance, apathy, and denial among the population. So, it's a very different approach because nuclear weapons are long-distance killing machines and, for most people, when they are out of sight they are out of mind. Without some specific leadership in drawing attention to the threat they pose, which is certainly as great if not far greater than strategic bombing, we're left with a population that would like to just set the issue aside and pretend that it's not there. One of the principal goals of the Nuclear Age Peace Foundation is to awaken ordinary citizens to the nuclear threat so that they be alert to it and put pressure on governments. It turns out that performing that function is very difficult because many people, even once they are awakened and embrace the fact that it really is a significant threat, don't know where to go with it. The discussion at governmental levels is so removed from the heart of the issue that there is very little place for citizens to take their concerns on these issues.

Falk: I think that is absolutely correct, but I would also try to make the point that the logic of nuclearism, apparent as it is, is not discontinuous with other practices that have been more or less uncritically accepted by the American people and our leaders as acceptable ways of promoting national security interests. That is why I brought up strategic bombing and the absence of any critical response to the fact that thousands and thousands, tens of thousands, of innocent people were being deliberately torched in a very cruel and unacceptable way, certainly from the perspective of international law or in relation to the just war framework. There was no pretense that such uses of force were discriminate or proportionate in the context of an armed struggle. The only consideration seemed to be military effectiveness, which was understood in World War II as waging total war.

Krieger: Does your argument take you to the place where you feel it's necessary to challenge the entire system of militarism? Do you think that's necessary before we'll be able to make progress on the issues related to stepping back from the nuclear precipice?

Falk: I think it's partly that and partly it's a broader attempt to go back to the earlier part of this conversation, namely: Why has there been so little reaction to the Kissinger group statement? Partly what I am trying to say is that one source of explanation is that nuclearism isn't that discontinuous from things that have long been accepted as part of what our government does in the name of national security. It's not only evident if you look back at World War II, but it is also more currently evident if you look at the kinds of debates about torture and counterterrorist strategy that have been emerging at the present time. So it shouldn't surprise us that the American people are prepared to live with nuclear weapons. As long as they are dormant, there is nothing about their potentiality that makes it seem worse than other forms of abusive uses of force.

Krieger: I see one exception. Mostly the American people are acquiescent in using these more extreme forms of militarism, such as strategic bombing and torture on others. They are not so likely to accept their use on Americans. Maybe there is some room for influencing the American people. With regard to nuclear weapons, they cut both ways. You can threaten others with nuclear weapons, which is a terrible thing to do, morally and legally, but nuclear weapons also threaten the American people and there is no physical defense to nuclear weapons. We have nuclear weapons, but we live in a world in which we are also challenged by nuclear weapons. A large number of American people and American cities may well end up being destroyed by nuclear weapons if we continue as we are. That seems to me to be the side of the equation that the Kissinger group was articulating.

Falk: I think that certainly is one part of it, but I wouldn't exaggerate the unwillingness of American people to see this kind of violence used against people in this country. If you consider the prison conditions that have existed here, many of the techniques that have been used in Guantanamo and Abu Ghraib have been used for decades against American prison population, mainly minorities, incarcerated in this country. Again, as with indiscriminate weaponry, these abuses on the home front have provoked almost no adverse reaction. Here the identity of the victims as members of the ethnic underclass helps explain the silence.

Krieger: The same class that is recruited and sent to our foreign wars.

Falk: Yes.

Krieger: All of this suggests to me that there is a serious need to reopen a discussion about the functionality of national security. My sense is that the concepts that drive national security have become dysfunctional and are no longer, if they ever were, serving the purpose of providing security to Americans. As you suggest, already the underclass of America is being brutalized in many ways. Certainly disparities are growing. Even in a military sense, the soldiers, mostly from the underclass, were sent off to Iraq under the false premise of preventing proliferation of nuclear weapons. Now we find ourselves entangled in a war that's creating more terrorism that's likely to come back and haunt the United States in future years and decades. And nuclear weapons seem to me to also fit into that slot of being dysfunctional forms of providing national security, and maybe that's the discussion that needs to be cracked open by this Kissinger group commentary. I have no idea if any of these men in the Kissinger group would want to go further than they have gone. It seems to me, though, that where our discussion has led is that national security has become dysfunctional and we need to look at a broader concept of security in which our security is entwined with everyone's security.

Falk: Yes, I think that is really important and, of course, there have been some efforts to talk about security in terms of human security or comprehensive security. National security is not really the true purpose of this military machine, both its nuclear part and its non-nuclear part. I think it has much more to do with a global grand strategy. And a global grand strategy involves not defending a society but projecting its power, as far as possible in order to exert influence and to safeguard some critical resources, particularly oil, and to engage in strategic partnerships with countries around the world. It has nothing to do, in other words, with national security, as the concept was connected with the homeland of a country against potential adversaries or enemies. Therefore, one has to ask the question: In the nuclear context, does the threat of using nuclear weapons still seem to be diplomatically useful for those who are devising these grand strategy scenarios that involve the projection of global power to all corners of the planet?

Krieger: It sounds as though you are suggesting that this grand strategy is largely to project power in order to reap the benefits of profitability for the few. To take control of resources, and to place our military bases strategically throughout the world in order to have greater degrees of control, sounds like a strategy to benefit corporate interests. In fact, if you look at it in that light, it would appear to be promoting the opposite of national security. Rather than to benefit the security of the nation, it's benefiting small groups of elites and, in that sense, it actually sounds treasonous.

Falk: Well I should pause at that word and let it sink in.

Krieger: Treasonous by the elites who are promoting it, if it really acts against the interests of the American people.

Falk: I think it is a betrayal of the interests of the overwhelming majority of the American people that is sustained in part by presenting the justification for these policies as necessary elements in a national security policy. The main statements by the government during the Bush presidency, for instance, have been labeled as National Security Strategy of the United States of America, in a way of probably accidentally or unwittingly fusing notions of grand strategy with more traditional conceptions of national security, putting them all into this one overarching conception.

Chalmers Johnson has written rather persuasively about this in his books *The Sorrows of Empire* and *Nemesis*, where he talks at some length about the degree to which this global military presence is unsustainable from a financial point of view as well as from a security point of view—and that it is in almost every respect dysfunctional. We see in Iraq that the consequences of trying to bring to bear this military dominance make us wish that its only role was to waste our resources. Whenever the military machine is used, the results are almost always worse than its nonuse. I mean worse for us, and worse, even more so, for those who are trapped within the arena where the conflict is taking place.

Krieger: I agree with everything you say, but I want to pull our conversation back to nuclear weapons, because I think they have a couple of distinct characteristics that set them apart. One of those characteristics is that they could destroy most life on earth; certainly they could destroy civilization and they could potentially destroy the human species. It seems to me that this puts them in a special category. The second characteristic is that once you have nuclear weapons, the decision to use them lies in the hands of a very small number of people, so in that sense they are antidemocratic. We have created a situation in the world where we have a very small number of people in control of nuclear arsenals—people whose competence is not necessarily proven, whose rationality is not necessarily at a high level, and whose ethical standards may or may not be acceptable. These people are in charge of making decisions about the use of weapons that could destroy civilization and most life on earth.

We are living in an extraordinary situation in that regard, and we have very little public attention to the issue. I think that somehow we need to sharpen our focus on how we can deal with this particular problem more immediately than the issues of profit and betrayal and the pursuit of hegemonic policies. For better or for worse it is going to require leadership from the United States. Without that leadership, we won't be able to eliminate the nuclear threat to humanity. If the United States stays on its present course, Russia will stay on its course, Britain and France will stay on their course, as well as the rest of the nuclear powers, and there will be more states like North Korea that feel that they must develop nuclear weapons for their own protection and deterrence against the United States.

Falk: So what would you propose in light of that assessment?

Krieger: I think the role of civil society is absolutely essential and civil society organizations that work in this area have a huge responsibility. They have a very difficult job and an enormous responsibility. I think we have to continue to expand the number of people who are involved; and to do it very much as an act of faith in the belief that small groups of citizens, as Margaret Mead suggested, can make a difference in the world, as they have proven on other issues. In certain respects the challenge of abolishing nuclear weapons has some similarities to the challenge of abolishing slavery that took place in the last century. It appeared to be an almost hopeless goal at some point in time and yet we were able as a species and as specific societies to meet that moral challenge. Today, I think we've got to understand that nuclear weapons may be the most critical moral issue of our time. They could foreclose the future. There may be other responses to your question. But my specific response is that civil society needs to continue what it is doing, and join hands across societies and try to become more effective than we have been in the past. And we must do so in the belief that we're creating some currents under the surface that may leave fissures in the existing structures of militarism and nuclearism. But let me toss the same question back to you, because I think it's an important question and a very difficult one.

Falk: I basically share your view that there needs to be something that awakens the energies of civil society in such a way that a real campaign emerges. And it may be that this defection of individuals, such as those that make up the Kissinger group, is indicative of a political climate more receptive to the antinuclear message. At minimum, a portion of the realist community of policy influential individuals can now be persuasively linked to a grassroots demand for denuclearization. It could cause a kind of mutual reinforcing of political development that would make it possible for mainstream media and mainstream politicians to finally take hold of this issue combining a pragmatic justification with a potent ethical and idealistic push for nuclear disarmament as a matter of highest governmental priority.

I would mention one distinction between the struggle against slavery and the struggle to abolish nuclear weapons, and that is that slavery was always embedded in the private sector. One of the problems with nuclear weapons, in my view, is this degree to which nuclear weaponry remains insulated within an anatomical bureaucratic structure. The people who are most attached to nuclearism are not amenable to rational argument or to being openly challenged. Partly this unresponsiveness arises because the guardians of nuclearism are hidden in the dark recesses of the state bureaucracy. What cannot be seen is impossible to engage in controversy.

Krieger: I think that it is largely true. Many of the decision makers involved in the nuclear weapons complex are not particularly receptive to arguments that would challenge their vested interests. But I also want to point out that there may be some ways to expose their vested interests in meaningful ways, and I think the recent student activities at the University of California to challenge the role of the university in providing oversight and management to the U.S. nuclear weapons laboratories is hitting at a vulnerable point in the system. If the students stay with their cause in trying to dissociate the University of California from the labs and get the university to stop giving its legitimacy to the labs, that could end up creating a movement that challenges the nuclear weapons establishment at its core. I don't know if that will end up being the case, but I see it as a hopeful sign that the students are reacting. I remember a conversation that I had with Ted Turner, many years ago, in which Ted said, that the only way that the American people are going to wake up to the nuclear issue is when another nuclear bomb goes off. I always had a great deal of trouble with that perspective, because it seems to me to be such an enormous failure of imagination that we would have to wait until witnessing devastation on the order of Hiroshima or Nagasaki or greater before the American people or people anywhere were ready to engage in serious action on this issue. So, in part, I think our challenge is to awaken imagination. In your terms, Richard, to try to achieve the politics of the impossible through our struggles.

Appendices

Appendix A: The Russell-Einstein Manifesto Issued in London, 9 July 1955

In the tragic situation which confronts humanity, we feel that scientists should assemble in conference to appraise the perils that have arisen as a result of the development of weapons of mass destruction, and to discuss a resolution in the spirit of the appended draft.

We are speaking on this occasion, not as members of this or that nation, continent, or creed, but as human beings, members of the species Man, whose continued existence is in doubt. The world is full of conflicts; and, overshadowing all minor conflicts, the titanic struggle between Communism and anti-Communism.

Almost everybody who is politically conscious has strong feelings about one or more of these issues; but we want you, if you can, to set aside such feelings and consider yourselves only as members of a biological species which has had a remarkable history, and whose disappearance none of us can desire.

We shall try to say no single word which should appeal to one group rather than to another. All, equally, are in peril, and, if the peril is understood, there is hope that they may collectively avert it.

We have to learn to think in a new way. We have to learn to ask ourselves, not what steps can be taken to give military victory to whatever group we prefer, for there no longer are such steps; the question we have to ask ourselves is: what steps can be taken to prevent a military contest of which the issue must be disastrous to all parties?

The general public, and even many men in positions of authority, have not realized what would be involved in a war with nuclear bombs. The general public still thinks in terms of the obliteration of cities. It is understood that the new bombs are more powerful than the old, and that, while one A-bomb could obliterate Hiroshima, one H-bomb could obliterate the largest cities, such as London, New York, and Moscow.

No doubt in an H-bomb war great cities would be obliterated. But this is one of the minor disasters that would have to be faced. If everybody in London, New York, and Moscow were exterminated, the world might, in the course of a few centuries, recover from the blow. But we now know, especially since the Bikini test, that nuclear bombs can gradually spread destruction over a very much wider area than had been supposed.

It is stated on very good authority that a bomb can now be manufactured which will be 2,500 times as powerful as that which destroyed Hiroshima. Such a bomb, if exploded near the ground or under water, sends radio-active particles into the upper air. They sink gradually and reach the surface of the earth in the form of a deadly dust or rain. It was this dust which infected the Japanese fishermen and their catch of fish.

No one knows how widely such lethal radio-active particles might be diffused, but the best authorities are unanimous in saying that a war with H-bombs might possibly put an end to the human race. It is feared that if many H-bombs are used there will be universal death, sudden only for a minority, but for the majority a slow torture of disease and disintegration.

Many warnings have been uttered by eminent men of science and by authorities in military strategy. None of them will say that the worst results are certain. What they do say is that these results are possible, and no one can be sure that they will not be realized. We have not yet found that the views of experts on this question depend in any degree upon their politics or prejudices. They depend only, so far as our researches have revealed, upon the extent of the particular expert's knowledge. We have found that the men who know most are the most gloomy.

Here, then, is the problem which we present to you, stark and dreadful and inescapable: Shall we put an end to the human race; or shall mankind renounce war? People will not face this alternative because it is so difficult to abolish war.

The abolition of war will demand distasteful limitations of national sovereignty. But what perhaps impedes understanding of the situation more than anything else is that the term "mankind" feels vague and abstract. People scarcely realize in imagination that the danger is to themselves and their children and their grandchildren, and not only to a dimly apprehended humanity. They can scarcely bring themselves to grasp that they, individually, and those whom they love are in imminent danger of perishing agonizingly. And so they hope that perhaps war may be allowed to continue provided modern weapons are prohibited.

This hope is illusory. Whatever agreements not to use H-bombs had been reached in time of peace, they would no longer be considered binding in time of war, and both sides would set to work to manufacture H-bombs as soon as war broke out, for, if one side manufactured the bombs and the other did not, the side that manufactured them would inevitably be victorious.

Although an agreement to renounce nuclear weapons as part of a general reduction of armaments would not afford an ultimate solution, it would serve certain important purposes. First: any agreement between East and West is to the good in so far as it tends to diminish tension. Second: the abolition of thermo-nuclear weapons, if each side believed that the other had carried it out sincerely, would lessen the fear of a sudden attack in the style of Pearl Harbour, which at present keeps both sides in a state of nervous apprehension. We should, therefore, welcome such an agreement though only as a first step.

Most of us are not neutral in feeling, but, as human beings, we have to remember that, if the issues between East and West are to be decided in any manner that can give any possible satisfaction to anybody, whether Communist or anti-Communist, whether Asian or European or American, whether White or Black, then these issues must not be decided by war. We should wish this to be understood, both in the East and in the West.

There lies before us, if we choose, continual progress in happiness, knowledge, and wisdom. Shall we, instead, choose death, because we cannot forget our quarrels? We appeal, as human beings, to human beings: Remember your humanity, and forget the rest. If you can do so, the way lies open to a new Paradise; if you cannot, there lies before you the risk of universal death.

Resolution

We invite this Congress, and through it the scientists of the world and the general public, to subscribe to the following resolution:

"In view of the fact that in any future world war nuclear weapons will certainly be employed, and that such weapons threaten the continued existence of mankind, we urge the governments of the world to realize, and to acknowledge publicly, that their purpose cannot be furthered by a world war, and we urge them, consequently, to find peaceful means for the settlement of all matters of dispute between them."

Max Born
Perry W. Bridgman
Albert Einstein
Leopold Infeld
Frederic Joliot-Curie
Herman J. Muller
Linus Pauling
Cecil F. Powell
Joseph Rotblat
Bertrand Russell
Hideki Yukawa

Appendix B: Abolition 2000 Statement

A secure and livable world for our children and grandchildren and all future generations requires that we achieve a world free of nuclear weapons and redress the environmental degradation and human suffering that is the legacy of fifty years of nuclear weapons testing and production.

Further, the inextricable link between the "peaceful" and warlike uses of nuclear technologies and the threat to future generations inherent in creation and use of long-lived radioactive materials must be recognized. We must move toward reliance on clean, safe, renewable forms of energy production that do not provide the materials for weapons of mass destruction and do not poison the environment for thousands of centuries. The true "inalienable" right is not to nuclear energy, but to life, liberty and security of person in a world free of nuclear weapons.

We recognize that a nuclear weapons free world must be achieved carefully and in a step by step manner. We are convinced of its technological feasibility. Lack of political will, especially on the part of the nuclear weapons states, is the only true barrier. As chemical and biological weapons are prohibited, so must nuclear weapons be prohibited.

We call upon all states particularly the nuclear weapons states, declared and de facto to take the following steps to achieve nuclear weapons abolition. We further urge the states parties to the NPT to demand binding commitments by the declared nuclear weapons states to implement these measures:

1. Initiate immediately and conclude* negotiations on a nuclear weapons abolition convention that requires the phased elimination of all nuclear weapons within a timebound framework, with provisions for effective verification and enforcement.**
2. Immediately make an unconditional pledge not to use or threaten to use nuclear weapons.
3. Rapidly complete a truly comprehensive test ban treaty with a zero threshold and with the stated purpose of precluding nuclear weapons development by all states.
4. Cease to produce and deploy new and additional nuclear weapons systems, and commence to withdraw and disable deployed nuclear weapons systems.
5. Prohibit the military and commercial production and reprocessing of all weapons-usable radioactive materials.

6. Subject all weapons-usable radioactive materials and nuclear facilities in all states to international accounting, monitoring, and safeguards, and establish a public international registry of all weapons-usable radioactive materials.

7. Prohibit nuclear weapons research, design, development, and testing through laboratory experiments including but not limited to non-nuclear hydrodynamic explosions and computer simulations, subject all nuclear weapons laboratories to international monitoring, and close all nuclear test sites.

8. Create additional nuclear weapons free zones such as those established by the treaties of Tlatelolco and Raratonga.

9. Recognize and declare the illegality of threat or use of nuclear weapons, publicly and before the World Court.

10. Establish an international energy agency to promote and support the development of sustainable and environmentally safe energy sources.

11. Create mechanisms to ensure the participation of citizens and NGOs in planning and monitoring the process of nuclear weapons abolition.

A world free of nuclear weapons is a shared aspiration of humanity. This goal cannot be achieved in a non-proliferation regime that authorizes the possession of nuclear weapons by a small group of states. Our common security requires the complete elimination of nuclear weapons. Our objective is definite and unconditional abolition of nuclear weapons.

*The 1995 Abolition 2000 Statement called for the conclusion of negotiations on a Nuclear Weapons Convention "by the year 2000." Recognizing that the nuclear weapons states would likely fail in their obligations to conclude such negotiations, this phrase was removed at the end of the year 2000 after member organizations voted and agreed upon its removal.

**The convention should mandate irreversible disarmament measures, including but not limited to the following: withdraw and disable all deployed nuclear weapons systems; disable and dismantle warheads; place warheads and weapon-usable radioactive materials under international safeguards; destroy ballistic missiles and other delivery systems. The convention could also incorporate the measures listed above which should be implemented independently without delay. When fully implemented, the convention would replace the NPT.

Appendix C: The Rome Declaration of Nobel Peace Laureates— The 7th World Summit of Nobel Laureates, November 19, 2006

We, Nobel Peace Laureates and Laureate Organizations, gathered in Rome, Italy, have for years been deeply disturbed by the lack of public attention and political will at the highest levels of state paid to the need to eliminate nuclear weapons. There are over 27,000 of these devices threatening civilization, with over 95% in the hands of Russia and the US. This danger threatens everyone and thus every person must work to eliminate this risk before it eliminates us.

We oppose the proliferation of nuclear weapons to any state. We are faced each day with a new crisis in proliferation exemplified by concerns regarding North Korea and Iran. However, our focus must be on the weapons themselves for the only sustainable resolution to gain security is the universal elimination of the weapons.

The failure to address the nuclear threat and to strengthen existing treaty obligations to work for nuclear weapons abolition shreds the fabric of cooperative security. A world with nuclear haves and have-nots is fragmented and unstable, a fact underscored by the current threats of proliferation. In such an environment cooperation fails. Thus, nations are unable to address effectively the real threats of poverty, environmental degradation and nuclear catastrophe.

Nuclear weapons are more of a problem than any problem they seek to solve. In the hands of anyone, the weapons themselves remain an unacceptable, morally reprehensible, impractical and dangerous risk.

The use of a nuclear weapon against a state without nuclear weapons is patently immoral. Use against a state with nuclear weapons is also suicidal. These weapons have no value against terrorists or criminals. Progress toward a safer future is not thwarted from a lack of practical, threat-reducing policy options. The problem is a lack of political will. As Nobel Peace Prize Laureates we commit to work collectively to achieve the elimination of nuclear weapons, which we believe are unworthy of civilization.

We have heard the impassioned warning from the Mayor of Hiroshima and survivors of the atomic bombs and join him and the over 1500 cities around the world, including Rome, in their call to all nations, including those with nuclear weapons arsenals—US, Russia, France, China, UK, Israel, India, and Pakistan—to immediately commence negotiations to obtain the universal, legally verifiable elimination of nuclear weapons. In past years we have set forth practical steps to bring us to such a better world, and we reiterate the need for such policies as an entry into force of the Comprehensive Test Ban Treaty, de-alerting of the hair trigger launch on warning arsenals of thousands of hazardous weapons deployed now by Russia and the US, obtain stricter IAEA controls over nuclear materials, and pledges never to use a nuclear weapon first. Such efforts will help to ensure that nuclear capabilities are denied to terrorists.

We issue a serious warning that without such efforts the Nuclear Test Ban Treaty (NPT) could corrode opening the way for dozens of states to become nuclear armed, a frightening prospect. The NPT is a bargain in which nonproliferation is obtained based on a promise by nuclear weapons states to negotiate nuclear weapons elimination and offer peaceful uses of nuclear technology. There is a fundamental dilemma which must end. Nuclear weapons states want to keep their weapons indefinitely and at the same time condemn others who would attempt to acquire them. Such flaunting of disarmament obligations is not sustainable.

The current situation is more dangerous than during the Cold War. We are gravely concerned regarding several current developments such as NPT stake-holders enabling rather than constraining proliferation, modernization of nuclear weapons systems, the aspiration to weaponize space, thus making arms control and disarmament on earth all the more difficult, and the declared policy of terrorist organizations to obtain nuclear weapons.

Given the critical nature of the situation, we pledge to challenge, persuade and inspire Heads of State to fulfil the moral and legal obligation they share with every citizen to free us from this threat. We declare our intention to participate fully in a world summit where leaders of culture, arts, sciences, business, and politics, will actively participate.

As Nobel Peace Laureates, conscience requires us to raise our voices, inspire humankind, and to demand change in state policies. We call upon the citizens of the world to join us in this work.

The 7th World Summit of Nobel Peace Laureates took place in Rome from November 17 to 19 and was held, as were previous Summits, on the initiative of Mikhail Gorbachev and the Mayor of Rome, Walter Veltroni.

The ceremony of the acknowledgement of Man of Peace 2006 took place before the opening of the Summit. It was awarded to Peter Gabriel.

The Summit was openend by Walter Veltroni, Lech Walesa and Mairead Corrigan Maguire. Those taking part in the Summit were: Frederik Willem De Klerk, Mairead Corrigan Maguire, Lech Walesa, Carlos Filipe Ximenes Belo, International Atomic Energy Agency, International Physicians for the Prevention of Nuclear War, International Peace Bureau, United Nations Organization, United Nation High Commissioner for Refugees, United Nations Children's Fund, International Labour Organization, Mèdecins sans

Frontières, American Friends Service Committee, Red Cross, International Campaign to Ban Landmines, Pugwash Conference. Guests of honour were: Mayor of Hiroshima and President of the World's Mayors for Peace Tadatoshi Akiba, Nobel Laureate for Medicine Rita Levi Montalcini, Man of Peace 2006 Peter Gabriel, Representative of the Weapons of Mass Destruction Commission Jayantha Dhanapala, President of the Foundation on Economic Trends and Greenhouse Crisis Foundation Jeremy Rifkin, Under-Secretary-General of the United Nations Nobuaki Tanaka and Under-Secretary-General of the United Nations Jose Antonio Ocampo.

Appendix D: Nagasaki Appeal 2006, October 23, 2006

THE 3RD NAGASAKI GLOBAL CITIZENS' ASSEMBLY FOR THE ELIMINATION OF NUCLEAR WEAPONS

The 2005 Review Conference of the Nuclear Non-Proliferation Treaty (NPT), held in New York in May 2005, the sixtieth anniversary of the U.S. atomic bombings of Hiroshima and Nagasaki, ended without progress toward nuclear disarmament. There was much disappointment in the atomic-bombed cities, especially since expectations were running high in that milestone year. North Korea's nuclear test on October 9 was another blow to people around the world who have devoted themselves to the abolition of nuclear weapons. However, we global citizens will never give up on efforts to achieve a world free of nuclear weapons.

Specific developments since the NPT Review Conference hold hope for the future.

Sensible governments, the United Nations, and NGOs have joined together, learned lessons from the setback, and boldly risen up as demonstrated by the following: The 60 recommendations of the Weapons of Mass Destruction Commission (WMDC) chaired by Hans Blix, which include the reaffirmation that the goal should be to "outlaw nuclear weapons"; the realization of a new and innovative Central Asia Nuclear Weapon-Free Zone (NWFZ), the first NWFZ of the 21st Century; growing support for Mongolia's nuclear weapon-free zone status; the increasing engagement of mayors and parliamentarians in nuclear disarmament through Mayors for Peace and the Parliamentary Network for Nuclear Disarmament; the Article VI Forum of the Middle Powers Initiative (MPI) convening likeminded states and nongovernmental organizations (NGOs) to bring about compliance with the nuclear disarmament obligation; and powerful citizen campaigns to stop the renewal of the Trident nuclear weapons system in the U.K.

Meanwhile, the surviving victims of the atomic bombings, the *Hibakusha*, although even today suffering from the aftereffects of radiation, are in their old age standing in the vanguard of the campaign to abolish nuclear weapons. Last year, the *Hibakusha* were nominated for the Nobel Peace Prize. Although they were not awarded the prize, the Selection Committee expressed the highest praise for their activities. In order to expose the realities of the atomic bombings, more and more atomic bomb exhibitions and *Hibakushas'* witness accounts are being presented around the world every year. Among them, it is significant that in 2006 one such presentation was made at a U.S. government-operated museum in Nevada, where the U.S. nuclear test site is located. Few words are needed to help those who think of the development of nuclear weapons as a victory for science gain an understanding of the hellish scenes that unfolded beneath the mushroom cloud.

This year marks the tenth anniversary of the historic Advisory Opinion of the International Court of Justice. The Court found that "the threat or use of nuclear weapons would generally be contrary to the rules of international law" and that *all* countries have an obligation "to pursue in good faith and bring to a conclusion negotiations" on nuclear disarmament in all its aspects.

This year, the sixty-first anniversary of the atomic bombings, is a new starting point. In Nagasaki, we have come together for the 3rd Nagasaki Global Citizens' Assembly for the Elimination of Nuclear Weapons and conducted enthusiastic discussions over three days. The opening day was marked by the dedication of a sculpture in Nagasaki Peace Park. "The Cloak of Peace-Te korowai Rangimarie" was presented as a gift of friendship from the people of New Zealand to the people of Nagasaki. We were greatly encouraged by the participation of young people in the Assembly, including high school and university students, who reported on their sustained and broad-based peace activities.

Bearing in mind the results of the activities and discussions we engaged in, and on behalf of global citizens everywhere, we make the following appeal to the peoples of the world.

1. We strongly proclaim that nuclear weapons are the most barbaric, inhumane and cowardly of weapons, and we call upon the governments of all countries, without exception, to renounce the practice of seeking security through nuclear weapons.
2. We strongly condemn the provocative nuclear test conducted by North Korea. We reject any use of force in response and call for a peaceful, diplomatic resolution based upon a return to the six-party talks as well as bilateral talks.
3. Japan, as an atomic-bombed country, has an extremely important role and responsibility to fulfill in the abolition of nuclear weapons. We call on the Japanese government to reaffirm its commitment to the three non-nuclear principles by giving them the force of law through enactment of legislation. We give our support to Japanese citizens calling on their government for a policy shift as soon as possible from that of dependence on the U.S. nuclear weapons umbrella and for its support of an international treaty to abolish nuclear weapons.
4. To address legitimate regional security concerns, underlined by the North Korean nuclear test, we call for establishment of a Northeast Asia Nuclear Weapon-Free Zone. In Japan, we support local authorities that have made nuclear-free declarations, and encourage citizens and local authorities to cooperate and strive toward this goal.

5. The control of weapons useable fissile material is necessary to prevent nuclear proliferation. We call upon the government of Japan to reconsider its nuclear fuel cycle program, including the production of plutonium.

6. Agreements reached at the 2000 NPT Review Conference, including the "unequivocal undertaking by the nuclear weapon states to accomplish the total elimination of their nuclear arsenals," remain valid today. These include a diminishing role for nuclear weapons in security policies; taking nuclear weapons off high-alert status; ratification of the Comprehensive Test Ban Treaty (CTBT); negotiation of a verifiable Fissile Material Cut-off Treaty (FMCT); and the principle of irreversible nuclear disarmament. We call on all governments to assure implementation of these commitments. A return to these commitments should be the starting point of the 2010 NPT Review Conference.

7. We oppose the double standards that accept some nuclear programs, and reject others. None are acceptable. We oppose the proposed nuclear deal between the United States and India. We appeal not only to the governments of those two countries, but also to all the governments participating in the Nuclear Suppliers Group (NSG) to reject it.

8. We oppose the development of missile defense programs, including those that will lead to the weaponization of space. The promotion of missile defenses is serving to escalate competition for armaments, including nuclear arms, on a regional basis and throughout the world.

9. We call for the implementation of the recommendations of the Weapons of Mass Destruction Commission (WMDC). Let us promote these recommendations to national governments, parliaments, local governments, and civil society. Though it is clear that the United States and Russia need to cut their arsenals more rapidly and deeply, each of the nuclear weapon states must undertake further substantial reduction in their reliance on nuclear weapons. All nuclear weapon states should commit not to develop new or replacement nuclear weapons.

10. We call for strengthened efforts to encourage parliaments and local governments to act for the cause of nuclear disarmament, and to organize wide-ranging mass movements around the world. Current positive examples, unfolding on a worldwide scale, include the Emergency Action Plan of the Mayors for Peace (2020 Vision), the ongoing efforts of the Abolition 2000 Global Network to Eliminate Nuclear Weapons, and the new IPPNW International Campaign to Abolish Nuclear Weapons (ICAN).

11. We endorse and support the campaigns and civil resistance by British citizens and others who are acting to stop the renewal of the Trident nuclear weapons system and to promote the denuclearization of Europe. Also we encourage and support the campaign of US citizens against the nuclear weapon policies of the US government aimed at the indefinite possession of nuclear weapons, such as the Reliable Replacement Warhead (RRW) program, and the development of new delivery systems for "global strike" capability. We further encourage and support the campaign of French citizens who are working to stop the development of new nuclear warheads and missiles.

12. We encourage and support all member states of Nuclear Weapons Free Zone (NWFZ) treaties, which constitute almost two-thirds of the community of nations, and call upon them to play even more active roles in promoting nuclear disarmament and non-proliferation. We encourage the establishment of single state NWFZs and other regional NWFZs, and especially call on the governments in the Middle East to commence negotiations for the early and unconditional establishment of a zone free of nuclear weapons as well as other weapons of mass destruction.

13. To promote peace education and learning, we call for the establishment of public education systems which incorporate the recommendations of the United Nations Study on Disarmament and Non-Proliferation Education, using a variety of teaching methods and content, to suit each sector of society, including youth, university students, the general public, opinion leaders and decision makers.

14. We call upon the media and entertainment industries as well as artists everywhere to help dramatize, graphically depict and awaken citizens of earth to the dangers posed by nuclear weapons.

15. We call upon citizens everywhere to add their voices to those of the *Hibakusha* in calling for the total elimination of nuclear weapons before these weapons destroy our cities, our countries and civilization itself.

Appendix E: Lecture at Princeton University, November 28, 2006

Kofi A. Annan

Let me begin by saying how delighted I am to have been invited to give this address by a School named after Woodrow Wilson, the great pioneer of multilateralism and advocate of world peace, who argued, among other things, for agreed international limits on deadly weapons.

Princeton is indissolubly linked with the memory of Albert Einstein and many other great scientists who played a role in making this country the first nuclear power. That makes it an especially appropriate setting for my address this evening, because my main theme is the danger of nuclear weapons, and the urgent need to confront that danger by preventing proliferation and promoting disarmament, both at once. I shall argue that these two objectives—disarmament and non-proliferation—are inextricably linked, and that to achieve progress on either front we must also advance on the other.

Almost everyone in today's world feels insecure, but not everyone feels insecure about the same thing. Different threats seem more urgent to people in different parts of the world.

Probably the largest number would give priority to economic and social threats, including poverty, environmental degradation and infectious disease.

Others might stress inter-State conflict; yet others internal conflict, including civil war. Many people—especially but not only in the developed world—would now put terrorism at the top of their list.

In truth, all these threats are interconnected, and all cut across national frontiers. We need common global strategies to deal with all of them—and indeed, Governments are coming together to work out and implement such strategies, in the UN and elsewhere. The one area where there is a total lack of any common strategy is the one that may well present the greatest danger of all: the area of nuclear weapons.

Why do I consider it the greatest danger? For three reasons:

First, nuclear weapons present a unique existential threat to all humanity.

Secondly, the nuclear non-proliferation regime now faces a major crisis of confidence. North Korea has withdrawn from the Nuclear Non-Proliferation Treaty (NPT), while India, Israel, and Pakistan have never joined it. There are, at least, serious questions about the nature of Iran's nuclear programme. And this, in turn, raises questions about the legitimacy, and credibility, of the case-by-case approach to non-proliferation that the existing nuclear powers have adopted.

Thirdly, the rise of terrorism, with the danger that nuclear weapons might be acquired by terrorists, greatly increases the danger that they will be used.

Yet, despite the grave, all-encompassing nature of this threat, the Governments of the world are addressing it selectively, not comprehensively.

In one way, that's understandable. The very idea of global self-annihilation is unbearable to think about. But, that is no excuse. We must try to imagine the human and environmental consequences of a nuclear bomb exploding in one, or even in several, major world cities—or indeed of an all-out confrontation between two nuclear-armed States.

In focusing on nuclear weapons, I am not seeking to minimize the problem of chemical and biological ones, which are also weapons of mass destruction, and are banned under international treaties. Indeed, perhaps the most important, under-addressed threat relating to terrorism—one which acutely requires new thinking—is the threat of terrorists using a biological weapon.

But, nuclear weapons are the most dangerous. Even a single bomb can destroy an entire city, as we know from the terrible example of Hiroshima and Nagasaki, and today, there are bombs many times as powerful as those. These weapons pose a unique threat to humanity as a whole.

Forty years ago, understanding that this danger must be avoided at all costs, nearly all States in the world came together and forged a grand bargain, embodied in the NPT.

In essence, that treaty was a contract between the recognized nuclear-weapon States at that time and the rest of the international community. The nuclear-weapon States undertook to negotiate in good faith on nuclear disarmament, to prevent proliferation, and to facilitate the peaceful use of nuclear energy, while separately declaring that they would refrain from threatening non-nuclear-weapon States with nuclear weapons. In return, the rest committed themselves not to acquire or manufacture nuclear weapons, and to place all their nuclear activities under the verification of the International Atomic Energy Agency (IAEA). Thus, the treaty was designed both to prevent proliferation and to advance disarmament, while assuring the right of all States, under specified conditions, to use nuclear energy for peaceful purposes.

From 1970—when it entered into force—until quite recently, the NPT was widely seen as a cornerstone of global security. It had confounded the dire predictions of its critics. Nuclear weapons did not—and still have not—spread to dozens of States, as John F. Kennedy and others predicted in the 1960s. In fact, more States have given up their ambitions for nuclear weapons than have acquired them.

And yet, in recent years, the NPT has come under withering criticism—because the international community has been unable to agree how to apply it to specific crises in South Asia, the Korean peninsula and the Middle East; and because a few States parties to the treaty are allegedly pursuing their own nuclear-weapons capabilities.

Twice in 2005, Governments had a chance to strengthen the Treaty's foundations—first at the Review Conference in May, then at the World Summit in September. Both times they failed—essentially because they couldn't agree whether non-proliferation or disarmament should come first.

The advocates of "non-proliferation first"—mainly nuclear-weapon States and their supporters—believe the main danger arises not from nuclear weapons as such, but from the character of those who possess them, and therefore, from the spread of nuclear weapons to new States and to non-state actors (so-called "horizontal proliferation"). The nuclear-weapon States say they have carried out significant disarmament since the end of the cold war, but that their responsibility for international peace and security requires them to maintain a nuclear deterrent.

"Disarmament first" advocates, on the other hand, say that the world is most imperiled by existing nuclear arsenals and their continual improvement (so-called "vertical proliferation"). Many non-nuclear-weapon States accuse the nuclear-weapon States of retreating from commitments they made in 1995 (when the NPT was extended indefinitely) and reiterated as recently as the year 2000. For these countries, the NPT "grand bargain" has become a swindle. They note that the UN Security Council has often described the proliferation of weapons of mass destruction as a threat to international peace and security, but has never declared that nuclear weapons in and of themselves are such a threat. They see no serious movement towards nuclear disarmament, and claim that the lack of such movement presages a permanent "apartheid" between nuclear "haves" and "have-nots."

Both sides in this debate feel that the existence of four additional States with nuclear weapons, outside the NPT, serves only to sharpen their argument.

The debate echoes a much older argument: are weapons a cause or a symptom of conflict? I believe both debates are sterile, counterproductive, and based on false dichotomies.

Arms build-ups can give rise to threats leading to conflict; and political conflicts can motivate the acquisition of arms. Efforts are needed both to reduce arms and to reduce conflict. Likewise, efforts are needed to achieve both disarmament and non-proliferation.

Yet, each side waits for the other to move. The result is that "mutually assured destruction" has been replaced by mutually assured paralysis. This sends a terrible signal of disunity and waning respect for the Treaty's authority. It creates a vacuum that can be exploited.

I said earlier this year that we are "sleepwalking towards disaster." In truth, it is worse than that—we are asleep at the controls of a fast-moving aircraft. Unless we wake up and take control, the outcome is all too predictable.

An aircraft, of course, can remain airborne only if both wings are in working order. We cannot choose between non-proliferation and disarmament. We must tackle both tasks with the urgency they demand.

Allow me to offer my thoughts to each side in turn.

To those who insist on disarmament first, I say this:

—Proliferation is not a threat only, or even mainly, to those who already have nuclear weapons. The more fingers there are on nuclear triggers, and the more those fingers belong to leaders of unstable States—or, even worse, non-State actors—the greater the threat to all humankind.

—Lack of progress on disarmament is no excuse for not addressing the dangers of proliferation. No State should imagine that, by pushing ahead with a nuclear-weapon programme, it can pose as a defender of the NPT; still less that it will persuade others to disarm.

—I know some influential States, which themselves have scrupulously respected the Treaty, feel strongly that the nuclear-weapon States have not lived up to their disarmament obligations. But, they must be careful not to let their resentment put them on the side of the proliferators. They should state clearly that acquiring prohibited weapons never serves the cause of their elimination. Proliferation only makes disarmament even harder to achieve.

—I urge all States to give credit where it is due. Acknowledge disarmament whenever it does occur. Applaud the moves which nuclear-weapon States have made, whether unilaterally or through negotiation, to reduce nuclear arsenals or prevent their expansion. Recognize that the nuclear-weapon States have virtually stopped producing new fissile material for weapons, and are maintaining moratoria on nuclear tests.

—Likewise, support even small steps to contain proliferation, such as efforts to improve export controls on goods needed to make weapons of mass destruction, as mandated by Security Council resolution 1540.

—And please support the efforts of the Director-General of the IAEA and others to find ways of guaranteeing that all States have access to fuel and services for their civilian nuclear programmes without spreading sensitive technology. Countries must be able to meet their growing energy needs through such programmes, but we cannot afford a world where more and more countries develop the most sensitive phases of the nuclear fuel cycle themselves.

—Finally, do not encourage, or allow, any State to make its compliance with initiatives to eliminate nuclear weapons, or halt their proliferation, conditional on concessions from other States on other issues. The preservation of human life on this planet is too important to be used as a hostage.

To those who insist on non-proliferation first, I say this:

—True, there has been some progress on nuclear disarmament since the end of the cold war. Some States have removed many nuclear weapons from deployment, and eliminated whole classes of nuclear delivery systems. The US and Russia have agreed to limit the number of strategic nuclear weapons they deploy, and have removed non-strategic ones from ships and submarines; the U.S. Congress refused to fund the so-called "bunker-buster" bomb; most nuclear test sites have been closed; and there are national moratoria on nuclear tests, while three nuclear-weapon States—France, Russia and the UK—have ratified the Comprehensive Nuclear-Test-Ban Treaty.

—Yet, stockpiles remain alarmingly high: 27,000 nuclear weapons reportedly remain in service, of which about 12,000 are actively deployed.

—Some States seem to believe they need fewer weapons, but smaller and more useable ones—and even to have embraced the notion of using such weapons in conflict. All of the NPT nuclear-weapon States are modernizing their nuclear arsenals or their delivery systems. They should not imagine that this will be accepted as compatible with the NPT. Everyone will see it for what it is: a euphemism for nuclear re-armament.

—Nor is it clear how these States propose to deal with the four nuclear-weapon-capable States outside the NPT. They warn against a nuclear domino effect, if this or that country is allowed to acquire a nuclear capability, but they do not seem to know how to prevent it, or how to respond to it once it has happened. Surely they should at least consider attempting a "reverse domino effect," in which systematic and sustained reductions in nuclear arsenals would devalue the currency of nuclear weapons, and encourage others to follow suit.

—Instead, by clinging to and modernizing their own arsenals, even when there is no obvious threat to their national security that nuclear weapons could deter, nuclear-weapon States encourage others—particularly those that do face real threats in their own region—to regard nuclear weapons as essential, both to their security and to their status. It would be much easier to confront proliferators, if the very existence of nuclear weapons were universally acknowledged as dangerous and ultimately illegitimate.

—Similarly, States that wish to discourage others from undertaking nuclear or missile tests could argue their case much more convincingly if they themselves moved quickly to bring the Comprehensive Nuclear-Test-Ban Treaty into force, halt their own missile testing, and negotiate a robust multilateral instrument regulating missiles. Such steps would do more than anything else to advance the cause of non-proliferation.

—Important Powers such as Argentina, Brazil, Germany and Japan have shown, by refusing to develop them, that nuclear weapons are not essential to either security or status. South Africa destroyed its arsenal and joined the NPT. Belarus, Ukraine and Kazakhstan gave up nuclear weapons from the former Soviet nuclear arsenal. And Libya has abandoned its nuclear and chemical weapons programmes. The nuclear weapon States have applauded all these examples. They should follow them.

—Finally, Governments and civil society in many countries are increasingly questioning the relevance of the cold war doctrine of nuclear deterrence—the rationale used by all States that possess nuclear weapons—in an age of growing threats from non-State actors. Do we not need, instead, to develop agreed strategies for preventing proliferation?

—For all these reasons, I call on all the States with nuclear weapons to develop concrete plans—with specific timetables—for implementing their disarmament commitments. And I urge them to make a joint declaration of intent to achieve the progressive elimination of all nuclear weapons, under strict and effective international control.

In short, my friends, the only way forward is to make progress on both fronts— non-proliferation and disarmament—at once. And we will not achieve this unless at the same time we deal effectively with the threat of terrorism, as well as the threats, both real and rhetorical, which drive particular States or regimes to seek security, however misguidedly, by developing or acquiring nuclear weapons.

It is a complex and daunting task, which calls for leadership, for the establish- ment of trust, for dialogue and negotiation. But first of all, we need a renewed debate, which must be inclusive, must respect the norms of international nego- tiations, and must reaffirm the multilateral approach—Woodrow Wilson's approach, firmly grounded in international institutions, treaties, rules, and norms of appropriate behaviour.

Let me conclude by appealing to young people everywhere, since there are—I am glad to see—so many of them here today.

My dear young friends, you are already admirably engaged in the struggle for global development, for human rights and to protect the environment. Please bring your energy and imagination to this debate. Help us to seize control of the rogue aircraft on which humanity has embarked, and bring it to a safe landing before it is too late.

Appendix F: The Power of Place— Citizens and Elected Officials Uniting to Create a Nuclear Weapon-Free World

Pamela S. Meidell

Good afternoon. I'm very happy to be here speaking with all of you, seeing the faces of many beloved colleagues and friends, and many new faces. I have the honor of speaking to you today as a concerned citizen on behalf of the Mayors for Peace 2020 Emergency Campaign to Abolish Nuclear Weapons, launched by the mayors of Hiroshima and Nagasaki. My organization, the Atomic Mirror, has been working in partnership with the Mayors Initiative as part of the Abolition Now citizens' campaign for over two years now. These efforts aim to achieve what 35 years of diplomatic negotiations have failed to achieve: ensure that Nagasaki is the last city on earth to suffer atomic bombardment, and lay nuclear weapons to rest forever. Thank you to Mayor Tadatoshi Akiba and Mayor Iccho Itoh for inviting me to represent them. Thank you to David Krieger and the Nuclear Age Peace Foundation for holding this conference.

THE NUCLEAR EMERGENCY ROOM OF OUR PLANET

I begin by focusing on the word, "emergency." My friend, Natalie Gehringer, a pediatrician in Wisconsin, once told me the three questions that doctors ask people when they arrive in the Emergency Room. Since the premise of the Mayors Campaign is that the world is in the Nuclear Emergency Room, I offer these questions to us:

1. Who are you?
2. Where are you?
3. When are you? (Often asked as "Do you know what time it is? What day it is?")

If you can answer all these questions, the doctors in the ER will consider you "Oriented X3—a basic quick evaluation of mental status. Not terribly meaningful as you can answer those questions and be completely loony, but if you can't answer them we know there is a problem!"[1]

So, who are we? Look around at each other. We are a group of people concerned about the nuclear issue, who have gathered together to reflect on International Law at the Nuclear Precipice—the title of our symposium. We are men and women, many ages, many backgrounds, ordinary human beings with ordinary hopes and fears who can probably each remember the first time we learned about atomic weapons.

Where are we? We are in Santa Barbara on the Central Coast of California. We are on the edge of what our friends in the Pacific call the "liquid continent." We are in the territorial homelands of the Chumash People, which stretch from just below Monterey Bay in the North to Malibu in the South. This resource-rich area includes unique species of Island Foxes on the Channel Islands; the great Condor; grey whales migrating through the channel; and landscapes of low hills, coastal mountains, strawberry fields, and vineyards. The *Strawberry Fields Forever* that the Beatles sang about is in Oxnard, just down the Pacific Coast Highway. This territory also includes what the Chumash call the "Western Gate," a sacred portal through which pass the souls of all who die on Turtle Island, or North America. It is Chumash responsibility to act as guardians of this gate, which sits within the boundaries of Vandenberg Air Force Base. Diablo Canyon Nuclear Power Plant lies with Vandenberg Air Force Base to the north. At the base of the Channel Islands sit many shells and missile nose cones of depleted uranium, the residue of many Vandenberg tests. To the south lies the City of Moorpark, which in 1953 became the first city in the world to totally switch over from conventional electric power to nuclear energy. A few years later, the nearby reactor (in Rocketdyne's Santa Susanna Field Laboratory in Simi Valley) became the site of the first nuclear plant catastrophe through a partial meltdown. Efforts to clean radioactive residue from this site are still ongoing.[2] One of our esteemed Chumash leaders, Pilulaw Khus, an elder in the Bear Clan of the Coastal Band, when asked about the nuclear sites on her peoples' traditional lands, said, "The remedy is so simple. Just stop. Don't add any more to the problem." But more on that later.

The third question is: "When are we? What time is it?" Today is Friday, February 24, 2006 and it is four o'clock in the afternoon. It is springtime here in the northern hemisphere of our planet. As a planet, we've been here for about 4.5 billion years. As human beings, we've been here on the planet for about 2 million years. About 10,000 years ago we began farming in the Nile delta. This is important because just 60 years ago, we entered the Nuclear Age, which requires us to think as far into the future as we have just looked into humanity's and our planet's past. The radioactive half life of Plutonium-239, for example, is 24,110 years. The radioactive half life of Uranium-238 is 4.5 billion years. We can honestly say that in the life of our planet, the splitting of the atom has created an emergency: "a sudden, unexpected occurrence demanding immediate action."[3]

From Hiroshima and Nagasaki to the World Court

What the Mayors Campaign has done is to inspire us to stand in the Nuclear Emergency Room in the very streets of our own cities. I first met Mayor Iccho

Itoh on the docks of Crane Harbor in his own City of Nagasaki. It was August 8, 1995, the eve of the fiftieth anniversary of the bombing of the city. Our small group of pilgrims had traveled from New Mexico over the route of the atomic bomb carrying gifts of healing. We had heard that the mayor would be meeting a group of traditional kayakers who had paddled all the way from Okinawa for the events. It was a bright and windy afternoon when we seized the moment and walked up to him, Mayumi Oda carrying a shell filled with the healing waters of Lake Shasta and I carrying a pouch of healing earth from Chimayo, New Mexico. Mayor Itoh had the grace to receive us. Three months later we met him in The Hague where he was the one bearing gifts: testimony from the people of his city and photographs of Yosuke Yamahata, taken August 12, 1945. We were all in The Hague to hear testimony at the International Court of Justice (ICJ) during the Oral Hearings phase of the largest case the court had ever heard—on the illegality of the threat or use of nuclear weapons.[4] The Honorable Takashi Hiraoka, then mayor of Hiroshima, joined Mayor Itoh in offering the following compelling testimony of their cities. Mayor Hiraoka:

> My wife, who was also a first-year student at a girls' school, happened to be sick that day and didn't go to school, so she was saved. Nearly all her classmates were killed. Even today the fact that her life was spared remains a heavy burden of grief deep in her heart. Those who survived will never escape the psychological and physical effects of the bombing.... The issue of nuclear weapons should not be a matter of political relationships among nations. We must approach this problem in terms of what nuclear weapons mean for the future of the human race.[5]

Mayor Itoh appealed to the judges with these concluding remarks:

> Nagasaki became a city of death where not even the sounds of insects could be heard. After a while, countless men, women and children began to gather for a drink of water at the banks of nearby Urakami River, their hair and clothing scorched and their burnt skin hanging off in sheets like rags. Begging for help they died one after another in the water or in heaps on the banks.... The unspeakable atrocity and agony suffered by the citizens of Nagasaki must never be repeated in this world. I can say with confidence that the use of nuclear weapons again will wreak havoc on the global ecosystem and threaten the very survival of the human race. To ensure that a curtain of darkness is not drawn on the development of humanity from time immemorial, I extend my heartfelt request for your decision based on the viewpoint of human love.[6]

A Renewed Call to Face the Nuclear Emergency

The Mayors of Nagasaki and Hiroshima compel us because of the power of place. They keep faith with where they live and with who lives there with them. The current mayor of Hiroshima, Tadatoshi Akiba, renewed the call for a world free of nuclear weapons in Geneva at the United Nations in April 2003. It was just one month after we all witnessed the "shock and awe" of the bombing of Baghdad, and barely two months after 11 million people had massed in the cities of our planet appealing to the United States not to go to war with Iraq. He invited all citizens, institutions, and governments to take action to make real the cry of the *hibakusha* (the aging survivors of the atomic bombings): "Never again!"

> It is incumbent upon the rest of the world, the vast majority of the international community, to stand up now and tell all of our military leaders that we refuse to be threatened or "protected" by nuclear weapons. We refuse to cooperate in our own annihilation...
>
> We cannot sit silently watching it happen....The time has come to go beyond words, reason and non-binding treaties. The time has come to impose economic sanctions on any nation that insists on maintaining nuclear weapons. The time has come to use demonstrations, marches, strikes, boycotts and every nonviolent means at our disposal to oppose the destruction of millions of our brothers and sisters, the destruction of our habitat and the extermination of our species. The time has come to fight, nonviolently, for our lives.
>
> All of us in this room today, blessed with extremely high levels of prosperity and education, are duty-bound to educate the rest of the population in our countries about the nuclear danger. We must inform them and mobilize them for their own protection. It is our responsibility to launch a massive, grassroots campaign that will make it clear that the people of all nations will accept only leaders who undertake unequivocally to eliminate nuclear weapons.
>
> Bottom-up change takes time and great sacrifice, but, unfortunately, people of moral and spiritual vision must again take up the struggle. The abolition of nuclear weapons is no less important and no less just than the abolition of slavery. We are not just fighting a technology or a weapon. As Martin Luther King, Jr. said, we are fighting nuclear weapons in our own minds. We are fighting the very idea that anyone could, for any reason that he feels legitimate, unleash a nuclear holocaust. We are fighting the idea that a small group of powerful men should have the capacity to launch Armageddon. We are fighting the idea that we should spend trillions of dollars on military overkill while billions of us live in dire, life-threatening poverty...
>
> Our immediate target is nuclear weapons, but our long-term aim is a new world order....We seek a world in which no man, woman or child goes to bed wondering whether he or she will live through the hunger, pestilence, or violence of the next day; a world in which we look around this room and see not murdering, thieving enemies against whom we have to defend ourselves but brothers and sisters on whom our own safety, security, survival and enjoyment depend.[7]

When Mayor Akiba called for a movement for nuclear abolition in Geneva, and said that Mayors for Peace "will work with anyone and everyone willing to help design, develop, and implement this campaign," he discovered a global network of over 2,000 citizen groups already committed and ready to join hands with him.[8] One of the immediate joint goals was to bring an international delegation of the world's mayors to the next Non-Proliferation Treaty (NPT) Preparatory Committee meeting in New York the following year. Like Mayor Itoh and Mayor Akiba who speak with authority from the streets of their cities, we citizens and Non-Governmental Organizations (NGOs) knew we had to start from where we lived. We all went home and went to work.

Over the next months, the 2020 Vision Emergency Campaign[9] took shape and was officially launched in Nagasaki in October 2003. It called for a Nuclear Weapons Convention (NWC)[10] to be signed by 2010 and implemented by 2020. Everywhere, citizens and mayors working together took root in the local landscapes responsive to the particular conditions of their places. Our aim was to bring 30 international mayors to the 2004 NPT Preparatory Committee meeting in New York City.

Several months before the delegation was due to arrive in New York, no U.S. mayor had yet agreed to be part of it. Literally two weeks before the meeting, I asked Dr. Gabino Aguirre, Mayor of Santa Paula, in Ventura County, California, and he accepted. He didn't even know until he arrived in New York and joined 29 mayors from all over the world that he was the only U.S. mayor.[11] Speaking as the guardians and protectors of the well-being of their local places—the cities of our world—the mayors made their case directly to the diplomats at the United Nations (UN), finding new allies and partners. Abolition 2000 activists launched the Abolition Now! campaign[12] as the citizen partner of Mayors for Peace, knowing that the citizens and the elected officials needed to work together on behalf of the inhabitants of our communities. Our mutual goal was to bring hundreds of mayors and citizens back to New York for the 2005 NPT Review Conference the following May.

In Belgium, following a visit to Brussels, Mayor Akiba and a diverse group of six Belgian mayors, including the mayor of Brussels and a former prime minister, sent a letter to all their 589 colleagues inviting them to join the campaign. Nearly half—250—said yes.

In Germany, the local abolition network linked up with the youth-led International Law Campaign, working with Mayors for Peace to run the "nuclear weapon free by 2020" campaign.

In the United Kingdom, the deputy mayor of London and the long active Nuclear Free Local Authorities movement based in Manchester led the way. In the United States, Mayor Aguirre and Mayor Akiba brought the campaign to the U.S. Conference of Mayors, resulting in the unanimous passing of Resolution #92, which became a template for local U.S. cities, including Santa Paula, California; Santa Fe, New Mexico; and Olympia, Washington.

In an America where the national leaders had no ears to hear the will of the people, the mayors reminded us that all politics is local and helped us to recapture public interest in nuclear issues at the grassroots level. We in Ventura County turned to our local leaders, who did hear us and took action: Two of the five county supervisors signed on, as well as five of the ten mayors in our county. We found new local partners, who included a high school principal, a youth organizer who runs a weekly open mike at a local coffee house, a legal aid attorney recently elected to the California State Bar Association Board of Governors, a development officer for the local Boys and Girls Club, plus local physicians and clergy.

THE POWER OF PLACE AND PARTICULARITY

The mayors reminded us of the power of particularity. The use of nuclear weapons destroys particular places, incinerates particular people, burns up particular trees, and boils particular rivers and seas. The creation and production of nuclear weapons poisons particular mesas and aquifers, sickens particular people and animals, corrupts particular democratic processes, and shields decision makers from the consequences of their decisions.

The people of San Ildefonso Pueblo, New Mexico; Hanford, Washington and Oak Ridge, Tennessee know these truths by heart because their lands were carved out by eminent domain to create the Manhattan Project. Shoshone and Paiute peoples in Nevada and Mormons in Utah, and island people of the Marshalls know them because they have seen the mushroom clouds of 1,000 nuclear tests and 67 hydrogen tests rise over their lands. Sixty years into the Nuclear Age, they are still feeling the downwind effects.

THE 2005 NPT REVIEW CONFERENCE: BEFORE, DURING, AND AFTER

In May 2005, hundreds of mayors and citizens came surging to the NPT Review Conference, from all of our various places and all under the shadow of the Iraq War, hopeful that our organizing and commitment would bear fruit. We all know now that the month ended in shambles.[13] The obstacles that we face became crystal clear in the subsequent days. In fact, in responding to a foundation's request to name the three largest obstacles we face "in creating the results we desire in our field," I replied:

- The entrenched nuclearism of the world's Nuclear Weapon States (NWS), and their rampant disregard of international law and the will of the world's peoples.
- A disengaged and fearful public, created by (1) above, and by an increasingly consolidated media. The overwhelming nature of the issue of nuclear weapons and power marginalizes it and relegates it to exclusive policy/political spheres. There is a lack of dialogue among citizens about the dangers of nuclear weapons and the risky course of U.S. nuclear policy, and a lack of confidence in the ability to influence and change direction.
- Funding for nuclear disarmament groups in the United States has suffered since the end of the Cold War, and particularly since 9/11. As a community, we have lost institutional memory and continuity while the nuclear issue has reentered the public stage with a vengeance.

Despite these challenges, I submit to you that a sea change happened in May 2005 in three important ways:

1. The citizens of the world and their local elected officials turned up in force—over 1,700 people stood in line the opening day, outside the UN and thousands more marched in Central Park, chanting "No Nukes! No War!"[14]
2. The *hibakusha* took center stage in the General Assembly Hall of the United Nations, on May 4, and the world listened. Just 10 years before, *hibakusha* were given no platform at events surrounding the NPT Review and Extension Conference.
3. Americans asked the world community for help. The last week of the conference, Thomas Graham, Ted Sorensen, and Robert McNamara

(a diplomat and former White House officials) appealed to the assembled countries to be brave and stand up to the United States.

This brings us to this afternoon's panel topic: *Domestic Strategies for Changing U.S. Nuclear Policy.* I would like to suggest a slightly revised topic: *American Strategies for Creating a Nuclear-Free World* (and I refer to all three Americas: North, Central, and South!). Within that changed title lies a potential path for getting us out of the Nuclear Emergency Room, and on the road to a flourishing, sustainable, and secure world community.

NUCLEAR WEAPON-FREE ZONES LEAD THE WAY

On February 14, 1967, the countries of Latin America and the Caribbean gave the world a valentine in the form of the Treaty of Tlatelolco, which created our planet's first Nuclear Weapon–Free Zone (NWFZ). It was created in direct response to the belligerent and fearful experience of the Cuban Missile Crisis mere years before, and demonstrated that the countries nearest the biggest nuclear power could still take effective and imaginative action. Now, nearly 40 years later, most of the Southern Hemisphere is nuclear weapons free by similar treaties, and the number of zones is climbing.[15] Little noted in the run up to the events of May 2005 was the unprecedented meeting in Tlatelolco, Mexico, in the previous month of all countries from the NWFZs of our planet, over 110 of them.[16]

Mayor Akiba addressed the opening of that meeting, inviting the support of the assembled countries. Mayor Aguirre, representing the only American city to send an elected official to the meeting, cochaired the Civil Society Forum of the conference. NGOs were invited to sit down with governments, and offer statements in the regular sessions. The conference agreed to meet every five years, just prior to the NPT Review Conferences, the next gathering to be hosted by the states parties to the Treaty of Rarotonga in the South Pacific. The conference established a new and powerful forum for the delegitimization and abolition of nuclear weapons, and offers a structure for the parallel process we all seek to negotiate a Nuclear Weapons Convention.[17]

Regional NWFZs are a significant and powerful strategy for achieving a world free of nuclear weapons. At a time when people and governments of nearly every persuasion look for better ways to be safe and create the conditions for their children and societies to flourish, the citizens and governments of the world's NWFZs have much to teach us. We should endeavor to link these zones for the express purpose of isolating the NWS into a planetary corner where the only option will be to abdicate before the collective voices of the other superpower— our organized communities—and make a commitment to total and unequivocal disarmament. Regional NWFZs form the heart of the untold success story of the road to a nuclear weapon–free world; they are one of our best hopes for bringing it into being. In a post-9/11 world, it is more important than ever to create regional zones of safety and security that foster cooperation and trust among neighboring states. With these three major initiatives—uniting the efforts of citizens (Abolition Now), local elected officials (Mayors for Peace 2020 Vision Emergency Campaign), and the countries of our planet's NWFZ—we can achieve nuclear abolition and the fulfillment of the NPT promises.

What Next? Accept the Invitation

Every two years, since 1967, the countries of Latin America and the Caribbean gather to assess the state of their NWFZ, created by the Treaty of Tlatelolco. Every two years, the administrative body of the treaty, the Organization for the Prohibition of Nuclear Arms in Latin America (OPANAL), invites NGOs and observer states and organizations to sit down as equals at the table with them. In November 2005, Mayors for Peace and the Atomic Mirror accepted the invitation, and sent a three-person delegation from Ventura County to Santiago, Chile. Of the nine NGOs represented there, only two came from beyond South America. Imagine doubling that number, and bringing 18 delegations of mayors and citizen diplomats from all over the United States to the next meeting in November 2007. Imagine doubling the number again in November 2009. Imagine bringing the signing of the NWC to this forum—after all, it was a country from this region—Costa Rica—that introduced the NWC to the United Nations in the first place. As Mayor Aguirre said in Santiago, Chile, "The work of this OPANAL organization is a very important parallel effort in this popular struggle for freedom from nuclear annihilation." The meetings of OPANAL can be the parallel pathway to nuclear disarmament that we have all been seeking, culminating in the NWFZ conference in the Pacific in 2010 just prior to the NPT Review Conference. The majority of the world's countries can use this pathway to sign onto the NWC and bring it to the NPT Review Conference as an invitation to the NWS to fulfill their disarmament promises to the world. The last point of that visionary founding document of Abolition 2000[18] calls for the creation of mechanisms to ensure the participation of citizens and NGOs in planning and monitoring the process of nuclear weapons abolition. OPANAL has been inviting us to do just that for years. Let's accept the invitation!

The countries of the Americas are the natural allies of nuclear abolitionists in the United States. Our neighbors to the south recognized early on that we are all on the nuclear precipice, and they took steps to use international law to protect their communities and their region. In doing so, they inspired others across the globe to do the same. (Malaysia has proposed the creation of a NWFZ in Northwest Asia at the International Islamic Conference in Qatar as part of the menu of solutions for Iran.) We know we are in the majority as nuclear abolitionists. The majority of nations have renounced nuclear arms and want them eliminated. Sixty-six percent of the American public believe the best way to prevent the proliferation of nuclear weapons is to outlaw possession by any country.[19] We represent a powerful majority of our society. Our task is to develop models for democratic action to assert our voice as the "other superpower," our organized communities.

Mayors for Peace have ignited and encouraged abolitionists worldwide to find new partners and allies where they live. We live in the Western Hemisphere, with three Americas. Let's unite them in a Nuclear Free America that extends from Barrow, Alaska, to Tierra del Fuego. In doing so, we can renew the energies of the hundreds of cities and towns that have declared themselves nuclear-free zones. Even though they don't have legal international status, these tiny zones help create a political sensitivity that promotes nuclear disarmament and the further expansion of such areas. Even though the NPT Review Conference of

May 2005 did not result in concrete recommendations, we should not forget that NWFZs create regional security, and provide a practical and proven model that promotes the principles of both nonproliferation and disarmament.

AWAKENING AND NURTURING LOCAL AWARENESS AND ACTION FOR GENUINE SECURITY

How do we plant this message and nurture it at the local level? It is at the local level where we find the purest aspirations for a better world with liberty, justice, and for life itself. It is the local level that feels the greatest impacts of negative top-down decisions and policies. Therefore, the involvement of our local communities is indispensable. I can only offer you some of our current initiatives in Ventura County, which we are organizing under the three themes of dialogue, democracy, and diplomacy:

1. Dialogue. Educate and express ourselves. All politicians, religious professionals, academics, writers, journalists, teachers, artists, and athletes have a role to play in establishing the climate and conditions that create genuine security without the threat or fear of use of nuclear weapons. Remember that we live in a nuclear world: awareness of nuclear weapons largely faded from the public's mind and heart at the end of the Cold War. Today, the Bush administration's policies of possible preemptive nuclear first strike, the targeting of the so-called axis of evil, and development of mini-nukes and "nuclear bunker busters" brings the issue center stage and threatens the well-being of our world. Local leaders and citizens have the right and responsibility to encourage the creation of new national and local security policies that are in harmony with our founding ideals as a nation, policies that secure a living wage, health care, education, affordable housing, and meet basic needs for all citizens. We need to talk about it, and raise awareness through education and dialogue with local partners.
2. Practice democracy. Because nuclear weapons are so closely bound to the power of the governments that hold them, promoting open public debate regarding nuclear weapons policies helps to reclaim the public space necessary for democracy to thrive, and can lead to its expansion and reinvigoration.[20] We know now, after Iraq, that democracy and freedom go hand in hand with ridding a country of weapons of mass destruction. Our government has told us so. Let us begin at home.
3. Be a citizen diplomat. In our interconnected world, we are all ambassadors when we leave our homes. Our Ventura County coalition of local organizations (which opposes military violence, the War in Iraq, the government's interventionism and advocates other struggles for justice) is sending delegations to conferences and meetings that address nuclear disarmament and related issues. These efforts focus on promoting a global citizen identity (in contrast to a consumer identity) with an awareness of a global perspective and understanding. Through these efforts we are developing a curriculum for citizen diplomacy. Based on leadership trainings on dialogue with government representatives, citizen teams are being organized to visit consulates in Los Angeles, California (which has the third largest concentration of country outposts in the United States, after

New York City and Washington, DC). We will also send local delegations to the OPANAL meetings in 2007, 2009, and the NWFZ meeting in the Pacific in 2010.

INSPIRING LOCAL-GLOBAL ORGANIZING

Last November, Terry Tempest Williams, a Mormon woman downwinder from Utah, visited our local California State University, Channel Islands, to address these themes, and to participate in the Campus Reading Celebration, which featured her book *The Open Space of Democracy*. She concluded by sharing *Guidelines for Community Organizing* offered by a friend of hers, Lily Yeh, a Community Artist and Organizer in North Philadelphia:

- Sense a need
- Have a vision
- Anchor with a local leader
- Present vision to more leaders
- Involve more leaders
- Create beauty and share it
- Create a structure from the ground up
- Identify the storytellers and set them loose
- Train leaders
- Involve elders
- Engage the children
- Be willing to change every day
- Await magic
- Anticipate transformation
- Remember to check our egos at the door of the community

We dare to dream of a world free of nuclear arms! Can we do it? As our leader of the farm workers in California, and a local Oxnard homeboy, Cesar Chavez, said: "Yes, it can be done! Come; let's get to work! Si se Puede!"

NOTES

I am indebted to my Ventura County colleagues Dr. Gabino Aguirre and Carmen Ramirez, who responded so immediately to the call for U.S. mayors to join the international mayoral delegation to the United Nations. Their partnership (and especially their speeches to the OPANAL (Agency for the Prohibition of Nuclear Weapons in Latin America and the Caribbean) conference in Santiago, Chile in November 2005) provides the inspiration for this speech and for our ongoing work.

1. Natalie Gehringer, M.D., in e-mail exchange, February 23, 2006.
2. Gabino Aguirre, Ph.D., and former Mayor of Santa Paula, California, in speech to biannual meeting of OPANAL in Santiago, Chile, November 8, 2005.
3. *American Heritage Dictionary of the English Language.*
4. See http://www.icj-cij.org/icjwww/icases/iunan/iunanframe.htm for all of the documents of the case.
5. See CR/95/27 - 07 November 1995, under Oral Pleadings on page http://www.icj-cij.org/icjwww/icases/iunan/iunanframe.htm.

6. Ibid.
7. See the full text of Mayor Akiba's speech to government and citizen delegates to the Preparatory Committee meeting of the Nuclear Non-Proliferation Treaty (NPT) at http://www.reachingcriticalwill.org/legal/npt/NGOpres2003/Abolish2005.htm.
8. The Abolition 2000 Global Network to Eliminate Nuclear Weapons, see http://www.abolition2000.org.
9. See http://www.mayorsforpeace.org/english/campaign/2020vision.html.
10. A Nuclear Weapons Convention is an international treaty outlining the steps necessary to ban and implement the abolition of nuclear weapons on the planet. A Model Nuclear Weapons Convention was introduced into the UN as a discussion document by Costa Rica as A/C.1/52/7 in 1997. See http://www.lcnp.org/mnwc/index.htm.
11. The 2004 International Mayors for Peace delegation included mayors and mayoral representatives from Tel Aviv, Israel; Waitakere, New Zealand; Hue, Vietnam; Laakdal, Belgium; Kyiv, Ukraine; Viareggio, Italy; Sarajevo, Bosnia and Herzegovina; London, England; Negombo, Sri Lanka; Athens, Greece; New York, New York; Honolulu, Hawai'i; and Santa Paula and Oxnard, California.
12. See http://www.abolitionnow.org.
13. To read Mayor Akiba's open letter to the NPT Review Conference, see http://www.mayorsforpeace.org/english/campaign/NPTopenletter.html For links to various NGO analyses of the outcome, see http://www.reachingcriticalwill.org/legal/npt/RevCon05/postRevCon.html.
14. The poster for the May 1 march was hanging on the wall of the meeting. See it at http://www.abolitionnow.org/site/c.lmK0JcNSJrF/b.1315057/k.E676/May_1_2005.htm.
15. See *Nuclear Weapons Free Zones: The Untold Success Story of Nuclear Disarmament and Non-Proliferation* at http://www.atomicmirror.org/nfz/briefing/index.htm.
16. See http://www.atomicmirror.org/nfz/mexico/index.htm.
17. You can download the final declaration of the Conferencia de Zonas Libres de Armas Nucleares at http://www.opanal.org/index-i.html.
18. For links to the Abolition 2000 Statement in seven languages, please see http://www.abolition2000.org/site/c.cdJIKKNpFqG/b.1316387/k.8918/The_Abolition_2000_Founding_Statement.htm.
19. "Atomic Bombs Still Stir Worries," *Ventura County Star*, March 31, 2005, p. 3.
20. For the draft *U.S. Abolitionist Statement on Democracy, Power, and Nuclear Weapons*, see http://www.unitedforpeace.org/article.php?id=2953.

Suggested Reading

Braun, Reiner, Robert Hinde, David Krieger, Harold Kroto, and Sally Milne, eds. *Joseph Rotblat: Visionary for Peace.* Weinheim, Germany: Wiley-VCH, 2007.

Burroughs, John. *The Legality Threat or Use of Nuclear Weapons: A Guide to the Historic Opinion of the International Court of Justice.* Münster, Germany: Lit Verlag, 1997.

Cirincione, Joseph. *Bomb Scare: The History & Future of Nuclear Weapons.* New York: Columbia University Press, 2007.

Gerson, Joseph. *Empire and the Bomb: How the US Uses Nuclear Weapons to Dominate the World.* London: Pluto Press, 2007.

Goldblat, Jozef, ed. *Nuclear Disarmament: Obstacles to Banishing the Bomb.* London: I. B. Tauris, 2000.

Graham, Allison. *Nuclear Terrorism: The Ultimate Preventable Catastrophe.* New York: Henry Holt, 2004.

Graham, Thomas Graham, Jr. *Common Sense on Weapons of Mass Destruction.* Seattle: University of Washington Press, 2004.

Kovel, Joel. *Against the State of Nuclear Terror.* Boston: South End Press, 1983.

Krieger, David. "Disarming Nuclear Weapons." In *America & the World: The Double Bind,* edited by Majid Tehranian and Kevin P. Clements, 131–140. New Brunswick, NJ: Transaction, 2005.

———. "Nuclear Disarmament." In *Handbook of Peace and Conflict Studies,* edited by Charles Webel and Johan Galtung, 106–120. London: Routledge, 2007.

Lifton, Robert Jay, and Greg Mitchell. *Hiroshima in America.* New York: Avon Books, 1996.

Lifton, Robert Jay, and Richard Falk. *Indefensible Weapons: The Political and Psychological Case against Nuclearism.* New York: Basic Books, 1982.

London Nuclear Warfare Tribunal. *The Bomb and the Law: Report of the London Nuclear Warfare Tribunal.* Stockholm, Sweden: Gunnar Myrdal Foundation, 1989.

Nanda, Ved P., and David Krieger. *Nuclear Weapons and the World Court.* Ardsley, NY: Transnational Publishers, 1998.

Pauling, Linus. *No More War!* New York: Dodd, Mead, 1983.

Rhodes, Richard. *Arsenals of Folly: The Making of the Nuclear Arms Race.* New York: Alfred A. Knopf, 2007.

Roche, Douglas. *Beyond Hiroshima.* Toronto, Ontario, Canada: Novalis, 2005.

Schell, Jonathan. *The Fate of the Earth.* New York: Knopf, 1982.

———. *The Seventh Decade: The New Shape of Nuclear Danger.* New York: Metropolitan Books, 2007.

Thompson, E. P. *Exterminism and Cold War.* London: Verso, 1982.

Weapons of Mass Destruction Commission. *Weapons of Terror: Freeing the World of Nuclear, Biological and Chemical Arms.* Stockholm. Sweden: Weapons of Mass Destruction Commission, 2006.

CONTRIBUTORS

Kofi A. Annan served from 1997 to 2007 as the seventh secretary general of the United Nations. The Nobel Peace Prize was jointly awarded to him and the United Nations in 2001 "for their work for a better organized and more peaceful world."

Aslı Ü. Bâli is the Irving S. Ribicoff Fellow in Law at the Yale Law School, where she also serves as the coordinator of the Yale Law School Middle East Legal Forum. Ms. Bâli is also an attorney in private practice in New York. She is the author of several articles on issues ranging from nuclear nonproliferation to the comparative legal systems of the Middle East to the tension between human rights and national security in the context of the war on terror. She earned her J.D. from the Yale Law School jointly with an MPA from the Woodrow Wilson School at Princeton University. She holds an M. Phil. in Social and Political Thought from Cambridge University and earned her B.A. at Williams College.

Jacqueline Cabasso has served as Executive Director of the Western States Legal Foundation (WSLF) in Oakland, California, since 1984. She has written and coauthored numerous articles for publications, including the *Bulletin of the Atomic Scientists* and the journal *Social Justice*. She is a coauthor of *Nuclear Disorder or Cooperative Security? U.S. Weapons of Terror, the Global Proliferation Crisis and Paths to Peace* (2007). She is U.S. representative of Mayors for Peace, an international organization headed by the Mayors of Hiroshima and Nagasaki.

Mohamed ElBaradei is an Egyptian diplomat and the Director General of the International Atomic Energy Agency (IAEA), an intergovernmental organization under the auspices of the United Nations. ElBaradei and the IAEA were jointly awarded the Nobel Peace Price in 2005 for their "efforts to prevent nuclear energy from being used for military purposes and to ensure that nuclear energy for peaceful purposes is used in the safest possible way."

Daniel Ellsberg graduated from Harvard in 1952 with a B.A. Summa cum Laude in Economics. He studied for a year at King's College, Cambridge University, on a Woodrow Wilson Fellowship. In 1967, he worked on the Top Secret McNamara study of U.S. Decision-Making in Vietnam, 1945–1968, which later came to be known as the *Pentagon Papers*. In 1969, he photocopied the 7,000-page study and gave it to the Senate Foreign Relations Committee; in 1971, he gave it to the *New York Times*, *Washington Post* and 17 other newspapers. Since the end of the Vietnam War he has been a lecturer, writer, and activist on the dangers of the nuclear era and unlawful interventions.

Richard Falk is the Albert G. Milbank Professor Emeritus of International Law and Practice at Princeton University and Visiting Distinguished Professor of Global Studies at the University of California, Santa Barbara. He serves as the Chair of the Nuclear Age Peace Foundation, and is a recipient of the UNESCO Peace Education Prize. He is the author, coauthor, or editor of more than 40 books on international law and the law of war. He received his B.S. in Economics from the Wharton School, University of Pennsylvania (1952); his LL.B. from Yale Law School (1955); and his J.S.D. from Harvard University (1962).

Thomas Graham, Jr. is Chairman of the Board of the Cypress Fund for Peace and Security. The Cypress Fund is a charitable foundation established to provide long-term, reliable support to selected arms-control, nonproliferation, and conflict resolution NGOs, support Ph.D. programs, and carry out other activities in these fields. He is internationally known as one of the leading authorities in the field of international arms control and nonproliferation agreements. Graham served as a senior U.S. diplomat involved in the negotiation of every major international arms control and nonproliferation agreement from 1970 to 1997.

Wade L. Huntley is Director of the Simons Centre for Disarmament and Non-Proliferation Research, in the Liu Institute for Global Studies, University of British Columbia, Vancouver, Canada. Previously he was Associate Professor at the Hiroshima Peace Institute in Hiroshima, Japan, and Director of the Global Peace and Security Program at the Nautilus Institute in Berkeley, California. He received his doctorate in political science from the University of California at Berkeley in 1993 and has taught at several universities. Recent publications include "Small State Perspectives on the Future of Space Governance," *Astropolitics* 2:3 (Fall 2007); "U.S. Policy toward North Korea in Strategic Context: Tempting Goliath's Fate," *Asian Survey* 47:3 (May/June 2007); "Rebels without a Cause? North Korea, Iran and the Future of the NPT," *International Affairs* 82:3 (July 2006).

Michael D. Intriligator is Professor of Economics at the University of California, Los Angeles (UCLA) where he is also Professor of Political Science, Professor of Public Policy in the School of Public Affairs, and Codirector of the Jacob Marschak Interdisciplinary Colloquium on Mathematics in the Behavioral Sciences. In addition, he is a Senior Fellow of the Milken Institute in Santa Monica and of the Gorbachev Foundation of North America in Boston. He is the author of more than 200 journal articles and other publications in the areas of economic theory and mathematical economics, econometrics, health economics, reform of the Russian economy, and strategy and arms control.

David Krieger is a founder of the Nuclear Age Peace Foundation, and has served as president of the foundation since 1982. He is the author of many studies of peace in the Nuclear Age. He is a recipient of many awards, including Global Green's Millennium Award for International Environmental Leadership (2005). He is a graduate of Occidental College, and holds M.A. and Ph.D. degrees in political science from the University of Hawaii and a J.D. from the Santa Barbara College of Law.

Mairead Corrigan Maguire received the Nobel Peace Prize in 1976 for her work to create a nonviolent peace in Northern Ireland. She helped found the Community of Peace People earlier that same year, which instituted marches across Northern Ireland encouraging a peaceful resolution of ethnic/political conflict. She also helped found the Committee on the Administration of Justice, a nonsectarian organization of Northern Ireland that defends human rights and seeks changes to the government's legal system. She received the Nuclear Age Peace Foundation's Distinguished Peace Leadership Award in 1991.

Matthew Martin is a program officer in Policy Analysis and Dialogue at the Stanley Foundation, bringing a wealth of experience working directly on nonproliferation, cooperative threat reduction, missile defense, and strategic security issues. Prior to joining the Foundation in 2005, Martin spent 10 years in Washington, DC, directing projects in the think tank world and serving as senior defense aide for former Senator Bob Kerrey. He has held positions with the British American Security Information Council; the Center for Arms Control and Non-Proliferation; the Henry L. Stimson Center; and Amnesty

International, United States. He has authored and edited briefs, reports, and articles on a range of nonproliferation and hard security topics.

Pamela S. Meidell is a writer and the founder/director of the Atomic Mirror, a United Nations–affiliated nonprofit program based in Ventura County, California, that is dedicated to reflecting the truths of our nuclear era and transforming them through creativity and the arts. She works with local organizations and elected officials to engage Ventura County's citizens in creating ways to help local democracy flourish, and keep our communities safe and awake to nuclear issues. She has created and produced four performance pieces on nuclear themes that have been presented around the world.

Douglas Roche is an author, parliamentarian, and diplomat, who has specialized throughout his long public career in peace and human security issues. Mr. Roche was a senator, member of parliament, Canadian Ambassador for Disarmament, and Visiting Professor at the University of Alberta. He was elected Chairman of the United Nations Disarmament Committee at the forty-third General Assembly in 1988. The author of 18 books, his latest is *Global Conscience* (2007). Mr. Roche has received numerous awards for his work for peace and nonviolence, including the Papal Medal for his service as special adviser on disarmament and security matters. He is chairman of the Middle Powers Initiative, an international network of seven NGOs specializing in nuclear disarmament issues.

Jürgen Scheffran is a senior research scientist in the Program in Arms Control, Disarmament and International Security (ACDIS) of the University of Illinois at Urbana-Champaign (since August 2004), and has adjunct faculty positions at the Departments of Political Science and Atmospheric Sciences. He received a physics diploma and Ph.D. at the University of Marburg in Germany. He is cofounder of the International Network of Engineers and Scientists Against Proliferation (INESAP), coeditor of two journals in conflict research, and coauthor of the Model Nuclear Weapons Convention. He served as science policy advisor to German parliamentarians, the Bureau for Technology Assessment, the Federal Environmental Agency, and the United Nations.

Alice Slater is the New York Director of the Nuclear Age Peace Foundation. She is a member of the Global Council of Abolition 2000, a global network working for a treaty to eliminate nuclear weapons and directs the network's Sustainable Energy Working Group, which produced a model statute for an International Sustainable Energy Agency. Ms. Slater is a United Nations NGO Representative and has organized numerous conferences, panels, and roundtables at the UN on nuclear and environmental issues. She has written numerous articles and op-eds and has appeared frequently on local and national media.

Christopher G. Weeramantry is the former vice president of the International Court of Justice. In the course of his professional career he has served as a lawyer, legal educator, domestic judge, international judge, author, and lecturer. He has written over 20 books and lectured extensively on a wide variety of topics essential to peace, cross-cultural understanding, and education, and his works contain a philosophy as well as a program of action to achieve these purposes. The Weeramantry International Centre for Peace Education and Research (WICPER) is based on this philosophy and has his vast corpus of research and writing as an informational base from which to develop its programs. He received the UNESCO Peace Education Price in 2006 in recognition of his commitment and concrete undertakings in support of the concept and culture of peace through his long and fruitful career. He also received the Right Livelihood Award in 2007 for his lifetime of groundbreaking work to strengthen and expand the rule of international law. He is the president of the International Association of Lawyers against Nuclear Arms (IALANA).

INDEX